We Fundamentalists

We Fundamentalists

Muhammad Dawud

To order additional copies of this book, contact:
Xlibris LLC
1-888-795-4274
www.Xlibris.com
Orders@Xlibris.com
551419

Contents

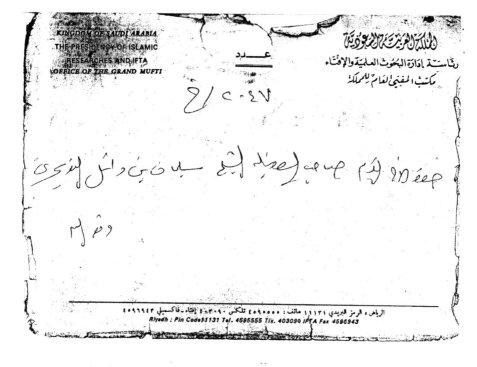

KINGDOM OF SAUDI ARABIA
THE PRESIDENCY OF ISLAMIC
RESEARCHES AND IFTA
OFFICE OF THE GRAND MUFTI

المملكة العربية السعودية
رئاسة إدارة البحوث العلمية والإفتاء
مكتب المفتي العام للمملكة

عــدد

٧/ق٠٢٧

صاحب الفضيلة سماحة الشيخ عبدالعزيز بن باز رئاسة الإفتاء

دمج

الرياض ، الرمز البريدي ١١١٣١ هاتف : ٤٥٩٥٥٥٥ تلكس : ٤٠٣٠٩٠ إفتاء - فاكسيملي ٤٥٩٦٩٤٣
Riyadh : Pin Code 1131 Tel. 4595555 Tlx. 403090 IFTA Fax 4596943

رئاسة إدارة البحوث العلمية والإفتاء والدعوة والإرشاد

التاريخ   /   /   هـ
المرفقات

مكتب الرئيس

من عبدالعزيز بن عبدالله بن باز إلى حضرة الأخ المكرم معالي الدكتور
عبدالعزيز أحمد الراجحي مدير جامعة أم القرى وفقه الله لما فيه رضاه أمين

سلام عليكم ورحمة الله وبركاته أما بعد :

فقد بلغني أنه وصل لمعاليكم رسالة موجهة إلى المسلم الجديد محمد داود
أمريكي الجنسية ، موضوع طلب الشفاعة من لدى معاليكم
في قبوله في معهد اللغة التابع لجامعة أم القرى ، فأرجو من معاليكم
التكرم بقبوله تحقيقاً لرغبته في طلب العلم ، ولما ذكره صاحب الفضائل
الشيخ ... مدير الكتاب المرفق الموجهة إلى معالي
شكراً لجهودكم مبارك في جهود وكم والسلام عليكم ورحمة الله وبركاته

الرئيس

لرئاسة إدارة البحوث العلمية والإفتاء والدعوة والإرشاد

بسم الله الرحمن الرحيم

المملكة العربية السعودية
رئاسة إدارة البحوث العلمية والإفتاء
مكتب المفتي العام للمملكة

الرقم : ٧٢٠٢٧/خ
التاريخ : ٢٨/٩/١٤٢٢هـ
المشفوعات :
الموضوع :

من عبد العزيز بن عبد الله بن باز إلى حضرة الأكرم صاحب الفضيلة
الشيخ سلمان بن فهد العودة مدير دار الحديث
الخيرية حفظه الله به

سلام عليكم ورحمة الله وبركاته وبعد

اطلع على رسالة في سلم الجديد عبد داود دترى
قبله في الدار في أي مرحلة ترونك ثم الإقدام
حتى نشفع له لدى سمو الأمير أحمد من مستحقاته في
ولدصكم بقدرًا من جهة النفقة والسكن وفقه الله
الجميع والسلام

عبد العزيز بن عبد الله بن باز

إلى إدارة الهجرة والجوازات

ع/ط رئاسة الجامعة

سجل الطالب .... المولود في ..../عام .... والمتمتع

بالجنسية .... طالباً في قسم تعليم اللغة العربية بجامعة دمشق للعام الدراسي ....

بتاريخ ٢٠.../ .../ ... ولغاية ٢٠.../ .../ ...

دمشق في ٢٠.../ ٢/ ٤

رئيس قسم تعليم اللغة العربية

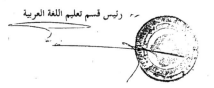

الجمهورية العربية السورية – دمشق – مزة أوتوستراد – مجمع الآداب – المعهد العالي للغات – قسم تعليم اللغة العربية
هاتف: ٣٣٩٢٥٨٤٣-١١-٠٠٩٦٣ فاكس: ٢١٢٠١٦٥-١١-٠٠٩٦٣
بريد إلكتروني: inquiries@arabicindamascus.edu.sy
موقع إلكتروني: www.arabicindamascus.edu.sy

When Muhammad Dawud, a Muslim American citizen, who was a student at Damascus University, Damascus Syria; a director and English teacher at a private English Educational Syrian school is thrown into a Syrian underground dungeon because he is a Sunni Muslim by the Syrian Alawite (Shiite) government at the beginning of the Arab Spring, he starts writing about the oppression and injustice he sees and lived with in the Muslim and Western World.

Muhammad Dawud is a world renowned Imam, and lecturer on Islamic and current international issues to both public, and private, Muslim and non Muslim audiences. London, UK. New York, New Jersey, USA. Mecca, Jeddah, Saudi Arabia. Damascus, Syria. Omdurman, Khartoum, Sudan. Karachi, Lahore, Dir-N.W.F.P., Pakistan. Fes, Morocco.

Dedication

To my mother, Thelma Edwich Hastings Hickson, and father, Constant Patrick Hickson. I thank you.

To my lovely wife, Houda H. Bassim, and children, Khaoula M. Dawud, Salah Eddin M. Dawud, and Abdullah Constant M. Dawud.

To Howard University and all my teachers here in America. I thank you.

To Imam Hamass Abdul Khaalis, Samwell Oliver, and all my Muslim brothers and sisters in this jihad struggle here in America, including Sheikh Omar S. Abu Namous from the Islamic Culture Center of New York, Dr. S. Sultan, and those true believers from Dar-Ul-Islah Mosque in Teaneck, New Jersey. I thank you.

To Dr. Fouad Rasheed and those true believers from the Islamic Center of Passaic, New Jersey, I thank you.

To King Abdullah of Saudi Arabia, Grand Mufti of Saudi Arabia Sheikh Abd Al-Aziz Abd Allah ibn Baaz, Sheikh Safar Al-Hawali, and all my teachers at Mecca University and all those believing brothers and sisters there in Saudi Arabia, I thank you.

To Sheikh Abdul Maged, from Sudan, and all my teachers and those believing brothers and sisters in Sudan, I thank you.

To Sheikh Ali, from Sham, Syria, and all my teachers at Damascus University and those believing brothers and sisters there in Syria, I thank you.

To King Mohammad VI of Morocco and all my teachers at Al-Quaraeen University in Fes, Morocco, and those believing brothers and sisters there, I thank you.

To Sultan Hassanal Bolkiah of Brunei and all those believing brothers and sisters there.

11

To Prince Saeed bin Maktoum bin Rashid Al-Maktoum, from the United Arab Emirates, and those believing brothers and sisters there, I thank you.

To Queen Elizabeth II of the United Kingdom and all my teachers and those believing brothers and sisters who aided me in England, especially those at Whitechapel East London Mosque, I thank you.

To Sheikh Yusuf Al-Qarardawi from Egypt and all those believing brothers and sisters there, I thank you.

To Ali Khamenei, Supreme Leader of Iran, Guardian Jurist of Iran, Leader of the Revolution, and those believing brothers and sisters there, I thank you.

To Doka Umarov, Shamil Salmanovich Basayen, Thamir Salen Abdullah Al-Suwailem, and all those believing brothers and sisters in Chechnya, we, the Muslim Fundamentalists thank you.

To Hakimullah Mehsud and all those believing brothers and sisters in Pakistan, we, the Muslim Fundamentalists thank you.

To Mullah Mohammed Omar, head of the supreme council of Afghanistan, and all those believing brothers and sisters in Afghanistan, we, the Muslim Fundamentalist thank you.

To those Teaneck, New Jersey, residents who lost their lives on September 11, 2001, at the World Trade Center in New York City: Daniel D. Bergstein, Gregory A. Clark, Fanny M. Espinoza, George Ferguson, Jennifer L. Fialko, Lillian I. Frederick, Edward Lichtschein, and Mark L. Rosenberg.

To Allah (swa). I thank you.

PART I:
The Enemy Near

I am compelled to put forth this book so that the heart, mind, and soul of the world body will be better informed.

> *Because Allah will never change the conditions he hath bestowed on a people until they change what is in their own hearts: and verily Allah is he who hears and knows all things.*
>
> —Quran 8:53

Oppressors

Oh, humble reader of this book. As I sit here silently in this underground dungeon located somewhere in downtown Damascus, Syria, watching from within the large crowded cell while the Syrian guards quietly did a head count, I pondered the fragrance of patience. The atmosphere is eerie; together with the stale smell of human sweat and anger that fills these chambers. This place is indeed inhuman, yet here we are. The semidarkness is not deep enough to hide the injustice; the sounds of Muslim prayers are just loud enough to overcome those words of foul contempt by those toward our Syrian guards. But what captivated me was that single point of cigarette light that was being passed around quietly clockwise illuminating the hard determined Arab faces of the young and middle-age men held in limbo, here behind the sun. Sadly, many of whom had been held here for months and years not even knowing the charges against them or seeing their families and loved ones to say that they are alive.

Yet what truly enthralled me in spite of my circumstances was that single loaf of bread that was being passed around counter clockwise amongst us, quietly illuminating the hearts of the Muslim brotherhood among us. I reluctantly but humbly broke off a small piece and pass the loaf onward to my right hand side to a bearded lean Syrian from Aleppo ending my three day hunger strike of protest.

I must be patient; revenge is best left to Allah (swa): "All praise is due to Allah." I am not in the company of murderers, thieves, kidnappers or the insane. This underground dungeon is not a place of rehabilitation center because of some crime against humanity. No!

This place, oh, humble reader, is an incubator of ideas that house religious and political prisoners against their will. Those whom that are suspected upright in their way of life called Islam, are thus, an abomination in the sight of the wicked and the apostates in many places of the Arab, Muslim, and secular world today!

It is Allah (swa) that underscores the true reality of our world we all live in for millennia, thus, enlightens those who seek to understand sincerely those descended responsibilities we as human beings had inherited from our lord as a fact of life that is widely ignored to our peril.

Therefore, there is no reason for me to harbor hate or revenge in my heart against my fellow Muslim neighbors for their failings on social graces and unlawful conduct towards me, or one another. *"Only Allah can forgive them for they just do not know what they are doing"* is just about the only prayer that comes to my mind as I sit here in this filthy dark underground dungeon, sardine along with more than a hundred and eighty other Muslims whose crime is thinking about the injustice in their lands, or pondering out loud that fearful relationship between faith and reason. It`s that I am in good company, which is that spiritual reply that comes to my heart; this is indeed one of the fruitful consequences of being spiritually aware to some degree, oh, humble reader, in this day and era. I must endure and pay my dues.

In the promotion of knowledge, this is where foreign and domestic Muslim religious scholars go to once that change in the conditions of their own hearts starts to glow in regard to justice. Yes, those students of knowledge whose hearts can contemplate the reality of the future of an Islamic change in their own Muslim communities are hooded, tied, and mailed to places of such behind the sun. Unsympathetically, peaceful Muslim travelers seeking the truth for their own hearts are also received here by the Syrian secret thought police in downtown Damascus to expel out without regard of karma.

As I lie here in these dim shadows, I cannot see the light of day or hear the busy traffic of cars, minibuses, and people going about their daily business above me in spite of being two stories down underground. They the Muslim people for now above us going about their daily affairs cannot hear nor wish to see our concerns, anguish, and torment in spite of them being Muslims for more than 1,400 years. Yet they the Muslim people above us also enslaved in regards to fear of the alternatives in their lives on the streets and in the cafes know we are down here.

It`s no legend that Jihad Salafi and/or Salafi are highly feared by despots, tyrants and secularist with Muslim names because there is no way an unjust person can capture a soul, destroy faith, and devotion at the same time, and cope with the fundamental threat of jihad against them in return. In spite of my American and British nationality, I got caught up in the early dragnet of the fear of Arab Spring. That Alawite (a Shiite sect branch of Islam) regime's growing fear of their own domestic religious Sunni Islamists' growing powers that's getting stronger by the day is real. Yes, I was arrested on the streets of Damascus by the secret police that held me in their underground prison for nine days until I was flown out of the country leaving my wife and children behind me. But it's why that Syrian Alawite regime that's now in power and is facing such a resilient religious Sunni jihad against them; it's why, the believers of this Islamic faith must be firm and vigilant against those who are unjust. We must be known to all oppressors whomever they are that we have not forgotten the sanctity of our faith!

Deemed persona non grata by the Syrian government in July 2009 may not be such a bad idea as far as Allah is concerned. Today, now the beginning of the spring season of 2014, the Alawite Assad government is in a full civil war setting; they would have killed me and my Salafi brothers on sight and vice versa—only highlights the upside of patience. Yet I shall never forget the Syrian government indiscriminate crackdown upon religiously conservative Sunni people and their abuse of me simply because I am a Salafi Sunni Muslim peacefully studying Arabic at Damascus University and working as a director in a private school teaching English to the local people.

There can never be enough said about oppression upon an Abrahamic monotheist peoples by their own governments because of their own hearts. Far too long this has been the norm and the novelty of the Muslim World, as well as the Christian and Jewish world! Oh, humble reader, please don't confuse today's populism with democracy in the Muslim lands. That Arab Spring the world is now witnessing is only the rippling effect of the Muslim people saying enough of the injustice and a time for a historic change of heart back to Sharia (the Islamic law) for the mercy of Allah!

"When rulers are wicked, their people are too, but good men will live to see the tyrants down fall." (Bible, Prov. 29:16)—these words truly suites and address the hard times we Muslims are facing in Muslim lands today when it comes to the wicked ruling and those who are good will be those who will see the downfall of oppressors.

These are the moments that mark your life; thus, time is unique in a dreadful kind of way. Though I often look for a pause button, I

finally had to admit to myself sometimes everyday that, there could be
no possible cure for a jihad whose time has come. We fundamentalists
are the stem cells of humanity who are ready without fear to stand
on the frontlines of the "heart, mind and soul war" that will happen
anytime and anywhere, which will be undertaken by anyone who
desires to stand up and fight with his sword or hands—fight with his
words, fight with his pen, and fight with prayers. We march all together
with hope in our hearts if need be. Yes, we fundamentalists of faith
and reason who are ready to be carried off to prison or even the grave
against those barbed wired barriers of social injustice, due process of
law abuse, human rights violations and the denial of equal rights for
all without fright. Yes, the world has come about begrudgefully and
is transpired by events of the peoples own hearts when in spite of
everyone in the accepted secular culture, political, and fashion media
said liberty could not be achieved when taking into account life's
apparent realities of oppression and greed, except our lord.

The true state of the Muslim world is awakening to the fact that
they are on the menu! The realization of this ongoing never-ending
human competitive societies competing for the dwindling world
resources exist. Please note that as our world population grows, so does
our problems and with less time to solve them. The true depth of the
social, economic, political and religious demands that is now pressing
upon the growing one and a half billion Muslims who are locked
in poverty is only beginning to bite. The awakening and growing
demands upon the Muslims like senior citizens and their pensions,
the working poor and their jihad of just chasing payments that leads
nowhere, and the youth with their dreams and aspirations seeking an
ever-more meaningful life, parents who are doing their best holding
families together in their capitalistic, socialistic, and class-driven
societies dreaming about good full health care in their lifetime and
an opportunity for a good and enlighten education that will help
themselves prepare for the competitive future at hand are dire and
real.

Indeed, I am only a human being like you, a family man with
three lovely children and a wife whom I greatly love now together over
seventeen years. We all have the same needs! So why cannot we be
frank with each other about the essential matters of our world? This is
far better than submitting and kneeling in the presence of this obscure
world together talking about the irrelevancy.

That true state of the Muslim world—it is quite clear—is fighting
for reforms. The Arab spring is nothing but a call for real change

from the old nationalistic ideal reforms, and habits towards Islamic leaders who advocate *Sharia* law (Islamic law), which is the best and only law for the Muslim lands. Such an awakening, with its priorities on justice and faith, is now in full worldview. Similarly, those Western secular democracies that exist parasitically—whose peoples, enjoy the freedoms of their civil liberties like human rights, equal rights, justice, and due process of law—but at the expense of the Muslim world and the third-world body cannot be sustained any longer. Not surprisingly, this hearts and minds war is old newspaper from one generation to the next in the mind`s eye of fundamentalists believers. First, the use of tyranny and oppression by Muslim-in-name-only leaders over their own people in the guise of fighting the foreign enemy, Israel, and/or those imperialist cannot also be sustained. Second, fighting that civil disobedient Muslim fundamentalist called jihadist at home cannot also be defeated. From the land of the Berber in the west to the ongoing jihad for an independent Islamic state on Mindanao, Philippines, in the east, the jihad war against the pharaoh`s rule continues!

As a Jihad Salafi[1] Muslim American citizen, who was born in the West and grew up in the Bronx, New York, United States of America, I am not surprised or fooled by my country's failing ideological struggles of the twenty-first century, their hearts and minds war. Nor am I misled or disheartened by those allied oppressors, Muslim-in-name-only leaders, those dictators, despots, tyrants, and presidents-for-life. Like Tunisia`s ex-president-for-life Zine El-Abidine Ben Ali, Egypt`s ex-president-for-life Hosni Mubarak, or now currently General Abdul Fattah Al-Sisi, Moammar Gadhafi, that dictator-for-life-only from Libya, President-for-life Abdelaziz Bouteflika from Algeria, President-for-life Bashar Assad from Syria, King Hamed Bin Isa Khalifa, a tyrant-for-life from Bahrain, as well as Ex-President-for-life Ali Abdullah Saleh, and currently President-for-life Abd Rabbu Mansour Hadi from Yemen. One does not have to be a military intelligence expert to correctly

---

[1] Jihad is ordained for you Muslims though you dislike it, and maybe that you dislike something which is good for you and that you like something which is bad for you. Quran 2:216. The word Jihad means "struggle." Salafism is based on three important pillars of creed. The first is the belief of one divine being (Allah). The second is the act of jihad. And the third is the missionary work or Dawa. This school of thought embraces a more purer and orthodox viewpoint of Islam thus "Salaf Al-Saleh" or "The righteous predecessors."

assess that American and European powers are losing this hearts and minds war; it's clearly because of their abandonment of human rights, equal rights, justice, and due process of law abroad. These foreign policy decisions of folly inevitably have their consequences, both domestically and abroad.

Today, it saddens me greatly to a high degree that the great majority of Sunni Muslim leaders are dictators, despots, tyrants, and presidents-for-life; likewise, I am continuously disturbed that the government of my country, America, has been and still is a prime supporter of oppression, injustice, and subversion in Muslim countries and Third-world. Throughout history, prophets of all stripes, shepherds of their nations or tribes, men such as Prophet Lut (Lot) who stood for the sanctity of family values, Prophet Moses who struggled for the emancipation from bondage, Prophet Jesus who beckoned for that divine revelation to be hearken, and Prophet Muhammad (sas): *"Peace and blessings of Allah be upon him"* who fought for the freedom of monotheist worship. Yet what has been gained in regards to the moral quality of spiritual life and justice that we the peoples of the Abrahamic faith have so longed for on this earth today?

As a free Jihad Salafi fundamentalist Muslim, the creed of my faith, which I recite five times a day, is my moral compass. Nowhere in the Quran does Allah (swa) say to the believers that they can oppress, be unjust, subvert, lie, steal, or murder anyone. Yet the enemy near has Muslim names. And to this I must ask *why*. The Quran twice states that "Allah will not change the conditions of a people until the people change the conditions of their own hearts."[2] My advantage, if indeed it is a favorable position only Allah (swa) knows, is that I choose this faith Islam of my own free will not because I felt that Christianity was bad or insufficient but by persuasion and example. Perhaps my next advantage is frankness. In controversial times like today, you require an interpersonal website of a strong mental and spiritual character to survive.

Where shall we begin in this journey of frankness? Let's start with the root of the problem, indeed one of the main causes of that monotheist social illness is that idea of "self-glorification," which is one of the true symptoms of nationalism, thus one of the many reasons it has no place in an Islamic society. Nationalism cannot unite people anywhere because it is based on quest for leadership on wrongful

---

[2]   Quran 8:53, 13:11

goals and methods. This conceited quest for leadership creates a wrongful desire for power between people that is based on race, family, tribal ties, and clans, whereas Islam binds people together, base on the purity of their faith in Allah (swa) and his messenger prophet Muhammad (sas). Thus, Islam calls for the loyalty to the faith of Allah rather than loyalty to the nation or tribes. This viewpoint is extremely important for the simple Muslim person to differentiate and for the straightforward non-Muslim person to understand. All Muslims are supposed to be treated under the law of Sharia with exactly the same rights in the sight of their brethren regardless of where that person was born or what tribe that person is from!

If by chance you just happen to be born last night and lived in a spartan cave all your life, these self-glorified Arab nationalist Muslims by name-only leaders are today's pharaoh's. Please, there is no need to turn that page once more to Exodus in the Torah or Al-Baqarah in the Quran and visualize. No, all you have to do is watch the Arab League live when they convene or observe the Muslim World League when its leaders flock and gather. Instinctually reactionary, they naturally prefer the shadows. But so unlike their ancestors of old, they put on a hubris show at the right time of crisis and Muslim suffering. How could you really dare not see, oh, humble reader? Their pictures are literally everywhere in their home countries, watching and displaying the evil eye if anyone should dare dissent. Their vanity is too deep to ever miss a photo-op. Their avarice is too high to miss a kickback.

After living and traveling in Muslim countries for more than fourteen years of my life, I am not fooled by what I see, read, or experience there. In fact, there is a sharp contrast between faith and what is practiced daily in the Muslim world. Imagine your father, mother, brother, sister, friend, or neighbor just disappeared without a trace because of a careless whisper of dissent. So what had happen to me in Damascus, Syria in July of 2009 is of no surprise to the average Muslim citizen living in a Muslim country in this modern time and in many regards it is a normal inconvenience because of that concept of injustice and the denial of human rights in their lives!

Naturally, you would want to run away from such places. But say I, our faith says take a stand and fear only Allah (swa). These events happened to the Hebrews before us: [3] *"Hast thou not turned thy vision to*

---

[3]   (Quran 2:246)

the chiefs of the children of Israel after the time of Moses? They said to a prophet that was among them: "Appoint for us a King; that we may fight in the cause of God." He said: "Is it not possible, if ye were commanded to fight, that that ye will not fight?" They said: "How could we refuse to fight in the cause of God, seeing that we were turned out of our homes and our families?" But when they were commanded to fight, they turned back, except a small band among them. But God has full knowledge of those who do wrong" (Quran 2:246).

So wipe away those tears and say to one self, "Where does the trail of redemption begin for those fundamentalists facing those enemies near?" Where to start? For me, it began in our Muslim countries, in our streets, and in our very own homes. All you have to do is look in the mirror. No, this book is not about demonizing people—not at all. We the Muslim people as a nation who celebrate that one faith called Islam must take a stand and be aware of our fundamental responsibilities not just to Allah, but also to each other.

Our prophet Muhammad (sas)[4] has said referring to "Nationalism":(*Asabiyyah*), "Leave it. It is rotten." (Hadith—Muslim and Bukhari). This is something I learned and experience personally in the summer of 1990 in Cairo, Egypt. Those who have eyes and see, understand those methods for leadership based on religious humbleness like wanting for others what you want for yourself. Sharia law and fear of Allah go a long way in regards to justice and human rights. Yet nationalism is all around me as I walked these streets of Cairo, Egypt. I was quite elated at the time; less than five years after embracing the Islamic faith, I am now praying for the first time, as one, with millions of my fellow Muslim brothers and sisters in a Muslim country in Raba`a Adawiya Mosque in Nasr City, Cairo, and many other mosques that is older than America. But it's that dominant secular nationalistic atmosphere that is the same here amongst it's people like back home in New York, United States of America, or in London, United Kingdom, or anywhere in Europe. This is an ideological power struggle between the people and their goals that produces conflicts of interest among various strata of societies for achievement and leadership. Whereas its "how" and "for what purpose," we Muslim are competing against each other "for" is what defines us in that eye of the

---

[4]   When a Allah fearing Muslim say`s Allah in his speech, then it is obligatory in many schools of Islamic thought to say (swa): All praise is due to Allah. The same respect is given to prophet Muhammad, to say (sas): Peace and blessings of Allah be upon him.

creator and human beholder who is Allah (swa) fearing that is under siege. Yes, mankind all has the same needs, but we call on different gods and sovereigns to answer them! All praise is due to Allah, Egypt is one of many Arab Sunni Muslim societies whose promise far outweighs its nationalistic poison. Yet self-glorification is one of the true symptoms of nationalism, and one of the many reasons it has no place in an Islamic society, but the people therein must see this poison for themselves in order to change their own hearts. I, Muhammad Dawud—a humble Muslim seeking knowledge standing on a Cairo street corner in 1990, a Muslim from the West preaching to them about this obvious poison—will only land myself eventually behind the sun. Their own sheikhs and imams for generations have said the same thing to them and was greatly ignored, imprisoned and even murdered because of their own people`s hearts. Many of the upcoming sheikhs and scholars with whom I studied in Saudi Arabia, and Sudan taught me that only Allah is to be glorified, and to be patient!

There are many caveat effects, and consequence, that are quite clear. So behold, for example that public servant, who is supposed to be the guardian of the Muslim state from foreign aggression; behold the Muslim generals today. They shamefully usurp powers unto themselves driven in part by their notable achievements and pride. That defender of the faithful then becomes the cancer of the very society they suppose to be guardians of! That fear of Allah (swa) concept, which is in our Holy Quran, but these Sunni Muslim generals in name only want it for themselves, so that their own people fear them, worship, and serve them totally. It is because of this conceit that our Muslim generals, Allah (swa) knows best, have not won a major war against the *kufr*[5] since the fall of the caliphate in Turkey 1924 until July 6, 2006, in southern Lebanon against an Israeli army!

But I humbly ask of you, oh, humble reader, what nation of people has not been tested? What tribe of people has never been admonished by their Lord? Yes, we all have gone through or experienced some form of social revolt in our human lives. Yet it`s those that have overcome who are the true authors of today`s history! Not one of my teachers can tell me of any one nation or tribe of people who has an exclusive monopoly of pain, suffering, injustice, betrayal, or holocaust by their own indigenous tyrants. If we are sincere with ourselves, then who

---

[5]   Kufr: Unbelievers of ones faith in creed and action.

doesn't know the truth when that imam, rabbi, or minister disappears after giving that sermon about injustice in the land? Who doesn't know the truth when that teacher at the university or college has been dragged off to prison with no trial because of intolerance? Who doesn't know the truth when that social worker for human rights, equal rights, justice and due process of law is assassinated?

The fact of the matter is it's what have they done, oh, Allah (swa), when their neighbor's door was kicked in, not by thieves at night but by the secret police with fright. What did the people there in the lands of the prophets do? Gone with the wind the family jewels—those beloved ones who spoke, who took a stand and tried to make a change with their hands and walk the talk.[6] *"Give this warning to those in whose hearts is the fear that they will be brought to judgment before their lord: Except for him they will have no protector nor intercessor: That they may guard against evil. Send not away those who call on their lord morning and evening, seeking his face. In naught art thou accountable for them, and in naught are they accountable for thee, that thou should turn them away, and thus be one of the unjust. Thus do we try some of them by comparison with others that they should say: Is it these then that Allah hath favored from amongst us? Does not Allah know best those who are grateful?"* (Quran 6:51-53). Yes, it is a sin to look and not see the wrong. To hear the *muezzin*'s call but only for prayers.

Prophet Muhammad (sas) is the man who saves you from yourself. The companions of this prophet and the prophets before him are the best examples and guidance for mankind. But we Muslims today are not teaching and showing the benefits of steadfastness and patience to our youths as a curriculum or possess it as a shield early in life, which is crucial.[7] *"By the token of time through the ages, verily man is in loss, except such as have faith, and do righteous deeds, and join together in the mutual teaching of truth, and of patience and constancy"*—(Quran ch.103).

At times, indeed, unfortunately, forcing people to look at the unspeakable we risk losing them, so we establish first the underlying seriousness of the issues so then we can awaken that moment of clarity that's in us all. Why, the Sunni Muslim world features so much despots in its leadership, most of whom rose to power from the military or from posts as public servants, but who was one of the best-known Muslim

---

[6]   (Quran 6:51-53) Muezzin: A male who issues an Adhan (call to prayer) to the muslim people five times daily.

[7]   (Quran 103)

generals who was both loyal to the faith and successful in his missions, who possessed that fundamental element of patience that is essential for a Muslim general sworn to be a true guardian of the Muslim state from foreign enemies? His name is Khalid Ibn Al-Walid, "The Sword of Allah." The point is not that he was victorious in his jihad against the *kufrs*—no. The point is the character of the man. For example, the Roman emperor Heraclius sent an ambassador to ask General Khalid to return his daughter who was captured during a battle; his ambassador gave Khalid the letter from the Roman Emperor, which reads as follows: "I have come to know what you have done to my army. You have killed my son-in-law and captured my daughter. You have won and gotten away safely. I now ask you for my daughter. Either return her to me on payment of ransom or give her to me as a gift, for honor is a strong element in your character." General Khalid Ibn Al-Walid said to the ambassador, "Take her as a gift; there shall be no ransom."

Before I go any further, I wish to share my insight with you, oh, humble reader, of the contested ground that men would defend if they faced other to please Allah (swa). Not only did General Khalid win every major battle he led against the unbelievers, but he was also known to be an honorable man by both friends and foes alike. He was a patient, charismatic, and a noble leader on and off the battlefield. However, when the Caliph Omar Ibn Al-Khattab dismissed General Khalid and thereby put an end to his successful military career in the autumn of 638 (17 Hijri), the Caliph Umar explained to the people: "I have not dismissed Khalid because of my anger or because of any dishonesty on his part, but because people glorified him and were misled. I feared that people would rely on him, and I want them to know that it is Allah (swa) who does all things and there should be no mischief in the land."

The message is clear: In a heart, mind and soul war, submission and patience to that civilian authority that is Allah fearing is essential in a *jihad*, as well as beware of people glorifying you!

Hum du Allah: (*All praise is due to Allah*). General Khalid Ibn Al-Walid understood that Allah is the *Ar-Rahman*: (The beneficent); therefore, trust is ruthless in the heart, mind, and eyes of Allah-fearing people. When people starts to sing you praises, start to add your name poetically in their books. Start to even publicly glorify you enthusiastically. Don`t take a bow! They are just cutting your throat by their ignorance. Therefore, he peacefully resigned without a fuss. Even though he was a heroic and noble warrior, yet this entire means nothing if people start to give you praise instead of Allah (swa). When people started to feel safer because of him not Allah (swa), therein lies the danger. General Khalid Ibn Al-Walid was well aware of this, so it seems, as well as what was said on the authority of Abu Hurayrah who said that Prophet Muhammad (sas) said of Allah (swa) who said: "*Pride is my cloak and greatness my robe, and he who competes with me in respect of either of them I shall cast into hell fire.*"

In a Monotheist faith called Islam, humility goes a long way in dealing with unfavorable circumstances that may turn out successfully in one's favor in the sight of a divine one who only demands gratitude. I honestly believe a high achievement of humility can only come about through training of submission and patience towards our own civilian authority that respects and worships a divine sovereign jealously. Therefore, indeed, the early days of pure Islam was a theocracy.

I bring this example up because it has a contemporary connection, especially to the holy month of Ramadan, the month the have-mores and the haves eat the most and throw crumbs—if that much—to the have-nots in this sad era of our times. This holy month of Ramadan in which the Quran was first revealed to prophet Muhammad (sas) as a mercy to the believers, is a month of fasting to remember both Allah and the plight of the poor amongst us. Ramadan is the month when Muslims must pay charity to the poor if they have a certain amount of funds. Yet today's reality bite is that the poor receives little if any needed funds or aid in the Muslim world. That sustained social economic policies by Muslim in name-only leaders that will truly help abate the brutal and harsh life of the majority have-not poor has only ended with conjecture, corruption and condemnation by their own citizenry. The one big question is I believe, does not the mainstream Muslim world realize that they are getting poorer? And if so, what will be the literal reaction of one and a half billion Muslims that sees and believes that that small ruling elite class as non-religious (secular), too comfortable (rich), and too out of touch (corrupt)? Thus, what will be the dire consequences if Allah should withhold more of his mercy from us Muslims because of our hearts? Is it a myth, or is it wrong to ponder that very probable thought?[8] "*When some of them said: Why do ye preach to a people whom Allah will destroy or visit with a terrible punishment? Said the preachers: "To discharge our duty to your lord, and perchance they may fear him." "When they disregarded the warnings that had been given them, we*

---

8   (Quran 7:164-5)

rescued those who forbade evil; but we visited the wrong doers with a grievous punishment, because they were given to transgression" (Quran 7:164-165).

Were not the Hebrew people before us Muslims also tested by the same lord oh, humble reader?[9] *"I set before you here, this day, a blessing and a curse: A blessing for obeying the commandments of the Lord, your God, which I enjoin on you today; a curse if you do not obey the commandments of the lord, your God, but turn aside from the way I ordain for you today, to follow other gods, whom you have not known. When the Lord, your God, brings you into the land which you are to enter and occupy, then you shall pronounce the blessing on Mount Gerizim, the curse on Mount Ebal."* (Deut.11:26-29). And *"when in their insolence they transgressed all prohibitions, we said to them: Be ye apes, despised and rejected." "Behold! Thy lord did declare that he would send against them, to the Day of Judgment, those who would afflict them with grievous penalty. Thy lord is quick in retribution, but he is also oft-forgiving, most merciful"* (Quran 7:166-172)

I don't really need to travel with you, oh, peaceful reader, we are already there at Tahrir Square in Cairo, Egypt. Standing there en masse defiantly against the tide of Muslim believers is Mr. Ayman Nour the party founder of the Egyptian secular Al-Ghad party and his followers. And that Nobel Prize winner Mr. Mohamed El—Baradei and his followers, along with hundreds of thousands of Egyptian agnostics, heretics, Coptic Christians, atheists, homosexuals, and Arab women who's creed is pagan European way of life style! They were banking on the idea that their Egyptian society can only tolerate one change at a time, so redemption should have waited a little longer. Unexpectedly that Egyptian field marshal Mohamed Hussein Tantawi, plainly a witness to all resigned quietly without a fuss, so he says, so it seems.

Was it not just two years ago they all together before with their allies "The Muslim Brotherhood" and the peoples of Egypt overthrown a president for life (Hosni Mubarak) who had taken sovereignty into his own hands for decades and murder and oppress them all for years in the name of security and Arab Nationalism?

Presently, in the case of leadership and social justice, the Egyptian people accepted the promise of democratic elections from Western powers. They the Western powers guarantee democracy will transform all their lives for the good by placing sovereignty unto all the people not just one person or one divine being.

---

[9]   (Quran 7:166-172) (Deut.11:26-29, 28:49-62)

Yet they had been warned that ingenious nature of those Allah-fearing people and their power to organize and unite. So it`s not hard to imagine that golden age of a free classical contest that elected Mohammed Morsi as president from the Muslim Brotherhood and place him in the presidential palace, who in turn proceeded to hand over sovereignty not to the people individually but to Allah in whole by way of Sharia law as the new Egyptian Constitution.

Please take a few minutes with me and consider the human debris of atonement, oh, humble reader, that is in under cover of darkness and ignorance. That human citizenry living in lands of known prophets who want power and sovereignty for themselves only, what has been gained—despots? Because of the peoples own nationalist desires and harden hearts, it was incomprehensible for them to have a leap of faith to appreciate their own countrymen in placing sovereignty towards an unseen divine being called Allah (swa) who only demands gratitude liken their forefathers before them.

You can still see them standing there defiantly no doubt with their souls on their shoulders shouting out against the human religious tide with posters in hand, their anger of events unfolding plainly a witness to all. It was their wish to falsifying the will of Allah, demanding that his people take once again a non-tethered walk across an unpopular void of the hearts for the sake of modernity. Truly it`s not really so far from here to there, oh, humble reader, people who wish to feel free like free people yet dreams go unfulfilled because of the lack of the will of change from pagan secular ways starting with their own hearts!

Perhaps, this upcoming holy month of Ramadan, the Islamic month of mercy, will be the catalyst that is needed to turn hearts around. It did work for me in prison in Butner, North Carolina Federal Correction Institute (F.C.I.) United States of America back in 1986. I was fasting with the Muslim inmates in the holy month of Ramadan, yet I was not a Muslim at the time, just praying for a change of heart in a month claimed to be the month of mercy from Allah (swa). A change of heart amid the mazes of human self-denials and pondering a grand leap of faith amid the mazes of religious deceptions had no doubt brought me spiritual clarity and peace. No, it`s not really so far from here to there, that conquest of one`s own heart, simply because it`s always a question of sincere intentions.

Yes, I am indeed fascinated and so should you. That millions of believers acted on their faith and voted to give sovereignty to a divine being sight unseen, and live by Sharia laws, the laws of their ancestors before them! It is captivating, observing a people throwing an anchor into heaven knowing that the litany of complaints against despots and those who follow their own desires is not sufficient towards acting on their faith in these so called modern times. The real question before the world audience is, how far are the believers willing to sacrifice to keep their victories in these lands of the prophets in order to please Allah (swa) now that they have their backs to Raba`a Adawiya Mosque in Nasr City, Cairo?

One of the golden rules I have learned the hard way in life is that providence is your rear guardian in whatever your endeavor is in life. As such, every citizen signs directly or indirectly into that social contract. For some, it is openly clear; for others it is a tacit consent. Thus, the idea permits in its government, disobedience and/or revolution, if their government breaches its side of the contract. Therefore, the duty to obey the law is a matter of degree. If all the people are not fully enfranchised members of a society, then they are not fully bound by its laws. However, that social contract cuts both ways. If we Muslims, whom by faith are not secular and believe sovereignty cannot be with the people but with a divine one whom we call Allah (swa), then "whatever good comes from Allah (swa), and whatever bad befalls us Muslims comes from our own hands." The ongoing dire consequences to our forward frontier is really long term and problematic. Being a spectator in this era is a true crime. For example, if you believe that Sharia law is a system in which Allah (swa) matters more than your personal freedom on this earth then you are saved, why? Because when people who don`t believe that Allah (swa) exists and should not be given sovereignty, in fact desires sovereignty for themselves (democratic-secularist) in vivid detail, they are in fact, destroying themselves (apostates-pagans) and/or conceiving by your simple presence what faith is all about, thereby bearing witness against themselves. Because knowledge is justified true belief amongst the confusion and the clutter of mankind's endeavors. In vivid detail a people and/or despot that is afraid to freely let its own citizen population judge the truth, and falsehood peacefully in an open free market of ideas and methods, of how to move forward in their lives positively, and stand by the merits of that decision whether they win or lose an election and/or decision knowing that it is with Allah whom they put their trust, but say—shamefully, to their neighbors, and themselves, 'go away, and let`s vote again.' Is a nation that is afraid of itself, knowledge, and justice.

Nations who live in bubbles are those who are afraid of religious, cultural, and political engagement. Indeed, how the people`s faith applies in their daily life in relative to their own hearts tells us the degree of success in their jihad. So we must beware that averse enemy's aim, which would be to attack with the idea that your faith has no freedom! For those who which to be truly free in their lives so why that Islamic way of life, what benefit can there be in avoiding that mutual harm in our society. Such a monotheistic life style would only limit our desires, right. Your faith supposes to enhance your freedom right? Then where's that freedom/that God, that has been brought onward by your faith, oh, Muslim living here in the east in the lands of the prophets surrounded by despots ignorant of the word jihad? Or is this that true condition of your overall hearts, in thus a promise land from your lord, one would sincerely ponder knowing that freedom isn't free and justice is not cheap.

Go East

*He who has a thousand friends has not a friend to spare, and he who
has one enemy will meet him everywhere!*
> —Ali, the fourth caliphate of Islam

How did America make me a better Muslim? Well, that`s a fair and
sincere question, but the real answer is that my first thoughts about
becoming a Muslim happened in America—in prison, in fact. Perhaps
what decided the path I had to take was reading about "*Al-Rahman*"
(Allah most Gracious) (Quran ch.55). It was then I decided to sincerely
answer the question imposed by its author, "*Which of the favors would
I deny my Lord?*" Since this is the holy month of Ramadan perhaps
there is some way I can succeed in getting Allah to work with my plans
knowing that there is none of the favors of my lord I could really deny.
Now it was my turn to reach down into my inner soul, and contemplate
about the Muslim brotherhood I left behind in America. Sitting on that
cool white marble floor inside the huge Al Masjid Al Haram in Mecca,
Saudi Arabia, I gazed at those large golden doors of the *Kaba* (earthly
house of Allah) and those golden words engraved into it. "*There is no
God but Allah and Muhammad is the messenger of Allah.*" The key is written
on those doors. With this key in hand, my mind's eye started unlocking
the painful firewalls of my memory.

I, F.C.I# 06654-016; I, D.C.D.C.# 200-750;—the man who had been
Dave P. Hickson from Teaneck, New Jersey, United States of America;
the man who had served seven years in the Federal Correctional

Institute at Butner, North Carolina—was now in Saudi Arabia two weeks after I finish my parole in America, November 27, 1992. Presently I am sitting in front of these golden doors, waiting soon to meet the Salafi Grand Mufti fundamentalist from Saudi Arabia, Sheikh Ibn Baaz, whom I had journeyed such a great distance to find.

I had first heard of the Grand Mufti when I was in prison, in the fall of 1982, from an African-American man named Hamaas Abdul Khaalis. He was the former national secretary of the Nation of Islam and the leader of a public uprising in the heart of Washington DC in March of 1977 popularly known in the media as the Halafi Siege. Khaalis was in prison for taking over two government buildings and holding over one hundred hostages at the Islamic Center and B'Nai B'rith headquarters in our nation's capitol. In the eyes of the United States government, he was responsible for two deaths during the three-day siege; a policeman, and a radio reporter, as well as the shooting of then-DC city councilman Marion Barry; but for me Hamaas Abdul Khaalis was the man who turned my troubled life towards Islam, and the reason I was now on a pilgrimage to meet the Grand Mufti of Saudi Arabia.

At the time that I met Khaalis, I had started serving seven to twenty-one years for attempt armed robbery and burglary. *I* was not yet a Muslim, but a Christian, a Seventh-Day Adventist but only in name unlike my father. Still Imam Khaalis chose to engage me, which I now consider an honor, because he only spoke with people he felt were worth his time. It has been famously said that when the student is ready, the teacher appears. That you do not seek him; he finds you. Along with another Muslim brother named Samwell Oliver, Imam Khaalis taught me the fundamentals of Islam, though at first only from a distance, since I was a Christian. My first lesson came through observing how the two men greeted each other and how they in turn greeted other Muslims along with an agenda in mind and a spiritual cohesion in practice giving forth a spirit of peace and sincerity, which in prison provided relative relief from a man's anxiety and fear. A man who always spoke seriously and considered every word heard, Imam Khaalis was a man of strong character who never once acted defeated by his incarceration; he was, likewise, a man who keenly understood both religion and the geopolitics of his times.

It was in the awaking fall season of 1982, my first year in Butner, and we were strangers when Imam Khaalis said, "Go to the East, black man, and learn and master that idea of a monotheist faith. Then and only then will you really be satisfied with life." He also said, "Your time is short here, so be patient. Seven to twenty-one years is not a long time, and it would be a disgrace for you not to rise from this prison. Get busy with more good books, take notes, and start a diary. Then go East. Fly East. America is not a place of the God-fearing anymore to learn about God. You will find out soon enough that Islam is the right faith to follow; you will find out soon, insha Allah [if it is the will of Allah]."

"Praise be to Allah" [Hum du Allah]." With a pause, he weighed his words carefully and looked me firmly in the eyes. The Imam Khaalis then said, "Meet the top scholars of our faith and spend your time in their company over there. There is much to learn from them that we need to utilize here at home for our people. But beware those Muslims-in-name-only and their leaders in those countries. They have taken our faith into disrepute and sold out, so stay away from them; they are corrupt."

With a firm whisper, he also said to me, "You went to Howard University a poor black man, then; make this place your sabbatical leave." He then smiled and continued, "You want an education, black man? Then start off with know your God, know yourself, and know your enemy."

The "enemy" he was referring to was the Devil and his human as well as inhuman advocates.

Why did Imam Khaalis spent some of his time with me? Only Allah (swa) knows. Perhaps it was because he knew I did not spend my time with homosexuals, I did not use drugs, or I did not gamble. My name was on nobody's enemy's list, I was trusted and knew how to mind my own business, and I did not betray anybody even for a lighter sentence coming into prison. Yes, I had spent a lot of my time with good books, and I choose my company well, which goes a long way in the sight of men in or out of prison whatever the era.

My third major lesson from Imam Khaalis was the subtle importance of having an Islamic faith in one's life like: "never be afraid of a book" and "not being indignant of any form of information." Faith is a discovery, which is why that golden rule if you want to hide anything from a black man you put it in a book. Faith is a gift from one's lord who only demands gratitude thus no one can put true faith into a person that isn't already there! Under this accord, those first few years of prison, this was a hard sell of having a belief concept that there is a divine being somewhere out there that cannot be seen that is worthy of worship that has not begotten any son (Prophet Jesus). And in spite of any event that may befall any human being that divine being still cares about you; and yet what good is it to spend one's time worshiping such a divine being who does not need your worship anyway.

To be frank, I was wary and sick and tired of white man's lies and those that carry them! Why should I then turn to the Arabs, or Africans, or the Asian beliefs, and put my trust in them and soul in jeopardy? I had truly believed that European Americans and Europeans were devil's advocates and that their track record speaks historically of itself of outright murder, greed, rape, kidnapping, racism, and theft, which is known to those of us enslaved in this modern society called America. I felt at the time during the early years of my life, that I would be a fool what say's insane for believing that there's a divine being out there somewhere that is all powerful plus sees all things and is aware of everything and yet the true reality is hell on earth!

I did not get that scholarship to continue my education at Howard University. I was the only person in the history of my family to ever make it to a university, and those white folks laugh me right out of their banks when I asked for a loan to continue my education. Till this day I never forgot that grinning white face of my banker in Georgetown, Washington DC, on the corner of Wisconsin Ave. North West and on M St. North West back in 1978. He told me they will gladly hold my college tuition funds for me but that request of mine for a student bank loan was totally out of the question for them!

Yes, I was informed by that grinning white bank manager, that at this time banks in this area are not giving out student loans to students who wish to continue their education and they did not know of any banks in the area that was. Depressed and dispirited, as I turned from those grinning white faces I noticed that the only people of color working in these banks in Georgetown, Washington D.C. 1978 were pushing a mop and that job was already taken!

I did not know how dark my skin was until I asked for a bank loan for a college education. I did not know how invisible that American dream was until I tried to work for it living in Washington DC when I was ready to make a difference, and a contribution to my society! Oh, humble reader, please take notice. A vacuum of hope is indeed a very violent place regardless of ghetto, regardless of race, regardless of dreams. The message was clear in those times to the black and minority poor as it is today: "Be all you can be. Join the military." Why did they say this? Because you will not be able to be all what you can be as a civilian that's why. These understood words was gospel then until a black man who had a white mother, whose name was Barack H. Obama became president and entered the White House in January 20, 2009; thus inheriting those ugly bags of wars, lies and corruption follies of our country!

Yes, at the age of twenty-three, I had attempted suicide many times. Yes, I too confess I wanted to be just dust like the millions unfortunate's out there who was sincere in their good endeavors in their lives. Getting a good education meant everything to me, just as important as the air I breathe. Within three years of my college odyssey at Howard University, I began to hate the very society I initially started out to benefit. All I knows for certain is there's no elbow room for me. Once the curtain goes up, it was a short walk. I stepped out into the streets from my dormitory (Carver Hall) that I could not pay for anymore, and walked the streets viewing the oppression and hopelessness that was all around me that I couldn't take anymore, walk to classes that I could not pay for anymore, I did not considered myself a fortunate young black man anymore. I was stealing food to eat at my University cafeteria and in my neighborhood supermarkets, selling my blood for fifteen dollars a liter over at the Children's Hospital to buy a book or something to eat taught me my first lesson about class hatred amongst black people and race deviations amongst white people. That lesson was hate is truly something else!

Oh, humble reader, I am sorry for knocking on your window frame this early on, but there's always a risk when you pick up a fundamental book.

A living wage job was not to be found in Washington DC from 1978 to1981. I was becoming sick to near death within three months after I first enrolled at Howard University in the fall of 1978 because of my worry of not affording to pay my tuition five months from now and no jobs. Then one day in November 1978, because of the stress to achieve, my health gave out on me. My appendix broke and I had to spend a week in Howard University Hospital after the surgery operation. Truthfully, I never really recovered physically or spiritually. I found myself dropping courses I had paid for as a full time student because I was too ill to continue. Now I am a part-time student with fading hope, going out the back door as a college dropout within two hellish years with no hope of a scholarship grant or a bank loan from my community. I was depressed; withdrawn, angry and suicidal. Too ashamed to admit failure or ask for help. I had to steal to eat, so I can get an education to live, this was the reality! I was living in the world's most powerful and richest nation on earth where the rich rob the poor and the poor rob one another. I was enrolled in a University that was made for those of us African descendents enslaved here in the West. So why should I believe in that slave masters God when it's clear that it's the devil that's bouncing the ball?

Now that I am sitting there in prison deemed persona non grata by my society was not a bad idea as far as Allah (swa) is concerned.

Baptism, at a cost of more than $35,000 a year at the time, I did not care anymore, I needed $3,500 a year or a living wage job to stay in the University. I am now in good company; along with hundreds of thousands of my fellow African Americans brothers and sisters who also had dreams deferred. There are more of us here in prisons in America than in American Universities and Colleges; more of us placed on death row than there are sitting Federal judges and Senators in America. The truth that I could not ignore is now who`s the enemy?

Yes, indeed, hate is something else, and no one has ever been able to fully conquer it but prophets. So please, oh, humble reader, do not confuse me with those "little house on the prairie" immigrant Americans. I am, unlike President Obama, a descendant of those millions who was "enslave" on the docks in chains who was brought to these Western shores so that the American dream will be a reality for others!

The United Negro College Fund says: "A mind is a terrible thing to waste," which till this day in the eyes of a reasonable beholder it is nothing less than a huge social scandal, an insult to the very same people it`s focus is aimed at. We as African Americans spend hundreds of millions of dollars on alcohol and cigarettes gladly and know the great harm they have done to ourselves, yet when it is time to invest in our youth and our future in the field of education here in America, we are truly niggardly. I realize this is hard for many of my people and even to me to accept personally, but this is the truth because we as a people lack true leadership and guidance since April 4, 1968. Because of our training, not education, we as a people think we can overcome oppression by way of individualistic ideals and deeds, not by focus to unite and invest together in order to achieve our goals as a nation of oppress people under one roof.

That idea from Imam Khaalis that I am on my "sabbatical leave" from Howard University was the mercy I needed. This was a true cause célèbre for my soul to stay alive and focus on the very merit of purpose in my life, in spite of being in prison, when, in fact, all around me was the living dead. I also became aware that prisons are a big business here in America; the ruling elite creates enough social and economic hunger in the ghettos, and then everyone is a criminal to exploit. For the lack of social graces, prisons are a place of cheap labor to exploit and a breeding ground of homosexuality.

Knowing about God (Allah) through the Quran also made me understand that I must change my attitude in my heart in my pursuit of accomplishments in my life. Like good intentions does not necessarily mean success.

It was Imam Khaalis who informed me that if a poor man has to steal because he needs food to eat and live, then he is no thief; he is just not patient with his lord. He also said, "Knowing when to walk away from an American dream because you cannot cash in the color of your skin is as well important in life in this Western world." Till this day I still remember walking along out in the prison yard on a bright sunny winter day in January 1983 with Imam Khaalis talking with him about some of my experiences and struggles when I was living in Washington DC as a student. Yes, he knew about the struggles of young African Americans and what we are going through in the urban ghettos of our country, particularly Washington DC in which he lives near with his family for many years. I told Imam Khaalis all about the false charges my government accuse me of just so they can get a conviction of attempt armed robbery and burglary; those false charges were armed robbery, kidnapping and rape. I told Imam Khaalis that the police tried to empty their backlogged cold cases on me knowing that I was some suicidal black young man stealing food to survive who did not care about life anymore. I was found not guilty of armed robbery, not even indicted for kidnapping or rape of white women. But the damage was done. My government was right: I did not care about life anymore. Their threat of life imprisonment was no threat to a dead man digging two graves, one for myself and one for them. Imam Khaalis remained silent for about fifteen minutes we just walked along that long dirt path inside the barbed wire fence of our prison together quietly for a while watching the world go by . . . then he said kindly an admonishment: "Hate is something else."

Yet Imam Khaalis aimed higher and said to me a (Hadith-Qudsi) related by "Al-Bukhari" on the son of Abbas who was one of the companions of prophet Muhammad (sas) the messenger of Allah who said that the prophet said: "Allah has written down the good deeds and the bad ones. Then he explained it [by saying that] he who has intended a good deed and has not done it, Allah writes it down with himself as a full good deed, but if he has intended it and has done it, Allah writes it down with himself as from ten good deeds to seven hundred times over. But if he has intended a bad deed and has not done it, Allah writes it down with himself as a full good deed, but if he has intended it and has done it, Allah writes it down as one bad deed." After another five minutes or so of silent walking letting me digest what he had said he continued: "Let success be your revenge, by increasing your good deeds and being more conscious of your intentions in not acting on your bad deeds in life. You had intended to do many bad deeds (attempted armed robbery, burglary and suicide) and had not acted on them on April 11, 1981 which you are now in prison for, so let that saving grace of those good deeds be beneficial in your life." "And ask for forgiveness from Allah"

Knowing myself means appreciating a gospel or good news from a stranger who has reverence for their lord who is generous beyond any deserts of their own. Understanding the difference of being misguided and guided, miseducated and educated, what is trained and what is educated, what is knowledge obtained from investigation and what is governmental or individual propaganda is a gift. This way I can better apply with success my goals and methods starting from now even in American prisons. I must learn to be patient.

It`s with that understanding that the fortunes of many deserts are raised by distant storms. Between the fall season of 1982 and the winter of 1984, I kept Imam Khaalis in my peripheral vision while we were together in Butner Federal Correctional Institute. Who can deny the healing rewards of mercy? We all want so much from that divine being whom we trust in heaven, but at the end of the day, we give so little compassion to our fellow human beings here on earth. For example, Imam Khaalis could have killed all those peoples and Jews he'd held hostage at B'nai-Brith in Washington DC but he understood "Allah (swa) orders us to be merciful."[10] "Allah (swa) loved not the transgressors" and "help ye one another in righteousness (Quran 41:33) "but judge ye not one another in sin and rancor" (Quran 95:8).

He was a Hanafi fundamentalist Muslim American who took a stand for a cause. He was a man that dared to take part in a religiously and politically public uprising in the heart of Washington DC back in March 9-11, 1977. For his beliefs and message, the courts there gave him multiple life sentences in federal prisons. He had led a determined group that held over one hundred people hostage there. It all started off as a sectarian dispute between the Hanafis Muslims led by Imam Khaalis against those who were members of the Nation of Islam, an African American Nationalist group who had murdered members of his family who was women and children. Imam Khaalis and some of his followers took over government buildings, the Islamic Center in Washington DC and B`nai—Brith also in Washington DC a Jewish organization.

---

[10]   Quran 42:25

Subsequently, they shot a D.C. city council man name Marion Barry in the chest, the future mayor of Washington D.C. killed a policeman and a radio reporter. His siege came with demands. Firstly that sacrilegious movie the *kufrs* producers wanted to show was *Muhammad, Messenger of God* to the world audience over the objections of many Muslim leaders here in America and the Muslim world. The main issue of concern and objection was that the *kufr* producers of this film was planning to put a human face in the role of prophet Muhammad (sas) in their movie which is seriously forbidden in Islamic jurisprudence and they the *kufr* producers had ignored many Muslim scholars warnings and objections worldwide!

Secondly, the American government was to hand over those convicted criminals over to them for punishment, those murders of women and children of their leader Hamas Abdul Khaalis. It took the combined efforts of three Muslim ambassadors—from Egypt: ambassador Ashraf Ghorbal; Pakistan, ambassador Sahabzada Yaqub; and Iran, ambassador Ardeshir Zahedi, may Allah bless them and other Sunni Muslim American leaders who helped win the release of all the hostages and help bring an end to the protest, terror, and anger.

Yes, I believe he was that other stem cell from the old Nation of Islam the Western news media and newspapers had truly wanted the African American people to forget about in our history.

Why? Because he feared no one, least of all, his own government! And he obeyed the calls of mercy from his own Muslim scriptures. Imam Khaalis was the Nation of Islam`s first national secretary and a dear friend of Malcolm X, Kareem Abdul Jabbar, Muhammad Ali, as well as many other believers who also had left the Nation of Islam and embraced mainstream Sunni Islam.

When I had last saw Imam Khaalis, I was still a Christian; but because of him and a group of other Muslim believers imprisoned with me, I started reading the holy Quran in earnest. I was truly surprised to learn that that Hanifa fundamentalist of the school of thought of the Islamic jurisprudence was founded by Abu Hanifa. He was born in Kufa, Iraq. He was truly one of the earliest and renowned Muslim Scholars in seeking new ways of applying Islamic tenets to people's everyday lives. But in his own life, Abu Hanifa was called an inventor of new beliefs, a hypocrite, a kufr, and humiliated by his peers and fellow Muslims as well as imprisoned plus poisoned. Today the Hanifa school of thought is Islam`s largest, numbering hundreds of millions of followers throughout the Muslim World.

I had to take advantage of my time in prison—I had no choice—and through a lot of research, debate and pondering the facts with

Imams, Christian preachers, and rabbi`s in regards to following a full monotheistic faith in life, it was Islam that had a lot of credibility, persuasiveness and truth in it that I could not ignore! Oh, humble reader, it is of no coincidence that Islam is the fastest-growing religion in and out of American prisons simply because if that individual is sincere at heart and wants a change in his or her life for the better and has some time on their hands to read and compare and weigh the truth of what is a monotheist faith really is without bias or fear of what he or she will find, it is indisputable that book will be the Quran.

That Muslim chaplain from Durham, North Carolina—his name was—Imam Muhammad who worked with Butner, F.C.I. as a prison chaplain at the time was for the lack of a better word "relentlessly authentic." If there`s anyone can best explain the three basic principles of the monotheist faith to those who are in prison that gave up on accepted social norms and who are ambivalent towards that idea of a divine being worth praying to, it was him. He said to us, "The first principle was that the creator of the heavens and the earth, that one divine being, does not pray to anyone, everything and everyone pray`s to him. The second principle was that the creator of the heavens and the earth, that one divine being, has no need of anything from his creation. The third principle was that the creator of the heavens and the earth, that divine being, does not die." In other words, knowing your God comes first in life. It is of the utmost importance not to confuse the boundaries of a Monotheist faith and its purpose with the pagan ideal and their aesthetics transcendence. For example,

"The Jews call Uzair a son of God, and the Christians call Christ the son of God. That is a saying from their mouth, [in this] they imitate what the unbelievers of old used to say. God`s curse be on them: how they are deluded away from the truth! They take their priests and their anchorites to be their lords in derogation of God, and [they take as their lord] Christ the son of Mary; Yet they were commanded to worship but one God: there is no god but he. Praise and glory to him: [Far is he] from having the partners they associate [with him]" (Quran 9:30-31). And *"Then the lord addressed Job out of the storm and said: Who is this that obscures divine plans with words of ignorance? While the morning stars sang in chorus and all the sons of God shouted for joy?"* (Torah-Job ch.38:1-7). *"Such was Jesus the son of Mary: it is a statement of truth, about which they vainly dispute. It is not befitting to the majesty of God that he should beget a son. Glory be to him! When he determines a matter, he only says to it 'Be' and it is"* (Quran 19:34-35).

So at the beginning of my fourth year of my sabbatical, leave I shifted into second gear and reverted to the Islamic religion from Christianity and also received an associate degree in optics at Durham

Technical Institute while I was still in prison hum du Allah. At the beginning of my fifth year, I shifted into third gear and started to study Arabic from the Quran. At the beginning of my sixth year, I shifted into fourth gear by studying and understanding the major schools of thought in Islam and Judaism. At the beginning of my seventh year, I dedicated myself to memorizing fifteen chapters of the holy Quran in Arabic, this was my fifth gear thou in reality the beginning of my compass.

Therefore, it came to pass. That Muslim chaplain of Butner, North Carolina, F.C.I., Imam Muhammad, from Durham N.C. and I sat down together in the last few days before I left prison and said he decided the best Muslim name for me would be Muhammad Dawud! He said this name best suits my character. Imam Muhammad was a Muslim African American like myself; he also went on to explain that my family name Hickson given to my forefathers in slavery by means of oppression and hate is not accepted in Islam. A person`s name means a lot in Islam; it is also an attribution of character. It was prophet Muhammad (sas) who was the first-known prophet to change people`s names from bad ones to good names. Prophet Muhammad (sas) said our names are attributes of ourselves and that a Muslim cannot inherit a name base on hate and/or oppression. So my slave name Dave P. Hickson is a name base on both hate and oppression because of the history of slavery here in the West; thus, I cannot carry such a name. And should legally change my name to Muhammad, which means "trustworthy" in Arabic, and Dawud, which means "beloved" in Arabic as soon as possible. Then Imam Muhammad looked at me sternly and said, "You will be placed on parole by this government for many years before you can again be a free man. Parole means, 'on your word of honor,' this should be an easy for you because of your name! I know you came to prison not because you are a thief but because you 'lack patience.' Go east, young man, and Allah will teach you how to be patient with him! Be a part of an Islamic movement!"

Getting a job on parole was the easy in January 1989. Finding Muslims friends only was also the easy. Finding a Muslim community I can work with was the hardest. Living an Islamic life style was also hard. Many Mosques here in America 1989 till the present day were built for show, a museum, only a few was built for brotherhood of worship who`s goal is to unite the hearts of the Muslim people here in America and live an Islamic lifestyle, which have methods that can be seen in the positive and whose aim is by rising the consciousness of the communities around them by producing high social achievements for society. Why? Cohesion is not our Muslim middle name in our relationships towards different Muslim communities here in America or even for that matter in Europe. Why? Too many Muslim leaders in the West put their culture in front of their faith, which is sabotaging our social Muslim lives in this alien secular society.

I realize my goal was to leave America as soon as possible after I completed my parole because the solutions in regards to achieving true social justice and social liberty here in America for one`s neighbors and one`s self rested in traveling and studying in the East. From the time I went to prison in 1982 to 1989, the people`s social conditions here in America has truly gotten worse. The poor has gotten poorer and the middle class has gotten smaller. Moreover, the rich has gotten greedier. It was a strange view, yes indeed. I was in prison for seven years, but hundreds of millions of my American compatriots are now living with dread of the future, and driving modern cars and living in modern homes, which are more and more base on a usury bubble! I knew I needed to learn more Arabic and study with Muslim scholars overseas; it was time to focus on going beyond the here and now-to getting it done.

A good message is an idea in motion, but in this modern Western society where tens of millions of people are working harder and falling behind faster, I simply asked myself a basic question. What can I do that will help make a meaningful contribution to my society, and who are the people that will help soothe that understanding in one`s soul, which will help me become more aware, and will tell me that we the Muslim community, who are here in this land are indeed special, with the true aim of helping their fellow neighbors accomplish their goals in life? Why? Because America is no place to dream petite nor is it a place for living in a bubble amongst the masses of secular people and move positively ahead.

Many of my Muslim brothers at the mosque Dur Al Islah in Teaneck New Jersey, my hometown was a great disappointment. Most was from Pakistan and India. Only a few was really religious, friendly and sincere at heart. Those who would invite you over to their homes or apartments to sit down and talk or even just for a cup of tea and explain how grateful they were of Allah`s bounties unto them and their families and why they are on this path here in America were few. I notice a lot of empty smiles, dead fish handshakes, and vain talk. Too much time was wasted on infighting about who gets to sit in the chair of leadership. Too much class and racial divide amongst them, not enough subtle social graces to go around I felt. Very little time was spent in (Dowa) preaching to non-Muslims in calling them into the fold of Islam, and a lot of time is spent talking and reminding Muslims how to be Muslims. The consequences was not enough Muslims leading the Muslim community by way of example and a lighthouse to those non Muslim communities all around us as an example to follow as well as answering that universal question: "What will makes a life so significant, is that Islam can make a great difference in your life in a positive way."

The Imam of the mosque then till this day has no power in the form of true leadership, sadly just a person to lead the prayers on time or someone you can go to, to talk about religious issues. The mosque is ruled by self-serving committee members and trustee`s in which they have the last and final word on the matter at hand based on their own self vested interests. The struggle here at home in Teaneck, New Jersey`s Muslim community in reality was not who was the most Allah fearing person amongst us, nor who are the most knowledge persons to be Imam to lead the Muslim community to a higher moral ground having the last word. But who has the most power and influence to be the President not Imam, to lead the Muslim community and direct the Muslim people in a Western democratic secular format. These immigrant Muslims had place their power base not on trust, of the example of the way of prophet Muhammad (sas), as a result, they, the early leaders of Dur al Islah mosque, dragged each other to court in shameful disputes of power sharing, making allegedly Jewish lawyers rich and kufr judges in Bergen County New Jersey courts pondering the very merit of their faith. On top of all the confusion here in my Muslim community in my hometown, they was unnecessarily divided along ethnical lines much like Christian churches and Jewish synagogues. Yet those few Muslims like (Dr. S. Sultan) and others that I had found there at Dar al Islah was enough to give me the Islamic guidance that I needed, Hum du Allah, they know who they are, may Allah bless them all. So, whatever good Allah fearing Muslim you find therein any mosque, you hold on to him like your life dependent on it, because it does in reality, and this is the truth I hope will help a new believer not give rise to anxiety to eventually walking away from the faith.

Living in this Western secular country is an era full of risk, grasping the possibilities of human fulfillment amongst that sea of material distraction is a jihad in of itself. So; I asked myself and my lord, what can I learn from these immigrant Muslims most of whom seeking worldly gain and liberties, other than a community is a terrible thing to waste. It sadden me greatly that only a few had travel to the West who`s interest is for the mercy of Allah first and foremost and not get so caught up in these abstractions in life which is another example of how America made me become a better Muslim! Yet those few that I had found was enough to give me the guidance that I needed.

Do not believe the hype; not all U.S. parole officials are encouraged to report a negative. When my parole officer heard of something genuine worthwhile like me requesting to travel to the Middle East for four months to study Islam, he responded with an eagle eye, by saying this is a challenge we can meet. He himself a Christian, his roots and family from Syria, which was ominous because he had a spiritual curious personality about himself, he knew what was Islam over there because he was born, and lived in a Muslim country as youth. He read my file, he watched me secretly like a hawk for months, did I really knew what`s behind my new Muslim name? Now I am asking him to go find Allah (swa) in the dark?

Promising the return of the Holy Grail I was granted permission to fly to Egypt and Pakistan while I was still on parole in the summer of June 1990 to meet with some Muslim scholars for the next four months. I was not aware that my first journey visiting Muslim countries would change my life in its perception of Islam greatly to the very core of my faith.

Those who have eyes and can see are reluctant to deny that I was not the only person walking the streets of Cairo, Egypt, on parole. Millions of people camouflaged in their worldly affaires are truly obsessed with staying sane and resisting the calls of jihad against their own despot leaders and straying countrymen was a shock to me. This ominous desert storm is not just lingering clouds passing over for the promotion of shade. Egypt was not just as I expected to be. They the majority of the people who wanted the modern world potentials without Allah`s negative consequences, yet that`s actually what`s been unfolding in their lives disastrously for decades! That signature trait of restraint is not the cost of bread on the street corners or the distasteful price of social injustice that is prominent but the olive character of their hearts in understanding what is at stake. "You cannot eat Sharia" is the byword of the ruling opposition. Now I realize the price of where this idea of not allowing the Sheikhs the last word on their matters of social justice and religious sovereignty in regard to custodianship of the state would lead to. Going East and seeing what happens to a people who don`t pay heed to their unseen sovereign lord was very important if the truth be told.

Those who have eyes and see are reluctant to deny that we don`t live by accident. Taking on the heat of the day is the only way Karachi, Pakistan, can melt into you. You want to really live? Then go nonstop through that medieval traffic on a cycle rickshaw from Karachi airport to the huge Medina mosque in downtown Karachi and check in for sixty hours!

Since it`s designed to meet the assume demands of lifelong Islamic learning, lectures are held day and night and led by Sheikhs and Imams who has power, knowledge, and influence over human events that will change how you think about the Islamic world. Catering mainly to the super poor, drug addicts, students of knowledge, and those who are spiritually risk averse that are going nowhere fast. Medina Mosque is that five star Islamic oasis in the center of a city that has taken the neighborhood and community around it into a high moral ground and bridges the urgency of hope towards its citizens!

I soon realized that I was indeed not the only student of knowledge with the idea of returning homeward with that Islamic Holy Grail. There, were other young men from the west whom I had met at Medina Mosque in Karachi who was also seeking Islamic knowledge in the Muslim world from widely diverse backgrounds. There was one brother—a Muslim African American from Los Angeles, California—whose name is Abdullah and another Muslim American whose family roots is from Pakistan. His name is Ahmed. We also met very serious-minded Muslim brothers from Canada, London, United Kingdom, and South Africa. We were a mix group of all races— white, black, Arab and Asian—about fourteen in all. Our group was a Tablighi Jamaat. Our mission was twofold: met those Muslim scholars in (Rai-Wind) near Lahore and met those Mujahideen up north in Dir, North-West Frontier Provence; talk with them and find out what is really going on in Afghanistan and in Northern Pakistan now that the Russians has been defeated and kicked out.

Three days later after early Morning Prayer service (Fajar prayer) at Mosque Medina, our native English-speaking group was given a Pakistani guide who was an imam who can speak both English and Arabic to shepherd us on our journey up north.

The journey from Karachi to Rai-wind about 30 miles south of Lahore, Pakistan, lasted twenty-two hours by a train that was full of hopeful optimism for all of us. Emerging from that timeless old vintage train in which you do not move, you just absorb the scenery as best as you can in this Asian scented world. These Asian peoples are not enforcing some social living code by a race of unseen demons or saints. It`s just why so many men like to wear the same type clothing I just don't know? Anyone can see they do have freedom here in this land called Pakistan; nobody is oppressing any one here. And as we travel further up north, I can see that to a greater degree their faith reflects the base of their freedom.

We as a group of foreign Muslim English-speaking travelers were united in the desire to contribute our time for a cause, for an idea, for a faith. The question is how we can channel the cause into the common ground of understanding for our fellow Muslim brothers and sisters back home.

Just up ahead a short walk north of the train station in Rai-wind stood an old man at the foot of a busy pathway leading to an open field nesting large buildings. He's holding a large cane upright conveying confidence and authority; this is where Muslim scholars, students of knowledge and curious visitors come to connect.

It was an Islamic jamboree of about 10,000 people from all over the Muslim world coming together to hear different viewpoints of liberal Islam. Once we checked in and registered to the authorities within. We listen to what the scholars had to say with an open mind. But those Muslim scholars from Pakistan and the Arab world knew that seven days of listening to standardize liberal discussions on Muslim way of life was our western limit. That dialogue about Allah presence that's all around us all the time was helpful to know. However, we come from lands that is ruled by kafr. Thus, progressive Islamic ideas are what we need behind enemy lines when mapping out and paving the road ahead, digesting the invisible foregrounds of faith and reason.

They the "underground" didn't expect us to either understand the nature of Allah or get the understandings of the nature of evil in a few weeks. That was for Allah's mercy. They just wanted to know whether we can take life's punches and stand back up not be counted out. Plus, are there any of us that are forbidden undercover intelligent agents from our western countries? That's all. Genuinely that task of getting people to see beyond reason and take that leap of faith is the most difficult thing to do, a daunting task, the real job, their ultimate concern.

Unceremoniously, we were broken up into three groups each with our own new permanent Pakistani guides. My group consist of three Americans and two South Africans. The other two groups were British and Canadians. We found ourselves placed back on our journey going up north on another train that was jam-packed with people that was standing room only on our way to a city called Rawalpindi. As we gotten into the rhythm and rhyme of our journey once again, I found it difficult at times to settle back and take it all in. It was hard, psychologically at the time to believe that just two years ago I was sitting in an American federal prison in solitary confinement. My meals were being handed to me between the bars in darkness and silence. Now the horizon is before me. Some young kid, not more than fourteen years old is running side by side our train and is handing me three whole hot roasted spiced chickens resting on a large flat oval baked bread through my train window for me and my comrades to eat and enjoy in this jam pack train full of amazing people with something in common to say in their humble lives. This scenery made me pause and reflect deeply how far I came from that hole in the wall isolation to this spiritual soul train on the other side of the world. It was when that Pakistani kid shouted with shock and joy when I handed him a twenty-dollar American bill that I realize that he did not see nor even could imagine that it was me who had gotten the real bargain, that extra in life; what's not to love? If you stay patient, it will come to you.

Upon our arrival in the city of Rawalpindi, our new and young bearded studious guide Muhammad quickly hired a mini-bus for us to continue our journey to the city of Abbottabad. He deeply assures us from the heart that we within the coming years, will indeed come to love this Muslim Asian world. He was right. The main road from Rawalpindi to Abbottabad are lined with large and beautiful eucalyptus trees which gives a rich aromatic comfort zone smell that helps put to ease any would be wary traveler.

I was not the only one to notice that as we have been traveling north since Rawalpindi. The forests of palm gave way to a forest of pine. Likewise, people gave way more thoroughly to distinctively Islamic religious mannerism. Such as, more and more men young and old, walking about with full beards and prayer beads in their hands and pockets, in a humble ongoing stride, whispering hushed utterance of prayers. Furthermore, more women young and old I notice particularly walking about in chastity in public, in proper hijab (head scarf) and in full nekab (head and body covering), going about their daily affairs in a humble manner, piteously not displaying their beauty and charms to the public eye. As well as, I notice, the streets and roads became further deserted of people during the times of Muslim prayers.

There is a happiness in an age of ideological anxiety in this Muslim Asian world which makes it safe from the looming tomorrow. I bear witness to this fact upon arrival when we met some community leaders in Abbottabad in the late afternoon. They live in simple large walled villas and some in small suburban non-walled villas. My group stayed and rested in our first night as guest with a man name Mr. Khan, who is a strong influence and member of Jamaat i Islami. He and three other

Pakistani religious men from the community held a small banquet in
our honor, consisting of delicious lamb, chicken and rice under a large
beautiful banyan tree.

They wanted to know about our viewpoints in the growing state of
Islam in America and in South Africa. I told them America is an idea
not solely a place on a map. And that idea of democratic secularism is
not compatible with that idea of Islam in America. The coin we all bear
in America say`s "In God we trust," yet it is not an idea lifeline that is
banked on with full conviction by all the people therein. There is still
a culture of hostility towards religious organizations playing a central
role in the political social arena there in the secular west.

The Muslim brothers from South Africa told a different story of
how Islam is not the cutting edge of that demand for social freedom
and justice in South Africa. Nor are the majority of Muslim leaders
therein are campaigning vigorously with a jihad spirit to end that
apartheid government. Instead, the attitude therein amongst the
millions of Muslims was how they can achieve financial success
dealing with the apartheid government in spite of the sanctions from
overseas. The fact of the matter is that they themselves suffer from
racism and class discrimination from within themselves. You don`t
have to be related to relate that very few Muslim are truly mindful to
that goal idea of "want for your brother what you want for yourselves."
Proselytizing is very weak amongst the Muslims towards their neighbors
whether they are black Africans or white Europeans who had made
it their home in South Africa, in spite of having a known charismatic
fundamentalist Muslim scholar who is a famous writer and public
speaker to lead the way whose name is Ahmed Deedat. Certainly there
is indeed racism problems with their black African neighbors in spite
of Muslims from South Asia living in South Africa for generations both
being oppress by the same enemy near. The problem is there is very
little demand by the Muslims living therein to make a sacrifice for the
mercy of Allah to make that change.

Consequently, when Nelson Mandela achieved his freedom on
February 11, 1990, it was the African National Congress a (Black
Nationalist Organization) that was given the full credit of bringing true
social justice and real change to all the South African people therein
that ended the apartheid way of life and government. No known
Muslim organization or Muslim person was given any honorary credit
or known contribution of sacrifice for social justice to end oppression
and apartheid in South Africa by all its people, in spite of their holy
books (Quran) that they have in the millions in their homes. They

said, (Muslim students of knowledge from South Africa) this was a true loss of a spiritual opportunity for the emancipation of a people (Black South Africans) under the same circumstances as they was under the same roof. Allah didn`t get an opportunity to take a bow therein.

I can tell by the way they hang their heads and balance their philosophy that precarious balance of power here in the central Muslim Asian world is now facing a crisis of inner intolerance. That being the case, it`s no accident that the Mujahideen get`s few moments of R&R (rest and recreation). Our guide Muhammad had awakened us on the third morning of our stay in Abbottabad saying it was time to move on. By the way, Abbottabad is a vibrant Pakistani military town.

Our group somehow got the green light to continue onward into the North-West Frontier Provence; a town called Dir was our destination. Perhaps it was that righteous insistence in our jihad, that interest in true public service that is putting us on an upward path to meet the subtle mountain warriors of Islam. Dir is a small quiet town tuck away up in the mountains less than fifteen miles from the Afghanistan border. Forgive me for not telling you more about the spectacular view; it`s just that time is short I am on parole. You can somehow feel it in the air. The grief, sorrow and betrayal in this whole region are real. When I reflect back on my own limited Muslim education at the time, as well as that idea of knowledge that guided me, and my society in the sense of what is significant in this ideological struggles we Muslims in the West are behind the curve. You can listen and talk all you want about the Islamic way of life, but you better be wise enough to sit and listen to those who know how to fight for it!

It was early in the evening after sunset (Maghreb) prayer while resting awhile in one of the guesthouses in Dir from a long mountainous trip when we got word of invite to come over and talk the hard talk. There was no need to frisk us for weapons as we entered their guest house which was a simple walled mud brick villa. Asalam Alakum (Peace be upon you) was the relief they needed as to our intentions. They all rise and said in unison, "Walaycom Asalam [And unto you peace]," which was the sign of welcome we needed as to their intentions. As we approached each other to shake hands and give hugs under the light of oil lanterns, I distinctively became aware that we wouldn`t need Muhammad, our guide for the help of translations. For this meeting of hearts, minds and souls was between countrymen, they were a platoon of Muslim Americans, British and Arabs (Saudi Arabia). The leader of their platoon was from Philadelphia, United States of America. His name Yusuf, a Muslim African American. My lesson at that moment of time was there are enormities of virtues in the visionary you simply have to make the first step forward.

Truthfully, tactfully, I cannot put down in words all that was said of those Muslims from our Western communities who had sacrifice their lives and time for the mercy of Allah whom I had met here in the town of Dir, Pakistan, because of today`s national security phobia and politics of fear here at home. But I was grateful to be in their company and to hear what they had to say.

The leader of their platoon, brother Yusuf, motions all of us to sit; and then he said, "All praise is due to Allah, and we thank Allah for sending to us Prophet Muhammad (sas) to us as a guide and mercy to all mankind. May Allah bless Prophet Muhammad (sas), and may Allah bless the Imam`s and elders of this town Dir, in NWFP, the people of Pakistan, and those Muslim believers in Afghanistan for allowing us to contribute in the fighting the invading Communist pagans, and now may Allah bless us and give us strength to fight the apostates of Islam."

Then he pause for three minutes, allowing us all to settle and be relaxed letting his words in the spacious scented room lined with thick rugs and a noticeable large black flag with white Arabic letters hanging in the far corner wall behind them, which says "There is no God but Allah and Muhammad is the servant and massager of Allah." He continues briefly by stating their epic victory is: 'Why' we are there fighting our neighbors not 'Who' are they?"

I knew from an early childhood in the Bronx, New York City, when you fight for a cause you better know 'why' first, not who. The most important thing above your neck is not for beauty, you have to really use it, or you lose it. Hum du Allah, owning to one of the natures of jihad we got a chance to tread through the minefields without walking through the door and learn from these western Mujahideen's on the front lines whom we share the same culture and faith about what`s going on in the moral and political significance of this asymmetrical warfare.

Brother Yusuf went on to say, "Fighting the Communist was the easy, hum du Allah. They were fighting using the mind-set of chess. We countered by fighting them by using the laws of Sun Tzu the 'art of war.' The moral battle had already been won because we was Muslims; the people was Muslim in many degrees of faith. And we was fighting against a pagan invading army who`s aim was to control our lives, faith, and lands."

"At this point and time my brothers, our main conflict and disputes are religious and social political rights. Now they wish to rule Afghanistan by democratic secular laws. This Ahmad Monsur and his

Northern Alliance organization—they who was our allies in war—are now enemies in peacetime. They did not wish to submit to the laws of Allah, the Sharia. Unfortunately, their sponsors are Western, and they believe Sharia law will deny them justice, wanting sovereignty for themselves and not Allah. At present this is the hard, the real secular opium that`s stirs in the hearts, minds and souls of some of our neighbors. This is a disease, which is a man made idea of faith that say`s it is best suited to handle your public affairs outside of your faith, outside your home and temple, because of so many different degrees of faith that we have amongst ourselves."

Brother Yusuf went on to say, "This has always been a fundamental foe of Islam, in regards to [Aqeeda], the purity of faith verses that secular man made idea, that tactic of dividing the private life from the social public life of the Muslim individuals. Namely to view and believe life and manmade laws outside of one`s divine sovereign's lord is best and modern. This secular faith concept of abstinence of one`s faith in the public arena, which the apostates believe, will ultimately nullifies cases of conflict in a tribal pluralistic society in terms of fulfillment of one's needs and aspirations in communion with the common good is a milestone that must be destroyed in Muslim lands."

He then pause for five minutes letting his words in the room be glowed by the light of lanterns find its way to our hearts and settle into our understanding. Consequently, the difference between his spiritual mental clothing and the ethical garments of the enemy near apostates is in the basic fundamental details of our faith. It`s, "Why" we are fighting our neighbors, not "Who" are they? The reason is that many of our neighbors has apostate the faith of Islam for political reasons!

Without a sound, our guide Muhammad stood up, and reached into his jacket pocket and pulled out some letters from their homes in the West behind enemy lines for these anxious battle—harden mujahideen. As we students of knowledge watched these mujahideen nervously open some of their letters from home, it is apparent in this great secular scourge, that dire reality here in the central Muslim Asian world is in a precarious balance of power of faiths. It`s agreed, that we are now facing a new crisis and that battle of jihad is far from over just because we the believers kicked the pagan Communist out of Afghanistan. This next battle chapter the Muslim world is now facing is secular apostasy, introduce by Western secularism.

We can tell by the way they hang their heads and balance their philosophy that the fighting and disputes is not an ignorant overt partisan warfare. But a deadly social religious civil war between those of a faith called Islam and why they wish to live by the laws of their faith in their Muslim country; verses, those that have Muslim names but wish to live by laws outside of their faith in their Muslim country as well. Islam and secularism are two different ways of life, a person cannot call himself a Muslim (one who submits to the will of Allah) and a secularist (a belief that promotes human values without religious doctrines) at the same time.

I am sure you will understand now, oh, humble reader, that serious blows to the head for most people is hearing talk without experience, and hearing philosophy without practicality is not a sacred thing to cherish. This trip to the Pakistani-Afghanistan border, a true civil war front lines, had a great effect on me and left me with a strong Islamic awakening impact on my life personally, because I understood clearly for myself that that hopeful outside conventional wisdom that many Muslim people been hoping for like a Gandhi style non violence approach towards the dire issues at hand will not work. Simply because this faith of secularism is being imposed from outside our faith by sovereign secular powers for political and religious reasons, not by Muslims themselves demanding justice within their faith.

Indeed, violence was the last resort and the believers were left with the only option of jihad against those that apostate their faith and did not submit to the will and sovereignty of Allah. The believers in the faith of Islam had to fight one and all, and never succumb to the temptations of letting the unborn be the recipient of long and desolate nights of despots with Muslim names and Secular laws that segregate a monotheistic people again. May Allah bless these Mujahideen, Taliban and Al Qaeda resistance fighters.

Yet what had astonish me was the lingering question of where do I go from here? By the time dawn came and the sun rose early above the mountains on the third day of our stay here in Dir with our fellow Muslim Mujahideen telling it like it is, akin to . . . "Allies in war, can never be enemies in peace time."

Deeply moved by what we had heard and experience we students of knowledge marched back down the mountains dispatched and resolved knowing more about jihad and what's outside the glare of faith and reason!

Upon my return back to America from my four-month Egyptian-Pakistani trip aboard in the fall of 1990, I reported back to my parole officer that I had completed my religious seminar. He did seemed quite surprise that I came back at all. He was inquisitive about my religious trip aboard, and I told him briefly about my experience I had in Egypt and in Pakistan except for Dir, NWFP. He was obliged to welcome me back and told me I must start working again as soon as possible and report back to him before the end of the month.

When a boxer steps out of the ring, that is when the real fighting starts, I kid you not. The backbone of faith verses your desires—this is the first jihad, controlling your inner desires. Yes, I got myself a job again and save money for a car and rented a room not far from the mosque. Indeed I stayed away from drugs, alcohol, women, parties, and bad company. And got closer spiritually to my Christian parents and those Muslims who was sincere in their faith at our mosque in Teaneck. Frankly, I went about salvaging my life. Gone was the slave master's family name Hickson I had been carrying for thirty years. I had by then legalize my Muslim name in the courts. Gone was the slave master's Western culture I had been following all my life; now I follow an Islamic one. And gone was the slave master's religion and viewpoints in my life, I now have a faith that I choose base on truth freely and a culture that will not clutter my life with falsehoods!

I made the right choices I believe, so now is the time to walk the faith and let my character profit from these new experiences in my life as well as learn from the experiences from my past life.

My horizons have indeed expanded physically and spiritually: Howard University, then federal prison, then homecoming, finally religious field trips to Egypt and Pakistan! Where do I go from here? I could get myself married once I get off parole. But no, not in America. I need to know my God more. Earning a living in a western secular society is no easy task. The economy is not that strong, and living wage jobs is still few yet real success doesn't come without sacrifice and discipline. Patience.

Then one day a Muslim man name Dr. Hassan Al-Turabi from Sudan came to New York City in the spring of 1992. So I made it my business to visit him at his Sudanese Embassy and have a word with him about Islam and perhaps visit him in Sudan. Dr. Al-Turabi's English was good enough, and he impress me with his creative cooperation ideas among peoples of different faiths and cultures but of the same needs. Dr. Al-Turabi, I felt, understood that the Arab-dominated north must overcome the racial and religious challenges that they face in their country and that time was not on their side but that ball of success was still in their court. I was very much impressed to meet a well—educated African religious and political leader who was conscious of the importance of the unity of Islam and the welfare of the black African peoples of sub-Sariah in Sudan as well as in America. In hindsight I am glad I took the opportunity to meet and talk with him about that new generation that is upcoming that has new ideas on how to govern Sudan with justice between the Arab north and their rivals the non Muslim black Africans in the south. I must confess that after my meeting with Dr. Hassan Al-Turabi, I indeed put Sudan on my list of must-see and learn about first hand. And I must confess that I am glad that Allah (swa) granted my prayers to go to Sudan. I was greatly rewarded with knowledge and wisdom in my quest there; also, I discovered a lot about my faith Islam, racism, and nationalism in action overseas to compare and ponder about in their adverse relationship together under one roof.

After three years and ten months, I was granted parole in November, 1992. By then my resolution was to take a firm leap of faith and go to Saudi Arabia, and sit with the scholars of Islam who can correctly explain what the meaning of this new faith is! For the record my Christen father and brother Clive, did not wanted me to leave home (America) and go east and learn about Islam, they did not trust the people therein at all. As far as they was concerned it`s the land full of Goliaths. My Christen mother was full of worry she did not know what to do other than say she will say a lot of prayers for me at her church we use to go to together as a family years ago in Teaneck.

Hum du Allah, I landed at Jeddah International airport just after Thanksgiving in late November, 1992; at the end of a mini sandstorm. The flight from New York Kennedy airport to Jeddah, Saudi Arabia nonstop lasted almost 12 hours. After passing through customs, I stood there in the middle of the huge gallery of the arrival gate with smiling and cheering faces of all nationalities welcoming their friends and family loved ones in joy. That golden rule of always travel light was not ignored by me. I had only one suite case, a backpack, and an index card in hand with the name Mustafa on it. I never met the man. I don`t know who he is. Just a day before I was to fly out to Jeddah, a Muslim brother from Egypt whom I never met he said his name is Ali; he was one of those who prayed with me at Dar-Al-Islah mosque in Teaneck. He approaches me in the mosque after prayers and said to me, "I heard you are flying to Saudi Arabia alone." I said, "Yes, tomorrow." He then said, "Then take this card. This person shall help guide you to the scholars you need to meet there in Saudi Arabia, if it is Allah`s will." Ali then said, "Asalam Alakum" and turned away! I never saw this person again even till this day.

As I stood there in crowed arrival terminal what seems like eternity thinking not where do I go from here? But how do I go from here? When suddenly a short light skinned middle age man wearing a kaffiyeh (head scarf) and a long white throb came up behind me and said "Muhammad Dawud"? I turned and said yes, are you Mustafa? He said yes in Arabic and greeted me with Asalam Alakum. My intuition, oh, humble reader, in overdrive was telling me welcome to the Muslim underground railroad.

Brother Mustafa drove me from Jeddah airport into downtown Jeddah towards his condominium apartment in the district of "Dar-ra-jar" (Bicycle), which is in northern Jeddah. Brother Mustafa insisted that I stayed with him and his large family for at least three days. He was blessed with a wonderful family consisting of a wife whom I never saw because she wore a veil and five beautiful children, three boys and two girls. I was given one of the four pleasant bedrooms to stay in, which had a magnificent north eastern view of the city of Jeddah`s background and surrounding dark mountains.

After a cool shower and some needed rest, there was a knock on my door announcing that a late-night dinner was being served of roasted baby lamb and rice. Smiling with joy and wonder, Mustafa and his young son`s and I sat on the thick and beautiful carpeted floor of their dining room. We was served by his wife and young daughters the amazing delicious meal and fruit drinks; then his wife and daughters went and sat separately in the living room behind a veil.

I was indeed surprised of the high level of respect and love the children had for their parents, the love and respect the parents had for each other, the fear of Allah in their lives, and the gratitude they had for their King. This honest mind-set captures your soul and reminds you of an era of prior honored integrated humanities of the Arab Muslim world. This honest mind-set captures your heart and mind and reminds oneself of a noble family with an agenda to impart.

Brother Mustafa was very cordial in his manner with me. He had studied in an American university majoring in Business. His father owns two gold shops in Jeddah`s downtown Corniche. Though his English is perfect he mixes his English with his Arabic words and helpful praises so as to help me in my quest of learning Arabic and Islam. In the first 24 hours of my arrival into Saudi Arabia, I was very shocked of the different Islamic atmosphere that awaited me. I traveled with him downtown to his work the following morning, and visited his family gold shops where I got to meet his father and brothers in the very busy Corniche which was full of active people of different customs.

I found Jeddah to be a very modest, modern, and religiously conservative city where you can hear the muezzin`s call to prayer anywhere clearly throughout this large city five times a day, echoing from hundreds of old and new mosques from all parts of this ancient Muslim city of trade and seaport. I watched fascinated in wonder as the Allah-fearing people in hundreds of thousands of their own free will, closed their stores and business and obediently walk to their nearest mosque for prayers. As Allah (swa) as my witness, this was the first time in my life I saw a modern city came virtually to a stop just to say a few words of thanks and gratitude to their lord on a regular bases daily. This level of religious appreciation far surpass Cairo, Egypt; and Karachi, Pakistan; whose Muslim populations numbered in the tens of millions, Muslim cities that I had just a few years ago visited. Deep down in my soul, I had always deemed the actions of a people as louder than words! And in this regard, coming from the western secular world where "In God we trust" is coined, I was truly astonished by this level of devotion. This is the first time in my life I saw a modern city become almost a ghost town in a matter of minutes on the simple account it`s time to offer prayer! People, stopping in mid stride, turn around and walk towards the call. A car thief back home would be a millionaire in days; these Arab people stop their expensive cars in the middle of the streets and step out of them and walk towards the call with the keys still in the car motor still running, reciting the words of the muezzin call.

There is no western secular city in America or Europe or Asia or even Africa that is greater or the same in comparison where the inhabitants possess such high degree of soulful religious ideals and actions that I know of. This is a new dawn for me to actually witness, such act of human humility in such a large scale in regards to a sovereign unseen. How can this happen in American cities back home is the dynamic bigger picture that brother Mustsfa and I had talked about together nonstop in our times together. It doesn`t help to complain. It`s about what would be the key inspired ingredient needed back home that can match this! It`s how can we start that Islamic implementation and propagation that will change the hearts of the Western people back home? We must start a campaign. That is simple to understand which any heart can grasp. That`s the key. Patience.

In the very early morning hours of my second day in Saudi Arabia, brother Mustafa and I left Jeddah and drove to Mecca both of us with intentions to make an Umrah pilgrimage with confidence and hope. Heading east on the new Jeddah-Mecca highway, we was in silent mode. I started to read the Quran under a light hazel sky, which helped me not get too nervous. Traffic was light, and I really felt that artificial

world of mental poverty and American dream slip away further and
further behind me with great relief. Then that large sign post up ahead
in the middle of the large light camel brown desert said Remember
Allah in Arabic came into view.

Oh, humble reader, an umrah pilgrimage to Mecca is not
obligatory for the Muslims, not like hajj is if a Muslim can afford
to make the trip. Yet the progressive fate of divine application of the
golden rule of law is the same, and that is "Mecca is by divine invitation
only!"

Descending down between the dark mountains from the North
West surrounded by a brown lifeless and timeless desert, Mecca is an
oasis in every sense of the word. The "forbidden city Mecca had me
in its grip from first sight. The scenery literally inspires and is a world
away from Jeddah or even any other city I have ever been to. This is
really the end of the road for the one who tracks by faith. This bee-hive
like city, Mecca, whose sole purpose is to worship a monotheistic
unseen divine being, only five times a day is a city of human spiritual
treasures. Treading our way slowly through the huge, lively, and
swarming crowd, buzzing with something positive to say, which increase
their faith and hope, Mustafa and I walked slowly through one of the
many huge bronze wooden doors facing south called Cavalry in Arabic;
the huge Al Masjid Al Haram had many of these doors all around it
with different special names. I was marveled by a sea of peoples bowing
together as one, immerse by a forest of huge grey white marble pillars
and large vast classical brass chandeliers overhead. We then began our
umrah pilgrimage inside the Al Masjid Al Haram with a short prayer
and a *tawaf,* which is a sevenfold counterclockwise circumambulation
of the Kaaba, which is the earthly house of Allah by us Muslim pilgrims.
This immense cubical stone house resting on a large wide white marble
floor in the middle of an open soccer-field size-stadium is ancient.
My prayers were twofold, not only for myself, friends, and family back
home in America. But also to remain here in Saudi Arabia and find the
Muslim scholars that would help me study Arabic and Islam.

Once our umrah obligations were completed, we sat down inside
the Al Haram and were joined by three other Saudi men who were
friends of Mustafa. They talked about the people I shall live with in
Jeddah and in Mecca until I meet the Grand Mufti of Saudi Arabia
and possibly be accepted at Mecca University. One of Mustafa`s friends
whose name was Abdullah, an engineer, turned to me and smiled
then said in Arabic, "Your journey is now of patience; you are in good
hands."

I did not have to wait long. The social net-workings amongst those who are fundamentalist in their faith is extremely strong here in Mecca. Regardless of season, they have everything to gain. For months I lived here, there, and everywhere—All praise is due to Allah—in people's homes, private mosques, the Al Haram, and out in the cool quiet and spacious desert that surrounded Mecca. Within a fortnight I got word from brother Abdullah that the Grand Mufti Sheikh Abdul Aziz Ibn Baaz will be in the Al Haram in Mecca. He will be attending the Friday (Juma) prayer service and have a sit-in question-and-answer session with the open public. Abdullah also said this is the best time and opportunity to meet the Grand Mufti, so we prepared a letter of request together and went to the juma service in the Al Haram. After the service we quietly sat in on the Grand Mufti `s lecture circle that he was giving; the crowd therein was huge with Muslim peoples of many nationalities. At least three thousand peoples sat in semi circle around the Grand Mufti. As he was finishing giving an open lecture on justice and the oneness of Allah, an interesting Arab questioner asked, "Oh honorable sheikh, there are some people who think that because rulers commit sins and major sins, this obligates rebellion against them and to try to cause a change even if this bring about harm to the Muslims in the land, and the events occurring in our Islamic world are many, so what is your view?"

The Grand Mufti answered, "In the name of Allah, the most merciful, the bestowal of mercy. All praise is for Allah, Lord of all creation, and may he extol and send blessings upon Allah`s messenger and upon his family and true followers and his companions and those who follow his way." Then the Grand Mufti said: *"O you who believe! Obey Allah and obey the messenger Muhammad (sas) and those of you Muslims who are in authority among you. If ye differ in anything among yourselves, refer it to Allah and his apostle, If ye do believe in Allah and the last day: that is best, and most suitable for final determination"* (Quran ch.4 v.59).

"So the Muslims must obey the rulers in what is good, not in sin. So if they order that which is sinful, then they are not obeyed in what is a sin. However, it is not permissible to rebel against them at all. Therefore, rebellion against those in authority causes tremendous corruption and much evil, unless the Muslims see clear and open unbelief, which is made clear as such by Allah. Then there is no harm in their rebelling against this ruler to remove him. If they have the capability! But if they do not have the capability, then they do not rebel; or if the rebellion will cause a greater evil, then they may not rebel in order to preserve the general well-being. It is not permissible to remove evil with that which is more evil than it; rather, it is obligatory to remove evil with that which will obliterate it or reduce it. But if rebellion will cause great corruption, destruction of security, and oppression of the people as well as killing of those who do not deserve to be killed and other types of great corruption, then this is not permissible. Rather, it is obligatory to have patience and to hear and obey in that which is good, to advise those in authority, to supplicate for them for good, to strive to lessen and reduce the evil, and to increase the good. This is the correct way which must be followed since therein lies the well-being of the Muslims in general."

Oh, humble reader, as I sat there listening to Grand Mufti speak about oneness of Allah, bad rulers, oppression, what to do about them translated to me in Arabic by Abdullah, I knew I was in the right place and company. Wisdom and good advice are life's masterpieces such that a person who seeks sincere knowledge should hold dear to himself. After his sermon and lecture, brother Abdullah and I worked our way through the crowd, right up to the old man. And brother Abdullah gave my letter of request to his aid.

"I wish to learn more about the Islamic faith and the Arabic language at Mecca University,"

I said.

The Grand Mufti looked up at me and smiled, and sensing my sincerity, give his reddish—gray goatee a light tug. "Yes," he said. The blind Sheikh Abdul Aziz Ibn Baaz could not see my black skin, my brown eyes, or my long black beard or could he see my white turban, my white robe, my American passport, and empty pockets. None of this mattered to him, though, for what he could see in me was sincerity.

An aid worker of the Grand Mufti approached Brother Abdullah and I after our meeting with the Grand Mufti and told us to come with him to the office of the Grand Mufti and wait for him there. The office of the Grand Mufti was here in Mecca not far from the Al Haram. He had a huge and spacious office; and it was full of Muslim students, scholars with religious complaints, Muslim judges and lawyers composing social justice into a coherent system of Sheria laws. Not surprising, the office of the Grand Mufti was very elegant and designed to make the visitors and petitioners rest at ease. The scented-50-by-120 feet room was laid with beautiful Arab rugs and lined against the walls was black leather sofas. This was literary a bee hive of human voices and aids running about serving Arab coffee and hot Indian tea to the more than 150 fidgety people who were the normal daily guest awaiting the grand Mufti to arrive from the Al Masjid Al Haram.

We did not have to wait long.

Upon arrival, the grand Mufti was lead into the huge office by one of his young grandsons, followed by his secretary and four police officers. The room suddenly went silent. We all stood up and sat down after Sheikh ibn Baaz sat in a simple leather chair; he Salam us all, and we all Salam him in return. A twitchy aid started to hand over opened letters of requests to the secretary who in turn read the letters in full into the ear of the Grand Mufti. He just sat there in deep thought in his leather chair, tugging his reddish short goatee listening to the many request one by one. Some he rejected with a short wave of his hand out of mind, and some he accepted and signed with his ring. When at last he reached my letter of request, I had a short verse from the Quran attached to my letter which said,

"Who is he that will loan to Allah a beautiful loan, which Allah will double unto his credit and multiply many times? It is Allah that gives you want or plenty, and to him shall be your return" (Quran 2:245).

The relaxed and smiling secretary read my note and letter of request into the ear of the Grand Mufti. He froze, then stared about into the audience around him, rubbed his eye lids, and let go of his goatee beckoning with his right hand to whomever to come near to him.

Brother Abdullah leaned over to me and said, "Go stand before the Grand Mufti once again." So I got up and walked across the large room to meet the Grand Mufti once again. Half way there his secretary read out loud the note and letter for all to hear. When I reached the Grand Mufti, he had a big smile on his face and was dictating a letter to go to the director of Mecca University for my acceptance into the school.

I realize suddenly the future had arrived and everybody knew it. I was a Muslim African American, descendent from kidnapped slaves from the west who came to this oil-rich nation requesting the wealth they had received from above in the heavens (The Holy Quran), not the wealth they had received from below in the earth (Oil)!

In January 1993, approximately a month after my encounter with the Grand Mufti, I was introduced to another Salafist sheikh, Sheikh Safar al-Hawali, then the dean of *Aqeeda*[11] at Mecca University, at his home in Jeddah. You will not see a white flag at his door, *insha Allah*. This was my first impression as well as his youthful manner of intelligence. He did not harbor a phobia of meeting of the minds in small or large groups even with foreign strangers. The second aspect about him was his inquisitiveness when it came to how people see God in their lives. He is a true advocate with a great depth of personal character to balance it all out. The problem like all high-caliber

---

[11]   Aqeeda: "Purity of Faith"

scholars and sheikhs is time. Their time is limited when it comes to having a rapport and learning the art of understanding your trade. In my opinion it is he the man to meet in the Muslim world that can clearly and plainly explain what a true monotheistic faith is. His collections of writings like *Kissinger's Promise, The Day of Wrath,* and *A Message to the President* are must reading for all who wish to know about Salafi, Islam. Except for people who have been living in denial Sheikh Safar Al-Hawali has address a crisis widely understood by mainstream Salafi followers which is opposed to United States or any other *kufr* military presence in their country and region. That Gulf War of 1990 was understood amongst many Muslim Arab rulers, Muslim people, and Muslim scholars themselves as a dispute within an Arab house that should stay within an Arab house. To invite non-Muslim army outsiders into their disputes of greed, oil and power would take Saudi Arabia and other Muslim Arab nations into peril. Latter within a year, because of these opinions Sheikh Safar Al-Hawali was thrown into prison in Saudi Arabia (Qur'an ch.100 v.1-11).

As I began my studies at Mecca University in Saudi Arabia in January 1994, with Sheikh Safar Al-Hawali, my first true mentor, I realize I was not alone in my seeking understanding of our faith from him. There were a number of other Americans the sheikh had nestled under his wing living with him in his home; most notable among them was the renowned American-born imam, Mr. Ammar Amonett from Denver, Colorado, who stood by his sheikh, which was the lesson I learned from him. You did not need Diana Ross's voice to reflect on the value of "Reach out and touch somebody's hand; make this world a better place if you can." You can see it in action when you hang around Sheikh Safar Al-Hawali. He was a man who spent his time with those poor Saudis and poor travelers from overseas seeking knowledge of Islam; this was the kind of man he is.

Well, when you are in a crowd of four million people, word gets around real fast. I was making my second Hajj back in 1994, this time at the personal invitation of Sheikh Abd Al-Aziz ibn Abd Allah ibn Baaz.

As we were driving through the desert from Mina, the Tent City, to the Hill of Arafat, a sea of chanting Muslims, hundreds of thousands, millions of people, engulfed our convoy of ten vans like a tsunami washing over a tiny island in the middle of the ocean. In every direction I could see people walking and praying (countless families holding hands, pilgrims both old and young men, women and children), drawn both by the spark of spiritual guidance in their lives and to the hope that every other soul taking part in Hajj—every Muslim on earth, for that matter—would find spiritual direction too.

Not long after we arrived at Arafat and could see the vastness of millions of Muslim worshipers congregate and praying for the mercy of Allah upon us all, we received word that Sheikh Al-Hawali had been "thrown behind the sun" by the Saudi government. In other words he has *disappeared*. With no lawyer, no judge, no trial, no due process of law, no writ of habeas corpus, he was simply gone. And the writing was etched permanently in stone all because he'd said, "*Hejaz* should not have foreign *kufr* troops on its soil." Suddenly, I felt like I was living on another planet; and those streets I loved of Mecca, Medina, Tiaf and Jeddah all seemed for a moment strange. Here, in the Land of the Prophets, as I was searching for the truth about my newly embraced Islamic faith, I again find the notions of freedom and justice disappointing. Sure, I had lost whatever faith I'd had in the political systems of the United States and the UK, and the Western world, but at least in those places I could express myself freely even if I just wanted to worship nothing, just pay the rent, the electric bill, seduce all the girls I desired, work a decent job, eat decent food, and pay my taxes like a good secular follower. Yes, I could do that there, and heaven can wait. And if on top of that I could add a good moral compass to that list to bless the fantasy, then the more the better. I also reasoned, I would achieve a certain sense of moral purpose in my life in denial and empty passions just living by the moment of the day, acting on the obedience of the now.

But in truth, all that wasn't for me, all praise is due to Allah. Yet in truth, faith without justice wasn`t for me either, all praise is due to Allah.

When a Muslim Saudi scholar that was with us requested to the Grand Mufti Sheikh ibn Baaz what to do, the Grand Mufti right hand ascended up to his reddish gray goatee and said, patience!

I was undergoing these moments of spiritual crisis when I learned of Sheikh Al-Hawaii's disappearance that I began, in earnest, to see clearly the social contrasts between Western Secularism and Islam, and Islam and the degrees of its faith in the hearts of its people! It isn`t the wind of the ideological warfare between them you see it is the havoc they cause. After two years living in Hejaz, in my campaign to learn Arabic and to embrace my Islamic faith with full understanding, it had suddenly become obvious to me, an African-American pilgrim from the Bronx, that those who lived in *Hejaz* and were sincere in their faith, were a group of people far different from the rulers of Hejaz, the Saudi royal family, who were decidedly not totally religious in their governorship. Essentially, they were secular Arab nationalists dressed in the costumes of the devout. These were the men who were in the driver's seat and the religious scholars and like-minded others who were the passengers. These men who loved their political power, their opulent palaces, their Rolls-Royces and Mercedes—Benz limousines, their excursions to five-star casino resorts in the world's most decadent destinations, their love of champagne, bars and prostitutes—this monarchy of the so-called devout. It is they who were truly the actual betrayers of true religious freedom and justice in Hejaz. And I came to understand, right there in the middle of millions of pilgrims at my second Hajj, that what had awakened my spirit in this holy land, were mostly the poor and struggling middle-class Saudis who hung onto their faith, every day, in spite of their corrupt rulers. It was these simple people, in their grace and courtesy, with their simple faith—much like the good simple folks one finds everywhere—that brought my daily reflections on the remembrance of Allah, our Islamic heritage, culture, and traditions, to a new higher place. These the Bedouins, who are the true keepers of fifteen centuries of Islamic legacy, I too now felt what it feels like to be one of the custodians of Allah's house in Mecca, Median, and Jerusalem yet knowing we as a people of faith we are spiritually leaderless not walking the talk, without an agenda in spite of our books.

"We do not all worship the same God, but we all worship for the same needs," so said Sheikh Muhammad Ibn Saleh Al-Uthaymeen, that Salafi fundamentalist from Saudi Arabia. "Does your reach exceed your needs in this life? That is the question. *"Say: He is Allah the one and only; Allah the eternal, absolute; he begetteth not, nor is he begotten; and there is none like unto him."*(Quran 112:1-4). [12] Then that first resolution you must hold on to is Tawhid (The oneness of Allah). I had first met Sheikh Al-Uthaymeen in January 1993 in the Al Haram with Abdullah who was translating his speech into English for me. He was preaching to a large crowd of onlookers and listeners sitting over on the northwest corner of the Al Haram. A short man dress in simple robes, nothing fancy, he was dark of skin by the heat of the desert which gives him the look of a kind and knowledgeable and distinguished Bedouin you can trust with your life. He also said, "Tawhid is a defining doctrine of Islam that declares the absolute unity and uniqueness of Allah as one divine being

---

[12]   (Quran 25:77), (Quran 39:7), (Quran 110:1-3), (Quran 112:1-4)

creator and sustainer of the earth and universe. This is what makes Islam an absolute monotheist faith." All the more curious, he showed, I believe a mystical ability to make things clear. Like, "Yes it is true mankind does not all worship the same God, yet we all worship for the same needs. So, the question is does your reach exceed your needs in this life, oh, Muslim? If not, then fine tune your worship with humility to Allah. What is it that you are doing in your life to fulfill your needs? Is this acceptable or unacceptable to Allah? And who is that sovereign to which reference is made to in your daily affairs?" He taught this lesson again and again to a group of young students from around the world back in the summer of 1994. Most of us, the majority of whom were from Saudi Arabia, answered yes. But a sizeable minority, however, including myself, who had raised our hands and answered no we were Muslims hailing from outside Saudi Arabia, including many from the United States, UK, Europe, and most Muslim students from the non Arab and Asian Muslim world.

It`s a bitter pill to be a man who lived all his life in America knowing that my country`s cornerstone is social justice for "themselves" and faith "secular Democracy" for all and making it work simply because of the aptitude and attitude of our own hearts! To be thus living in a monotheist super power country ruled by a monarchy whose corner stone creed is justice "for all", and faith "Islam", but faking it. It is uncanny that we Muslims have the best holy books I believe and the best scholars yet we the Muslim communities are not reaching our full potential simply because of the aptitude and attitude of our own hearts. Yes, the relationship between faith and reason is a marriage called hope. So when the challenges and circumstances of life confront us Muslims and we deny ourselves justice and make our reach not enough for our needs, then we can have the best imams and sheikhs who can reflect a thinking and adopt a capacity that gives life from our own printed holy text while in these trenches, but this means nothing when that capacity is called jihad is pushed aside by a demand of show me the money! These basic idea fundamentals is how one wins the hearts, minds, and soul war par excellence anywhere on earth and how one loses that heart, mind, and soul war fiasco in the sight of that divine one for the lack of a coin.

As I said previously, I am a free jihad Salafist Muslim. No one tells me what to think or say against my will. That is because I am from the West where my enslaved forefathers stood with nothing but rags to wear and bound in the chains of their oppressors. Nor am I from the East, where hundreds of millions of Muslims live enslaved by their own tyrants because of their own hearts. Here in America the thought police has not, as of yet, knocked on my door inquiring about some speech I have given about human rights, equal rights, justice, and due process of law for the time being. Nor have they bundled me off to jail, or buried me in some side of the road pit because of what I say or write.

Simply because these same Christians from the West who are ignorant of the ways of my fellow Muslim brothers and sisters in the East in regards to a true monotheist faith, these same ignorant Christians, have freedom and justice in their lands because they did inherit their faith and know the meaning of jihad. Not just accepting their faith as sufficient but daring to make their faith work for them in their lives but, unfortunately, only for themselves and countrymen as a domestic policy, not for others as a bold foreign policy.

Just why am I telling you all this drama, oh, humble reader? You think it`s just a passing storm this Arab Spring? Well, twenty-five thousand people (human beings) die a horrifying death every day on this green earth we all call home of hunger-related causes and poverty; sadly most are children (*www.poverty* ticker.com). This is not one of those enduring paradoxes of death that the followers of the faith of prophet Abraham (sas) shall accept as normality of life here on this earth. No, we cannot. Just why am I telling you all this for? You think that weather vane is not pointing at you? Every sheikh and imam I had ever met who is sincere living in the Middle East knows what we are saying is true. But only a few have the courage or faith or both to tell their people the consequences of not acting on your faith. The blame game runs deeper than quicksand. The reason you do not have freedom, liberty or certain basic civil liberties is the Jews, Christians, *kufrs*, the blood thirsty Americans and greedy Europeans; any one will do just fine and hundreds of millions will sit there every Friday service (juma) and listen to their boring sermons and only a few conscious Muslims will put the dots together and have the audacity of courage to look in the mirror and see why they live under dictators.

Yes, it was this same Bedouin Fundamentalist Sheikh Muhammad Ibn Saleh Al-Uthaymeen who can melt you with his elfin smile that first gave me a true lesson in *Ihsan*, the worshipping of Allah as if he can be seen by the human eye. This idea of faith is one of the highest state of worship in Islam, the constant idea that Allah`s presence is always near. Personally speaking, I call it the twin. To go any further if I may, the Sheikh said it`s that remembrance of Allah that is the fortress of the believing Muslim. This level of worship of ihsan is a sanctuary that only a gifted few who dare to perform that jihad of the self. Since you are never alone, not even from the earliest moments of your life. That formality relationship with respect is a cohesive engagement with that divine being personality called Allah whom you cannot see; which becomes the main persistent reality in your life. Not just bearing good news but also good company. This ishan raises your level of awareness and consciousness in your certainty of Allah and your communion with your Lord will be far from trite and trivial. Why? Because the Islamic religion is not just about beliefs and ethics. No it is not. It is about a whole way of life. When Allah (swa) says *"It was we who created man, and we know what dark suggestions his soul makes to him: for we are nearer to him than his jugular vein."* (Quran 50:16), for the believers, this is no sacrifice or leap of faith. This is a fact of life.

There are moments that I wish that every major Islamic charity organizations on this earth had a dime for every Muslim man who falls asleep in Friday`s juma service in a Mosque when he suppose to hear the Imam or Sheikh talk about this serious issue of ihsan in the Muslim world. I also wish in this holy month of Ramadan that every widower and orphan of a believer who died in Jihad fighting against the kufr and monafics, shall receive a blessing from every imam and sheikh who fails to establish clearly to his congregation at his Mosque when he speaks about Islam and how it is capable of solving the problems of the twenty-first-century Christian calendar, fifty-eighth-century Hebrew calendar, and fifteenth-century Islamic calendar that is now facing all of mankind. Failing to marshal that idea, that collective will, and understanding by connecting day-to-day life experiences with the moral Islamic order of life benefits with the idea`s of individual responsibilities and understand the human values and aspirations of the *Ulmma* that the caliphate must transcend has its consequences.

Therefore, we as Muslims have no one to blame but ourselves when our caliphate, king, president, or leader becomes corrupt. Why? The good farmer cultivates. The good citizen fosters.

Once your worship is of that degree that you are conscious of Allah`s (swa) presence at all times, a level of conscious as if you can see him. Then how much of a change of character for the better has your worship done for yourself and others? Since you know he is your sovereign lord, creator of the heavens and earth, who is all powerful, most graces most merciful, then why be the beggar unto the world when something that is divine is at your caprice? Therefore knowledge is the justification of true faith, so all we Muslims have to do is be just to ourselves.

One village at a time, the future is still in our hands because all the natural ingredients are there in our own books. Those days of our non-accountability within our own gardens are over. You simply have to look at the fruit of Islam today to see the reality on the ground; undoubtedly those voices on the streets of Tahrir Square, Egypt, is only an example of a heralded revolution of humanities and public welfare demanding change and *Sharia* law versus those demanding freedom to sin and/or secularism. The days of village and town hall meetings for all who are willing to face the hard issues that must be addressed and be Allah fearing who are sincere, mature and transparent are upon the Muslim Arab and Muslim non Arab world to face boldly and wisely.

But is this now the moment of change already too late to be heard by those authoritarians? Did not King Abdullah of Saudi Arabia who sent into Bahrain more than a thousand troops to aid that despised King Sheikh Hamad Bin Issa Al-Khalifa, against the will of the majority of the people there in the eyes of March 2011, to preserve the oppression of the Shiite majority, to silence those voices of freedom, liberty and justice? Did not this same King Abdullah of Saudi Arabia tell those fossil Arab leaders that flocked to the Arab League in Riyadh, Saudi Arabia in March 17, 2007 "The American occupation of Iraq was illegal" and warned "That unless Arab Governments settled their differences foreign powers will continue to dictate this regional politics." The King also said, "In the beloved Iraq the bloodshed is continuing under an illegal foreign occupation and detestable sectarianism. The blame should fall on us the leaders of the Arab nation, with our ongoing differences, our refusal to walk the path of unity. All this has made the nation [people] lose their confidence in us."

Please, just how do you hold on to your faith, your creed, your laws when no one is around with the power to compel you to? I submit to you. I plead to you, oh, king, where are those tenets in action that we the Muslims hold dear during this Arab Spring, which is a time of "interest" verses "values"? What is strange to me and to many Muslims from the West who are looking for real leadership is that these Eastern Muslim kings in these days of sorrowful era of leadership forget nothing, learned nothing and do nothing.

With assurance, oh, humble reader, I am truly compelled to describe the world as it is. This is a wakeup call or an admonishment if you will. Please let's be frank and honest with ourselves, oh, humble reader, if a mountain of justice was to blossomed in the Muslim world because of the efforts of that Arab Spring what would the Muslim people do with it now that they have a locomotive call Islam to drive it? Would they break down those barriers of trade between the Muslim nations themselves and face the need of economic and social prosperity together by electing the next caliphate who will stand on a quilt of many nations and tribes of Muslim peoples. Thus, on top of his shortlist is a constitution that guaranties tenets of social justice and liberties for all. As well as having all of the Muslim oil and petroleum products under his tent including OPEC under his management and control unconditionally. Indeed, the currency of our oil and petroleum products shall be under the currency of all Muslim states per annual, not under the currency of the dollar or euro nor any non Muslim currency; the poorest of our Muslim states amongst us shall be first. Therefore, all the oil and petroleum products for one year will be sold under the currency of a Muslim state only until all Muslim member states have had their turn. Then we will continue this cycle again and again for the mercy of Allah because it all came to us Muslims from Allah by means of a test. It`s called wanting for your brother in faith what you want for yourself essentially—"self interest" verses "moral values." This courageous step of ihsan by the next caliphate shall, insha Allah, strengthen the bond of brotherhood among us and financially with transparency uplift the economical and social prosperity of all the people in the Muslim world thus putting an end of depending on the tourist industry from the West or Far East as a main avenue of economic uplift for the poor, middle class, and the young, which breeds lewdness, alcoholism and other social vices. *Ihsan* is the currency of your faith. As well as an end to depending on those notorious usurers the International Monetary Fund and so-called World Bank carpetbaggers.

Outrageous? Did we hear somebody say irrational? "A currency you can trust is us" is not too far a leap of faith! With certainty I am truly compelled to describe the world as it is but being frank and honest with ourselves has its price. Consider for a moment, oh, humble reader of this book, if a mountain of gold was to be discovered in Colorado United States of America today, would the American government sell that gold for riyals? Of course not. How outrageous to even consider the thought! It's the currency of oil and petroleum products that matters most of all, not its price! I beg you to bear in mind oh humble reader of this book why is the custodians of the faith of Islam selling the main natural resources of the Muslim world under a currency not of its own currency but under a currency of a nation whose faith is secular democratic, as well as refuses the right of the Palestine people to have a sovereign state of their own and its capital Jerusalem to be shared with the state of Israel?

Would that courageous fundamentalist king Faisal Bin Abdul Aziz Al-Saud from Saudi Arabia may Allah bless him with heaven, continue once again that oil embargo unto America like he did before in 1973, because of its injustice policies in the middle east in the spirit of the *Intifada* in spite of his own self interest if he was alive today? I would say yes, because he would have time and time again say unto the western powers that they must respect the will and sovereignty of the Muslim people worldwide. Would he king Faisal Bin Abdul Aziz Al-Saud, change the currency of his oil and petroleum products to match his faith if he was alive today seeing the deficit of justice in western nations towards nations of Muslims and third-world peoples under the banner of secular democracy? Again I would say yes, so why patronize and fuel an enemy's interest? Why heaven couldn`t wait I just don't know, I only feel that this Arab king could had made the world truly a better place if he was still alive today! *"Say: Nothing will happen to us except what Allah has decreed for us: He is our protector; and on Allah let the believers put their trust"* (Quran 9:51).

The writing is on the wall. Indiana Jones was in Iraq because it had much to do with Ghawar oil field in Saudi Arabia dying and that oily fundamentalist Mr. Marion K. Hubbert`s principle of Peak Oil who said, "Our ignorance is not so vast as our failure to use what we know." Now that Saudi Arabia will not market their new oil fields for years to come, a seventy thousand plus American and N.A.T.O. army is running around in Afghanistan looking for the Taliban and Al-Qaida drinks more than a million barrels of oil a day! So something had a give. It`s about oil and who controls the future oil and gas pipeline from the Caspian Sea through Turkmenistan, Afghanistan and south into Pakistan. This is why we have a war in Afghanistan today. Western nations and Western corporate oil barons where being excluded from these Asian markets with the possibility of currency of trade not Western at all but under a Muslim countries` currency of trade to benefit the people therein by Islamic resistance groups.

Addiction to oil is worst than addiction to heroin, I feel, because it`s not just the threat of national collapse domestically but also the urge to habitually take by force if needs be its life`s blood which is oil. A Mr. Hyde foreign policies from the West towards nations that has large oil and petroleum products, is the inevitable endgame that will expose the moral weakness of the monotheistic faiths from all strips to successfully avoid another major war amongst themselves.

The consequences today of these oil-rich gulf states with their burgeoning cash-and-carry oil revenue which is now buying Western overseas assets in the blue chip corporate world that's worth tens

of billions of dollars and euros, as well as the same amount in arms
trade deals, is enormous. They are blindly stowing the seeds of greater
conceit and greed among themselves towards their own devastation.
For the love of money, that degree of contempt is astounding towards
one's fellow Muslim human being not just because he is not of the
same class but also of the same faith yet oblivious to his brethren's
needs! That inconvenient truth is they are simply out of touch of the
lives around them; when they do give, it's mostly for the cameras or
press or a bribe to just get out of their way—for you to just move on!
That golden rule that says, "Everybody is a beggar in the sight of Allah"
is what keeps you sane when it is your turn to ever ask or in need!

Now I painfully realize why Imam Hamaas Abdul Khaalis—who was
in prison with me back in America in 1982, now more than twelve years
ago—told me to go East, so I can get a balance digest of the Islamic
faith and Islamic world issues in true earnest. *"Let not their wealth nor their
following in sons dazzle thee: in reality Allah's plan is to punish them with these
things in this life, and that their souls may perish in their very denial of Allah.
They swear by Allah that they are indeed of you; but they are not of you: yet they
are afraid to appear in their true colors"* (Quran 9:55-56). Those dictators,
kings, emirs and princes are not investing with the same billions of their
currency in hand to match their faith, in the lives of the Muslim people
at home and their neighbors like medicines, hospitals, clinics, schools,
libraries, colleges, universities, R and D, and Islamic bank loans to
small-and-middle size business to Muslims of Asia and Muslims of Africa,
because of the state of greed in their own hearts. You would want these
essentials for others your brethren first before yourself, that opportunity
for others before oneself. This idea and will is not that difficult to
fathom if you are led by a prophet and have that fear of Allah in their
lives that what they have is only a test of their faith.

This so-called viable alternative, which we all see today in the real
world, is, in fact a collapse of courage. A leadership led by a profit. The
evidence is evident in their actions—smart money follow intent. Smart
money says that ex-slave fundamentalist Frederick Douglass was right
when he delivered a lecture called "Will it Pay?" He said, "Can money
be made out of it? Will it make the rich richer and the strong stronger?
How will it affect property? In the eyes of such people, there is no
God but wealth, no right and wrong but profit and loss. Our national
morality and religion have reached a depth of baseness that which
there is no lower deep."

You can see the remains of yesterday and the jewels of our faith
all around the world almost. In spite of 9-11, you can literally feel the

zeal pulsating in our *madrassas* (Islamic schools), large or small in Asia, Africa, Europe and the Americas. Sense those Sheikhs and Imams in these far continents overcoming tremendous obstacles reaching the unreachable poor, homeless and the growing hungry masses of humanity with a simple massage that which is impossible with mankind is possible with Allah (swa). With hope for Allah`s mercy, they endeavor onward. Yet in the eyes of the beholder and owner of these numerous palaces, wealth, and political power in the Arab Muslim world, it is neither prudent or desirable nor is it a reasonable good return on their investment to invest their Sovereign Wealth Funds (SWF) which is more than one and a half trillion dollars. That`s correct, that these Gulf states countries, Saudi Arabia, Qatar, U.A.E., Bahrain and Kuwait—could not give a loan to Allah (swa) at least half of their (SWF) to Allah (swa) for his mercy only. Could not even they these few leaders say, "let`s make Damascus University, Syria; Al-Azhar University Cairo, Egypt; Katsina Islamic University from Nigeria; Omdurman Islamic University in Sudan and Jamia Darul—Uloom in Karachi Pakistan our standing pillagers into our Ivory League Schools of the future Muslim world?" Not their own universities first. No. It`s their neighbors these gulf states countries want first. So be it a loan to Allah for his mercy only. I behold that if you do not want it for your neighbors what you want for yourself then do not tell me about your faith keep it to yourself. Because then their only answer to the debate is "will it pay?"

Let`s just raise the stakes significantly and globally. Fooling yourself will be the news, brought to you by a few very rich, very powerful American and European secular Western media, like the B.B.C. or CNN who have their own vested interest at heart. Yes, talk is cheap, we Muslims say we believe in Allah but I Hum du Allah have learned that a divine being is to be served, not just praised. Manna from heaven comes with a price and often an opportunity to restore redemption or respite or both. But will this pay? To imagine 10 billion dollars to those universities in Syria, Egypt, Sudan, Nigeria and Pakistan is also raising the fruit of Islam. By putting their neighbors first because a brotherhood starts with your neighbors globally. But will this pay?

The importance of being earnest during this Arab Spring is that Muslims are living very difficult lives that promised neither the certainty of having food, clothing, or shelter for oneself, bride, and/or children. Yes, we expected more, from our kings and princes to imaging themselves once more as nobles of the faith not clients of a faith! Yes, we the Muslim *ulema* expected more from our unattainable emirs and princes fiddling on their rooftops daydreaming about more oil, gold, horses, wives, cars, and palaces on top of what they already have! While the salt of the earth marches onward, begging crumbs from their nobles, pleading like a beat that needs a heart. Calling out to these nobles in long white dragging robes to do the right thing and invest their hundreds of billions of dollars of their (SWF) into the lives of hundreds of millions of Muslims who are their neighbors. Cynically the ruling Arab noble elite response is "Will it pay?"

Hearts of Mankind

The vanguard (of Islam) is the first of those who forsook (their homes) and of those who gave them aid and (also) those who follow them in all good deeds. Well pleased is Allah with them, as are they with him: for them hath he prepared gardens under which rivers flows, to dwell therein for ever: that is the supreme felicity

— Quran 9:100

Since it is Allah (swa) who is beautifying this earthly garden one soul at a time, I write as one, oh, humble reader, who intends to enrich and deepen that human moment of clarity. If you wish to bring a trenchant critique to what is said, you are free to do so. Therefore, who are those people for whom the *fatwa*[13] reflects the true pulse of an Islamic movement that begins in the hearts of mankind? Who says "We hear and we obey?"[14] *"The apostle believes in what hath been revealed to him from his lord, as do the men of faith. Each one of them believes in Allah, his angels, his books, and his apostles. "We make no distinction they say, between one and another of his apostles." And they say: we hear, and we obey: We seek thy forgiveness, our lord, and to thee is the end of all journeys"* (Quran 2:285). Who are those ordinary people who wish to believe in and submit to a divine force outside of themselves?" (Quran 9:100).

---

[13] (Fatwa): A formal legal opinion by a mufti, in answer to a question of a judge or private individual.

[14] (Quran 2:285)

This was at the heart of my questions when I started my journey to live and study Islam in the Middle East in November, 1992. If you are going to take some of that time that Allah has given unto you on this beautiful earth upon which we live, then at the very least find out who that divine one is, your purpose, and who are the Salafis really are? Are they from *Ahlus-Sunnah wal-Jamaa`ah?*[15]

Who is better placed than the *Salafi* to understand the revelation of Islam than these disciples of the prophet Muhammad (sas), the same men (companions) who accompanied him throughout his life? Furthermore, in fact, any understandings of the Islamic religion that does not follow in their footsteps will be necessarily deficient and hopelessly flawed. Why? It's those sincere Islamic orthodox fundamentalist imams of old like Imam Al-Asbahaanee who said, "The sign of *Ahlus-Sunnah* is that they follow the *Salafus-Saalih* and abandon all that is innovated and newly introduced into the religion."[16] or Imam Abu Haneefah who said, "Adhere to the narrations and to the path of the *salaf* and beware of newly invented for all of it is blameworthy innovations"[17] or the words of Imam Ibn Taymiyyah who advised that "there is no criticism for the one who proclaims the way of the Salaf, who attaches himself to it [by calling himself *Salafi*] and refers to it. Rather, it is obligatory to accept that from him by unanimous agreement because the way of the Salaf is nothing but the truth."[18] [19]

From the first time I heard of them, I have found these words by my prophet Muhammad (sas) to be true, even to this very day. Hum du Allah I made the correct decision to fly to Saudi Arabia and study the Arabic language at Mecca University and immerse myself with the scholars there. Truly it was a mercy from Allah to give me, the great-grandson of freed slaves from America, an opportunity to learn not only more about his roots but to also learn about the correct

---

[15]   The United Body of Sunni Muslim People

[16]   Al-Hujjah fee Bayaanil-Mahajjah 1/364

[17]   Reported by As-Suyootee in Sawnul-Mantaq Wal-Kalaam p.32

[18]   Majmoo al-Fataawaa 4:149

[19]   The Salafi are the companions of Allah's messenger prophet Muhammad (sas) and the Imams of Guidance of the first three generations, those whose goodness has been testified to by Allah's messenger prophet Muhammad (sas) who said: "The best of mankind are my generation, then those who follow after them, then those who follow after them." (Reported by Imam Ahmad bin Hanbal, also by Al-Bukhaari and Muslim.)

understanding of monotheism, or *tawheed*.[20] I thank Sheikh Abd Al-Aziz Abd Allah ibn Baaz, the former grand Mufti of Saudi Arabia who aided me in my path of seeking knowledge, may Allah bless him. It was these Arabs from the east who truly freed me spiritually, with not only the faith of Islamic belief but the proper understanding of my faith and adhering to the path of purification from false practices and innovations that have crept into Islam over the centuries. In short, a Salafi Muslim adheres to the fundamental principles that the companions of the messenger prophet Muhammad (sas) and the early generations were upon in totality, inwardly and outwardly, in their daily lives to please Allah.

It is those who understand the importance of being spiritually aware, those who are conscious and understand the responsibilities mankind faces, who are truly successful.[21]

Most of our Muslim leaders by name only have self-imprisoned their people for the love and power of this world; their true aim is to take the very taste of faith out of the mouths of their very own subjects so that they can rule yet another day, knowing once you take away that inspiring spirit of our purpose here on earth the rest is just wet clay and brine. Removing those veils of gauze denials is only one of the purposes of this book, which chronicles the struggles of our spiritual human world governed by the fear of Allah until we don't fear him anymore followed by the consequences of our decisions, followed by our pleas of mercy, then perhaps followed by respite. Likewise, our material human world is governed by the fear of today`s despots until we don't fear them anymore. *"Therefore be patient with what they say, and celebrate constantly the praises of thy lord, before the rising of the sun, and before its setting; Yea, celebrate them for part of the hours of the night, and at the sides of the day: that thou mayest have spiritual joy. Nor strain thine eyes in longing for the things we have given for enjoyment to parties of them, the splendor of the life of this world, through which we test them: But the provision of thy lord is better and more enduring. Enjoin prayer on thy people, and be constant therein. We ask thee not to provide sustenance: we provide it for thee. But the fruit of the hereafter is for righteousness"* (Quran 20:130-132).

---

[20]   To single out Allah alone for worship with the negation of anything that is worshiped besides Allah.

[21]   Quran 17:62-74

In 1995, I was blessed by Allah (swa) with the opportunity to travel
to Al-Khartoum and Um Durman in Sudan during my summer recess
as a student at Mecca University. Yes, I was blessed with an opportunity
to sit down with an old sheikh for ten weeks in the hottest summer in
my life. This cool dude was as black as a plum and just as wrinkly. He
must had been about eighty-five, an imam, and when I asked him his
name, it took him about twenty seconds to finish because he started
with his great-, great-, great-, great-, great-grandfather`s name, Abdual
Maged. He knew I was a poor man from American, had come a long
way seeking knowledge about Islam, and maybe to find myself a sweet
wife while I am at it. He treated me like family and over some hot sweet
tea, huge delicious fried Nile fish with fual (beans) and long walks
together along the banks of the rapid Blue Nile River. Such was the
hospitality of my Sudanese host, which help me feel that African spirit
of home away from home. We shared our fears and concerns about
the Muslim world and the troubles we Muslims have in the West. The
sheikh had a lot of respect for Dr. Hassan Al-Turabi but felt there is
little that can be done now to heal the hearts of the Sudanese people
both north and south from the destruction of colonialism and despots.

Sheikh Maged`s background, demeanor, and culture is totally
African. He comes from a family of Sufi Sheikhs until he first made
Hajj fifty-five years ago. Now he is a die-heart Salafi sheikh that likes
to stay under the radar for political reasons here in Sudan. He`s also, I
feel, a spiritual hunter.

Sitting very much at ease in his private chambers in Um-Durman
part of the capital of Sudan, he seems content with his self-built
recession-proof voluminous bungalow and enjoying every moment
of his buzzing small grand children wandering about us playfully. He
initiated our dialogue together by at times by frowning and joking
about myself being unmarried as of yet, thin in frame and wondered
what do you give to a Muslim African American beggar sitting on
a mountain of gold. All praise to Allah I keep my mouth shut and
had the foresight to just smile and bow. The sheikh was highly
recommended by some Muslim African scholars I had met in the Al
Haram in Mecca, Saudi Arabia who valued his knowledge, wisdom, and
Islamic pragmatism.

Sheikh Abdual Maged pause for a few moments just looking at
me with his keen eyes; somehow satisfied of what was delivered unto
him, he started off by saying to me in Arabic (reported by Mu`awvah in
Shahin Muslim [hadith]), "Whosoever Allah decides to show goodness
to he gives his the understanding of the religion." Then he leaned
forward and read to me the Quran 4:59 *"O ye who believe! Obey Allah,*

and obey the apostle, and those charge with authority among you. If ye direr in anything among yourselves, refer it to Allah and his apostle, if ye do believe in Allah."

Thereafter, Sheikh Maged looked up from the Quran, turned to me with firmness in his voice and said to me, "The problem in the Muslim community lies with obedience with whomever is in authority amongst them." I then said after a moment of silence, "May Allah bless you, oh, Sheikh, but what if that that leader is oppressive and sinful?"

Thereupon Sheikh Maged gave a long sigh, lean back in his black leather chair, mumbled to himself and reached over to his night table and picked up Al-Barbahaar (hadith) and slowly turn to page (d. 329h) and read in Arabic: *"It's not permissible to fight the ruler or rebel against him even if he oppresses."* This is due to the saying of the messenger of Allah prophet Muhammad (sas) to Abdu Dharr Al-Ghifaaree. *"Have patience even if he is an Abyssinian slave."*

After a moment of hiatus, I said, "May Allah bless you, oh, sheikh. The grand Mufti from Saudi Arabia Sheikh Abdul Azeez ibn Baaz had related to me about fighting oppressive leaders the hadith of ibn Saad in Tabaqaatul-Kubraa [7/163-165], please what is your opinion?" The verse started out by saying: "A group of Muslims came to al-Hasan al-Basree [d110H] seeking a verdict to rebel against al-Hajjaaj. So they said: *"o Abu Sa'eed! What do you say about fighting this oppressor who has unlawfully spilt blood and unlawfully taken wealth and did this and that?"* So al-Hasan said. *"I hold that he should not be fought. If this is the punishment from Allah, then you will not be able to remove it with your swords. If this is a trial from Allah, then be patient until Allah's judgment comes, and he is the best of judges."* So they left al-Hasan, disagreed with him and rebelled against al-Hajjaaj; so al-Hjjaaj killed them all."

About them al-Hasan used to say. *'If the people had patience, when they were being tested by their unjust ruler, it will not be long before Allah will give a way out. However, they always rush for their swords, so they were left to their swords. By Allah! Not even for a single day did they bring about any good.'*

I remained sitting upright on the rugged floor cross-legged in front of the smiling but thoughtful minded sheikh silently for a while digesting the coherent spiritual doctrine that has been given to me. In my mind's eye many Muslims, Jews, and Christens sees a faith and creeds and nothing else more. Therefore, they complicate conversations about faith and forget to pause on the merits of justice.

Then the Sheikh said, "Doctrines—doctrines are designed to get around that corner before you do! Patience gets you there before you understand!"

Thereupon Sheikh Maged suddenly sat forward in his chair thrusting his arm frontward with an imaginary spear, and recited from the Quran 18:65-82, "*So they found one of our servants, on whom we had bestowed mercy from ourselves and whom we had taught knowledge from our own presence. Moses said to him "may I follow thee, on the footing that thou teach me something of the higher truth which thou has been taught? [The other] said: 'Verily thou will not be able to have patience with me! And how can thou have patience about things about which thy understanding is not complete?'*"

After a period of silence giving me some moments of pondering thought, the Sheikh continued and said, "The Jewish, Christen, Muslim communities` understandings was already completed when they the Hebrew people had their Torah in complete text before the destructing of their temple and banishment to Babylon." "*But the thing commanded I to them, saying, Obey my voice, and I will be your God, and ye shall be my people: and walk ye in all the ways that I have commanded you, that it may well unto you. But they hearkened not, nor inclined their ear, but walked in the counsels and in the imagination of their evil heart, and went backward, and not forward*" (Jer. 7:23-28). The Christens had their *Injaal* (Gospel of Jesus) from Prophet Jesus in complete text before it too was lost, and their destruction of their holy temple in Jerusalem was followed by the Romans. From Jerusalem the followers of Jesus and all Hebrew people therein they was both banished by the Romans army because of their hearts. The Muslims do have their Quran in complete text today, which is the best examples of guidance for all mankind, yet many are going astray in spite of it again because of their hearts!"

"Do not lament, Muhammad Dawud, the Sheikh would say to me. "Just follow the hearts of a people and you will discover the true life of a community. Their leaders anywhere on this earth are a punishment or a trial from Allah. If indeed their leaders are a punishment from their lord they obviously can't remove what is in their own hearts with their own swords, thus, upping the ante of non-repentance upon themselves for punishment before their lord to judge! And if indeed their leaders are a trial from their lord then, "*And hold fast, all of you together to the rope of Allah and be not be divided among yourselves*" (Quran 3:103). Upping the ante of patience, and respite for those who are wise!

Immediately Sheikh Maged`s glowing smile gave me clarity and ease because determining what is right is paramount and primary in the fortress of the Muslim instead of who is right in regards to appreciation. From the tip of his neatly trimmed white goatee to the bottom of his long white throb, his adept body language and reasoned psyche matched his mental humility, characteristics I found to be very real and stimulating. The sheikh said to me, "Patience. There are seventeen different important examples of patience in the Holy Quran just having an understanding of a few of these principals and applying them to my life then to his understanding, everywhere its déjà vu" (Quran 2:45; 3:17; 6:34; 7:87; 8:46; 10:109; 11:11; 12:83; 14:05; 16:42; 19:65; 20:130; 25:20; 30:60; 40:77; 52:48; 103:3). While a great majority of normal people are controlled by the terra firma of hindsight, the one who is patient with his Lord and himself are of those who are truly successful in this world and the next. You mature faster in your life ventures he feels if you exercise more patience in your life and unto others as well. The fragrance of patience is hope. Hope is a plan that does more than smells the coffee; hope is a breath of fresh air that we positively need in our daily lives. Hope for the mercy of Allah. But, nevertheless, for that person or organization that is determined and confidant enough, then "victory is only being patient for one more year or one more day or one more hour or even, one more minute "[22] *"And the apostles whom we sent before thee were all men who ate food and walked through the streets: We have made some of you as a trial for others: Will ye have patience? For Allah is one who sees all things"* (Quran 25:20).

Then Sheikh Abdual Maged said to me words which gave me an understanding of a deep seated awareness of the Islamic life we need to live by "Taken from Al-Ma`loom Waajib il Ilaaqah bain Al-Haakim wal-Mahkoom, p. 22-23), "When changing the evil of the rulers, then this should be done by the scholars and not openly as is mention by a clear hadith of the prophet Muhammad (sas): *"When you wish to correct the sultan then take him by the hand in secret and advise him."* (Aquidah at-Tahawiyah)." Yes, it`s been a harried millennium. The life we live is driven by the attitude of our very own hearts. "Overstay your patience!" The Sheikh will say this over, and over again to me.

Yes, Sheikh Abdual Maged is right, and I can bank on it; we the Muslim people are morally obliged. It has been a harried millennium for a reason. And it does not seem likely to let up without a whisper or a fight any time soon. Thus it`s hard to believe in the mind`s eye of the naive and the covetous that they still cannot navigate smoothly in the tumultuous deserts of their own despots. But of course, oh, humble reader, you must not worry, we are going to look at all the scenarios that we possibly can, including that delicate art of saving people from themselves!

---

[22]   (Quran 25:20)

In the fall of 1995, after two years of studying I returned to Mecca after my insightful and fruitful trip to Sudan. When I had landed back in Mecca, Saudi Arabia, where I was studying Arabic Language and purity of faith (*aqeeda*) at Mecca University in the fall of 1995 from Sudan, I had shared many of these religious concepts and possible solutions with a few sheikhs and scholars I knew and trusted at the University and also not too far away in the Al Haram.

I said to them, "If this dire condition in the Muslim world is the punishment from Allah . . . then we will not be able to remove it with our swords. But with submissive hearts! If this dire condition in our Muslim world is a trial from Allah, then we Muslims must be patient until Allah`s judgment comes, and he is the best of judges."

Many sadly and quietly agreed that numerous segments of the Muslim world has itself separated the connection between day-to-day order of life and the moral order of life by adopting an old pagan faith into their hearts: secularism. Upon this I realized that we had strayed far from the original monotheist faith that prophet Muhammad (sas) brought to mankind. I further realized that once we as a people change the conditions of our own hearts then Allah (swa) will change our conditions here on earth.

The onus is on us, as a people, that we must establish our individual responsibility before Allah (swa) whom we cannot see and worship Him alone. In doing so, we make Allah (swa) the lone "executive branch" and thus bring divine existence here to earth into our very lives. To establish Sharia law is to swear an oath of allegiance to one's Lord. At this point, our individual responsibility intact, we will no longer bow before the men we can see and worship them along with Allah (swa). Once making Sharia law the executive branch over men in regards to our social, economic and political life, we will no longer foster the cancerous growth of dictators, despots, tyrants and presidents-for-life that we find in the Muslim world today.

Religious Freedom

Therefore all things whatsoever ye would that men should do to you,
do ye even so to them: for this is the law and the prophets.
                                                    —Bible, Matt. 7:12

The mainstream Salafiya Muslim, like myself, are opposed to U.S. or any kufr military presence on our Muslim and holiest lands. This was self-evident by the bombing of the United States Army barracks at Khobar Towers in Saudi Arabia in 1996 by their own Saudi Salafi citizens, which only highlighted the degree of public opposition. Why? Because it`s one of those golden rules that just wouldn`t go away on its own, which says that once you have foreign troops in your country contrary to your creed of faith, you have lost your sovereignty. We are also opposed to any establishment or demonstration of pagan or un-Islamic faith institution on the Arabian Peninsula. Contentious, yes, but the prohibition of churches, synagogues and pagan temples for the more than six and a half million non-Muslims who live and work in the Saudi kingdom is rooted in the command by the Prophet Muhammad (sas) not to have any house of worship in Hejaz[23] that is not Islamic: Narrated by Omar ibn Al-Khattab, may Allah be please with him: (Hadith—Muslim 1637, and 1767and Hadith—Bukhari 2888). I have no right to dispute an order of Prophet Muhammad (sas) before Allah or anyone for that matter and as a Muslim knowing that this command

---

[23]   The Arabian Peninsula

by him is true, I must obey him even if I were a king. I believe Prophet Muhammad (sas) had a very good reason for issuing such a command. I know it is sound. My only duty is to obey him without concern for the future and its consequences, which only He can see.

I also believe it was not by chance that Allah welcomed me to Mecca for umrah and then for hajj followed by an opportunity to study there for almost four years both at their University in Mecca and privately with religious scholars. It was also an act of mercy from Allah to be able to live with and be loved by his people, those custodians of my faith Islam. Yet I am fully aware that once you live with a people, you are then expose to many truths about yourself and about them.

Once, during the first few months I was living in Saudi Arabia a knowledgeable and blind sheikh said to me, "If you are looking for the rose you will find the rose; if you are looking for the mud, you will find the mud." This blind Sheikh Ibn Baaz then turned and looked at me and said, "You will find what you are looking for, *Insha Allah.*" Then he also shared these words with me, "When you speak, speak the truth, perform your promise, discharge your trusts, commit not fornication, or adultery, keep away from impure desires, withhold your hands from striking, and from taking that which is unlawful and bad. The worst of Allah`s servants are those who carry tales about to do mischief and separate friends as well as seek for the defects of the good. Acquire knowledge, and patience, this way you can ensure religious freedom."

"Heavy is the head that wears the crown" is a true statement in this enlighten era, especially if your name is King Abdullah of Saudi Arabia, one of the richest men on earth and one who has been endowed with great insight by Allah (swa). The responsibilities he holds are enormous, obligations that reach far beyond the borders of his kingdom. Domestically, however, one of his most pressing problems—in the minds of the Salafiya, that is—is that the kingdom has invited a large, non-Muslim labor force to help build their homes, roads, schools, and industry; a labor force from Europe, India, and Philippines that also works beside native Saudis both in business and as servants in their homes. There are now more than six-and-a-half million non-Muslims living in Hejaz, compared to the four million Muslims that come for hajj yearly and leave. With another three and a half million non-Muslims living in the neighboring Arabian Peninsula states of Bahrain, UAE, Kuwait, Oman, Qatar, and Yemen, the leaders of these nations have created a society that effectively defies the

Prophet's original edict in my opinion and in the opinions of many Muslim scholars.

Considering America, which houses every faith on this earth under its roof, religious freedom is the norm and a prideful standard. Yet one does not eat apples and oranges in the same manner. If you are appreciative of delicious fruit, then you eat an apple, never wishing it was like an orange; you eat with contrast in mind. Likewise, having been blessed to grown up in America, I have been deeply aware from an early age that every faith has its own flavor and atmosphere. Therefore I worship today as a Muslim with contrast in mind. This is indeed one of the ways how America has made me a better Muslim! Knowing that if a prophet wishes to sow his particular brand of faith unto a tribe of people in a land promised to them, the question then remains: "Are those chosen people spiritually appreciative of what they have received from their Lord and his command to not intertwine that faith with the faith that others have chosen?" In this context, religious freedom means that the people are free to practice their faith freely without interference from a foreign faith. Secular democracy and Abrahamic monotheism are two very different kinds of fruits, atmospheres, and faiths.

So mind the gape! It makes no sense to me, I feel, not to affirm that every person is a living temple of their own faith regardless of what it way be or where they are.

What makes sense to me, a humble student of knowledge, is why bring a person into a land that my prophet has forbidden him or her to build a temple and to worship therein. If I really want for that person what I want for myself, then I would say to them I am sorry but you cannot enter this land because I, myself, would not want to enter a land that I could not pray in together in a mosque with my fellow Muslim brothers and sisters regardless of the wage. So why should I deny you this right of freedom of worship given to you by that same divine one just so I can extract labor from you knowing that I am surrounded by a sea of Muslim neighbors all around me in need of work and opportunity? Why invite a people into your lands when you, yourself, would decline the same invitation under the same rules? Heavy is the head that wears the crown indeed. Denouncing the bias against religious freedom in Saudi Arabia because of a decree given to them sincerely by a Prophet that is dear to them is not the wise. Denounce the act of a people of faith who did not want for others what they want for themselves is the perfect self-portrait. And pity their king who is aware of this sad situation before him I believe, as well as the answer to this situation is that these millions of non-Muslims who must leave his land by order of prophet Muhammad (sas) depends on the will and faith of the people therein to act.

When on March 15, 2012, the Grand Mufti of Saudi Arabia, Abdul-Azeez ibn Abdullah Al Ash-Sheikh may Allah (swa) bless him, said, "All churches on the Arabian Peninsula must be destroyed," one without knowledge of the Salafiya might assume a brutal reality that the destruction of all churches in Hejaz would be the simple solution. Admittedly, the act of sending millions of non-Muslims back to their home countries with pay and restitutions simply because the Muslim people therein want for them what they want for themselves may likewise sound extreme to some "secular democratic" ears or "Arab Nationalist" ears. Yet it`s a message that says their world is not according to money and profit but faith and obedience to a prophet; this is truly a hard definition of reality that is envious, or impossible to infused in the eye of the beholder. An objective person who is seeking the truth, however, and not ashamed to admit freely what they find, will conclude that much can be accomplished in life once people realize you truly want for them what you want for ourselves. Being the inviters of Islam we must all be conscious of both our behavior and truthfulness in our dealings with people from outside our faith so that those who will observe us from afar will say we are a just people in spite of their strange faith.

Sincerely, that hard contentious definition of reality and religious freedom can only, I believe, be bridged by wanting for others what we want for ourselves. Islam, being intolerant to those who are not of the Abrahamic faith, is a reality! We are not tolerant to polytheist or atheist or secularist or those who are practicing witchcraft; this is the truth. We Muslims are not even tolerant to Communism or today's capitalist based on usury. Yet the majority of Muslim scholars know the saving grace is can we all "humanity" be "just" to each other in spite of our different faiths and creeds? This is the hard-core question worthy of addressing to ourselves and to the world public.

With contrast in mind, those who have a false sense of their own creativity, it is they who cannot bridge the gap towards a more harmonious world that is dearly needed.

For those of us Muslims who has consider challenging the myths, the excessive pagan cultures, secularism, the political correctness, and the hate, sure religious freedom is important in life. But the real battle is can "justice" be in lockstep with "religious freedom"?

Let`s be frank because time is important. When people cry out for religious freedom, is it really at the expense of their neighbor`s human rights, equal rights, justice, and due process of law? Yes or no? Or is this demand rightfully by us, that this idea is a component of a whole for a complete civilize way of life between peoples of different faiths living side by side going about their daily public lives without a secular law insisting we all remove our faiths given to us by that divine one, from the state and public arena in which we all live in?

Or is this demand rightfully by them, that Islam is like a strange window exposing a forbidden world yet privileged and honored faith? So when nonbelieving individuals cry out from within Muslim countries or outside Muslin countries for religious freedom, it`s an opportunity for those of them that blaspheme conviction in the name of ignorance a pardon from a death-row verdict or even an outright pardon because of the ignorance in their lives, yet sincerely wishes justice and truth; people are free individuals, and such is the pragmatism of this life. Oh, humble reader with experience in mind, truly humanity lives in a gated globe so that we may learn more about each other with tolerance.

With contrast in mind, conceivably, oh humble reader, it`s those who make such a sincere call of religious freedom are those whose hearts lie the fear that they will be brought to judgment before their lord on earth and those who believe they will be brought to judgment before their lord in heaven.

The SHAM CRESCENT

And those who, when an oppressive wrong is inflicted on them, (are not cowed but) help and defend themselves. The recompense for an injury is an injury equal there to (in degree): But if a person forgives and makes reconciliation, his reward is due from Allah: For Allah loves not those who do wrong. But indeed if any do help and defend themselves after a wrong (done) to them, against such there is no cause of blame. The blame is only against those who oppress men with wrong doing insolently transgress beyond bounds through the land, defying right and justice: For such there will be a penalty grievous.
—Quran 42:39-42

Moving forward with our knowledgeable sheikhs whose fatwa's reflect the true pulse of an Islamic movement, that great promise of Sharia law is finally being put to the test. The trenches are in our mosques, schools, universities, libraries, courts, town halls, parks and front doors, through the efforts of ordinary people who wish to believe in and submit to a divine force outside of themselves. The eyes of the world are watching to see if we can muster the will, if we are the true ambassadors of our Lord, chosen to restore opportunity and prosperity here on earth. Can we, the believers, restore that hope that humanity so desperately needed from the grass roots up? We do believe that having more people coming to the mosque to pray every day, every year, is not enough. Yes, we want the people to become actively engaged in the affairs of our movement connecting faith with works and new ideas; indeed, the key is winning neighborhoods one block at a time. The key is organizing, plus having the youth play a major role in our Islamic campaign for the hearts, minds and the souls of humanity. The results have been a network of trained professionals working in cohesion at brigade strengths.

All praise is to Allah; my fourth tour of duty into the Muslim world was traveling into the heart of the Sham[24] Crescent with my wife and children and enrolling at Damascus University in Syria to study Arabic and learn more about my Islamic faith in January 1998. Oh, humble reader, this jihad of mine is a combination of important goals. I must see, and experience for myself that Arab Shiite-Sunni lifeblood of rivaled networks of jihad; truthfully I am sick and tired of hearing all that bias talk about one religious group against another from Muslims and non-Muslims alike, when, in fact you are free to go about this world, sit down with the scholars, and find out the truth for yourself. It's that commerce and way of life of a people committed in uplifting as well as liberating themselves by their faith that must be seen and experience firsthand before one talks about jihad unto others.

The people of Sham throughout history are a people not "waiting for change" in the Asian Muslim Arab world; they are one of the carriers of this civilize old world who believe their time has come. After ten thousand years, forthrightly, they know who they are and lived that. Yes, they know who their God is and learned from it; that's why they are now fighting for his mercy. They know who their enemies are and been there before when it is time to make that sacrifice; simply put, these Asian Arabs are a different stripe. Their base is the mosque, and that's how it came to past.

Exiting my apartment in Ruk-ul-Deen, the heart of down town city of Damascus, walking in the twilight early mornings towards masjid Kuwaiti for Fajar (morning) prayers, I long realize I am not alone. I was incredibly lucky to witness and join those men who will leave their homes and form a line of determination and faith and be grateful to that unseen sovereign lord. Indentifying that undercover postal carrier amongst us who has that air of certain confidence in himself is the hard part because of my nationality and culture; yet in time, being patient is truly a revolutionary act of faith. Because trust is ruthless on the front lines, it's "who you know" that believes you are a legitimate

---

[24] Sham: the region bordering the eastern *Mediterranean Sea*, usually known as the *Levant* or *Greater Syria*, comprising modern *Syria, Lebanon, Israel*, the *Palestinian Territories* and *Jordan*

believer who is "grateful to his lord" is what counts in this part of the old spiritual world. It's then you get a route heading northeast towards Beqaa Valley, Lebanon. I am not a tourist nor do I wish to be a farmer, oh, humble reader. I am just a student seeking knowledge, yet sometimes that road that is less traveled is the one that surprises and enriches you. Now that I am in this part of the Muslim Arab Asian world, I also wanted to know why Hezbollah feels they will overcome!

The clearest evidence that I had that Hezbollah was an aspirating winnable force, that victory was its middle name was when Sheikh ~ Ali stride into the courtyard gave his Salam's and sat down before me. He is two meters tall and looked like a middle-aged Arab Anthony Quinn with a heavy long black and gray beard, an olive tan wearing a black turban and long white robe. But it was his voice that was most impressible; he sounded like Charleston Huston but in Arabic, and you can feel the gravitational pull of influence that is alluring in such a way that it fits right into your plan of conversation and manifesto.

From his manner, I knew and he knew I was not an enemy in spite of my American passport on the small table before us, or even that I was a Sunni Muslim and he a Shiite Muslim. I've began breaking the ice by telling short stories of the lives and the odysseys of my enslaved peoples and our faiths back home; after a short while I then relented, one can sense if you are spiritually conscious that Sheikh ~ Ali is no bartender, it's "why I am here" not "who am I" initially? So I asked him frankly how did Hezbollah make him become a better Muslim?

I can see my words touched a nerve. He smiled for the first time and only time; then he finally displayed a bodily ease after which he responded by saying in a prophetic pragmatism kind of way, "Hezbollah helped illuminate patience in me." Sheikh ~Ali continued by saying, "The pace of social life here in Lebanon is not as fast as in America or Europe, but we all still have the same needs. We Muslims are evolving out of the first stage of the decolonization of the Muslim world from the creative revolution of identity into an Islamic revolution of purpose. But not everybody is going to be happy in letting go of the imperialist past." "Because of Hezbollah, millions are rediscovering what it means to be free from foreign Western powers and distinguishing the values between that delicate matter of justice and peace amongst ourselves. All praise is due to Allah; our history is not as ancient as you think. European invasions is not something new to us nor were they bound by rules of religious or pagan dignity. But by Allah we Muslim believers here in Lebanon and in Sham had to be patient when facing oppression and death; even in the best of our Muslim worlds there will be tragedy. So we must fight onward in spite of the suffering and hardships that will come and have faith in our lord. However, all praise is due to Allah it is ironic to have a Muslim man coming from the land of the imperialist enemy inquiring sincerely about the blessings of Allah upon us!"

Then the Sheikh went on to state, "For as long as I can remember death and oppression generates an amazing amount of faith. I just don`t care who your enemies are, Muhammad Dawud; such understandings is not beyond your cognizance. I am not being superstitious; it`s just that so much of life is unscripted whereas that surety of death and oppression only maximizes our potential in faith, which usually gives it a keener zest, if, off course, you don`t scare easily. Thus, I slowly came to the realization that the best defense to our human frailty here in Sham against death and oppression by imperialist is to aspire with faith, unaware and regardless of the time you have left." "This is how Hezbollah helped me be a better Muslim."

I just sat there in his large garden full of olive and pomegranate trees in momentary silence with Sheikh ~ Ali, appreciating and absorbing what was being said to me whilst an elderly aid strolled up to us with cups of hot Arab coffee, served us, and went back into the beautifully large villa without a word. Thereupon Sheikh ~ Ali then averted his gaze from me and stared into the westward sky and seemly yearned for the relative safety of jihad; he then stated, "Our attacks on invading American and French imperialist forces in Beirut, Lebanon, on October 23,1983, is still a lesson not well learned by them, Muhammad Dawud. Why they did not care?

I felt this was a very loaded question pointed at me to see where my heart rests. It was time to earn my attendance. And see where his motives lie in such a question? So I left it with Allah and said, *"O ye who* believe! *Take not the Jews and the Christians for your friends and protectors; they are but friends and protectors to each other. And he amongst you that turns to them "For friendship" is of them. Verily Allah guideth not a people unjust* (Quran 5:51).

But the Sheikh wanted more and said again in a higher tone still looking westward, "Why they did not care?"

So I said, "Because many peoples in Sham have made their enemies rich buying cigarettes and alcohol."

The Sheikh wanted still more and said again in even a higher tone still looking westward, "Why they did not care?"

"Because the love of usury in the Arab lands."

"Why they did not care?"

"Because the Philistine intifada is only news."
"Why they did not care?"
"Because talk is cheap."
"Why did they not care?"
"Because of the people`s fear of death."
"Why did they not care?"
"Because what do you give to a beggar sitting on a mountain of gold?'
"Why did they not care?"
"Because Allah is forgotten!"

Thereupon Sheikh ~ Ali returned his gaze upon me as if he was looking at me for the first time leaned back in his chair folding his arms with a light sigh. "I am indeed very surprise to meet an orthodox Sunni Muslim American student of faith who has travel to meet me coming from Damascus seeking to understand our creed of faith Shiite Islam, which is based upon two pillars. The first pillar is theology: [1] oneness of Allah; [2] justice [Addel]; [3] prophethood [Muhammad]; [4] devotion to the imam [Walaya], which is the most excellent since through it and through the imam (Wally), the true knowledge of the rest of the pillars can be found, and [5] the day of judgment.

The second pillar is [1] prayer [salat]; [2] alms tax or poor due [Zakat]; [3] fasting [Sawm]; [4] pilgrimage [hajj]; [5] Islamic governmental allowance [al-homs], funds that are given to persons who are related to the prophet or early followers of Muhammad (sas); [6] promotion of virtue; [7] prevention of vice; [8] loyalty to Allah (swa); [9] aversion from bad things, and [10] holy war [Jihad].

"Thus, faith consists in word, deed, and belief. There can never be word, deed, and belief without faith and affirmation, for then alone is faith completed. He who asserts, acts, and believes in other than the faith and the truth [we have delineated] cannot be a believer. His works will not benefit him, howsoever he abases himself."

"It is not correct to assert, like the Murjia (Sunni Hadith books of evidence) that faith consists in profession without action, or is it correct to say, like a group of the commonly Amma (Public) that faith consists in 'word and deed' only."

Homeward bound back over those mountains to Damascus and my family from that beautiful Beqaa Valley oasis, I must say Sheikh ~ Ali was a generous host. I also realize nobody ever joins Hezbollah; they join you and that they are a popular resistance organization. This is why they shall overcome; their affair is with Allah (swa).

Following my journey into Beqaa Valley, Lebanon, where I was visiting and talking to Hezbollah leaders about their resurgence and faith, I was quite surprise that one early morning seeing a large crowd of young people marching and chanting words of protest who walked westerly by my apartment in Ruk ul-Deen Damascus. But at the time I thought nothing of it; perhaps they were some religious sect on a purifying mission that needed a public processing. It was a splendid day though traffic was backed up because of the chanting marchers up ahead that numbered about hundred people of all ages, which spilled into the streets. I was on my way to my morning classes at Damascus University, but from what I can see from the now large gathering groups of protesters that I was going to be delayed and this engender was impossible to bypass. Such as life would have it, curiosity compelled me to follow along since they were traveling my way. It felt more like a parade than anything else; walking along behind them down the wide avenue between the angry beeping outmoded cars, obsolete taxis, and crowed minibuses, I did notice some of their few signs some of them was carrying. It read in Arabic, "House of Satan" and "Go back home, Satan." Now I really marveled and wondered, what Shiite sect is this, or perhaps maybe they are a Sufi sect by some unknown order I just don`t know or heard about? Possibly a holiday for sure because now their numbers was growing, and spectators that was looking on from the sidewalks and windows of their homes was cheering them onward. I did not had to walk far, just a few blocks behind the Turkish embassy, the young and chanting leaderless crowd which even had school children with them, had stopped in front of a small but elegant mansion like house and started to throw small stones, tomatoes, eggs, and even their own shoes at the house! The people just showered the house with what garbage they were carrying in their bags or picked up in the streets and started shouting obscenities at it.

Totally shocked by what`s happening, I dared to interrupt a Arab man with his daughter that was beside me as they were throwing small stones and eggs at the poor house whose windows were now broken and looked really ransacked from the outside. I asked him, "What custom is this that you are doing so that you can get the devil out of somebody`s house?" But I was disregarded. Being ignored by the busy crowd but unabated, I continued to look for an ingenious face and said out loud to whomever will hear my words, that with a surety, I am sure there is a hadith by our prophet Muhammad (sas) that there is a better way to get rid of a evil devil or jinn that enters a home, that this action is nothing but a sad innovation of our Muslim faith! Upon hearing my humble Arabic words of earnest inquest and concern, a simple old

Arab man turned to me and looked surprisingly at me and somehow sense that I was a Western foreigner not an African foreigner, and straightforwardly explained with an air of contempt with simple Arab words that the house is the residence of that American ambassador to Syria, a Mr. Ryan Crocker, who is but a disgusting kufr devil here in their country, an enemy to the Muslim people and we want him and his ideas out!"

Standing there staring at the awful event before me, I now realize how deep the hatred there was for American polices and ideals in the Sham Crescent. Surrounded by ordinary people and children in the hundreds shouting in unison that my ambassador from my country should get out of their country deeply made me ponder about why so many nations of peoples have such a distain for America I love and grew up in. What is there to hate?

If there was any doubt about how out of touch the people of Sham and the American people were, this was the moment. Living here in this beautiful city called Damascus now more than a year and half, I realized that we the Muslim people of America needed to be properly introduced. I am still a believer that "soft power" turns angry skeptics into pools of amazement and admiration. Till this day I feel the people here in Sham just don`t know who the people are in America and vice versa. So I walked away from the growing angry roaring crowd before me with a plan, a marketing plan, a plan that I submitted to the American Culture attaché at her office in Damascus, Syria, with the hope of making a change. The marketing plan was called Islam in America. She looked at my plan in shock and disbelief. Later on, I learned she was a "political spin doctor of a high order," so it is not strange the best advice to my government then did not go unheeded, yet I was surprise that I was unappreciated.

I had the audacity to submitted a proposal that I and a few friends of mine name *Jihad Brown* from America (New Jersey) who had was also studied at Damascus University and Imam *Zaid Shaker* who is also from America (Connecticut) who was studying privately with Sufi Sheikhs in Damascus, that we respectfully request to present a program at the American Culture Center in Damascus called "Islam in America" so that the people here in Damascus would truly know what we the religious Muslim people of America was all about and what we have to say.

My proposal was denied not only by the culture attaché at the time but also by our ambassador Mr. Ryan Crocker himself when I went directly to see him at the American embassy. As fate will have it, four months later, I found out through a Syrian student at Damascus University that there was a program tomorrow evening at the American

Culture Center here in Damascus about Islam in America. I was truly shocked by what I heard. In disbelief, the following day after the American governmental version of Islam in America program was over upstairs in the American Culture Center, I stood in front of my ambassador Mr. Ryan Crocker and looked him in the eyes; he subsequently looked down at his feet in humble apology. He stole my ideas and made it out as his own credit and was hoping to keep me in the dark about it. Being patriotic, I let this offence by my own ambassador pass by; but in the back of my mind, I notice the kind of Western secular image my government wanted to portray to the Syrian people of Islam in America; they wanted a nationalist secular viewpoint. My government did not want a religious Muslim Americans to speak at an open forum to the Syrian people. This was a living proof to me that harvesting influence is worthy of its final destination and that my government is not apprehensive about its Muslim American citizens studying Islam and Arabic in Muslim countries privately, thus willing to block us every step of the way as possible with suspicion and or ignorance.

The following weekend I found myself wanting to put behind me that selfish betrayal from my own ambassador. So my lovely and patient wife decided that we should take the children with us and visit some special religious monuments for a change of atmosphere and do some shopping in Damascus old markets (*Suks*). On our way to the bountiful markets, we felt that we should first stop by and visit one of those famous martyrs of Islam for the first time. Subsequently we all together got off the minibus at the University of Damascus (downtown) and went behind the old building of the faculty of dentistry near a quiet clearing surrounded by old tall pine trees and uncut grass. Therein lies the grave of Sheikh ibn Taymiyah. May Allah bless him with heaven! As my wife and children and I quietly stood there by his lonely white marble grave and paid our respects with prayer, I wondered about his noble life and destiny. Yes, in many ways he is still forgotten, and ignored, because of his audacity in calling out in public acts of innovations. Exiled, even in death to such a lonely place that only word of mouth can find. One can only ponder standing there looking down upon this solitary grave of a man who was Allah fearing and stood against innovations (Bida) in our Islamic faith and let come what may in his life. And yet because of his outspokenness against innovations incorporated into the Islamic faith by Muslims who are ignorant as well as arrogant, he died in prison here in Damascus, Syria one of three great learning centers of the Islamic world at the time. That sheikh, that scholar, that Muslim imam who stood up and said this is a dangerous thing to do when you innovate and incorporate man made ideas and desires into our faith; thus we felt he must be remembered and respected. His warnings about innovations in the Islamic faith was one of those stepping stones of understandings about guarding ones faith I truly appreciated but learned a great deal about it in my own studies in Mecca University, Saudi Arabia. But I am now a minority; many here want the freedom to be ignorant or arrogant. In this ancient city of religious humanity many wish to hang on to their deep-rooted innovations in spite of the warnings and clear evidence against it in accepted hadiths or Quran (Quran 23:53-54). Considering the great power of sin and how it gets hold of the hearts of men, and considering all the wrongs that men have done, I too feel it is the height of true recklessness and injustice on their part to turn away from warnings, which are given expressly for their own good so that they will not rendered themselves impervious to Allah`s grace.

All that hype talk about fifty thousand mourners who marched back then almost 640 years ago and came to this very spot to oversee the burial of this pious Allah (swa) fearing Muslim man who said the truth but was ignored by his own people because of their quest of invented desires to be placed into their faith means nothing to me. Simply because out of the fifty thousand people, five could not be found from amongst them who had the courage to act on their faith on getting Sheikh Ibn Taymiyah out from that prison of injustice alive before he died in it!

Those who strive and suffer in Allah`s cause are never forgotten. If you think not in today`s geopolitical world that your goals go not beyond your borders, that your methods is based not on conventional popular opinions on the next wave, then you are gravely mistaken. Sheikh Amed Ismail Yassin and Dr. Abdel Aziz Al-Rantissi, may Allah (swa) bless them both with heaven, were true Islamic Palestinian fundamentalist martyrs that inspired a nation of people under oppression and illegal occupation by an apartheid Israeli regime, and both were assassinated by American helicopter gunships sold to Israel. In 1987, they started the Islamic resistance movement called Hamas. In January 2006 the Palestinian people elected Hamas as their government and Mr. Khaled Mashaal, who had lived in Syria and now lives in Jordan their leader. Mr. Mashaal wished to liberate the Palestinian people from the apartheid Israeli regime because I feel he truly loves his people, justice and fears Allah (swa). Shame and the curse of Allah (swa) on Mahmoud Abbas, that leader of the corrupt and traitorous Fatah, which is that enemy near organization. He and other members of Fatah have forgotten so it seems that other Muslim stem cell fundamentalist Sheikh Izz Ad-Din Al-Qassam and what he stood for and fought for and died for.

In October of 2000 I had the good fortune to visit again Beirut, Lebanon, once considered the "Paris of the Arab world." As I walked the streets of Beirut with my wife and young children, and watched the people live and work together with the knowledge that they had come a long way from the abyss of civil war, I had the sense that the refreshing air of hope for the future was the talk of the town. My wife, and my children and I strolled past the picturesque hillside homes, along seaside boardwalk, then across to the American University campus and main market centers; and I cannot doubt the great historical past of the city, nor deny the great historical future of a people who out of many faiths all have the same needs. Those days of civil, religious and class wars between the faiths, that bitterness and desire for recriminations among the different groups, all look to me as if they are finally over. I believe the devastating past was a lesson learned painfully well, a lesson that has made people desire to communicate better with one another. Even though they have been speaking the same language to each other for thousands of years and look the same to me, it seems, only now, that they, as a people, are truly listening to each other with real concern.

That contrast to be noted here in the Middle East for that Western humble reader who has yet to venture to the land of the prophets, it is not the importance of the color of one`s skin but the creed of one`s faith that dictates success and opportunity. Many people here were indeed surprise that I was a Muslim African-American enjoying the blessing of what Allah has endowed upon the people here in Sham. That America has Muslims who are conscious of their faith and are humane in their actions! Sham is inhabited by sincere people who`s faith demands proper orientation for the future of living a humble Allah-God fearing life as they know it. So when I meet people anywhere the first thing I notice that comes to their hearts is just how did America made me become a better Muslim? Sincerely I feel we Westerners have been sending the wrong ambassadors abroad with outrageous goals and methods, which only compounded the hatred towards us with unnecessary selfish interests.

When Sheikh Hassan Nasrallah said, "The angels are above the planes" in that refreshing summer day of July 6, 2006 in Beirut, Lebanon, his staggering words were a seismic wave thundering through a relatively conscious Islamic world. Till this day my Muslim brothers, those Shiite brothers of ours, gain confidence and momentum by being black turban ferrets of Sham. Yes, some people cannot see the cedar from the trees, that Hezbollah has won broad-based grass roots support by lessons learned by cultivating an innovative social welfare network along with the building of hospitals, schools, and housing in Lebanon in equal par with their military wing. This quilt has won them huge popularity in the Arab Muslim world today. But why did Allah (swa) grant Sheikh Hassan Nasrallah victory over the apartheid Israeli regime after so many had tried and failed? Is it because he feared Allah (swa) first, as well as the hearts of the people truly changed knowing that victory will only come from Allah (swa) not from nationalistic slogans, desire for power and greed! Perhaps it`s that ongoing historical challenge of tolerance towards each other, no matter if our neighbors are Muslims or Christians or Jews, that we fundamentalists have before us. For these moments, however, one might hardly believe in the need to propagate a secular state government just so we all can get along together and walk these beautiful streets together in peace. Patience.

I bear witness to Allah (swa) I saw a similar change in the hearts of the Palestine people, those stateless and dispossessed people forced to lived under an alien citizenship in the millions, forced to live in the ghettos in the millions and forced to live by the millions in refugee camps throughout Sham. Still, these people have not given up in their fundamental faith in Islam or in Christianity.

Yes, I thank Allah (swa) for making me one of those believers to see with my own eyes a people who have endured such oppression by their neighbors, neighbors who believe they have a valid mandate from Yahweh to do such acts. I heard the call for the second intifada while I was living with my family in Damascus, Syria, where I was studying Arabic and teaching English at Damascus University, from 1998 to 2001. Leaving my wife and two children, Khaoula and Salah Eddin, behind me at our apartment, I set out on my five-day fact-finding journey down that Damascus road that first led to the graceful but expensive city of Amman, Jordan. On the first day of my journey, I visited Sheikh Nuh Ha Min Keller from America for the first time at his home. He had been on my short list of Muslim scholars I had to meet in the region for some time who had written the book *Reliance of the Traveler*. He lived out in a beautiful modern villa in a quite hilly suburb of Amman with his family. I wanted to know from his point of view his understanding of this new crises called intifada. Sheikh Min Keller explain to me as we went for long walks in the late evening night that this intifada will be long and ongoing what say`s undoubtedly bloody. I had asked him will the Palestine people end their oppression with greater sacrifice and work together and face the common enemy with victory? He says he does not know. The Sheikh then ask me about why I embrace the Islamic creed of Salafi. I told him that following the orthodoxy of Islam was best for me in light of what can happen to a person who strays from the straight path. Sheikh Keller has a gentle persuasive tone and way about himself, which I liked, and is wary of the Salafi, his own school of thought is Sufism but he accepted the wisdom of my decision. I believe he is a knowledgeable Sunni Muslim scholar who has lived here in the Muslim Arab world for many years and has made it his home away from home, yet sadly, I doubt that he has any plans to come back home to America and help proselytize Islam in person. The following morning, just before I left him on my way to Jerusalem, Sheikh Keller warned me about the risks of going to Jerusalem and the hearts of the people overall therein telling me many times to make my journey there as short as possible because of the lingering crisis and to remember Allah much.

Committed, I rode a minibus down a vast, winding, and ageless rainbow-colored canyon. Crossing the shallow river Jordan into Palestine and heading up the other side of that large canyon. I was indeed mesmerized by that malevolent, forbidding maze of rocks and broken promises not shaped by nature but by men. Suddenly I had lost myself in that timeless, barren landscape; yes, it`s easy to get lost on that road to Jerusalem, a city that's designed to reveal your soul, a place where abstract theologians and evil idle spirits rule till this day with hopeless desires.

It is true that the vultures of this forsaken dry landscape are fat and numerous, constantly high on the wing and keenly watching; they loathe both the sinner as well as those truly devoted and humbly searching on the path for that divine one who only demands gratitude. After many hours of travel, I could see Jerusalem clearly, that walled brooding medieval city, which is called City of Peace; awaiting patiently those on the path who are whispering final goodbyes to their worldly endeavors. Beware. Don`t be a fool. Give something in charity no matter how small before first entering the gates of this contested holy city for your own protection. Yes, this is that contested holy city of the three great monotheist faiths that truly reveals a dark-hearted tale of serial killings and oppressions in the name of that divine one and ancient idols. As I made my way downtown onto the plaza on the

Mount my six sense felt that familiar peaceful calmness descended upon me like that same peaceful atmosphere as in Medina and Mecca but not as strong as them but a person who is conscious about a radiance outside of himself can nonetheless feel that presents of peace.

I knelt there praying inside El-Aqsa Mosque with my Muslim brothers inside the old city of Jerusalem for juma[25] services on an early spring April day. The diligent, popular and beautiful medieval Mosque was full long before noon, hum du Allah, and the whole plaza on the Mount was full of worshipers of all ages deep in prayer; tall old pine trees swaying are the only pillars here. It was kneeling room-only as tens of thousands of people prayed to Allah (swa) to make successful their intifadas! That spiritual magnetism of Hamas was self-evident all around me from social to sacred to the soul behind that Arab human face. It was there that I first heard that Palestine Imam called out in a loud voice to the humble people in Arabic something that was also said in Hebrew to the Hebrew people not too long ago that seems long forgotten: "The Promise Land is for those who keep their promise to Allah!"

---

[25] Juma: Is the weekly Friday day of prayer that is an obligation upon the Muslim people.

The Shiite Resistance

"Moses said: "O my people! If ye do [really] believe in God, Then in him put your trust if ye submit [your will to his]." They said: (the Hebrew people), "In God do we put our trust. Our lord! Make us not a trial for those who practice oppression; and deliver us by thy mercy from those who reject [thee]."

—Quran 10:84-86

In this age of misinformation, there are times when elections are not always so pleasant and appropriate! It is not so hard for those of us religious fundamentalists to understand what that other American fundamentalist said, "What country before ever existed a century and a half without a rebellion? And what country can preserve its liberties if their rulers are not warned from time to time that their people preserve the spirit of resistance? Let them take arms. The remedy is to set them right as to facts, pardon, and pacify them. What signify a few lives lost in a century or two? The tree of liberty must be refreshed from time to time with the blood of patriots and tyrants. It is its natural manure." [26]

We understand quite clearly that paralyzing fog of denial America and their allies had in Iraq. That fiasco till this day just will not go away. The writing in the sandpit said quicksand, but American and European political leadership ignored the warnings even from their own Muslim

---

[26]   Thomas Jefferson, the 3rd President of the United States.

citizens. Now catapulted to front and center stage because of their conceited and blithe foreign policy adventurism—the rainmaker on their Operation Iraqi freedom in Baghdad, Al-Najaf, Al-Basrah, Fallujah and other cities in Iraq that honorable fundamentalist Sheikh Moqtada Al-Sadr and his grass root resistance guerrilla fighters, the Mahdi Army. If there is any doubt on his religious, or political intelligence, it was he who said, "Never negotiate under occupation." As the current head of one of the leading Shiite dynasties, whose father was Iraq`s Grand Ayatollah Mohammed Sadiq Al-Sadr, whose teacher was Iran`s Ayatollah Khomeini and who was murdered by Saddam Hussein under the oppressive Baath party. In an apparent bid for more grassroots support it was he who denounced continued American and western troop occupation in their country and waged a war of attrition against coalition troops saying: "Iraq should be governed by those who did not flee Saddam Hussein`s rule."

I truly believe that Islam urges all Muslims to stand with those who are oppressed.[27] *"The believers are but a single brotherhood: So make peace and reconciliation between your two contending brothers; and fear Allah, that ye may receive mercy"* (Quran 49:10). But what happens when we Sunni Muslims oppress our Shiite Muslims brothers because of their school of thought?[28] What happens when we Sunni Muslims assassinate the character and faith of our own neighbors because they are Shiite or Sufi Muslims?[29] The consequences are dire and catastrophic, I believe. It is self-evident that president for life Saddam Hussein was a Sunni Muslim-in-name-only till the last seconds of his life. In fact, he was a bigot, an Arab Ba'ath Party secular nationalist, as well as a renegade to his Western secular masters.

Yes, Sheikh Moqtada Al-Sada is nobody`s fool. He understood the dynamics of the political weather in his country. Those American, British and European Christian crusader armies that had invaded his country and overthrew Saddam Hussein they was truly his patrons. The fact that he went renegade against them is the true reason why they are in his country. The invasion of Kuwait in the summer of 1990 and Saddam Hussein`s decision to sell his oil not for dollars but for Euros in Iraq was the real reason of the break in relationship with Iraq. Not by any means, Western armies where in his country because of "weapons of mass destruction," or even because this despot had

---

[27]   Qur'an ch.49 v.10

[28]   Qur'an ch.49 v.10

[29]   Qur'an ch.49 v.10

denied his countrymen civil liberties. It was for the control of those oil fields in Iraq. Indeed, now that the puppet masters have gotten rid of the troublesome Sunni Arab puppet they wish to manage the troublesome affairs directly with a Shiite Arab puppet. I am well aware that Sheikh Moqtada Al-Sadr has learned in life that Allah (swa) has tested every nation or tribe of people with their leaders from their very own scriptures. How can it be that hundreds of millions of Muslims who can read, write and speak Arabic and who have the Quran in their homes, fail to take heed of Allah`s warnings in their own books? Now at this stage of horror with over two hundred and fifty thousand Iraqi people dead, a nation divided along ethnic lines, thanks to their Western liberators who after more than eight years of military foreign occupation, ethnic cleansing is now almost completed in virtually all of Iraqi cities and provinces. I ask of you oh humble reader of this book who is seeking the truth and straight talk not hype and propaganda who will Sheikh Moqtada Al-Sada call for help in his time of intifada against foreign puppet installed leaders and foreign Western occupation troops? The Sheikh has called on Allah (swa) for help which is no surprise. For years now after the invasion of Iraq by foreign Western troops those Shiite brothers in Qum, Iran and Najaf, Iraq have been working together to forge a new Iraq without unwanted foreign Western influence and troops. Those Shiite scholars in Qum, and Najaf knows their time has come; they remember after the overthrow by the Sunni dominated military back in 1958 over the British who installed King Faisal II, the first goal of the Sunni ruling class was to unite the majority Shiite Muslims and the minority Sunni Muslims in a way that the Shiite would submit to Sunni ruler ship. This was done by secularizing the Muslim state, which took their religious differences out of the picture as well as Allah`s mercy and protection and replace it with Arab nationalism. Such arrogant fools, with Muslim names only, how convenient; instead of holding onto their faith when it mattered and resolving their disputes with the laws of Allah when a mutual enemy faced them all, the Sunni leadership in Iraq adopted Arab nationalism as a way to rule over all the people with the aim of benefiting themselves and the goal to have power for themselves. It hurts me greatly that my Sunni Muslim brothers in name only went after the poison. Prophet Muhammad (sas) told his true followers to avoid "nationalism." It`s trademark is devotion to the sovereign interests of one's own nation.

What we Muslims who adhere to the fundamental principles of our Islamic faith, no matter if we are the majority or the minority, a Sunni or a Shia, the answers to all of our problems lie in our holy books. It is likewise a mistake to call on those whose creed is outside of our faith for aid. Now more than ever before in the history of Islam that focused call of intifada[30] are those Muslims who are true believers of the faith and who are now demanding justice and Islamic law in their lives, contrary to those Muslims-in-name-only who are nationalist and demanding the reins of power to stay in their despotic hands. Our enemies far call this movement the "Arab Spring," but in all actuality the awakening of the Muslim masses of all denominations which demonstrates a more mature dialogue between the people and their leaders with candor, frankness and reasoning in an admirable way that will please Allah (swa), whose mercy will show the way to overcome the disparities in wealth, health, employment, class prejudice and education in our Muslim societies, that we all have common hopes and that our dreams do not come at the expense of our Muslim neighbors again.[31] *"And hold fast all together, by the rope which Allah [stretches out for you], and be not divided among yourselves; and remember with gratitude Allah's favors on you; for ye were enemies and he joined your hearts in love, so that by his grace, ye became brethren . . ."* (Quran 3:103).

What is troubling for me and anyone else out there who is Allah fearing is all this operation Shock and Awe. Strange is it not that hundreds of millions of Muslims who can read, write and speak Arabic very well and do have the Quran in their very homes, yet they fail to take heed of Allah's warnings in their own books. *"To such as Allah rejects from his guidance, there can be no guide: He will leave them in their trespasses, wandering in distraction"* (Quran 7:186). Sectarianism? Iraq? Camel feathers; where they a people who had been neighbors for more than 10,000 years, a people who has been Muslims for more than 1,400 years, a people without a caliphate, Shiite, Kurd and Sunni who stood together and fought, successfully defeated the invading British Army with nothing but "Allah is Great" on their lips with inferior arms to carry less than a hundred years ago! *"Ye are the best of peoples, evolved for mankind, enjoining what is right, forbidding what is wrong, and believing in*

---

[30]   "If two parties among the believers fall into a quarrel, make ye peace between them: but if one of them transgresses beyond bounds against the other, then fight ye all against the one that transgresses until it complies with the command of Allah; but if it complies, then make peace between them with justice, and be fair: for Allah loves those who are fair and just"— Quran 49:9-10.

[31]   31 Quran 3:103

Allah. If only the People of the Book had faith, it were best for them: among them are some who have faith, but most of them are perverted transgressors. They will do you no harm, barring a trifling annoyance; if they come out to fight you, they will show you their backs, and no help shall they get" (Quran 3:110-111). Yes, I am still in shock and awe. Thanks to their Western liberators, this historic nation today is divided along sectarian lines in the sand who after more than eight years of foreign military occupation, ethnic cleansing is now almost completed in virtually all of Iraqi cities and provinces along with nearly three quarters of a million people dead and hundreds of thousands gravely injured!

Now that the Sunni despot Saddam Hussein, that enemy near, has been hanged, memories of pain, death, humiliation, doubt of faith, and fear have not truly gone away. Nor has the hate and revenge of those times disappeared. The grievances of our Shiite Muslim brothers rights by Allah (swa) are legitimate. Empty promises to our Lord and to each other will only make the disaster unhealed in Iraq for generations. Yes, Sheikh Moqtada Al-Sadr, and that Honorable fundamentalist Grand Ayatollah Sayid Ali Al-Husayni Sistani have a heavy obligation, unto all the people that live in Iraq that they will not be the new Shiite enemy-near unto the Muslim people. With the mercy of Allah (swa), the many tribes and faiths of Iraq will come to acknowledge that their diversity is, in fact, their strength. Now that our Shiite brothers are at the helm in Iraq, they must lead however painful it may be, knowing that Allah`s (swa) mercy is greater than His wrath. Momentous choices lie now before these Shiite leaders, so can they, the Shiite branch of Islam, be the better brother`s keeper? We the believers of this faith called Islam are asking this central core question to ourselves.

Perhaps they can. But what troubles me, oh, humble reader, is a *hadith* (Sahih Muslim) from Prophet Muhammad (sas), the narrator: "Ubay ibn Ka`b # 2895": which says: "that there shall come a time when a mountain of gold will be discovered between the rivers Tigris and the Euphrates and there will be such a demand for this gold that out of every one hundred people ninety nine people will die fighting for it." Cautiously and fearfully many knowledgeable Sheikhs in the region from all schools of thought I hear are whispering with a nervous realization that this mountain of gold is inverted, "black gold" . . . "oil".

I believe the only recourse the Grand Ayatollah Sayid Ali Al-Husayni Sistani and Prime Minister Nouri Al-Maliki have in obtaining peace through justice and ending sectarian violence in

Iraq is together they must show to the Muslim world for the mercy of Allah (swa) their true sovereign lord that they are the better brother's keeper!

However time is not on their side; violence is truly rising again to the delight of the enemy far Western powers that was forced to leave Iraq empty-handed in December 14, 2011. Furthermore, those monafiq advocates in the gulf states—those advocates of greed, hate and oppression are hedging their bets that the Shiite community in Iraq cannot be just to their own domestic minority Sunni community in finding someone who can sit in that empty chair of Vice President Tariq Al-Hashemi and help govern all the people with justice.

That art of do-it-yourself challenges of confidence in Islam is not forgotten by all. I know, somehow intuitively, if you think faith comes and goes and the healing prescription is simply being in the right place with the right light, think again. You have to rub that lantern, not just wishes, prayers, and alms! What does this mean, what I am saying? Good works are what counts because the whole world is watching to see what is the fruit of Islam in such a crisis is?

Yes, this book is part personal, part analytical and part sermon. If history is to be a true guide, beware, oh, peaceful traveler with an inquiring mind, of that curious thirsty one who is exploring the many shades of religious truths among the huge grayish white marble pillars in the Al Haram[32]. Take note of the man who may pass your way with an encyclopedic mind, but it is those laden caravans from afar from which unthinkable wisdom may emerge. For instance, back in 1997, I remember speaking with an Ayatollah in the Al Haram just as I was my finishing (tawarf)[33] together with millions around the *Kaba* (house of Allah). The sun was setting on that Ramadan day when that tall man with the long, silvery-white beard and wearing a black turban surprised me with his guarded English. He said, "Once an empire it will always will be," and gazed at me, and continued wisely, "Though sometimes enchanted, some go to sleep, while some awaken." It's amazing those Persians brothers—champions of intrigue, the inventers of chess, seldom do they travel empty-handed. True to my creed as a student seeking knowledge, I stayed close by. What he said was an old golden

---

[32] Al Masjid Al Haram: The House of Allah the forbidden place to all who is not Muslim.

[33] Tawarf, is a sevenfold counterclock-wise circumambulation of the Kaba in prayer."

rule that I needed to know more about, so instinctually I bartered. Yes, he was Shiite. And no, he was not an enemy. He spoke freely in his guarded English and Arabic, bearing no grudge that my nationality was American, for I was not his enemy. I was a brother in the Islamic faith.

We sat afterward our towarf together on the huge, cool white marble steps inside the Al Haram, in Mecca, with four million people on the same channel, experiencing the same intonation of wonder and worship, an atmosphere of spiraling peace that can be felt in only two other cities in the world: Medina and Jerusalem. There are no spectators here. Only, just enough breathing, and kneeling room for the four million people that has family concerns, fragile dreams to build on, scandals to erase, and those who live off hope for a better tomorrow. Yes, there are no spectators to be seen here, so there is no need to be shy or ashamed here in this place of what you have to say out loud your private needs because everybody is a beggar in the sight of Allah (swa).

Following a hush of the masses, I wanted to know how the Shiites in Iran won the mercy and pleasure of Allah (swa), which gave them the faith and the understanding of the importance of sacrifice to overcome the Shah and fulfill their Islamic revolution. For a long while, he just sat there silently on the cool white marbled steps, his sight buried at the golden door of the Kaba for some time. Then the sunset call for prayer was announced by the muezzin, breaking our fast; thereupon, the revolving counterclockwise masse of believers ceased with a hush. As the Imam of the Grand Mosque in Mecca (*Kaba*) Sheikh Abdul Rahman Ibn Abdul Aziz Al-Sudais may Allah bless him, led four million Muslims in prayer, I knew this was a special day for me in the month of Ramadan.

After the prayers were over, his glaze now focused on the revolving mass of believers slowly gaining momentum as if in a trance, the ayatollah calmly said to me, "We held on to our Faith." We were soon joined by at least ten other Shiite pilgrims who sat cross-legged in a semicircle, the silence in their eyes uncompromising. What this Ayatollah then said, as he leaned against one of the huge marble gray-white pillars for support, I placed in my heart forever.

"For the mercy of Allah only, if you love each other more than your enemies hate of you. You will always be victorious *insha Allah.*"

I stayed as long as I dared with these Shiite fundamentalists from Qom, Iran. In my mind's eye, I was thinking how to package what was being said and send it westward for safe keeping for the right time. As I wished them salam and started to rise, the sheikh raised his hand and motioned me to sit back down. We were then joined by seven more pilgrims, four of whom were Shiite, and three Sunni. The Shiites wore long black robes with black turbans the Sunnis wore long white robes, kaffiyeh`s and white turbans. A few onlookers also sat down to join us, one of whom brought bottles of cool refreshing *zam zam* water to drink and a large bag of sweet dates to cure our hunger from the fast. After five minutes of talking in Persian to his comrades, he fell silent, as did the others around him. He then looked at me with those uncompromising eyes and asked in Arabic, "How has America made you become a better Muslim?"

That Shiite Spring

Allah will judge between you on the Day of Judgment concerning the matters in which ye differ.

—Quran 22:69

Justice does begets peace is a true doctrine of reality worth standing up for. So when the first raindrops of the Persian Spring commenced thirty-six years ago, in October 1977, the majority of Sunni despot leaders and kings hoped that the torrential rains of justice to come would not spill over into their countries. These "enemy near" leaders understood clearly the Iranian Revolution, and the campaign of civil disobedience at its core, as a human epidemic of faith and ideas that could potentially spread across the Muslim region. Yes, of course, the leaders of the Sunni Muslim world saw the Shah of Iran as oppressive, corrupt, murderous, and extravagant; but the true fear was that if those poor and middle-class Shiites could free themselves of their own domestic despots tyranny and of the Western Imperialism afterward, for the mercy of Allah, change their hearts, then hold on to their faith, then the corrupt Sunni leaders could be next on the short list. A dirty word amongst today`s Arab Sunni governments is that the uprising of dispossessed Shiites in the Muslim world is not by chance but by design!

For the emerging Ayatollahs in Qom, Iran and Najaf, Iraq, jihad against discrimination begins first within the Muslim world itself. The late honorable fundamentalist Sheikh Abdul Amir Al-Jamri and the honorable Fundamentalist Sheikh Ali Salman, both Bahraini

leaders of the El-Wefaq National Islamic Society, hum du Allah, have
been mapping the essential issues that have divided Sunni-Shiite
world. The true aim of the recent Shiite uprisings in the nations of
Bahrain, Kuwait, Oman, Qatar, Iraq, Saudi Arabia, and the United
Arab Emirates—countries known also as the Gulf Cooperation Council
(GCC)—is to uncover the ideological elements that are destructive
to the spiritual Islamic values that all true Allah-fearing Muslims hold
dear. Working alongside the Shiite fundamentalist, Sheikh Hassan
Al-Saffar from Saudi Arabia, the leaders of these Shiite uprisings
are effectively entering the avenues of power through the media
and public platforms, stating the ineffective use of sectarianism as a
resistance against discrimination.

Yes, it is true between Sunni and Shiite Muslims there are
significant differences in their understanding of the concept of
Aqeedah.[34] Yes, these differences regarding our understanding
of aqeedah have been exaggerated by an exploitative media and
convoluted by scholarly public debate forums who`s goal is to ill inform
the public. But where we agree, unequivocally, is in the understanding
that Islam can develop and cultivate the hearts, minds, and souls of all
human beings in these so-called modern times—that Islam can speak
to the heart and spiritual strength in human beings and give the world
an authentic example of moral leadership, one that begins with true
cooperation between Sunni, Shiite and Sufi Muslims, that we, the
believers, are uniquely qualified to resist the evils of discrimination,
oppression, racism, xenophobia, sectarianism and secularism. But just
what are those issues that have been mapped by our Shiite brothers in
their uprisings of dignity because talk is cheap?

1.   An end to state sponsored anti-Shiite propaganda, the breeding
     ground of intolerance and hatred in our Muslim lands.
2.   An end to discriminatory state and local policies; the release
     of all political and religious prisoners, and as well as the
     implementation of meaningful constitutional reforms.
3.   The ban on *ashura*[35] processions and the proscription of the
     Shiite call to prayer to be lifted. Also allowing construction of

---

[34]   Aqeedah: the purity of a Monotheist faith.
[35]   Ashura: "Tenth day of the Muslim month of Muharram. This is
       a commemoration of the martyrdom in 680 of Husayn, Prophet
       Muhammad grandson and the third Imam of Shiite Islam. Shiite
       communities annually reenact the tragedy in a passion play, including

Mosques and community centers in Shiite neighborhoods if the people therein so desires.

Truthfully, I feel, if these Shia demands are not addressed, the world village in which we live will simply not take Islam seriously. Likewise, we must be sincere in professing to ourselves, and to the world, that our creed of faith has merit and is tolerant! Moreover, the Muslim world's emerging media must have more depth in its coverage of the serious issues that confront Islam, as well as be willing to propose difficult solutions to them the (people) rather than merely idle talk. A more independent media provides the enduring voice that will reflect the hopes, concerns, and dreams of all the people across Islam. We Muslims can`t afford to project a one-or even a two-dimensional image to the world, to be seen as unchaste and corrupted, wearing suit and tie like the pagans in an attempt to be something which is not part of our true character or rich heritage! We, as a people who believe in that one divine being, must renew our efforts and announce to the world that our lives are fit to print, fit to broadcast, and worthy of the beliefs we so deeply espouse! For the truth is nobody else is going to do the job for us! Similarly, we as a nation of Allah-fearing people must learn to lower our wings towards one other and be more tolerant to those who harbor different opinions, viewpoints and ideas outside our fundamental creed and text. Most of all, every Muslim brother, sister, and neighbor must feel safe from the tongues and hands of others, for as is the will of Allah, we are all here on this Earth for a purpose, not by chance.

With all due respect, I profoundly disagree with Sheikh Abdul Rahman Al-Barak, that honorable Saudi Salafi fundamentalist, when he said, "Shiites are infidels, apostates, and hypocrites, and are more dangerous than Jews and Christians." As a Salafi student of knowledge, I am aware that faith is the property of Allah, not of the people that reflect Allah; it is, strangely, a sensation that arises within the heart. Because Allah is the only one that knows that which arises from within the hearts of every Muslim brother and sister, we are slave servants of Allah not of each other. My task—our task—is to impart the message of

---

self-mortification and displays of sorrows and remorse intended to unite them in Husayn`s suffering and death as an aid to salvation on the day of judgment. Shiite communities experiencing deprivation, humiliation or abuse today understand Husayn`s martyrdom as a paradigm for the struggle against injustice, tyranny and oppression.

Islam as best we can. To those Muslims who may differ with my ideas, and understanding of Aqeedah and/or Hadith, it is only Allah who knows my true heart and yours. I have no right to oppress anyone, nor deny anyone human rights, equal rights, justice, and due process of law because of the nature of their faith. I lead by example and persuasion; likewise, in all matters of faith, we must all lead the people by example and persuasion, for the greater truth is that, on this earth, each of us are merely servants of Allah, endowed with the mission of urging the people onward with objective guidance. Only in the eyes of Allah may one be better than another. For the truth is, "We the believers in view towards each other are but patriots of various rank and degrees unto our Lord."[36]

---

[36] Quran 22:67-69/Munafiq: A "Hypocrite"; a word applied to Muslims who profess faith while secretly working against it.

Arab Spring

So Moses returned to his people in a state of indignation and sorrow;
He said: oh my people! Did not your lord make a handsome promise
to you? Did then the promise seem to you long [in coming]? Or did
ye desire that wrath should descend from your lord on you, and so ye
broke your promise to me.

—Quran 20:86

There are moments when I feel that this beautiful earth we all call home is actually the playground dare. The aims are the same: "The Promised Land is for those who keep their promises to God."[37] To this day, clearly I remember that crowd of teenagers on a bright Saturday afternoon standing around that new sky blue 1964 Cadillac on the corner of East Tremont Avenue and Prospect Avenue in the Bronx, New York. It was a cold February day just after my sixth birthday, and like all the other kids I could not walk past that car and the song playing from its radio, "I Want to Hold Your Hand" by the Beatles. The melody stopped me midstride the first time I heard it, and I, like everybody else was held as if we were in rapture. None of us held each another's hand that day, but the message was out of the bottle and into our hearts. The larger truth is that Muslims have been holding each other's hands for more than a thousand years now, a custom practiced in the Muslim and eastern world whenever a person feels that he is

---

[37]   Quran 20:86

in public with someone dear, regardless of gender. Two men walking down the street in hand in Muslim lands does not mean they are homosexual; it means that they are treating each other like beloved brothers for the mercy of Allah. In fact it was the Prophet Muhammad (sas) who said, "Do not be the first to let go off his hand." For me this custom of hand holding in public indicates that we Muslims in the Middle East, are well ahead of the West in this sense of demonstrating brotherhood amongst the masses in public without the phobia of homosexuality, in spite of this, still so many of my Muslim brothers have been too quick to let go in times of adversity. Algeria, Iraq, Egypt and Syria are but four examples where Muslims have dropped their brothers' hands; and the whole fabric of a harmonious Islamic society has been ripped apart, simply because serious religious responsibilities were abandoned.

Yes, you can hold my hand, but it is not for show! It is serious to us. My Western culture does not call for it. The act itself is not necessary; it is my Islamic faith that says that it is the intention behind the act itself that matters most. A bond that means peace and trust is not culture, it is deeper than that, it is a brotherhood of faith. I saw this in Buraydah bus station in Saudi Arabia. Two men locked in a handshake then an embrace neither wished to be the first to let go.

Try something new in your life that can benefit your character like looking that person in the eye when you are giving that greeting of peace. Yes, put a few of these ideas and its direction to habit will be like planting a seed. A seed if by the will of Allah will help many of our Muslim brothers to lower their wings towards each other, *"And lower thy wing to the believers who follow thee."* (Quran 26:215) And show people a smile from the heart from time to time. Our Prophet Muhammad (sas) said that a smile is a form of charity.

Arab spring sprouts from the hearts of the people, oh humble reader. And I ask of you who can truly market Islam to the world but a true believer of it? It is he the believer who has not forgotten the sanity of the sacred or scripture nor how to address the issues at hand from one`s own written spiritual text. But if we as Muslims fail to heed to the fundamentals of our own religious books because of the lack of faith within our own hearts we have our own selves to blame not the kufr. Our campaign stalls because we are not adopting or adjusting using our own creed of faith to face the evolving new frontiers that mankind is challenged with on a daily basis. For surely this is a campaign and we must be charismatic and elaborate in our thinking and marketing towards ourselves as well as towards our neighbors, whose goal is to build our relationship with our lord and with each other as Muslims living in Muslim lands. Building that rapport is essential to success as well as a requirement in our ongoing personal jihads. *"Who is better in speech than one who calls (people) to Allah, works righteousness, and says: "I am of those who bow in Islam?"* (Quran 41:33).

In the land of the banana republic, thought, crime is the only crime that matters. Those Muslim-in-name-only despots who govern by fear the problem now is that their people don`t fear them anymore. When will the era of fear and oppression—which has been apparently used to divide, demoralize, and disenfranchise the Muslim people in the east—be over totally? "I believe when men fear only Allah, not mankind! Indeed, it has already started with a single match and a fruit seller in Tunisia; by a Egyptian googleist" in Tahrir Square in Cairo, Egypt; followed by a Libyan lawyer Fathi Terbil in Libya, accompanied by those collage students in San`a, Yemen; next by those young juveniles in southern Syria being tortured because they spray painted words of freedom and justice on the walls in their hometowns; complied by those Shiite marchers at the pearl roundabout in Bahrain weary of years of discrimination by their own so-called religious Sunni neighbors. That moral global Islamic conscious field is becoming more aware, and becoming more visible to the duplicity in spite of their oppression which reveals that sobering consequences of having to cry out for justice amidst the day to day brutality and terror which is part of their lives is now easily assessable on Facebook, Twitter, You tube, Al-Jazera and the Internet to behold that freedom is not free.

Seeing beyond the establish moments helps keep the issues of jihad where they are ladies, and gentlemen. Fundamentalist Muslims viewing the great betrayal of the Western democratic nations upon the Democratic aspirations of the Muslim Brotherhood in Egypt as of July 3, 2013, are now aware without doubt who their enemies are come near or far. So it is best to clear one`s calendars when mixing religion with justice and politics with so called allied unbelievers and stay focus. Hum du Allah, it is refreshing to hear that on September 25, 2013 Brother Mohannad Al-Najjar and his Al-Tawhid Brigade, The Al-Nusra Front, The Islamic State in Iraq Syria, along with many other Islamic religious groups that is fighting in Syria has rejected the Western opposition spokesmen Ahmad Al-Jarba group known as the "National Coalition of Syrian Revolutionary and Opposition Forces" who is backed by France, United States, Jordan and Turkey, saying, "We the opposition could only be represented by people who have "lived their troubles and shared in what they have sacrificed" and "We are not a call

for a Democratic, civil government to replace Mr. Assad. We call on all
military and civilian groups in Syria to unify in a clear Islamic frame as well
as "What we are after is Shariah Law."

Be assured, oh, humble reader, that honorable Islamic fundamentalist
Sheikh Yusuf Al-Qaradawi knows that civilizations not only clash; they also
compete and conspire. He said returning to Egypt addressing the people
in Tahrir Square, Cairo, after 50 years living in exile in Qatar, "Don`t let
anyone steal this revolution from you those hypocrites who will put on a
new face that suits them." He went on to say, "The revolution isn`t over. It
has just started to build Egypt. Guard your Revolution."

Keeping your friends close and your enemy near closer is a
mentality and rational that reveals the shocking truth about our
heart, minds and soul counterinsurgency war. Tuned in, he knows
the Arab world has changed from the inside out; their revolution is a
revolution of morality, faith and justice. With the example of Algerian
killing fields in Sheikh Al-Qaradawi`s rear view window along with the
ongoing plight of his Palestinian brethrens just around the corner
in mind. We could begin by asking ourselves what kind of leadership
Egypt needs at this vibrant juncture.

We believe the answer is candidates that will fear Allah first
and foremost and will work in jihad to bring together a country
that is divided, who will create a sense of unity and transcend the
over-shadowing divisions within the nation. The promising leader
in this contentious campaign trail in the land of the banana republic
who has won our endorsement as well as the endorsement of Sheikh
Al-Qaradawi and millions of Egyptians who wish to be free from
dictatorship is that granite Islamic fundamentalist, Mr. Mohamed Mahi
Akef chairman of the Muslim Brotherhood. Whose credo is, "Allah is
our objective, the prophet is our leader, Quran is our law, jihad is our
way, dying in the way of Allah is our hope." Why? It`s axiomatic, you are
only as good as your last promise.

The true geopolitical reality today in the Egyptian world is which
party can best govern the people with respect of basic human rights for
all citizens and the protection of civil liberties and due process of law.
Behind the scenes, we know the devil attacks through poverty. Behind
all that cheer about liberation is that full eye view idea of democracy,
it does not have a monopoly on justice, not by far or near at home.
Behind that siege of the national banks by Islamic forces, grows
unsettled accounts and international debts are piling up. Concerning
practical matters it`s the 'economy stupid', it`s who can inherit Egypt`s
recession, breadlines, unemployment and survive politically on an

economy built on sand, bribes, usury, consumerism and racketeers? Plus how to seek justice for the more than 840 people killed during the start of the Arab spring revolution in January 2011. How do you seek justice for the more than 1,200 people killed during the military coup of July 3, 2013 to the attack on Raba`a Adawiya Mosque on August 14, 2013? Will General Abdul Fattah Al-Sisi pay the ultimate price for treason and betrayal upon his own people for love of rule and power? Also will the ex-president for life Hosni Mubarak and his two sons stand trial for murder and corruption under the Judicial Investigation Commission a so called independent office set up by the government prosecutor? Or will they live hidden behind the palace walls with solace under discreet house arrest pulling strings of power?

Looking past the script, at stake right now is beyond Egypt`s revolution of morality and faith, but the ability of a religious party organizations in Egypt to take on a colossal corrupt power of Arab secular nationalist, and military generals betrayals, and turn it into a triumph of a leap of faith by millions of believers who believe they have a heritage worth fighting for, and sacrificing their lives for. The hearts, minds and soul counterinsurgency war is an unconventional war fought with human intelligence in fifth gear. The people are the prize the objects Islam, Allah the goal. For some people discussing this is a sin, or a one-way ticket to the gulag, or both. For some people it is better to take the "river path of least resistance", ignore the situation at hand go back to the sweatshops and pay the rent on time. In that approach so the Egyptian military government feels, it avoids issues that require a direct answer. Whereas the believers should diversify their campaigns of attack against their indigenous despots and give their people a clearer picture and way of how they will govern plus face those daily social, economic, and political challenges in their lives. At stake right now is the path of the Islamic revolution in the Middle East, which is an evolution of ideas: "In Allah we trust versus in despots we fear." If truly the people are willing to make that sacrifice of their lives for that change of heart for Allah`s mercy, then the most largest Arab population nation in the world will be the example and main stream beacon for other Sunni Muslim nations to follow. If the Allah fearing people are truly successful in taking back the reins of power in their society and place it before Allah then the plagues of future pharaoh`s are over.

It is not surprising that the scarecrows of the over turned regimes must be confronted and removed from established offices of the new formed governments whomever they are. Their actions and words are illegitimate no matter how high or honorable and prestigious that public office may be. The political reason that General Nabil Farag of the Egyptian Giza security forces was shot dead in the town of Kerdasa, Egypt, on September 19, 2013 was that he is only a scarecrow unto the people whose aim was to serve their despot masters for survival. In this revolution era, the shameful cabal of Egyptian Generals and secular establishment insiders who has been running the country since July 3, 2013, know that time is not on their side. Such as life, there are many paradoxes associated with a brutal coup in the land of the promise, one of which I feel is the devil and the details. Going beyond the pagan and monotheist world of conflict that foreshadowed civil war many has feared has already begun, the Islamic organization Al-Gamaa Al-Islamiya is now on the same hate list as the Muslim Brotherhood in Egypt; thus, the Egyptian military interest is not for the true public national interest anymore but fighting for their own survival against an Islamic agenda.

Oh, humble reader, it is an inconvenient truth and a genealogy of pragmatism that the era of the management of savagery is upon the Muslim world. Reasoning is of four kinds: the rejection of human rights, equal rights, justice and due process of law by Muslim-in-name only despots and secularist who refuse to give up power by a democratic ballot or the call for Sharia law by their own people. So now what lies frankly before the believers is it`s just a matter of time when you are dealing with a despot who imposes martial law in order to rule for another day and desires peace and security who is willing to face a patient enemy that is resourceful and don`t mind dying for a cause just as long as their enemies understand that death is mutual.

That secret of a successful revolutionary jihad force within a civilian sea, which you will never hear on the radio or T.V.; is the meat of success when facing despots is now universal: (1) discipline; (2) training (rethink your focus); (3) tactics (work in cohesion, being flexible); (4) weapons (well hidden); (5) commitment (until the mission is accomplish); (6) Organization (in depth); (7) careful (small independent groups of five or less); (8) patience; (9) attuned (gathering intelligence); (10) scholars of guerrilla warfare (where are they?); (11) respectful (of firepower and mobility); (12) asymmetrical warfare (must master); (13) the plan (the end game); (14) communication (couriers); (15) logistics (self-owned independent business); (16) commanders (no visible insignia); (17) persistent (the policy of paying the price); (18) prepare (the battlefield well); (19) jihad (for Allah`s mercy); (20) the message (resistance); (21)

keep abreast (facts and situations); (22) leadership (obey); (23) the basement (counter intelligence).

I cannot help but wonder about how deep the hypocrisy can go once a nation of people take their faith for granted and submit to oppression and a sovereign other than Allah. For example: Elected by the government of President for life Mohammad Hosni Mubarak who has ruled Egypt for 30 years, who had won a landslide election of seven percent of the vote in 2005. Appointed to be the "Grand Sheikh of Al-Azhar University in Cairo, Egypt," a Mr. Ahmed El-Tayyed, who has long been a critic of the conservative Muslim Brotherhood, appointed by former President Mubarak but also served as high ranking member of his National Democratic Party who believed it is permissible for Muslims to sell alcohol to non-Muslims abroad in non-Muslim countries, that secularism and Islam can live together, is now calling for the "emancipation of the university from the State" a declaration of Independence from the Egyptian government. Maybe my analysis is not perfect but my gut feelings tell me ignorance. Why? It was the great Islamic polymath, Abu Hamid Al-Ghazali, who bemoaned the lack of intellectual independence, integrity and critical distance from the state. He said in his book "Ayyuhal Walad" to his young disciples: "Neither to get too close to the princes and sultans nor to praise them excessively, but even more than that not to accept generous gifts from rulers. Coveting things from the rulers and those in power will spoil and corrupt your religion since there is born from it flattery and kowtowing to those in power and unwise approval of their policies."

Sheikh Yusuf Al-Qaradawi, president of the World Council of the Union of Muslim Scholars, is well aware that he must be patient, a corrupt regime and those who follow it will not fix what it ruined. And Mr. Muhammed Badi, the ex-supreme guide chairman of the Muslim Brotherhood in Egypt says, "The brotherhood wants America to fail. It tells its followers to be patient because America is heading towards its demise. The United States is an infidel that does not champion moral and human values and cannot lead humanity." The Muslim Brotherhood claims Western democracy is corrupt, unrealistic and false. As well as calls for jihad against the Muslims real enemies is not only Israel but also the United States waging jihad against both of these infidels is a commandment of Allah that cannot be disregarded.

The leader of the Salafi movement in Egypt, Sheikh Sayyid Abd-Al-Azim, has said, "I want to say that Democracy is a bad idea.

We should not feel ashamed to say it. It is bad, backwards and a retarded idea. Even the freedoms, what are they? Among the freedoms inherent in the democratic system are freedom for women, freedom of ownership, freedom of homosexuality, personal freedom, freedom of conscience and expression, freedom to disbelieve in the creator of heaven and earth. There's mixing of men and women and usury. All of this is in Democracy, which is why I condemn it."

That leader of the Islamic Jihad in Egypt, Abboud Al-Zumar—who was sent to jail for 30 years for his role in killing that other President for life Anwar Sadat now released on March 12, 2011, with other leading Islamists—said, "The revolution created a new mechanism: The mechanism of strong, peaceful protest. Public squares around the Arab world are ready to receive millions who can stop any ruler and expose him!"

Perhaps that passive fundamentalist Sheikh Abdel Moety Bayoumy from Egypt, who did not wish to be religiously insensitive said, "They didn't arrest them because of their ideas alone. These ideas constitute a movement that has political goals and can cause sedition. Politics always starts with an idea, and sedition starts with ideas."

This is the reason why, oh, humble reader, there are no draws in a religious, political, social and economic campaigns here on this earth; and you would be dead last if you are so foolish enough to accept it. Yes, civilizations conspire, but to have an strong Islamic diplomatic corps within one's society that knows how to walk that rice paper is not unreasonable to demand by the people to safeguard justice so that never again the Muslim people be alone in facing homegrown despots! The question is how do you build such a guardian institution like in Iran but in a Sunni Muslim society, whose purpose is to defend the rights of all the people under Sharia law even those people in the millions who are citizens of the land as well and not Muslims? Our neighbors who live amongst the Muslims cannot fear for their lives because of Sharia law. No, they cannot fear the Muslims because of their own faith of Christianity or Judaism.

It is a horrible view to look at, those true colors of Western secular nuclear powers and Eastern communist nuclear powers the enemy far, and their support for such allied dictators is shameful. For anyone familiar with not being in the bubble of the accepted establish power when it comes to civil liberties, less is more; and how to beat the growing maddening crowd with laws that do not apply to interrogators, laws that do not apply to justice and due process of law is the key. In a world full of ideas, there is no such thing as a little bit of sanction torture. I can never fully paid tribute to the more than 75 thousand Egyptian political and religious prisoners in prison languishing because of ill suspicion and shady notions called dreams and Sharia law. The proof, if proof is needed, is the acknowledge statement by former Secretary of State Condoleezza Rice. She said at the American University in Cairo on June 20, 2005, "For sixty years my country the United States pursued stability at the expense of democracy in this region here in the Middle East, and we achieved neither! Now, we are taking a different course. We are supporting the democratic aspirations of all people."

Yes, there are conflicting imperatives at work; Western secular civilizations and Communist civilizations do conspire, pursuing talks of worthless peace and stability at the expense of Democracy and Socialism so that they can rape a nation at night, and sell their stolen wares in the daytime, and preach about peace on earth in their lifetime to their own citizens! But why these allied despots and dictators did not see the writing on the wall? Was it because of that old golden rule "The enemy of my enemy is my friend" or *"Those who reject Allah and hinder men from the path of Allah, their deeds will Allah render astray from their mark"* (Quran 47:1). Surely, American and Western Europe (NATO) would not dream of making peace with those Islamic forces they got locked up in their prisons, now that Osama bin Laden is dead, Al-Qaeda is on the run, Islamophobia is bring in great returns to their war industry, and stability has been a myth in the Muslim world in spite of their own corruption, greed, and injustice throughout their lands? So, why the change of heart President Obama? Why the change of plan at this time? Why do you feel that the call for democracy be heard amongst the people in the Muslim world is worth the risk of another Islamist state? Indeed, time is not on the side of America or Western Europe, in the eyes of the average Muslim on the street who is becoming more anti-Western and more anti-Socialist because of the rising awareness of that support towards the dictators and despots from these very same secular democratic and Communist Socialist forces that profit from their oppression in their daily lives. The American military withdrawal from two strategic important countries in the Muslim world of Afghanistan and Iraq has not been easy in the name of regional stability. Under the cover of Arab Spring the carnage will only end when American and Western Europe (NATO) troops are removed totally from Afghanistan as well as their proxy leaders. A justified war? You got to be kidding; we are in Afghanistan because of revenge, we have killed more innocence civilians there in the hunt for Taliban and Al-Qaeda by a factor of two. Iraq—a justified war? An episode of outright greed for oil, and the U.S. media was in complicit in the governmental lies. A true Pandora's box opened because of outright imperialism.

Following that long shadow of pain of taking care of business that fatwa from Sheikh Yousef Al-Qaradawi, that Islamic fundamentalist who had said from August 2004 "It is not suicide it is Martyrdom in the name of Allah." Diverse Islamic theologians and jurisprudence of many stripes have debated this issue referring it to a form of jihad, under the title of jeopardizing the life of the *Mujahideen*. It is allowed to jeopardize your life and cross the path of the enemy and be killed. Is still valid and ingrained. Thus, it is permissible for a Muslim to sacrifice his or her life in order to kill that imperialist invader in their homelands.

Jihad Salafi in my opinion is largely motivated by a strong desire not to let paganism, nor western cultural practices and secular ideas as well as ideals to invade into the religious, social, cultural and political affairs of the Muslim lands. The fact of the matter is that in the Muslim lands we oppose democracy in the Western secular form in general. Jurisprudence derived from the mind-set of human beings rather than Allah (God) is an obvious heresy. We reject such man made principle in favor of the principle of divine laws. It is true when our ancient Hebrew brothers achieved their miraculous liberation from Pharaoh many yearned in their hearts to go back to him in spite of his lash and kufr lifestyle, but also yearned in substance for example their worship of the modern day golden calf was more exciting and thrilling than Prophet Moses sermons and official miraculous acts. *"Here in the desert the whole Israelite community grumbled against Moses and Aaron. The Israelites said to them, "Would that we had died at the lord's hand in the land of Egypt, as we sat by our fleshpots and ate our fill of bread! But you had to lead us into this desert to make the whole community die of famine!" (Exodus 16:2-3).* Therefore, our Hebrew brothers wandered in the desert wilderness as if asleep for 40 years. That generation thou liberated had to die out before they were able to wake up and remember their promise to their Lord. We, Jihad Salafi and other known and unknown Islamic groups are presently facing a very daunting but similar precedent in our present-day Islamic crises. Many millions of Muslims have been asleep for generations under the spell of secularism and materialism since the fall of that corrupt caliphate Abdul Mejid II and those confederates (Arab nationalist) who fought their Muslim brothers and killed them for their kufr allied masters. *"Those who believe fight in the cause of Allah, and those who reject faith fight in the cause of evil:*

So fight ye against the friends of Satan: feeble indeed is the cunning of Satan" (Quran 4:76).[38]

Drawing the battle lines in the sand is that once again Islamic fundamentalist Sheikh Yousef Al-Qaradhawi, a highly respected scholar in the Muslim world, wrote another fatwa which is an accepted religious legal opinion "permitting the abduction and killing of American and NATO soldiers and civilians in Iraq because they the civilians abets the soldiers in Iraq`s occupation." He also said in August, 2004 at the Egyptian Journalist Union in Cairo: "Those that abets the occupiers their status is identical to the soldiers they are not civilians." This fatwa was signed by ninety-three known and highly knowledgeable Muslim scholars from around the Muslim world as well as leaders from Hamas, Islamic Jihad, and Hezbollah.

This fatwa has truly gone global throughout the Islamic world. That debate between moderate and orthodox Muslim schools of thought whether Sunni or Shiite, of what to do with citizens of kufr oppressors captured within Muslim countries is over. They are to be treated as invading soldiers!

It`s not that Sheikh Qaradhawi had an ax to grind against Americans and secular Western Europeans who invaded Afghanistan and Iraq under a false flag mandate. Oh no! Nor that *Lancet Medical Journal* report published in October, 2006 that said between March 18, 2003 and June, 2006 There were 601,027 deaths due to violence in Iraq`s occupation and the war is going on till that very day. Or that Halliburton and their war profiteers associates who made billions of dollars off the blood of our Muslim brothers and sisters a debt that shall be repaid in full *insha Allah.* Or that America had ordered in November, 2001 sequestered of Sheikh Qarahawi private properties and belongings at Al-Taqwa Bank because of his association with Hamas who is now democratically elected by their people. Nor declared persona non grata in the U.S.

It`s just that some of my brethren within high circles of our brotherhood are of the fundamental opinion that old Persian golden rule that fatwa`s are like hinges: they can swing either way. I tend to

---

[38]   That civil Muslim war between the Ottoman Empire (Turkey) and Arab states (Syria, Saudi Arabia, Lebanon, Jordan, Philistine, and Egypt) wanting independence supported by kufr European governments and armies after world war one in 1918.

agree. Does these fatwa's speak unconditionally? There are American military bases and intelligence offices in Egypt today working in support and cohesion with the Ex-Mubarak's military regime against the will of the people and Islam. Like in Beni Suef Air Base, North Base Camp in El-Gorah and South Base Camp near Sharm El—Sheikh. Which is housing thousands of American and foreign Western troops, as well as support and logistics and training of Multinational Forces and Observers in spite of a peace treaty between Egypt and Israeli. Using so-called peacekeepers as a front to hide and buttress an imperialist agenda is an old hat, when in fact military despots are using these foreign forces in one's owns country to train one's own forces to suppress domestically a despots own opposition forces, and parties is an old quid pro quo being used in many sell out Muslim-in-name-only banana republic's and third-world countries to stay third world class.

Every week it becomes more and more apparent keeping your friends close and your enemy near closer is best. A few more have dared to give a Friday Juma Sermon and talked about *kufr* troops in their own country, which deeply undermines the people's sovereignty in their own countries. Now that Ramadan is upon the Muslim world again, every day is a Friday Juma sermon. That American and foreign Western European military and intelligence base in Bahrain known as the Host to the United States Fifth Fleet is becoming more and more an apparent insult to the very dignity of Muslim sovereignty within the GCC countries. When will these inspiring and meaningful fatwas that is spoken so equitably within the human breast reflect their own domestic agendas? When will the words from our own Holy Quran bridge that relationship between faith and reason within the hearts of those who call themselves Muslims? *"And obey not the behests of the unbelievers and the hypocrites, and heed not their annoyances, but put thy trust in Allah. For enough is Allah as a disposer of affairs"* (Quran 33:48).

That uprising of the Shiite Muslims dispossess in the Muslim world is not by chance but by design. For the Ayatollahs in Qom, Iran and Najaf, Iraq—that jihad against discrimination and oppression starts first within the Muslim world. The late honorable fundamentalist Sheikh Abdul Amir Al-Jamri and the honorable fundamentalist Sheikh Ali Salman both from Bahrain, leaders of El-Wefaq National Islamic society, they hum due Allah had been mapping the essential issues that have become more and more contentious in the Sunni, Shiite Islamic world we live in. That Arab spring of ideas of freedom and justice has now turned into an open revolt for liberty in this hot Ramadan Arab summer. Yes, in many Arab revolutions that is now happening spontaneously since the Arab spring began, they are inclusive of all the people of one's homeland like the poor, the middle class, the youth, and the women against their authoritarian governments. But that human rights and equal rights storm gathering over at Pearl Square, Bahrain was in the mind's eye of Bahrain's King Hamad Ibn Al-Khalifa a Sunni Muslim, a sectarian revolt demanding freedom of expression, justice, and an uprising of dignity by the Shiite majority in the land oppress by their Sunni Muslim minority.

Bahrain's main Shiite opposition party leader Sheikh Ali Salman of the El-Wefaq has now withdrawn from the so called "National Consensus Dialogue" stating that the rulers are not "sincere." The call for the release of hundreds of political prisoners, an end to torture, human rights, and promised constitutional reforms has fallen on deaf ears. In light of the current situation Hassan Mushaima a Shiite and a leader of the (Haq Party) has now called for an Islamic republic, who said: "The dictator fell in Tunisia, the dictator fell in Egypt and the dictator should fall here." Sheikh Abdel Wahab Hussain leader of the Shiite Wafa Party in Bahrain, as well as Abdulhadi Al-Khawaja a major leader of Human Rights Advocate also in Bahrain, and Dr. Abdulhadi Alsingace for human rights—all prisoners of conscience—and many others condemned for life in prison by Bahrain's military tribunals courts.

Oh, humble reader of this book, yes that sectarianism is in the air in Bahrain like in Iraq, Syria and many other Muslim gulf countries for a reason, please if you can, pass the word to these Muslim kings and rulers that the confidence of all the people is worth more than the money and oil at hand. We know that a ruler must look past his own prejudices for the greater good and this is by no means an easy thing to do in such turbulent times. So, for the wise ruler who wish to enjoy these Arab spring moments, that hadith reported by Abu Malih in Sahih Muslim (1:82) Prophet Muhammad (sas) said, *"A ruler who has been entrusted with the affairs of the Muslims, but makes no endeavor for their material and moral uplift and is not sincerely concerned for their welfare will not enter paradise along with them."* And as well as that hadith reported in (Al-Tirmidhi, Hadith 1011) which say's, *"It is better for a leader to make a mistake in forgiving than to make a mistake in punishing).*

I must truthfully say I had never experienced that painful vision of religious sectarianism here in America at any time in my life living here in America. Though, I had experienced those ugly moments of race riot and the angry mass episodes of violence, hate, lawlessness and vengeance. Perhaps because I know what it is like to be discriminated because of the color of my skin as an African-American, I can understand to some degree that feeling and affects of discrimination simply because of a religious idea I may hold to be true. I became a Muslim by choice here in America while I was in prison. I first learned how to live a Muslim life by Muslims who were free and also imprisoned with me. As far as my government was concerned, my faith has changed, but what about my character? I was not imprisoned because of my faith but because of my character. The color of my skin had a lot of influence and effect on my character in my American society which reflected my perception of my own government and my level of contribution to it. It is the very pursuit of knowledge and sincerity that I realize that the power of true faith can change character. Thereby, it is strange and somewhat alien to me to see and or hear a Muslim discriminate against another Muslim whither he or she be Sunni, Shiite, or Sufi school of thought. Simply because we all know that every Quran that we read is the same. Yet it's what's our intentions in our hearts are, as we open the holy books that makes us view each other differently! I am well aware that the social problems here in these Western secular pluralistic societies are truly based on race and class because of the accepted ignorance and greed that propagate our lands! Whereas in the East the overwhelming problems is sectarianism, ignorance and lack of patience because the people are not just to each other in spite of their faith and good character that propagate their lands! That right of freedom of expression with respect, that ability of people to agree to disagree with patience, is in our holy books. But sectarianism base on hatred and ignorance is what's keeping the Middle East from emerging as a world leader economically, culturally, politically, and religiously. Will Arab spring help resolve these problems? Truly this all depends on the hearts of the people!

What can I say that has not been said before by those believers in Algeria, those believers whose *raison d'etre* is "There is no God but Allah, and Muhammad is the prophet and messenger of Allah" has not been lost. Those believers who decided to change a wrong with their hands. Not just change a wrong with their tongues. Nor just change a wrong with their prayers. Yes, those believers who saw their national uniformed guardians firing into the peacefully demonstrating people. Yes, those believers who felt those made-in-Europe bullets. Those believers who witness the World Bank (WB) and the International Monetary Fund (IMF) put billions of dollars and Euros into the pockets of those treasonable and murderous Algerian generals in support of their despotic regime. Yes, those believers on the front lines amid the despair who condemns that expressionless condolences from that Algerian secret service the (D.R.S.) and it's sub-department the counter intelligence agency the (D.C.E.) for their massacres upon the people they was suppose to defend who's strategy was of attrition and their measurement the body count in mass graves. Why? Sovereignty! Then whose law? The renegade secular Algerian military junta's marshal law or the Sharia? Who's rules? The regime of president for life Abdelaziz Bouteflika who wants a process of national reconciliation and pardon under his terms, like get out of jail free cards to some not all of the believers. Plus blood money to shut up those families who are still waiting to hear from their loved ones went missing under military custody. Or the Sharia! So, it should come as no surprise that scriptural reasoning says those mass graves in Algeria shall soon speak a lot louder. Insha Allah, those faceless voices out in the sandbox shall remind all of us in the Muslim world why they 250,000 people are there and what is our purpose as believing Muslims who fear Allah!

What do I know about oppression in my life here in America, the land of the brave, and the home of the free? To even understand other people's desire for true liberty, human rights and justice? What I will say is this to the world. There are two men who taught me about oppression. The first is Dr. Martin Luther King when I was 10 years old—what he stood for, and why he had his jihad. The second person I learned more in depth was at Howard University when I was a student there from 1978-1981. His name was Frederick Douglas, that black Afro American ex-slave fundamentalist who said, "The limits of tyrants are prescribed by the endurance of those whom they oppress. Men may not get all they pay for in this world, but they must certainly pay for all they get. If we ever get free from the oppressions and wrongs heaped upon us, we must pay for their removal. We must do this by suffering, by sacrifice, and if needs be by our lives and the lives of others."

Freedom is not cheap or free—it never was. And justice is not born without labor it never can be. Human rights are not given freely; one must take it. Therefore an objective person trying to earn his keep and prove his worth in this world, who is seeking the truth, will indelibly conclude that not all men are the same in rank, courage, and spirit. My teachers in the East have indeed told me that if half of the people in a nation are to be sacrificed so that the other half can be free, then that is the price to pay. But because of the limited will of supply of justice, human rights, and freedoms the Muslim people must be willing to pay extra for the removal of their Sesame Street dictators, despots, tyrants and presidents-for-life in their lands. To pay in blood, not sweat, or tears. Yet to satisfy demand of such precious civil liberties will the Muslim people be willing to change their conditions of their very own hearts which is the real cause of their problem? Time will tell.

We believe that when the government fears Allah, there is liberty, justice and mercy. When the people fear Allah, there is favor, mercy and guidance. This is the true Islamic course of rightful action and the way to success in this world. In this early era of Arab spring the working lower masses of Muslim people are demanding that their custodians in the apex be a reflection of their hungry development of truly Islamic change, and their awakening movement is the soul of the Muslim masses true leaders. This belief is important in establishing the favor of Allah who is sovereign to be blessed with an Islamic government and state. The way forward in our sacred ideal principle of *jihad* is relying on our pure religious values, which will compel the believers to stand their ground and face their enemy near and far without fear. If we wish to truly analyze effectively any primetime civilization one must carefully consider its social and its intellectual foundations and judge correctly without prejudice what they are saying about themselves and what they are saying about others outside of themselves and where do they stand on the world stage on which we all live. It is these foundations which holds and molds our Islamic society and our outlook on life. It is our actions and deeds between two or more very different civilizations of faiths when they do meet eye to eye which is crucial. For example: That beloved fundamentalist from the Maghreb, vice-president of the Islamic Salvation Front (F.I.S.) from Algeria, Imam Ali Belhadj, who said, "There is no democracy because the only source of power is Allah through the Quran and not the people. If the people vote against the law of Allah, this is nothing other than blasphemy. In this case, it is necessary to kill the non-believers [Muslims only by name, apostates] for the good reason that they wish to substitute their authority for that of Allah." *"Hast thou not turned thy vision to those who declare that they believe in the revelations that have come to thee and to those before thee? Their real wish is to resort together for judgment in their disputes to the evil one, though they were ordered to reject him. But Satan`s wish is to lead them astray far away from the right. When it is said to them: "Come to what Allah hath revealed, and to the apostle": Thou see the hypocrites avert their faces from thee in disgust."* (Quran 4:60-61). *"Those men, Allah knows what`s in their hearts: So keep clear of them, But admonish them, and speak to them a word to reach their very souls"* (Quran 4:65). *"It was we who revealed the law (to Moses): therein was guidance and light. By its standard have been judged the Jews, by the prophets who bowed (as in Islam) to Allah`s will, by the Rabbis and* *the doctors of law: For to them was entrusted the protection of Allah's book, and they were witness thereto: Therefore fear not men, but fear me, and sell not my signs for a miserable price. If any do fail to judge by (the light of) what Allah hath revealed, they are (no better than) unbelievers"* (Quran 5:44, 53:23-25).

Yes, it is a reality that our divine laws handed down to us from the prophets are dear and worth while defending; and yes, it is shocking to the consciences of the nonbelievers who lives in our Muslim lands with us as citizens to what we hold dear in our lives. The Allah-fearing slave servants knows that the divine laws that we have called Sharia by themselves cannot clean the hearts of mankind nor stop the heartless. They are but a reminder to one who fears that divine one and an admonishment to the ignorant.

Those arrogant amongst us must submit to the divine laws of Allah willingly or unwillingly by the sword if this needs to be, then so be it. Surly, as Muslims, regardless of nationality out of many one people in faith, those arrogant apostates who call themselves secularist, Democrats, Communist, Socialist, pagans and agnostics; cannot lead the believers in anything, nor can they with Muslim names only, rule over us. *"These are nothing but names which ye have devised, ye and your fathers, for which Allah has sent down no authority [whatever]. They follow nothing but conjecture and what their own souls desire! Even though there has already come to them guidance from their lord! Nay, shall man have (just) anything he hankers after? But it is to Allah that the end and the beginning (of all things) belong* (Quran 53:23-25).

Please abide with us. How does this all end this latest crusade into the Maghreb lands by the Western secular countries that was ensured by that golden rule of supporting their allied despots in the Muslim countries as proxy beachheads? Their aim is to ethnically cleanse the corridors of power towards those who are non-secular in belief. Today we have a banana republic here in Algeria where elections amount to nothing because the stakes is so high, the will is not as high, and no one publicly who is somebody who wishes to see their name on the menu. In this early era of Arab Spring this is a battle ground country now in the end game mode with Al-Qaeda against the notoriety. Magnified from behind the curtains we find General Smain Lamari (died 8-28-2007) who said, "I am ready to eliminate three million Algerians if necessary to maintain the order threaten by the Islamists." Thus the motto of the (D.C.E.) We also find shamefully the head of the military Security General Mohamed Median codename (Tawfik) who breaded army death squads upon the believers, those people from the shadows those (D.R.S.). *"Think not that Allah doth not heed the deeds of those who do wrong. He but gives them respite against a day when the eyes will fixedly stare in horror"* (Quran 14:42-43).

Beware of the perspicacity of the believers since they see by the light of Allah, may he be only exalted![39] Beware when a Muslim government relies more on external support and friendship from kufr governments than their own constituents in regards to overcoming constant internal pressures and challenges like religious, economic, social, and political core issues. Why should we pattern ourselves of a people of different faiths and creeds we had vanquished from our Muslim lands? Why should we seek advice from *kufr* governments whom Muslims had fought with to gain their independence? Why should we lock up our mosques after the prayers like the secularist Christians and Jews? Yes, there is that old wave of required change going on now in the Muslim world that is fighting us, simply to deduce the consequences of ignoring fundamental principles of our Islamic faith without being destroyed by it! Only by educating our citizens to be more aware of the dangers of our enemies premise can we be victors. For example, defeating and expelling the French, British, Italian, Spanish, Russians and Americans from our lands is only the first part of the strategy, the next obvious step is the removal of the remains of their kufr ideals and secular residue in the land, whether it is in the form of cultural, economical, religious or political ideology. As well as all those who stood with the kufr must be re-educated. Ignorance of our respective societies, and the lack of faith, and test of patience is what is making us Muslims fall prey into the hands of bad leaders, we are then in mass lied to, manipulated, slaughtered, then enslaved simply because we as a people, as a whole, have yet today recognize that the enemy near has a body, a face, a plan. *"Therefore shun those who turn away from our message and desire nothing but the life of this world. That is as far as knowledge will reach them. Verily thy Lord knows best those who stray from his path, and he knows best those who receive guidance"* (Quran 53:29-30). and *"To those against whom war is made, permission is given to fight, because they are wronged; and verily Allah is most powerful for their aid"* (Quran 22:39).

I must be frank; I believe that the true measure of a nation is not just what road it chooses but what decisions they make along the way. In the absence of popular support I do not believe that despot Abdelaziz Bouteflika does not care what is going on in the lives of the

---

[39]   Quran 16:71

Algerian people. I just feel and think that he is just not repentant. Thus, the enfolding misery and pain is ahead of him not just in the past. His national reconciliation program's true colors is just to extend an unconditional amnesty to members of his own security forces who committed crimes under international law as well as a needed fig leaf of shame to bar Algerian court members from the World Court and world opinion from considering crimes-against-humanity charges against Algerian judges and civil servants. Amnesty International—what a true play on words! They sent a memorandum not a "Crimes against Humanity" indictment from the World Court on April 13, 2006, to that Algerian president for life Abdelaziz Bouteflika who now also holds the position of minister of defense, in which capacity he oversees the D.R.S. This is the service most frequently associated with extrajudicial executions, torture, secret detentions, and disappearances. *"Let those fight in the name of Allah who sell the life of this world for the hereafter. To him who fights in the cause of Allah whether he is slain or gets victory soon shall we give him a reward of great value. And why should ye not fight in the cause of Allah and of those who, being weak, are ill-treated and oppressed? Men, women, and children, whose cry is "Our lord! Rescue us from this town, whose people are oppressors; and raise for us from thee one who will protect; and raise for us from thee one who will help! Those who believe, fight in the cause of Allah, and those who reject faith fight in cause of evil: So fight ye against the friends of Satan: feeble indeed is the cunning of Satan"* (Quran 4:74-76).

Yes, to differ and disagree amongst ourselves is only natural, but it's the way we differ and disagree which is a matter of attitude, discipline and grace. It's when the lights go out for whatever reason a cadence is lilt that helps guide the way somehow that is pleasing to Allah. *"Now then: for that (reason), call (them to the faith), and stand steadfast as thou art commanded, nor follow thou their vain desires; but say: "I believe in the book which Allah has sent down; and I am commanded to judge justly between you. Allah is our Lord and lord. For us [is the responsibility for] our deeds, and for you for your deeds. There is no contention between us and you. Allah bring us together, and to him is [our] final goal"* (Quran 42:15).

What is troubling to me as a Muslim student of knowledge from the West, who grew up all his life believing in human rights, equal rights, justice, and due process of law was the icon of my land. Yet why was there was no roar of injustice from American and European citizens upon their own leaders demanding support for those Algerians who were demanding justice and liberty from their own despots back in the 1990s when that other Arab Spring tried to blossom in their lands? Nobody here in the Western media, or in the Western political correct circles at the time felt that the people in Algeria did not deserve their desire for justice and liberation under the system of Democracy simply because they are Muslims and they will elect a leader that is Islamic in creed? It was moneyed Western secular nations, that told the Muslim world audiences where their hearts stood in regards to an Islamic Revolution based on civil liberties and justice! This revealing act of where the true colors of the hearts of Western leaders lie as well as the citizens thereof when it comes to justice and freedom outside of themselves must never be forgotten. The inactions of those Muslim Gulf state nations who ignored the cries of *Sharia* and justice for all from their Muslim Arab neighbors and continued to count their oil profits this too must never be forgotten and a lesson learned.

But the lesson was forgotten! The Muslim Brotherhood leadership in Egypt on July 3, 2013 thought that idea that the road ahead to governorship of the people by way of a fair democratic ballot would be respected by Western secular democratic nations was imprudent and unwise. Behind the scenes it was all about secular Western democratic vested national interest and greed verses an Islamic government coming to power through the ballot box who adhere to one divine sovereign. Welcome to our world of that ideological warfare where there are three kinds of pain for a creed lesson forgotten. Holocaust, slavery, and diaspora!

All you got to do is follow the money, what that despotic Algerian government, and it`s generals paid to those in Europe (Spain, France, Italy, England) and America to all those Western governmental arms merchants for all the guns, bullets, tanks, planes, helicopters and advisers that they can buy so that they can fight and murder their own people, their own so-called insurgents because the less the Muslim world knows about justice and freedom the more they can make a profit off their blood! Less is more when it came to civil liberties in Muslim Arab counties, this was the norm accepted by the Western New World Order, and so called Muslim Gulf state nations even more so, until their surprise wakeup call from Al-Qaeda on September 11, 2001.

What was troubling me deeply, oh, humble reader, as a humble student of knowledge from America, was that, did not all of the above named western nations at one time in their own history had a civil war where their own people fought and died in the tens of thousands, hundreds of thousands, and millions, just so that they can breathe free today and enjoy their civil liberties, their justice, and their human rights from their own indigenous tyrants? These enemy-far Western secular governments that poise as arbiters of freedom and justice with one face toward their own citizens and with the other side of their face, poise as arbiters of oppression and injustices towards citizens of lands outside their borders and outside their faith as well as abetting tyrants for profit and gain cannot be forgotten anymore!

Did they believe they will not lose their sovereignty and legitimacy from that upcoming divine retribution? So, it was no major brainwave for me or anybody else to hear from my Salafi Sheikhs in Mecca, Saudi Arabia that a nation of people who want for themselves what they don't want for others are imposters of such ideals such as, "human rights, equal rights, justice, and due process of law" and the more precious that value what they want for themselves only, the more hypocritical they truly are in that eye of the divine beholder. *"So lose not heart, nor fall into despair: For ye must gain mastery if ye are true in faith. If a wound hath touched you, be sure a similar wound hath touched the others. Such days [of varying fortunes] we give to men and men by turns: That Allah may know those that believe, and that he may take to himself from your ranks martyr witnesses [to truth]. And Allah loves not those that do wrong. Allah`s object also is to purge those that are true in faith and to deprive of blessing those that resist faith"* (Quran 3:139-141). And *"Do to others whatever you would have them do to you. This is the law and the prophets"* (Matthew 7:12).

Riding on that crest of that Arab Spring wave facing forward is that newly elected President Mr. Rached Ghannouchi, leader of Tunisia`s Islamist Al-Nahda Movement. He had spent more than fourteen years in Tunisian prisons and was forced to live for twenty two years in exile in London. Now just a few months in power after open and free elections it is clear that what his moderate Islamic party says is true, and that is "The Revolution here in Tunisia has two goals: freedom and development." In the mind`s eye of this Jihad Salaifist the first part of this revolution has been achieved and that is freedom from oppression. Yet, it is the second part of that goal, "development" that is ambiguous to many who are Allah fearing, and worrying some to an important majority who wish to have *Sharia* law in the land now, as well as those powerful secular minorities who are now being assured justice in their lives so that there will be absolute peace, not civil war. This newly formed government of President Rached Ghannouchi and his Islamic Al-Nahda party in Tunisia is truly walking a tightrope I believe. His "development" must lead to an end to intolerance towards all citizens and a beginning to a dialogue based on trust towards all its citizens. The method he is using in achieving his goals is of great concern to me and a true uneasiness to many of my Muslim brothers who are knowledgeable in Islamic guidance. *"It is not fitting for a believer, man or woman, when a matter has been decided by Allah and his apostle, to have any option about their decision: If any one disobeys Allah and his apostle, he is indeed on a clearly wrong path"*(Quran 33:36).

Mr. Ghannouchi methods on moving forward with the aspirations of all the people is based on keeping the first article of the 1956 Constitution in the new basic law now being drafted. This article says that "Tunisia is a free, independent and sovereign state, its religion is Islam, it`s language is Arabic, and it is a republic." President Ghannouchi has reportedly said that, "We are not going to use the law to impose religion." And he also states that "This article is the object of consensus amongst all sectors of society, preserving Tunisia`s Arab-Muslim identity while also guaranteeing the principles of a democratic and Secular state." President Ghannouchi has also been reportedly stated that "His Islamist party would not introduce ambiguous definitions into the constitution that risk dividing the people."

On the other hand, Sheikh Hechmi Haamdi, leader of the so-called hard line Islamic Al-Arydha movement in Tunisia has said that "this is a betrayal of all those who voted for that party." As well as, Sheikh Abd Iyadh Al-Tunisi, a powerful and knowledgeable Salafist Jihadis who also has been struggling for *Sharia* law to be also recognized as the main source of law in Tunisia also feels that these actions by the Al-Nahda party has also betrayed the people's revolution. My prayers is "will Allah be pleased by the actions of these new leaders and has the hearts of the people really changed for the good?" I can only say, oh, humble reader, time will tell, "patience" perhaps this is a test from Allah their true sovereign lord to see their true hearts and are they grateful.

It is not nonsensical to believe that once your enemy near is overpowered, that your enemy far will try to attack you by means of economics and subversion! Yes, it`s that morning after the revolution that is critical, because, people, all individuals are really trying to go through the motions of normal life and picking up the pieces of what matters to them after the rebellious social storm. Freedom cannot be sustained without justice for all. Now that the people have been freed those who had stood with those who where oppressors with Muslim names and secularist with Muslim names it is a time for reconciliations with those who are very devoted to Islam with Muslim names. That is the hidden agenda in spite of all the hype and talk I believe.

Yes, there are millions of people living in Muslim lands with Muslim names who are afraid of *Sharia* rule in their lands because it is a way of life different from the way of life that they had been living freely by their desires all their lives under despots. So it's going to take some time to get everybody back on track faithfully; what has been done unto the Muslim people by way of imperialism, followed by nationalism, will take years and generations of true Islamic teaching to undo.

Submission to the will of Allah is not an easy thing to do, especially if you have been living a life of foreign moral goals, heathen values and pagan methods all your life. We cannot force those who went astray to walk the straight path in terms of faith overnight, but we can force laws of justice and the mercy of reconciliation to avoid a civil war— patience. Now that the believers is growing in power in the land of the Muslims they must by example show those who has not submitted it is in their interest to do so willingly. Humanities' is an art form that counterpoints the drama of justice which must be seen on the street level to keep the peace. Time is always unique in a dreadful way I feel. We mustn't waste it by losing track of the deeper sense of formal struggles of this life and our true purpose in it. What happens between the hearts of developing men who fear Allah and those whose hearts fear the loss of power at the table of dialogue and change is a human gallery of values of faith versus the self interest of now and human needs!

Patience—those ambiguous definitions in Tunisia will sort themselves out in the framework of openness and justice insha Allah. What matters is that state of heart therein the Muslim people in the eye of the beholder, who only demands gratitude.

Given that this Arab spring era all started because there was a real change of heart in the Muslim world, then that pragmatic truth becomes ever more clearer in the lives of that common layman to the housewife to that child right onward to that mujahideen in regards of how they should respect each other and what is demanded of them from that divine one whom they call Allah (swa). The genius of a people are those that are innovative in their thinking but not in their faith in overcoming tremendous obstacles that lies before them.

For example, Global Capitalism unchecked within Muslim lands today cannot stand. Not just simply because the will and law of Allah in our own lands is weak not strong enough to counter the homegrown cartels and monopolies plus the eventual conflicts of interests that flourishes unbounded. But because only a fool fights his own money, having an economist that is Islamic in nature that is the head of your governmental finances is wise. *"O ye who believe! Fear Allah, and give up what remains of your demand for usury, if ye are indeed believers. If ye do not, take notice of war from Allah and his messenger: but if ye turn back, ye shall have your capital sums; deal not unjustly, and ye shall not be dealt with unjustly"* (Quran 2:278-279). This western Global Capitalism culture that was brought into our Muslim lands by the imperial colonist is a fundamental threat to the Muslim people there.

This capitalistic culture has established itself on the basis of pure benefit and it makes benefit the criterion of actions. Whereas Islam is established on the belief in Allah (swa), which is the criteria of all actions in one`s life and governs all the actions and values according to the commands and prohibitions of Allah (swa). It is time that the finances of the Arab Spring bring sweet fruit that is blessed and is pleased by Allah (swa). That the bounty of Allah will be increased upon all because that desire for wealth and prosperity will not be at the expense of others. This is one of the reasons why that American trained economist Mr. Mahmoud Jibril from Libya who was the nominal prime minister of the Libyan interim government cannot stand with the fundamental believers!

Riding on the crest of that Arab Spring wave face up that other president-for-life Muammar Gaddafi from Libya, who was captured, tortured and murdered by his own people for the sake of revenge in his own home town Sirte on October 20, 2011; ending almost forty years of Arab despotic Nationalism and Muslim-in-name-only rule there. How ironic that his last known words to his captures that day is to be treated fairly under Islamic law. The question now remains can Abel Al-Rajazk Abu Hajar, a leader in the New Tripoli Municipal Governing Council, Abdel Hakim Belhaj, the new Military Leader of the country; and Ali Sallabi, that Islamic Fundamentalist as well as Islamic Scholar who lead the spiritual Libyan mass uprisings, can they with the help of Allah, find a way for their people who had been oppress and wish to be governed according to the commands and prohibitions of Allah? May Allah help and guide them as well.

That Human Scourge

S.A.D.: By the Quran, full of admonition: [This is the truth]. But the unbelievers [are steeped] in self glory and separatism. How many generations before them did we destroy? In the end they cried [for mercy] . . . when there was no longer time for being saved!"

—Quran 38:1-3

That mysterious epidemic called colony collapse disorder does not only affect honeybees. It also affects countries like Turkey. To assume that it was Islam that lost World War I for Turkey is offensive to me. To assume that it was Islam that brought about the downfall of the caliphate in Turkey is a lie unto Allah (swa). Because every epidemic has its causes and effects, then the golden rule is truly global when it comes to corruption! These timeless consequences are universal and dire when ignored. This sad phenomenon is not that difficult to observe and ponder when a person wishes to see beyond the moment of his times. We fundamentalist embrace the idea of many Muslim scholars today that the root cause of the backwardness of Muslim states lies not in the people's failure to embrace Western secular modernism and its ideas. Rather, this backwardness lies, on the individual level, in tolerating the rampant corruption in our Muslim lands, and the people's failure to fully embrace their Islamic faith collectively and unconditionally.

By not taking your fundamental principles of your faith into action working for your mutual benefit as a nation of people of a monotheistic faith on a universal level thus it has its consequences. That's why we must firstly look objectively at the grass roots of a society.

Corruption cannot only decide the fate of a family, it can also decide the fate of a nation and an empire!

Likewise, it`s that act of abetting corruption which is a total eclipse of the heart in a monotheistic faith; thus, tens of millions of believers get left in the dark because of it. The pragmatic truth, whether we like it or not, is that corruption in a society is brought about by those who have forsaken their dignity and self-esteem. In turn, the one who denies his own accountability before his true lord, becomes a slave to his own instincts and desires. The one who sells out a trust, takes a bribe or offers a bribe, has lost respect for himself and for others in his community and nation. You do not have to have a PhD to correctly make the assessment that that avenue of perdition is lined with iniquity and vice; it is also the debasement of human dignity in the eye of a true beholder.

Corruption is a major interference and obstacle in the development of true prosperity within a nation of people who believes in and wishes to live under the law of that one divine sovereign being.

There are many Muslim scholars today in the Middle East now that Arab spring is awakening who don`t mind telling it like it is, let come what may who will say to you that the down fall of the Ottoman Empire was the lack of trust and faith firstly within the Sultan-Caliph Suleyman own family culture. This was the root cause we believe that affected the Muslim community and empire. The obvious effect was corruption and suspicion, which brought about the whole down fall of the Ottoman Empire.

Looking back at the etiquettes of the era with all the advantages of hindsight, I can see clearly those same bonds of universal family affection becoming unraveled, which has a true devastating effect regardless of faith, nationality or empire. The best sincere example is my own family as well as the millions of families that surrounded us in America back in the 1960`s till this present day because of the lack of trust!

The real front lines of a nation at war with itself in this human scourge whether you realize it or not are domestic violence. Whether you like it or not, it has been observed, but not enough to end the silence coming from within households, both rich and poor, that is no longer larger than life.

Lend me your ear, oh, peaceful reader of this book, and ponder, where is the love?

Too many years gone by, which strikes me with sad amazement how empires including American have fallen into depravity and the lost of strong family bonds within its own communities. My own parents were also afflicted with that epidemic called colony collapse disorder. Back in the day when I was two and my brother Clive one, our parents separated, then they divorcee each other with great malevolence. Yes, we were at a young age bedside observers to desertion and estrangement in the promise land called America.

Like millions of other parents, our parents at the time did take their marriage vow promise to that divine one in a church full of cheerful witnesses. Yet after the honeymoon our inner family theater relations lost their fervor of faithful obligations of true believers of the faith as temptations of life and it`s Western pagan reigning fashions over came that idea of commitment and dedication before their lord overcame them.

I have discovered growing up living in a one parent home where my father may come by once every fortnight weekend, that unless you have the right perspective it`s hard to imagine an ideal family. As culture would have it, few men today are born or raised to love that girl; fewer women ever catch that occasional soul mate that may come their way. Life as my family knows it back in the early days was a daydream without love or trust. In the twilight 60`s I learned about love by listening to the music on the radio. I learned about trust by reading the bible, love and trust was from outside in not from inside within my home. How strange that so many parents don`t realize that parents are like gods in the sight of a child. Hence, love and trust is ruthless behind the enemy`s lines!

My advantages truly only Allah (swa) knows if it is truly an advantage are the love and trust my wife and children have with each other. I believe that this era of colony collapse disorder within human families is nothing new, for generations divorce after divorce after abandonment is the secular cultural answer to hard times and desires. The pain is more acute, and contentious in poorer neighborhoods, the heartache and despondency are more known in the ranks of the middle class, the consequences are more severe and dire upon the elite. Any empire that throws away with disregard their God given family values and moral compass in order to obtain those selfish desires of sovereign independence from their lord and the material glitter things in this life shall indeed reap the grapes of wrath.

Seeing the world as it is, I bear witness that the spiritual well being of the human family in spite of today`s human diversity do have their backs up against the modern wall.

So what is the cure? In a non-secular society more and better shepherds are needed in our communities, not just more and better sheriffs initially, but those who must be eternally vigilant in their civil mission in addressing this problem of corruption. Any shepherd worth his salt can stage a spirited charge down a darkened road on a moment's notice, and with a whispered invocation step into the lives and hearts of his countrymen, and sort out the maggots from the rice without throwing away the bowl. Those shepherds who can speak with a fluency to their countrymen that this seemingly ageless malady of selfishness and greed is an outright violation of the sovereignty of Allah (swa)—from whom all life, wealth and property come. Yes, those shepherds who can find Allah in the dark shadows of human hypocrisy, and arrogance are few. They, who can unplug all your ignorance by nightfall are fewer. Otherwise, this life is just a long walk in the solitary dark looking for a good journeys end without a true moral compass that leads to death.

Yes, it is strange, till this day, I remember still, on any cloudy day, with joy, that church priest (Father Wane) from Saint Simeon's Episcopal Church on 165th Sheridan Avenue in the mid 60's who stopped by our simple home in the Bronx back in the day, carrying hope inquiring . . .

Truly, you don't have to be related to relate, it's not so hard to know whether to laugh, cry, or frown from this great *Topkapi Palace*[40] this unassailable ground where no kafr dared to challenge is a mixed blessing of confidence. We accept the premise that those two, severed grinning heads of traitors resting on display together on a black stone block, for the Sultan-Caliph Suleyman's eyes only, are truly guilty. Although, I do not think the evidence is so clear cut against them that the punishment upon Sultan-Caliph Suleyman's older sons Mustafa and Bayezid who had conspired against their elderly father was justified.

Victor's justice predetermines so much in all our lives that only a few understand how history is no longer a true guide in today's geopolitical world. Yes, Sultan Suleyman was called the lawmaker and his main central function of the Sultan-Calipate in the Ottoman Empire was to guarantee social, economic, political and religious justice across his lands. Rooting out and purging heterodox and heretical practices within our faith is no easy jihad. Ultimately,

---

[40]   The Topkapi Palace was the primary residence of the Ottoman Sultans. Construction of the palace began in 1459, in Istanbul, Turkey, by Sultan Mehmed II. It's primary propose is to strengthen the peace and tranquility of the Muslim lands.

the crown of caliphate goes to that individual person who is most fundamentally qualified.

Yet eventually that crown was under siege. Where in the Holy Quran and accepted hadith does either Allah or prophet Muhammad (sas) permit the taking of life of one's brothering and or family members is the price to inherent a global kingdom of Islam?

Till this day trust in Muslim leadership has been so barricaded in its own bunker for so long from the grassroots of its own society then and now that it's beseeching human shrill has waned pending payment of bail. Trust is one of the greatest gifts a father can give to his family, which is a home grown product of love. The first family of the Nation of Islam is a family that is the envy of the world, I believe. Yet, the down fall of the Ottoman Empire was the lack of trust within the Sultan Caliphate family culture which mirrored the family culture on the layman's level in its regard to treatment of women and the relationship between husband and wife or wives, father and son, father and daughter. This was the cause! The effect was corruption which brought about the whole down fall of the Ottoman Empire. It's a shameful thing men's reluctance to be dutiful within their own homes! That only a few men know how to be that loving husband; that understanding father that teaches that golden rule of trust deftly within his home to his wife or wives and children and fear Allah! Before we go blazing saddles over yonder off the unbeaten path, as men we should start a grand tour within our families' right at home.

When your enemies call you Sultan Suleyman the Magnificent, it's just spit on your face in my opinion. And in the opinion of the Prophet Muhammad (sas) who said: *"They are cutting your throat"* Only Allah is the *Magnificent!*

When you cull members of your own family because of the lack of trust, this is a curse. When family members within your home are in a cherished coma amid fears of assassination by each other, this is a curse. When an absent father with no sense of love, trust, brotherhood, kinship, and patience enters the room, this is a curse. When greed for power and that political bureaucracy which promotes fratricide to suit its own ends, this is a curse. When your religious scholars are fearful of taking that high moral ground with you in private or public under whatever essential context not just because of certain death ordain by you but because of the thirst for justice has been lost in their societies, this is that curse.

The problem can be distinctly seen that when a drowning Sultan and governmental bureaucracy which is both corrupt they will be

privilege to fight you just to hold on to that which they are familiar
with. This corruption of trust and faith is especially horrendous when
it is correlated just in order to stay in power, regardless of the Sultan or
layman.

You can surely see everything from here. Allah gets the blame.
Since the Copper Age, Yahweh got the blame. Since the Bronze Age,
Jehovah got the blame. Now it`s Allah`s turn. Blessed is the man who
does not blackmail the divine one, but instead feels that it's a gifted
personal responsibility, as well as a virtue, to be a spiritual bondsman
to his countrymen in times of need. That man who will say to his
fellowmen in dire times, 'We must search our own hearts for our own
shortcomings in our lives, our communities, and in our nation, and
with the help of Allah (swa) move onward.' This is why many Islamic
scholars today see General Mustafa Kemal Ataturk as an apostate
to the faith of Islam. General Mustafa Kemal Ataturk has said: "We
don`t take our inspirations from the heavens and the unknown"
Some knowledgeable Sheikhs have said that he is a *munafiq*. I agree
sadly with those fundamentalist Muslim scholars. Yes, the Ottoman
Empire had to change in order to survive. But what General Ataturk
did in order to survive as a nation of Turks, rather than an empire
of Muslims, was change, by force of arms, the faith of Islam to a new
faith of secularist apostasy! Why? Because they was corrupted by
centuries of arrogance, greed, neglect, and his people and leadership
being Muslim-in-name-only that's why. Yes I, too, agree that Turkish
secular fundamentalist Gen. Ataturk was opposed to the merchants
of our faith, and as well as our theocratic ideals. In addition, he that
public servant who believed the miracle is in their human minds and
hands, who believed his victories on the battlefield, meant the time
for eclipsing of religious social justice and Islamic law. Which now
shall be base on prudent logic, science, and tested human knowledge
so that the new rising republic nation would stand on modernism
and protected by secularism, shall be the new theme and era. Not to
be ruled by religious fundamentalists with their superstitions and
fears over the will and worldly desires of the general public. Then he
General Mustafa Kemal Ataturk also changed the national calendar,
which was Islamic for more than a thousand years to the solar calendar.
Allah got the blame!

Yes, Allah got the blame, but they are only fooling themselves.
How ungrateful they are. It was Allah who gave the Muslim world the
example of General Khaild ibn Al-Walid and the Caliph Umar ibn
Al-Khattab those early followers of prophet Muhammad (saw) 1,350
years before them to pave the way that idea of submission to the ruler

and leader of a society by the civil servant. Yes, the Ottoman Empire had to change for a variety of reasons; nevertheless, only a sincere and inquiring mind can assess the true hell on earth for a people who had lost that immunity from their Lord. To hear those misfortune walking and talking about 'If only their weapons where more modern' when in fact it was their hearts and aim. But to see those self-misfortunes of an Islamic Empire refusing to throw up an anchor unto heaven is an ultimate fallacy. Indeed, that heartless mysterious epidemic called colony collapse disorder does not only affect honeybees. It also affects human beings!

Islam and Secularism

A.L.M. Do men think that they will be left alone on saying, "We believe, and that they will not be tested? We did test those before them, and Allah will certainly know those who are true from those who are false. Do those who practice evil think that they will get the better of us? Evil is their judgment!

—Quran 29:1-4

Today it`s the turn of the Justice and Development Party, or AKP, to find Allah in the dark, and cauterize the ugly wound of secularism in Turkey. The AKP, under Prime Minster Recep Tayyip Erdogan and President Abdullah Gul are faced with monumental challenges in addressing the centuries of corruption, arrogance, greed, spiritual neglect and apostasy. They amongst others know they must stand that moral high ground and continue their dominance of the public discourse. Focusing on domestic issues, AKP's platform stands on "Islamic Ideals" that, given the opportunity, could solve any problem that might arise in the lives of the Turkish people. Essentially, they are saying that Islamic principles and virtues are the symbols of the human spirit. As such, their message was clear to the base of their supporters: If, as a society, we do not live by our creed of faith then we will not appreciate the value of Islam. Consequently, for Muslim people living in secular Muslim societies and accepting its dogma as a better way of life, the sin is that they have quit the faith—not that they have lost the faith. Likewise, it is their loyalty to the state that is in conflict with loyalty to their faith. Absurd? No, in fact, there is a generation of

Muslims today, which believes the miracles lie in science, in the arts, in economics, in their minds, and hands, that have made them freer in their lives. Since a man can only have one master, so-called secular Muslim states, like Turkey, cherry-pick whichever laws of Islam best suits their interests, and follow human laws that best suits their desires, because in their hearts the leaders of these states consider the laws of Islam irrelevant and medieval in today's so called modern times. Loyalty to the state means subordinating religion to the state. So the results of their propaganda are that the most important thing in one's life is not religion, not one's faith, but rather what can a person do in sacrifice and/or duty for my sovereign country not my sovereign divine lord Allah.

Yes, it is undisputed that there are more secularist journalist who are in jail in Turkey for slander and libel than in America or Europe. Undoubtedly, Prime Minister Mr. Erdogan has imprisoned whole staff colleges of generals who had plans of revolt because of Turkey's political fault lines have shifted more towards an Islamic ideal. Prime Minister Mr. Erdogan had once said, "that democracy is a train from which you get off once you reach the station." Is that station an Islamic state for Turkey? Time will tell, but it sure looks to be that way.

The problem also is ethics. The secular Muslim state of Turkey, like other deviant secular Muslim states, force upon its citizens this ideal of secular law versus the notion of religious ethics and principles. Those promises of ensuring neutrality and tolerance to all their citizens are just only talk and worthless daydream. On rice paper, all these secular Muslim despots today and before Arab spring, it is their wish to arrogate unto themselves the right to be sovereign, the freedom to sin, and control the legislation of all fashions and deeds of their people's daily life!

Oh, humble reader, we fundamentalists don't need to go undercover to expose that shameful record of the secular religious political establishments in Turkey; it's already a clear milestone. They the apostates, are a living tribute for all Allah-fearing people to see in regards to human rights abuse and injustice. The apostates just simply wanted the freedom to sin as they please. For example, gagged, while standing in the gallows on the isolated island of Imrali off the north-west coast of main land Turkey and 100 miles south of the city of Istanbul, with a noose around his neck to better ensure there is no last words is Mr. Adnan Menderes the most popular Prime Minister in the history of Turkey. He won three national election victories in a row, the second of which was greater than 57% of the vote. His political party was called the Democrat Party (DP) known for its famous motto: "Enough. It is the Nations turn to Speak." Hum du Allah, Prime

Minister Adnan Menderes had the metaphorical audacity of faith to campaign in his election platforms of legalizing the Arabic language call to prayer (adhan) which was banned by the secular Kemalist followers. He reopened thousands of Mosques throughout Turkey that was closed by orders of the ex-President of Turkey, Mr. Kemal Ataturk as well as countered the secularist with the winning social revolutionary Islamic idea that shaped society from the grass roots up in advocating the truths of our faith into their daily lives.

Running out of ideas to survive, the secular Turkish military junta stage a coup d'état; those traitorous civil servants who believe they have a monopoly on wisdom and administration established martial law. Subsequently, on September 17, 1961, they hanged the Prime Minister Mr. Adnan Menderes. His crime: violating the constitution. The charge: empowering religious retrogrades. They also hanged with him was Mr. Fatin Rustu Zorlu, his foreign affairs minister and Mr. Hasan Polatkan his finance Minister. May Allah bless them all with heaven!

Let`s be frank. Under Islamic creed of faith and Islamic law (Sharia), there is no such thing as a secular Muslim state. A secular state and a Muslim state are two very different protocols of societies and ways of life (religion) that are very distinct and opposed to each other in doctrine.

As an Islamist, I realize that what's most important in life is what a person stands for, not only what he or she stands against! I stand for justice: what I want for myself I want for you; what I don`t want for myself but if it is lawful in your books (Torah-Bible)—for example, "wine in wedding ceremonies, holidays and festivals only" I want for you! *"He will love and bless and multiply you; he will bless the fruit of your womb and the produce of your soil, your grain and wine and oil, the issue of your herds and the young of your flocks, in the land which he swore to your fathers he would give you"*(Deut 7:13). *"Wine is arrogant, strong drink is riotous; none who goes astray for it is wise"* (Prov 20:1), also the wedding at Cana: *"Jesus told them: 'Fill the jars with water' So they took it. And when the headwaiter tasted the water that had become wine"* (Jn. ch.2:7-11) *"And do not get drunk on wine, in which lies debauchery"* (Eph. 5:18-20). Islam means peace. There`s no peace without justice. If a Jew or a Christian wishes wine then yes, he or she can have the wine for their religious services this has been ordained by Jehovah in their creed of faith in their own books as part of their religious ceremonies only! Thus, no Jew or Christian can stand before a Muslim and demand a barroom or a saloon within our neighborhoods or state that we all live in and say he is God fearing!

Secularism stands for a vacuum of active religious faiths in civil policies and public education, a belief that promotes human values without religious doctrines.

Quite plainly, secularism is a faith that calls for a vacuum of active religious faiths in civil policies outside of homes and temples under the conviction this will cause divisiveness and polarization within communities! Fundamentally, a belief that stands on humanity being not humanely mature enough to resolve our worldly and religious disputes and move forward if we all wish to hold on to our active faiths in a public arena and in civil policies. Essentially, a belief, that humanity as well is not capable enough to address wisely those life hurdles that will confront humanity in a positive and resourceful manner while adhering to their faith in an active public arena and in civil policies. An inconvenient truth is that secularism is a pagan and/or atheism faith of self-worship that promotes human values. Therefore, "Basically, what I do not want for myself, I do not want for you!"

Consequently, secularism stands for itself and cannot compete in an open field of contenders in the light of day in a Muslim environment simply because it is a faith unto itself. Politically, deviant secular Muslim states allow the citizenry no input in public debates, practice no fair and open politics, nor permit any intrigue within their countries in terms of the process of obtaining power or governorship. Secular Muslim states stand for one-party rule—their party—and believe in a free and fair vote, so long as it is for themselves only. Legally, deviant secular Muslim states stand for outlawing any homegrown rival source of sovereignty for legitimacy in their lands. Culturally, deviant secular Muslim states believe that they are the only true guardians of the ethnic minorities living in their countries, protecting the rights, liberties and heritage of these peoples. In reality, however, these secular Muslim leaders must divide their populations in the name of ethnic liberty, and likewise rule with an iron fist if they wish to survive.

Since the differences between Islam and Secularism are substantial, the issues here are none other than the difference between a monotheism faith and polytheism and/or atheism. We monotheist Fundamentalists believe Secularism is a faith that robs humanity of its soul outside the home and temple in the field of civil policies and in public education thus humanity stands on dangerous skeletal ground in the sight of their lord. The effect in the field of mass communication and mass commerce between citizens is the promotion of blasphemy polytheism and/or outright atheism towards the faith of the Muslim believers in Muslim lands or in any lands. Oh, humble reader of this book, this is where we have that clash of civilizations. Islam is a complete way of life and does not restrict itself to home and or temple. Thus the enemy near truly has a secular face with a systematized exploitation of freedom of thought and speech agenda in hand out side of home and temple arena; thus his domain.

We the believers have been warned from every point of view. Secularism in Muslim countries is the cornerstone of legitimacy for the apostates and *kufr* who have lived in the region for centuries. The secularist's motto is always *"in the name of personal liberty"* because they wish to differ from the Islamic masses whose motto is *"In the name of Allah,"* demanding continually those terms of fundamental right to exist within Muslim lands and keeping sovereignty unto themselves. Secularists adhere to a doctrine that appoints mankind as the lord and ruler, one who holds the right to dismantle the laws of Allah (swa) and replace them with their own. This line of thinking makes human desires divine, and the human mind a master that must be fully obeyed fully, an ideology which takes precedence over the faithfull's submissiveness and obedience to Allah.

Secularism makes adultery not punishable by imprisonment or death if the man and the woman are consenting adults; the fine is divorce perhaps alimony. Secularism makes alcohol lawful for the public consumption without adherence to a creed of faith, and makes selling it lawful business; the fine is decadence in the land. Secularism makes usury (*Riba*) lawful, which is the basis of the majority of financial transactions in the world today—the fine debauchery. Secularism makes homosexuality an acceptable lifestyle choice with rights; the fine, lewdness in the land. Indeed, on the issue of abortion, the secular elite have made abortion legal even if the unborn child does not threaten the life of its mother—the fine, the value of morality and life is cheapen. Hundreds of thousands of unborn children are murdered every year in abortion centers in secular Muslim countries in the name of a woman`s personal liberty; even though the child does not threaten the life of its mother is of no matter. However, the Quran clearly states that *"In the name of Allah you shall not murder your children due to fear of poverty. We provide for them as well as for you. Murdering them is a gross offense."*[41] Also, Prophet Muhammad (sas) said on this issue of abortion "What crime did the unborn child commit for this child to die?"

Kufr, that enemy near with the secular face, and its apostates living in Muslim lands, now realize that on these issues they cannot weather

---

[41]   Quran17:31

the growing storm of ideological conflict of interest that they represent and to think that this Arab spring that this Islamic awakening will continue to tolerate these laws against the growing demand for Sharia (Islamic Law) in the people's lives is only denying the geopolitical Islamic reality that is confronting them all.

It's what you stand for and what creed you represent in the light or dark of the day outside your homes and temples which determines true guidance when it is time to take an unequivocal stand regarding a monotheist faith.

Let the prayers rise as they may. Sovereignty is with Allah (swa) only, not with the people.[12] *"To Allah belongs the dominion of the heavens and the earth: He forgives whom he wills, and he punishes whom he wills: but Allah is oft-forgiving, most merciful"* (Quran 48:14). When these "enemy near" leaders and their allies hear in public squares the roar of millions of their citizens demanding justice and Sharia law, they should realize that their citizens, their countrymen, are demanding that sovereignty to be returned to Allah. This is Islam. What the enemies near fears is that the people no longer fear them, but only Allah. That the people no longer put their trust in each other, but now put their trust only in Allah. Sovereignty then lies not in the hands of their leaders, nor in the hands of the people, but exclusively with Allah. The result is that the most important thing is not the life of a human being on this earth, but a divine being in one's life on this earth. Whereas secularism in Muslim countries or non-Muslim countries the result is that the most important thing is not religion in one's public life but life being a human being today!

---

[12] Quran 48:14

Sovereign

*To Allah belongs the dominion of the heavens and the earth; and
Allah hath power over all things.*

—Quran 3:189

At the sound of the Christian bell and the muezzin`s call for the past
one hundred years the former keep their promises to each other
in some degree of domestic human rights as citizens in the text of
national civil liberties but not in the text of Christian and Protestant
faiths (secular-nationalism) and (World War I and II). Case in point;
Christian nations fighting and killing each other (France-Italy),
Spain a civil war. Protestant nations fighting and killing each other
(England-Germany), and Protestant and Christian nations killing each
other (France-Germany, Germany-Poland-Russia). Whereas the latter
did not keep their promise to our sovereign lord (Allah) as citizens in
the text of national civil liberties (human rights) and (justice) nor in
the text of Sharia law towards their only lord and sovereign Allah (swa)
in the text of the Quran and example (*sunna*) of prophet Muhammad
(sas). Case in point: Tens of millions of Muslims apostate their faith of
Islam by following nationalism, and practicing secularism.

The inevitable result is that the masses of Christians, and
Protestants benefited from their benefaction towards each other
nationally, and assented as players on the world stage in spite of more
than 45 million dead (World War I and II) (secularism-nationalism),
and over 30 million dead within one year because of that Influenza
Pandemic of 1918-19 brought to them as punishment by their lord.

By contrast, the latter, Sunni, and Shiites, lost their benediction from Allah (swa) their true sovereign lord, and being punished, descended, resulting in invasions and oppressions upon almost the whole Muslim world of one billion people (except Mecca and Medina) by their colonist enemies, their illegitimate nationalistic benefaction towards one another was fruitless. Consequently, the Muslim peoples ended up being more cursed after rising up against the colonist, which was followed by being ruled by their own despots.[43] Because of their own hearts. *"Evil as an example are people who reject our signs and wrong their own souls. Whom Allah doth guide, he is on the right path: Whom he rejects from his guidance, such are the persons who perish"* (Quran 7:177-8).

Welcome to the era of ideological warfare, one in which the people in complete obedience with his God, Allah, or Yahweh have the true edge over rival ideologies. That sensible person of a known cause utterly in obedience with his government and fellow man is silver since you cannot fight your own shadow of desires and expect to win abetting a body of lies against the will of a divine being. Beware, being patriotic to a king, president, or nation has it`s blackout dates. Whereas being patriotic unto a divine being has its reward even beyond the grave.

Yes, handing over total sovereignty to a divine being to rule over his subjects is a bit too much of a summit to climb for billions of Monotheistic peoples. So here we are. We do know what you are pondering. Truly, it is a damning conclusion out here on the ground floor called earth, that billions of lives can begin, and end, without notice, beautiful lives so full of hope, and contribution, and yet quite a majority of people would rather call a dog to bring a bone than call on that only divine one to bring a miracle to them in need. So here we are, simply because billions of Monotheistic people forget or ignore who their sovereign lord really is and go about their daily business as if tomorrow is promised to them. It`s that imparted social message of today`s reality in which billions of people are now faced with in their daily lives in whether to throw an anchor into heaven so as to overcome social, economic, political and religious barriers that can help make empty ideas and ideals real and tangible in people's lives, other than putting forth ideas and ideals towards their fellow neighbors (nationalism, secularism, communism, paganism, atheism, capitalism and democracy) that are simply scarecrows in the field of human survival.

Yes, it is a bitter irony, having this volition imposed upon us. Whether to acknowledge and submit sovereignty to an unseen divine

---

[43]   Quran 7:177-8

being or not is truly a leap of faith, a leap of faith that can reduce the risk of serious injury in this dark and ignorant world if that person would only have a gram of faith to act on. In life, becoming self-aware, such as it is given unto all, one has to be pragmatic in all endeavors; as such, mankind can achieve a guarantee of justice and rights from an unseen yet merciful divine being, one who only demands gratitude. Considering this to contemplate on in contrast to the drafting of a constitution of ideas, one that promises justice and rights, put forward by men desiring to rule other men and who demand allegiances and sovereignty. This very essence of the Arab Spring metaphor is the awaking of Islam in the Sunni Arab world. Because it was Islam— loyalty to a divine being, versus loyalty to the state—that united and enlighten the Arab world unlike any Arab leader, nation, or ideology, the Muslim people want justice and rights through Sharia law throughout the Middle East and the larger Muslim world. And it's not just the Muslim fundamentalists but also the youth denied a hopeful future and the women denied the opportunity of living the faith inside a loving family home, who are willing to fight for it.

Simply put, brought to life by a divine sovereign being above, and beyond our understanding warrants commendation and allegiance. We as human beings did not choose the time, place on earth or created the human vassals in which our souls reside, so answering the purpose of a divine sovereign lord is best learned when it is lived in earnest demand.

Our pursuit of happiness starts right at the hearts of our own Muslim countries. I am not writing this book to churn the already-bloody waters to attract more sharks; instead I wish to bring to your attention a dose of realism, from a fundamentalist Salafi Sunni Muslim perspective, which explains how we perceive ourselves and our neighbors in this global village and what path people of our faith need to take, in these extraordinary times. The issues I have addressed needs no spyglass; they have, in fact, loomed large before you waxing in its resistance to that new world order. Close your eyes if you wish or dare. These Islamic priorities are no longer in a flux fueled by that nosebag of discontent.

Real change by way of the Arab Spring has truly emerged now as a rallying cry in the jihad debate amongst the top Salafi and mainstream Islamic scholars, thanks to a rising majority of enlightened Sunni Muslims who call for the sovereignty to be placed only with Allah. They harbor a deep suspicion about America and Europe's secular policies as well as ideologies, most notably the "war on terror" and "globalism." The Islamic backlash to these policies and ideologies has produced a worldwide call amongst Muslims for human rights, justice, and due process of law (Sharia), one that must be heard, understood, and acted upon according to our faith in Islam.

The reality speaks for itself; faith and justice are not always neighbors. What has happen to the Jews in Europe's concentration camps is not by chance or arrogance; it is a sign of Jehovah's punishment of those who ignore his laws and what happens when you forget who is sovereign regardless of where you stand on this earth or nationality you may possess. Those of us Monotheistic peoples, across the globe who are struggling to keep what's left of our lives together, and as the numbers of our oppressed Muslim poor grows, eats less, and has its hopes forestalled, each of us must consider that cookbook theory of dire social justice: "Either we are all innocent or we are all collateral damage" in the eyes of our more merciful lord. Likewise, we fundamentalists are not deaf to the cries of the world's citizenry or intimidated by media magician propagandists or strong-armed spooks in our home countries, as well as those thought police that lurks in the sinister dark, those who are skilled in the art of darkness, transmitting that vast neglected shadow of human perpetual drift of fear of the alterative, that their time has now ended. We all know the rescript is the same then as it is now: "You must not say this because we will think you mean that!" "You must not think this because we will say you mean that!"

We understand clearly those Muslim-in-name-only leaders are merely tools used by our external enemies to further launch their war on Islam. Today's Muslim-in-name-only puppet leaders, whether they are in exile or under siege, are only interested in their lives, wealth, and power, and the forces that threaten these. Much the same, we fundamentalist believers remember all too well the ideals of those Yahweh-fearing fundamentalist Jews, led by Prophet Moses, who fought for religious freedom and demanded that Pharaoh "let my people go."[44] Likewise, we recall a psalm of David, the prophet who, on the day the Lord delivered him from the hand of all his enemies, spoke unto the Lord the following words:

> *I will love thee, O Lord, my strength. The Lord is my rock, and my fortress, and my deliverer; my God, my strength, in whom I will trust; my buckler, and the horn of my salvation, and my high tower.*

---

[44]   Exodus 5:1-3

*I will call upon the Lord, who is worthy to be praised: so shall I be
saved from mine enemies*[45]

We also recall the command of Prophet Jesus who said, *"Sell your
clothes and buy your swords,"*[46] as well as the words of Samson, who
famously said, *"Let me die with the Philistines."*[47] Yes, we also remember
Patrick Henry, that God-fearing fundamentalist Christian, who said,
"Give me liberty or give me death"; and the General John Stark who
said, "Live free or die. Death is not the worst of evils"; or what John
Brown, that beloved abolitionist crusader fundamentalist said, on
his hanging day, "It is easy to hang me, but this question, this slave
question, remains to be settled."

Ultimately, neither I, nor my Afro-American brothers can
forget those heroic and grave events of that visionary black slave
fundamentalist Nat Turner, which lead to his hanging day. Simply
put, the jihad of the Christians and Jews "people of the book" is no
metaphor nor, was they the least bit ashamed of their faith and the
doctrines that define it. They weren't cowed by *their* enemy near, or far,
so why should we? They did not forget who was their sovereign lord was
in times of troubles, so why should we?

It is deemed a sacred mission to purify Muslim lands in our faith. So
the onus before us as believers of the Muslim faith lies in the following
question: does an unabashed purge of kufr military bases, soldiers,
agents, customs and pagan faiths from our lands warrant the savagery it
entails? We Fundamentalists of this Islamic faith believes it does.

The emerging truth is that the Middle East is now the awakening
battleground of the twenty-first century. The contending rivalries like
America, the United Kingdom, and their European allies, as well as
Russia and China; all of whom are more thirsty for oil than ever before,
are now pitted against Afghanistan, Iran, Iraq, Egypt, Syria, Libya,
Somalia, Algeria, Yemen, Sudan, Pakistan, Bangladesh, Mali, Palestine
and other Islamic movements in a hellish proxy war spearheaded
by autocratic, despotic Muslim-in-name-only governments to thwart
change in the direction of their countries against the will of their own
Allah fearing peoples who wish to make Allah (swa) their sovereign
lord only here on earth.

---

[45]   Psalms 18:1-3

[46]   Luke 22:36

[47]   Judges 16:30

Hum du Allah, Muslims across the globe are making renewed efforts—not through Western ideologies, but through the Islamic faith— to find solutions to their social, economic, and political deprivations and return that rightful sovereignty back to Allah who only demands gratitude. "*So, glory to him in whose hands is the dominion of all things and to him will ye be all brought back*" (Quran 36:83)

Suspended Rights

Allah doth command you to render back your trusts to those to whom they are due; and when ye judge between man and man, that ye judge with justice: Verily how excellent is the teaching which he gives you! For Allah is he who hears and sees all things.

—Quran 4:58

In my twenty years of *dawa* (preaching), I have heard the voices of our Islamic resistance and the words they have been saying unto the people. One does not have to be a member of the United States 345th Military Intelligence Battalion or a psy-ops expert, to understand that the human race faces a humanitarian crisis that pits faith against reason. The stark reality of today's Muslim world is that not all of the Muslims living in Muslim countries are zealously patriotic to Allah. These shameful munafiq leaders of Muslim lands, their sons and faithless allies, many of whom are shameful politicians, generals and colonels who consider in their hearts the laws of Islam to be irrelevant for these modern times and is willing to suspend the rights of Allah fearing people. Their souls, Allah knows best, are not true public servants to Allah. Sadly, for many Muslim-in-name-only people, the Islamic religion is too binding, its embrace of spiritual and moral wholesomeness just not their cup of tea, something they have not freely submitted to or chosen in full. Yes, those who are born into the faith only then to quit it because of those deadly "pursuit of happiness" temptations, for them earthly responsibilities are too great and the faith seemingly too rigid to help them meet the growing challenges in this world. So for many, they feel, why shouldn't one accept an inheritance in full here in life, rather than the promise of paradise after death?

Paradise? It`s only sky in any case for the apostates; such a understanding concept of a promise of a life after death then they will be in paradise is truly too much of a great leap of faith at any rate. Better still, "Why not just walk away from too much drama and get busy living the now?" is the word that`s going about town. Got bills to pay, need a bigger shoe, which is the accepted Western culture insight. Since we are only human and being what life is, it is wise to choose one`s own hurdles and pleasures in life is the norm; so they hope and plea.

I am one of those believers who, in this holy month of Ramadan 1435 (*hag*), have managed to put aside nationalistic differences to face a common enemy near. I believe that the caliphate shall soon return to Islam, *insha Allah,* but the Muslim world must see this value for themselves, and fight for it themselves, and must also understand why we lost the Caliphate and the mercy of Allah in the first place. The deeper conflicts inside most Muslim countries today are not just between the ideas of extremism, intolerance, and authoritarian governments fighting to hold on onto power, against a popular and powerful sentiment amongst the public for Islamic reforms. Nor are these conflicts simply a result of the rich and powerful living inside a sea, of Muslim poverty. As Sunni Muslims, we believe these ongoing revolutionary conflicts are the clear symptoms of the effect. The true cause of the revolutionary jihadist discord inside Muslim countries today lies with the emerging scriptural Islamic fundamentalist leaders and their wealthy Muslim traditionalist allies in conflict with those secular nationalist despots and their Western secular *kufr* supporters who are willing to suspend the human rights of Allah fearing people for their own personal causes.

Oh, humble reader of this book, who is seeking the simple truth of the matter at hand, how can I explain to the real world that it is quite nearly impossible to describe a hellish life to a nation of people who have been living a life of human rights, equal rights, justice, and due posses of law all their lives, benefitting in their home lands all their lives, because their ancestors before them fought for these civil liberties all their lives, to comprehend, a nation of people who do not have these same civil liberties all their lives, because their ancestors of old was not successfully vigilant in understanding the value of maintaining with their very lives these important creeds that`s in their very own holy books!

It is only when people like myself, a student of knowledge, or some simple backpackers from the West, looking for new humanitarian archaeological oasis aboard, then comes face to face with a people in the Middle East, Africa or in Asia who say`s they believes in one divine being that only demands generosity, but these very same people are living in a state of emergency with suspended rights, declared by banana republic's because of their own hearts! I, who now comes back home to tell the awesome tale, that this is what happens when a people who live by their desires, and ignore that divine being that they swear to that only demands generosity!

Indeed, one thing is obvious: this book is no gossip. Nowadays, hundreds of millions of Muslims from many nations are living in a world full of ideas; yet they are still impoverished, impotent and tamed. In my mind`s eye I see the beloved masses of Muslim people venturing out of their hives with the same look for years on their faces, a people who are working hard but are really just chasing payments under vows, seemingly getting very little in return for their endeavors. The established power of their pharaohs is far from their hands, yet these simple people who are living ordinary lives and make less than $10 dollars a day still hear the muezzins call and pray for Allah`s mercy. They do not act on their faith with a jihad as if in a trance until now that Arab Spring a clear mercy from Allah.

From 1990 until the day I was released from an underground Syrian prison in July 2009, because the government of that country knew I was a Jihad Salafi Muslim, I became part of the ideological warfare preformed by Muslim-in-name-only governments, where a sensible person in search of his God can be questioned as to the merits of living the Islamic faith. For most of my life, I'd lived in the West, believing that justice is the true life blood of our humanity; in fact, this is how we define ourselves in the West with the understanding that justice allows one's soul to breathe freely when freedom is extra dry.

Whoever told you that the dead does not suffer the living to past are liars. All you got to do is look at what is happening now in the land of the prophets. What really yanked off that Band-Aid was that very first day walking the streets of a Muslim country Cairo, Egypt, back in the summer of 1990 and beyond. Oh, humble reader, I hope you don't mind if I put down in words what my heart, mind and soul has truly seen and experience. It`s that stunning DNA of a people en masse seized is no superstition. That reality-bite consequence of mixing an atheist faith (secularism) within an Islamic faith en masse held in check by their unseen divine sovereign lord cannot be ignored. That reality-bite consequences of justice denied towards their fellow neighbors en masse is no superstition! *"Allah will not change the condition of a people until the people change the condition of their own hearts"* (Quran 13:11) is jolting but not beyond human understanding!

I am not one of those zealots who demands perfection from others, but it doesn't require much insight to realize that the actions and policies of these Muslim-in-name-only leaders and their constituents have severed the Islamic world from the sovereignty of Allah. The continued brutality of these despots and dictators have hardened people's hearts towards one other, making them reluctant to lower their wings for Allah's mercy. In turn, millions of educated Muslims have fled to non-Muslim lands in pursuit of happiness and justice, thereby depriving their native countries and constituents the essential intellectual capital that can translate into economic and spiritual success of revolt. Likewise, the economic consequences in Muslim lands are the brain drain of tens of millions of educated elite Muslims fleeing into non-Muslim lands in their pursuit of happiness and justice. Instead of taking a stand, and fighting their own repressive governments at home, if needs be, these educated elite had fled, like rabbits with visas in hand, to places like New York, Los Angeles, London, Paris, Rome, Bern, Berlin, Madrid, Stockholm, Brasilia, Singapore, and Sydney to name but a few, in search of profit and peace in their lives, not a prophet, his message, and a jihad.

These shameful asylum seekers and political refugees had run for their Muslim lives, their families in hand, fearing oppression by those self-invented despots, not Allah's admonishment. These so-called elite have not stood their Muslim ground with their money and their swords in hand in order to inspire their countrymen onward—those nobles, the youth, the working class, the shackled poor—to inspire a campaign of jihad that would bring Allah's mercy upon them all. In fact, these educated Sunni, Sufi and Shiite elite and their rich cousin nobles have failed to envision the power of our diversity, regardless of the oppression we have individually or we collectively faced.

In spite of their intelligence, still even till today, so many feel it is best to sit in foreign cafés with newspapers and black coffee in hand comfortably reading about their poor compatriots' struggles, even as "over five hundred Arab refugee boat people every year wash up dead on European beaches."[48] The sad truth is that the Muslim people are being tricked and led astray by homegrown tyrants who are encouraging their citizens to relocate to non-Muslim lands in the hope

---

[48]   As reported by the German Institute of Human Rights

that those citizens of theirs abroad will continue to send remittances
back home to their families and love one`s, and thereby help the state
economically. Yes, at the same time, in foresight, one more person in
a foreign land is one less person to worry about turning jihadist, or
worse, starting a true Islamic resistance movement at home!

We Fundamentalists ask of you to take into account when Europe
was in the grasp of dictators like Stalin, Mussolini, Francisco Franco
and Adolf Hitler, how many hundreds of thousands, or even millions
of Europeans swarmed the shores and borders of Muslim countries
seeking both asylum and political refuge? So then, why would a nation
of Muslim people prostrate themselves, eyes wide open, to both Allah,
and their enemies at the same time? What would free men, and women
do otherwise? We the believers of this fundamentalist monotheist faith
are aware that whatever human devil is ruling over Europe and denying
the people there in their human rights, our enemies far would find
the morale somewhere, somehow and take a stand. The very idea of
themselves in our Muslim lands as political refuges and or fugitive's en
masse because of their own despots is not in their vocabulary!

Justice is that catalyst masterpiece of human civilization, the
same demand virtue that has fueled the Arab Spring, which has now
turned into the Arab summer, and will continue into the month of
Ramadan, the month of mercy and beyond, the month of opportunity
for repentance from their Lord. The people in Algeria, Yemen,
Bahrain, Egypt and Syria are now asking how long they must wait for
their hearts to be purified by jihad so that they too can taste justice in
their lives. How long, they ask, will a nation of people stop relying on
justice from the *kufr* (U.N.) and the *munafiq* to cover the cost of faith?
How long, they ask, until a nation of people stop carrying their holy
books on their backs just for show? How long will Muslim have to wait
for their nations to stop economically boycotting and ostracizing each
other, and unite with reciprocal interest, respect, and commerce with
each other? How long will it take to change the conditions within
their breasts into submissive hearts of more than a billion and a half
people who call themselves believers in the Islamic faith? How long
the world must wait to see a people act on their faith in spite of their
circumstances?

How long? Only Allah knows. Or is it again Allah who gives and
forgives and mankind who gets and forgets?

Whether or not the Muslim world can achieve critical mass by
means of settling accounts due to, or by the consequence, of jihad
remains up to the contribution of each individual. The only question

that matters then is what is your contribution? Yes, there are many number of people who are fond of floating belly-up down the river of denial, even when the tributaries are clear and numerous. Why then should you follow them, face down, those advocates who want to live for everything and die for nothing in this cynical world in which we all live? The simple truth is, your sincere demand for justice for all may just turn the tide of sovereignty to Allah`s way.

Now and then you have to write your own script and stop imploring the world—or the United Nations for that matter—to do the right thing and having stage fright when it is time for jihad. We all have known for the longest time that the notion of democracy by those "enemy far" states was far from perfect as a foreign policy. For decades, this institution called the United Nations has sailed against the winds of human dignity just to continue business as usual of denial of human rights and justice, revealing a true blind eye to the vast expanse of human suffering. In fact, the UN, under the control of its secular Western and Communist pagan masters, have supported numerous human rights restrictions, many of which have come in declared states of emergences by illegitimate Middle Eastern governments. The list is long and shameful and includes denial of the following:

1. Protection of life and liberty
2. Freedom of speech
3. Freedom of assembly
4. Freedom of expression
5. Human rights
6. Equal rights
7. Due process of law
8. Habeas corpus
9. Bail
10. Protection of property rights

The cure? You`ve got your favorite justice; they got theirs.

Oh, humble reader, I sincerely believe that justice is best learned when it is lived, not only talked about. Sadly, justice has not been an article of faith in the lives of millions of Muslim people living in Muslim lands some of whom now, for more than five generations. This is why Islam is so full of stories of success, failure, suspicion, and discovery here within the dominion of their lord and aboard within the dominion of their enemies.

The grim scenario is that by learning how to be just to each other, we as Muslims must be patient with each other. So if there is a spot in your heart where you do not want for others what you want for yourself seen by that divine sovereign and witness by our own holy books. Then we will be cursed with the lack of love and trust and that dark domestic violence within closed doors and your favorite despots ruling outside our homes and temples will only get worst. Thus we will be ignored like the Hebrews before us, rightly so, by a divine sovereign lord who only demanded gratitude, which could had enlighten and inspire our lives as we dreamed it and more!

Even though it`s a terrible thing to live in fear and oppression, there`s no place like home! In the wake of Arab Spring, it is therefore poetic justice that Nigeria, one of the most corrupt governments in the world, has declared a "state of emergency" on May 14, 2013. President Goodluck Jonathan has announced that Islamic extremist is now in control of many Northern provinces, towns, and villages. He has ordered more troops to be sent into the northern region to fight the peoples therein because of their open rebellion lead by that determined fundamentalist Abubaker Shekau and his "Boko Haram" (Western Education is Sinful) organization.

Yes, it is true; and please do not doubt this fact for a *second—that* injustice makes your world full of terrorist. And for the millions of Allah-fearing Muslims living in Nigeria President Goodluck Jonathan`s luck has run out. I say this, oh, humble reader, with a heavy heart knowing that the road ahead will be filled with an even greater human rights abuse and more suspended rights upon the peoples in their time of civil war and liberation.

However, it seems like only yesterday, twenty years ago, my first day in class at Mecca University in Saudi Arabia which ironically gave me a true perceptive of what`s going on in Nigeria. Sitting beside me on my right was a smiling young Muslim from Nigeria who was also a student who also traveled far to learn about Islam and the Arabic language to better his people back home. His name I shall never forget was Shryib. He tells me he was from Kano, Nigeria. His father and his father`s, father`s father were all Imams in his country. Now he has been blessed by Allah to travel to Mecca University to study Arabic and Islam to better himself so that he can help his own people as a more knowledgeable Imam and contribute in the fight against governmental corruption and oppression that plagues his country.

From day one, I like him very much, and we bonded very well in spiritual pursuits. I was surprised that his English was perfect, and he can read and write Arabic well; but his speaking and understanding the Arabic grammar and language was not so good. Still, I felt it was strange that he along with many other foreign students were being put into my Arabic 101class as if they knew no Arabic at all, when, in fact, they did. But that was not that important for the moment.

For more than three years, Shryib and I was great friends together at Mecca University and it was primarily he and other Muslim students studying here from Nigeria who informed me of the serious corruption and oppression that goes on in their country in spite of the fact that the two great majorities of faiths of the peoples therein are Islamic and Christian. Nigeria, I am told, as a whole itself has not truly benefitted actually from the two great monotheist faiths living side by side one another complementing with each other to gain that mercy from their same lord. Sadly, the faiths of the people overall is small compared to the growing natural wealth of the country that they had been granted over to them by their lord, a place where no vice is legal but every vice is tolerated are nearly ubiquitous.

I first heard the term Boko Haram from Shryib back in 1993 when he was talking about his own Muslim leaders and people back home. This came about as he was explaining the level of faith and corruption in the hearts and lives of the Nigerian masses. Because of him, I became more aware of the dire consequences of Muslim communities that 'souled-out' in his words, for Western material gain, secular Western education, and political military power. As well as, those Christian communities that also 'soul-out' for the same Western material gain, secular western education, and political military power. Boko Haram`s jihad, is a life in revolt from blasphemy that has earned an international reputation of decadence, corruption, and greed. And is now on a soul-searching road trip into the hearts of the African people.

Yes, it was my good friend Shryib, who portrayed that reality image of the need for spiritual and moral renewal in Nigeria and sub-Saharan Africa as a whole. The walking dead of AIDS, he believed, was the least of Africa`s worries; as a matter of fact, it was the continuing effect of the secular western imperialist`s lewdness and cultural rape that bothered him most of all.

For a young man then of twenty-five, he was very strong in Sunni orthodox Islamic faith, intelligent, and well rounded in world affairs. Shryib did not harbor any hatred toward us his fellow students who came here to study the Arabic language and faith because we were from the West. No. Our nationality was not the enemy. Nor did he speak in any way that was abhorrence towards Christians and their faith. No. His revulsion was towards the indoctrination of hell-bent nationalist exploitation ideals that many people from the Western secular countries carry with them into Africa as unnecessary baggage.

From him and other Africans scholars and students living here with me in Mecca, I had learned that sub-Saharan Africa was a three-tier Eden world of the hopeless poor, corrupted capitalist elite, and those military Junta generals with their guns. I heard Shryib say many times the "real intifada starts at home in Nigeria, the most populous and diverse country in Africa not here in the Middle East" these Arab beggars sitting on a mountain of gold, the thought of jihad just theater.

In spite of the suspended rights of the peoples that's been going on for decades now in Nigeria and in the sub-Saharan Africa as well, like Mali; invaded by foreign kufr forces. Deep down in my heart I know that brother Shryib is earning his degree by playing a major role within the Boko Haram organization, fighting against the corrupt Nigerian government and all those who support it. Brother Shryib is not a person I know who will burn down a church simply because they are Christians—no. This is not the creed of the Islamic faith that he lives by. The enemy is not the Christians or their churches as the Western media wishes to portray it to be. The enemy is the corrupt Nigerian state and those Western patrons of the corrupt Nigerian state, as well as the state of the hearts of the Muslim and Christian people in regards to social justice!

The Islamic Community Fundementalist, Imam Ustaz Mohammad Yusuf, a Salafi Muslim, may Allah (swa) bless him with heaven began the organization "Boko Haram" in Nigeria back in 2002. [*"Jam'at ahl us-Sunnah Ii'd-Da'wah Wa'l-Jihad"*]—*"The group of the people of the Sunnah for Preaching and Struggle"*, was a popular non-violent social-religious organization, which was against the corruption, and the oppression of human rights in their society. Imam Mohammed Yusuf wrote an open letter to his government to stop the corruption and oppression upon his Muslim people and urged them to respond to them within forty days. The only response was more brutality. Imam Mohammed Yusuf was arrested by the police and para-military, tortured and publicly executed in August 1, 2009. Without public trial, without fear of injustice, and without fear of Allah's retribution.

Yes, it is an inconvenient truth; injustice makes your world full of terrorist! Therefore, a civil war in Nigeria is a country lost well beyond ransom. Just ask Imam Mohammed Yusuf, those thousands of Muslim families' members that disappeared in police and military custody. As well as those three hundred Christian, school girls kidnapped in retaliation.

Now and then, my thoughts and prayers are focused towards my old friend Shryib who now has to write his own script in the middle of a civil war that is unfolding into a jihad without borders. Yet because we are free men the world is subject to change, this is my prayer. So I am sure he knows it`s certainly a matter of your level of contribution when you have to un-suspend your rights and deal with ending the indignity of an African nightmare with all its tortuous complexity once and for all. May Allah bless him and keep him safe in his Jihad.

Al-Qaeda

Think not of those who are slain in Allah`s way as dead. Nay, they live, finding their sustenance in the presence of their lord.
—Quran 3:169

Is it not enough that an elite organization of highly educated and motivated Muslims, one dedicated to the unified cause of establishing an Islamic state, has taken the path that many have forgotten? Who knows how to follow all the pain and the other ugly business of war back to their adversary's doorstep, and understands the grim cost of winning and the consequences of failure in the West's war on terror? Who values martyrdom cherishes liberty, and the pursuit of all who threaten Islam? It was the martyred fundamentalist, jihadist Osama Bin Laden, who said, "Under what grace are your victims innocent and ours dust, and under which doctrine is your blood, blood and our blood water?"[49]

Walking that rice paper and writing the prescription for millions of Muslims is that doctor of Islamic fundamentalism, a war pioneer puritan and CEO of management of savagery is Sheikh Ayman Al-Zawhiri, the leader of Al-Qaeda. It was Al-Zawhiri, who with too much of unfinished business said, "When we wage jihad in Allah`s path, we aren't waging jihad to lift oppression for Muslims only. We are waging jihad to lift oppression for all mankind, because Allah has

---

[49] Quran 3:169-171

164

ordered us never to accept oppression wherever it may be." As far as the question of savagery goes, a question which no longer remains in doubt, Al-Qaeda's Al-Zawhiri also said, "You gave us legitimacy and every opportunity to continue fighting you."[50]

May Allah protect him and forgive us Muslims living here in the West, where apathy runs rampant and the thought of jihad for the mercy of Allah is often running dead last in this materialistic era.

As American, Western and Russian policymakers try to figure a way out of this unwinnable war on terror they had gotten themselves into; an old nemesis, and what he had to say comes to my mind that suits the climate of our present times. It was on November 13, 1974, which feels like just like yesterday, as Mr. Yasir Arafat, another Arab nationalist fundamentalist, who spoke to the United Nations assembly, and thus the world community, for them to decide between an olive branch or a freedom fighter's gun. It was he, who brought that revolutionary idea to the West in a portrait for all to see of why injustice is making the Western world and communist world full of terrorist. In his own words, Arafat said, "The difference between the revolutionary and the terrorist lies in the reason for which each fights. Whoever stands by a just cause and fights for liberation from invaders and colonialists cannot be called a terrorist. Those who wage war to occupy, colonize and oppress other people are the terrorists!"

At the present moment, sadly, when it comes to fighting terrorism and or aiding revolutionary struggles that is ideal, common sense for justice is not resolute everywhere or even in the breast of everyone. The reasons that organization or individual is fighting for is greatly clouded by all branches of today's Western media. Truthfully, the average individual out there in the West trying to maintain a living wage, pay the rent, and rise a family is not going to know the truth of the matter at hand if he or she relies on their governmental media for information. They must outsource like everybody else who is thirsty for the truth and knows that the revolution will not be televised. Scornfully, humanity has been haunted by Western nations` selfish imposed illusions of peace and misdirections of other peoples own liberation for benefit gain at the expense of their neighbors regardless of creeds or faiths for ages. Yes, we are all surrounded by illusions of imperialistic realities of their own existence. This is why the arrogant and the ignorant are greatly inclined to persecute that obdurate God-fearing person who dares to take a stand. Thus so, that ongoing

---

[50]   Quran 42:39-42

human barbarism ideals and civilize savagery demands is constantly tired of that modern novelty idea of justice and peace outside of themselves; slaves of their desires and self interest, they prefer to go about their daily and nightly business of sin by proxy and oppression for profit and gain. Save for a few howling human voices here and there barricaded in their bunkers discussing strategy for what to do next, those die hearted religious fundamentalists continue to struggle, plan and organized, lead, and inspire.

This is why, oh, humble reader, "injustice makes the world full of terrorist" because that common sense of why, the reasons those so-called terrorist are fighting us is greatly ignored to our peril. Oh, humble reader, you don't have to just take my word for it that "injustice makes the world full of terrorist." Just look at those countries that have to worry about terrorist haunting them and their own record of injustice towards others. This is how that imperialist air of innocents came to pass undeniably a long time ago.

So far, as I can reasonably make it clear to you, mankind has not lived in vain. This is more than a fight for generations to come. I agree Al-Qaeda does stands by a just cause and fights for the liberation from invaders and colonialist and is speaking truth to that illegitimate power that be here on this earth from a moral authority. Yet the tactics of this Islamic resistance does raises a question. But who am I but a descendant of African slaves brought to these Western shores in chains, trying to stay in touch with tomorrow have to say about how those who are oppress shall rightfully respond to affliction.

The Five Essential Pillars

Let's take a good hard look at those essential pillars of society that are the guardians of the Islamic faith. For those who walk by faith, and not only by sight, the answers are mightier than the questions. If you close your eyes and try to imagine those despot Muslim leaders making sure that the imams are vigilant when they speak about the serious issues of ihsan[51] and jihad, and how Islam is capable of solving the problems facing the ulama,[52] then you might as well keep them closed. Simply because, these ideas and faiths enacted would only remove themselves (despots) from power regardless of era.

Those great concepts of ihsan, jihad, and how the teachings of Islam that can benefit one's life are not how these secular, Muslim-in-name-only despots came to power! Rather, they came to power with the help of guns from abroad, by overthrow, by assassination, by oppression, by greed, by treason and by the weight of the corruption in the very hearts of their own people. So is it really proper to demand these Muslim-in-name-only despots to implement

---

[51] The Muslim responsibility to obtain perfection, or excellence in worship, such that Muslims try to worship Allah as if they see Him, and although they cannot see Him (due to the belief that Allah is not made of matter), they undoubtedly believe that He is constantly watching over them, and near by.

[52] Ulama: The Muslim Community

the essential Five Pillars, the key human resources which nourish and protect Muslim society?

I introduced these loaded questions and all their implications to a Salafi Saudi Sheikh in the Al Masjid Al Haram, in Mecca, back in the fall of 1999, after most of the Ramadan crowd had departed and flew home. He sized me up with one long glance, and after a pleasant glimmer of amusement subsided, hope and recognition crept into his face; he bid me to come forward. The sheikh knew I was no African, but from the West, and that I had been haunting the Al Masjid Al Haram for many years. Soon it was his turn to be daring. He sat down in the shade and blew his nose as daintily as possible, then looked over his right shoulder, and bid me once again to snuggle closer to him. In broken English and in perfect Arabic he said, "You cannot serve Allah and that temple of *mammon* together!"

The sheikh then looked up at the notes in my hand and took them into his own as I quietly sat before him on the cool white marble floor and thankfully I had the presence of mind to keep my mouth shut. I knew that he was the lonely planet Sheikh that the Muslim grape vine been talking about, a connoisseur of idealize warfare, whose writings and lectures are known, respected, and feared by the Salafi establishment in Saudi Arabia.

The five essential pillars are the following:

1. A national library
2. An independent and private Islamic university system
3. An independent and private hospital and medical centers
4. Independent and private research and development centers.
5. Independent and private Islamic banks

These essential pillars are paramount to an authentic Islamic society, as they espouse the tangibility of jihad in the hearts, minds, and soul war. In turn, they aid the people's search to know Allah's commonwealth, their world, and themselves. It is not in my interest to throw stones into the Islamic well that quenches my spiritual thirst. But those of you who have eyes to see, ears to hear, and have been to hell and back alive like I have, know that I am speaking the truth. I ask then: Is it wrong to ponder in our innermost hearts the sins we the believers, we who pray with our eyes open in prostration five times a day, have committed unto our Lord? But what of the ignorant, those who are secular in their worship, who pray once a week with their eyes closed, yet build libraries in their nations that are second-to-none in the Muslim world today? If I am postulating, then let your fingers surf the Internet and find the Library of Congress in Washington DC with its more than thirty million books and fifty-eight million manuscripts in total. Truly millions of my Muslim brothers and sisters with their families should visit the Library of Congress on their vacations, rather than to Disneyland, or Las Vegas, or New York City. For surely, they will see for themselves, what jihad really is! That the real sin is ignoring the Archangel Gabriel's mandate to Muhammad (sas) to "read." Even so, after more than 1,400 years, we remain the most illiterate amongst the monotheistic peoples on earth. I believe for those who are poor and oppressed libraries are the life-blood of liberty.

I defer to you without demur: is it wrong to ponder, in our deepest hearts, what sins we Muslims have committed unto our Lord? To ask why there is no independent private Islamic University in the Muslim World, one comparable in academic prestige to Catholic University of America, with an endowment totaling more than $148 million, or the Duke University (Methodist) with an endowment of more than $4.5 billion, or Fordham University (Jesuit) with an endowment of $450 million; or Notre Dame University (Catholic) with an endowment of over $6 billion? or Georgetown University in Washington DC (Catholic) with an endowment over $1 billion. We might also add Hebrew University of Jerusalem, whose endowment is purported to be in the hundreds of millions of dollars, to the aforementioned list of American institutions. The truth is, it is not in the best interest of a dictator to establish an academy of independent and free thinking in his country. So, call me delusional then when I attest that we have no independent private Islamic Universities comparable to those in the West is because hundreds of millions of Muslims-in-name-only ignore the call of the muezzin— *"Allah is the greatest!; Allah is the greatest!; I bear witness that there is no deity except Allah; I bear witness that Muhammad is the messenger of Allah; Come to prayer!; Come to Success! Allah is the greatest! Allah is the greatest! There is no deity except Allah!"* and then do not answer the call to pray after hearing the humble call to prayer, thereafter the whole community suffers!

Instead, they go freely about their worldly affairs and mind their own business. Oh, Sheikh, Allah is not blind to the fact that more money is being spent on cafés than on universities in Muslim countries. Is it that we are not grateful enough to Allah for his favors?[53]

---

[53] Quran ch.55

Just as the educational system is inferior in the Muslim world, so is the quality of medical care in spite of the more than $7 trillion earned from oil revenues in just the past four years. Every year, countless Muslims need to leave their home countries and go to a hospital in the West for medical treatment because the quality of medical treatment is far superior. Is there, in any Muslim country, a private or governmental hospital medical center comparable to Mount Sinai Hospital or Beth Israel Medical Center in New York, or the Mayo Clinic in Rochester, Minnesota? Why is more money being spent building five-star hotels to entertain wealthy guests than building five-star hospitals to aid their own ill citizens? Why is curing the diseases that afflict mankind being put solely into the hands of the non-believers around us throughout the world?

Prophet Muhammad (sas) said, *"You are not truly a believer of this faith if you do not want for your brother what you want for yourself."* Is not the sin that prevails is, live and let die for those who cannot afford to fly with a visa in hand to seek treatment.

So then, I ask: Who is the enemy?

Oh, honorable, and noble sheikh, who knows that every why has a therefore. Where, too, are the Silicon Valleys in the Muslim world? Why are there no research and development centers, comparable to those in the West, in our lands? For how long will the idea persist that the Muslim people are content to be consumers of foreign goods and products? Why are the people, encourage to blindly patronize foreign franchises and institutions? When will the goods from Muslim countries find equality in foreign markets? Why don't Muslims know the power of the boycott or the economic sanction and tools of international politics and trade that will help the development of character, discipline, self-reliance, and self-respect? Where are the funds for both the light and heavy industries which encourage a country's citizenry to emerge out of the twilight of unemployment? Where is that campaign that promotes pride and self-satisfaction in work performed by Muslims? Where are those Muslim stem-cell scientists, aerospace engineers and nanotechnologist along with their new ideas and inventions? Will not the Muslim economic miracle come from their hands? Or is the fate of an economic miracle coming from the hand of Allah not of these people, in fact, a mercy from Allah?

So perhaps it is the greed, the collective tolerance for the material and fashionable things from all levels of Muslim society that is the great sin, one that has produced the obvious consequences.

My dear and esteemed sheikh, it is truly the promise of profit, not the promise of the Prophet, that is motivating the great majority of banks in the Muslim world today. The Muslim public can no longer tolerate the clear conflicts of interest employed by those scoundrels in suit and tie that live amongst us. The underlying problem of this disease of usury is that the great majority of government and private banks in the Muslim world, although they know it is forbidden, are using the Western banking model of charging usury in all of their transactions. As a result, these institutions are wrongfully devouring their people's wealth and substance. They are likewise heedless to the warnings that the usurer will be deprived of Allah's blessings. Much the same, the leaders in these Muslim countries refuse to allow themselves to be admonished by the Quran, from both Allah and his Prophet, for not forbidding the practice of usury in all of their country's banking transactions—a simple enough ultimatum, it would seem, by one who is truly Allah-fearing, yet one that is impossible by one who is *munafiq* in faith. In fact, despite the warnings from believers, despite the trillions of dollars these Muslim countries have profited from their export of petroleum products, there is not one bank from any Muslim country that is currently rated as one of the top one hundred safest banks in the world!

Sheikh, as we both know, the bank—in a Muslim country, or in any country—is an institution which undoubtedly lies at the heart of a society's financial and economic security is an institution that both nourishes and protects the society. Since every bank operates under the laws of its land, it is therefore not permissible to use Western religion, culture, and law, and the secular systems that emanate from them, as the models for our own banks. This is a direct contradiction of Islam, as we are aware that the religion and culture of the West is based on the creed of separating religion from life and separating religion from the state, thus secularism! In contrast, Islam is based on the creed obliging that both life and state should be governed by the commands and prohibitions of the Quran, authentic hadith and Sharia law. The law of Islam is Sharia law; thus it is prohibited for any Muslim, leader or citizen, to introduce, practice, or implement any kufr law or system in a Muslim land.[54] For Allah ordered the believers to take everything from the prophet Muhammad (sas), and that every believer should stay away from what Allah has forbidden. Western culture has established itself on the basis of pure benefit and makes benefit the

---

[54] Quran 2:275–279

criterion of all actions. Islam, on the other hand, is established on a belief in Allah, which is the criteria for all actions in one's life, and it is this belief in Allah that governs all the actions and values according to his commands and prohibitions. Obedience, then, is the supreme and fundamental price.

Perhaps it is that, humble reader of this book whom may be more endowed than I to understand the present day strategy, and logic that has been presented before the Muslim ulema by the ruling dictators and authoritarian judiciaries, legislatures and executives branches of Muslim governments since the fall of the caliphate. Yes, you know that you only have one divine lord to call on for help, protection, strength, knowledge, guidance, and wisdom. You are surrounded by enemies near and far. You did not create yourself or your soul. You did not asked to be here on this earth, which is only an invitation to the truth. You do have needs, don't we all? That divine one who placed you here on this earth made it clear and known to you by way of prophet or prophets certain laws to live by so you will not go astray. You realize that you will die and be in that state like before you was born yet standing before your lord. You are the leader of your people, tribe, or family; so the stakes are higher. What to do? What do you do?

It is from Allah, is it not? The divine one that you invite curses on your national wealth by circulating usury in your banking institutions. Likewise, that same divine One consigns curses upon your soul by inviting profiteering kufr banking institutions into your sovereign lands, and to allow these same institutions of usury to trade the wealth of our divinely-granted national resources on the open market under a foreign kufr currency. So then, is it wrong for me to be suspicious, knowing that the Promised Land is for those who keep their promise to Allah and not condemn the hearts of those exploitative Muslim-in-name-only custodians?

Who then, I ask, is the true enemy near when you fail to heed the demands of the believers for private Islamic banks and Islamic banking laws in our lands? Who are the true betrayers of the Islamic public trust?

The lonely planet Saudi Sheikh looked up at me from my notes in his callus, dry, and austere hands. Nodded and smiled, looked over his left shoulder for a moment, bide me to be patient and snuggled even closer to me. Whispering in his inspiring and awakening voice said in Arabic, *"Do they not travel through the earth and see what was the end of those before them? They were even superior to them in strength, and in the traces they have left in the land: But Allah did call them to account for their sins, and none had they to defend them against Allah." "That was because there came to them their apostles with clear signs, but they rejected them: So Allah called them to account: for he is full of strength, strict in punishment"* (Quran 40:21-22).

Then the lonely planet Saudi sheikh leaned back against the tall white grayish pillar, and tugged lightly his gray beard in deep thought and sighed, setting his sight on the golden doors of the Kaba, letting the meaning of those words sink inward, then again whispered, "When we make wrong alliances and put our trust in fallible sources we suffer the consequences. This jihad struggle on the front lines is not your fight; our quite comfortable days on the front lines here in the Middle East will soon end." "So tell me soon about those five essential pillars and how they will be implemented while living behind the enemy's lines in the secular West?"

Then the Sheikh went on to say, "The five essential pillars that you write about Muhammad Dawud, rest upon five basic Islamic pillars of faith; without them the five essential pillars will not be able to stand. The problem our Muslim community faces regardless of nationality is rooted in the neglect of the five basic Islamic pillars of faith in the lives of its people. The first is the profession of the faith [shahada] Testifying that there is no God but Allah (saw) and Muhammad (sas) is his prophet. The second is offering the five daily prayers [salat]. The third is paying the alms-tax or welfare-tax [zakat]. The fourth is fasting [sawm] in the month of Ramadan from sun rise to sunset. The fifth is performing the pilgrimage to Mecca [hajj] if the Muslim person has the means."

The sheikh continued by saying, "At the present time many years into the Arab revolution, disturbing events that the whole world is witnessing, this is the true essence of what the Muslim world is demanding is simply the authentic implementation, by its own people, of these 'five pillars,' as well as the aforementioned notions of justice and civil liberties. The question remains: how strong is the willingness of the Muslim people to take that stand and fight for the true creed of their faith? In particular, will enough Arab Muslims commit through both social networks and the Quran to fueling that power of justice and liberation from despots and apostates that have repressed them for decades?"

Yet the sheikh was right, this is not my fight! I am a native from behind the enemy lines!

Equally important is that question in the back of my mind? What will the face and soul of the Muslim world look like after the tyrants are swept away by their own people? Have the conditions of the hearts of the Muslim people in the East sufficiently changed?[55] Yet again the sheikh is right; this is irrelevant to those of us who are on a jihad right here behind the enemy lines!

In my assessment, the hearts of the hundreds of millions of my Muslim brothers and sisters in Islam are awakening and engaging in an internal jihad over its core values, its own identity, and its rightful place on the world stage. In my assessment, the hearts of the Arab people are changing in the right direction in regard to who shall be sovereign over their lives. Ultimately, however, the main question to ask is if the Muslim world is willing to make those hard and bloody sacrifices, not only to achieve their political and economic goals. Will they also be submissive to Allah and be guided by his rightful methods in order to sustain this victory? Likewise, now that the Muslim people have lost their fear of tyrants, of kings, of living with nondivine sovereignty, and fear has been rightly and willingly handed back over to Allah, will they now be dutiful in establishing their creed of faith and essential pillars?

Nevertheless, if those Muslims in the East are not awakened and do the right thing, we Muslims living here in the West are the true vanguard of Islam and must do the right thing in spite of the times. What`s happening in the front lines is truly a problem for the unseen to handle and deal with. The sheikh is right, indeed, when it comes to jihad here behind enemies lines the Islamic resistance now must enact a plan to bring into life those five essential pillars here, without the neglect of those five basic Islamic pillars of our faith were we stand, and live, even such a society as this in the lands of the secular West!

---

[55] Quran 8:53,13:11

Allah`s Short List

Therefore listen not to the unbelievers, but strive against them with the utmost strenuousness, with the Quran

—(Quran 25:52).

Allah`s short list is getting shorter by the day. Yemen's President-for-life, Ali Abdullah Saleh, was exiled to Saudi Arabia and currently resides in America suffering from wounds of a June 3, 2011, bomb attack he received from his own people demanding justice, liberation and Islamic law. Now the Yemeni people are fighting his sons and his family clans, who are secretly supported by the American CIA, and other nearby Arab monarchs, each fearful of an Islamic Yemeni revolution which will transform the country into a Sunni Islamic version of Shiite-revolution Iran. The Yemeni people are also fighting against American, British and Arab Gulf state agents who has violated their sovereignty with the use of drones and who are also undermining their human rights with the use of torture. No wonder so many Shiite brothers from Iran are coming full force to the aid of the Yemeni Sunni resistance fighters regardless of their Muslim school of thought!

Similarly in Bahrain, King Hamad ibn Al-Khalifa planted the kiss of death upon himself by calling into his country troops from Saudi Arabia and the United Arab Emirates! By this action he was attempting to avoid the sectarian problems he'd created by his own hand, and in turn he initiated a brutal and bloody crackdown on native Muslim peaceful protesters and opposition Shiite organization movements.

His rule will not last long, I believe; Allah is neither blind nor deaf to those who are unjust. These Muslim kings, who heed neither the Quran nor the dustbins of history, they have no advantage over any boy who cannot read them or value them.[56] *"How many generations have we destroyed after Noah? And enough is thy lord to note and see the sins of his servants. If any do wish for the transitory things of this life, we readily grant them-such things as we will, to such persons as will: in the end have we provided hell for them: they will burn therein, disgraced and rejected"* (Quran 17:17-18). Likewise, that naval base that harbors the United States Fifth Fleet must forever leave Bahrain and never return. Yet this is what these faithless despotic Sunni leaders in the Gulf States fear the most, to stand on their own faith for protection. That question on the naval base must be answered like why would a Muslim state allow a foreign power to build such a base on their land in the first place? It would not be reciprocal.

The next bitter farewell mythology of these Presidents-for-life on Allah's short list is Syria's Bashar Al-Assad, a despot willing to bomb every major city of his own country just to avoid defeat in an open and fair election he could not possibly lose. This is because of the integrity of the hearts of the people therein in regards to justice. Rather than have, multi-town hall meeting with his own countrymen and resolve their disputes with each other with honor and fear of Allah (swa), have a fair election to decide who will be the legitimate leader of the people in their country and count the votes himself with public transparency to decide who had won, knowing that his opposition is greatly fragmented with many different untested opponents, on how to govern the country with justice! There is no doubt in my mind and heart he would have won an open and fair election back in January 2011, it would had been an election that`s his to lose! What a bitter irony, this was at that point in time; now he has order his secret police to shoot peaceful protesters in the streets on sight and fill mass graves with their dead bodies. This is the only road back from the calamity that faces him so his heart believes. Assad tortures and "disappears" his enemies, both ignoring worldwide sanctions and denying, to any extent, the actions of his regime, if that is what it will take for him to hold onto power in Syria then so be it so his heart believes. No less disturbing is the fact that many members of the Syrian military are under no illusions that the situation in the country cannot be resolved by military means or the full weight of the secret police. It`s just that there is no retirement plan for them other than death if President for

---

[56] Quran 17:17-18

life Assad and his regime should fail, this they are fully aware of. Simply because there is too much blood and brutality on the ground, thus the calls for blood vendetta against the Assad regime cannot be paid with gold or surrender.

Even with the aid of Hezbollah fighters, the Russian ground-to-air missiles and arms as well as poison gas, Iranian weapons and trainers all is lost for President Assad and his regime. This is a civil war Assad can't win simply because it is becoming a sectarian religious civil war in which case tens of thousands of Sunni Muslims from Iraq with ax to grind is pouring in to aid their Sunni Muslim people in Syria who are a majority. By Allah, I believe this is a historic ironical downfall, of a Shiite despot ruling over his Sunni Muslim people because of his injustice, like the downfall of Saddam Hussein an Iraqi Sunni despot ruling over his Shiite Muslim people who were a majority because of his injustice next door.

One by one the regime's notorious secret police headquarters in Aleppo and Damascus as well as other places even the one that imprisoned and abused me back in July 2009, are being blown up by the free Syrian resistance fighters, truly all praise is due to Allah. The worry, however, within the ranks of the military, merchants and those sell-out religious imams who choose to remain silent about the ongoing atrocities, is the looming reality of sectarianism and outright civil war like what happen in Lebanon, if the people's demands for human rights, liberation, and justice continue to be ignored after Bashar Al-Assad and his followers are removed from power.

Either way that Sunni-Salafi up rising is now a war of growing attrition that is now expanding, a civil war which is gaining ground like the Nusra Front who's fundamental leader is Abu Bakr Al-Baghdadi, Al-Tawhid Brigade under Mohannad Al—Najjar and The Islamic State in Iraq and Syria org. may Allah bless them all. Terror is not a novel life style there in Syria, I believe, yet that political, religious culture of violence still remains if all other voices and means fail!

In Algeria, perhaps in response to the situations in Yemen, Bahrain, and Syria, another president-for-life, the renowned authoritarian Abdelaziz Boutefika, has seemingly promised a host of constitutional reforms in the name of justice and human rights. He and his entrenched governing cronies are the living example of denial of what Sheikh Zayed bin Sultan Al-Nahyan that endowed fundamentalist from the United Arab Emirates, meant when he said, "Arab blood is more important than oil." Similar to the words of truth spoken by that black American fundamentalist, Mr. Frederick Douglass when he said,

"Power concedes nothing without demand." It never has and never will. Show me the exact amount of wrong and injustices that are visited upon a person and I will show you the exact amount of words endured by these people." Boutefika's iron grip in Algeria follows on the heels of his Arab Gulf friends, as he bribes, raises the pay of governmental workers, and stabilizes the price of bread and food, to both forestall unrest and head off this Arab spring revolution that surrounds him. As Muslims, we must have true patience even with these despots.[57]

If indeed, mountains of justice were to blossom in the Muslim world because of the efforts of the Arab Spring, what will the Muslim people do with it now that they have a locomotive called Islam to drive it? In truth, once they too have justice in their lands, I believe they will do the same—or perhaps even more—than the Christians and Jews. An end to institutionalized discrimination and repression of Sunni, Shiite, Sufi Muslims, as well as other minority groups in Muslim lands, and an end to racism between Arab Muslims and African Muslims, Arab Muslims and Persian Muslims, Asian Muslims and non-Asian Muslims, would herald a new chapter in social justice in the Muslim world. Not only will the non-Muslim world witness the emergence of a true genie from the bottle offering wishes to sincere prayers, they will also come to see the ascent of a noble race of people pulling itself out of the mire of hate, self-genocide, and crimes against humanity. Only then do I believe that America, Europe, Russia, China and the rest of the non-Muslim would start taking Islam more seriously. The golden rule says, "No one respects anyone until they respect themselves"; as such, a chorus of events amongst the world's Muslim countries would signify a great historic achievement of human faith and a triumph of freedom and justice that hasn't been seen on Earth since the time when Omar ibn Al-Khattab and Khalid ibn Al-Walid were united together. [58]

The idea of a Pan-Islamic community whereby any Muslim citizen can travel freely, without a visa, to and within any Muslim country, and once there have all the inalienable rights granted unto him or her by

---

[57]   Quran 18:68

[58]   Omar ibn Al-Khattab is a Theocrat- a person who governs as a representative of Allah and head of the Islamic ecclesiastical authorities. Khalid ibn Al-Walid is a Muslim civil servant-general, the protector of that Islamic Theocracy; who submits to the will of the theocrat that abides by the laws of Islam.

sovereign Allah, would indeed force the non-Muslim world to take Islam seriously. For when the Muslim people finally take themselves seriously on the world stage, this idea of a Pan-Islamic reality whereby all its citizens experience justice, freedom, and human rights, the power within, and without, will be greater than any weapon—be it a knife, a rifle, or an atom bombs—in hand for its defense, insha Allah. The down to earth significance idea of a Pan-Islamic community is continents of fulfill dreams for the people therein. The prospect of free travel between citizens thereof without visas opens the door to free trade between nations like the European Union. That Pan-Islamic community will reach from Morocco Northwestern Africa to Indonesia Southeastern Asia. Thereby uplifting the social and economical potential in more than two and a half billion people, Muslims as well as their non Muslims neighbors investing more with each other and develop and grow together because of mutual interest. African and Asian nations does not need Europe and American nations to survive, they need more trust and trade with each other to survive.

Today, despite the Arab spring, the main rival schools of thought in Islam—the Sunni and the Shiite branches—are now contending openly for spiritual, social, political and economic dominance in the Muslim world. They both wish to get and to stay on Allah's short list, but clearly it has been the Shiite Muslims—most notably in Iran, Lebanon and Iraq who have taken the lead in liberating their people from domestic puppet tyrants and from foreign *kufr* occupation. The establishment of a true Islamic theocracy in Iran is the by-product of the rich heritage of the Iranian Revolution. They the honorable Shiite fundamentalist Ayatollah Seyyed Ali Khamenei and the President of Iran Mahmoud Ahmadinejad are winning the battle of change, justice, governorship and ideas in the Muslim world. In achieving *Vilayat-El Faqh*, or guardianship of the jurists, the revolution has worked to fight against political, economic, and moral corruption in their lands, and has achieved *Equaniny Muslimie*.[59] Which is their other revolutionary foreign vanguard working in cohesion with other honorable black turbaned Shiite fundamentalist like the Grand Ayatollah Sayid Ali Al-Husayni Sistani of Iraq who refused to have a dialogue or speak with American or Western occupiers in Iraq since the invasion of his country by them in March 19, 2003. It is not to me, a surprise that millions of Muslims in the Middle East in the Shiite world branch has

---

[59]   "Want for your brother want you want for yourself."

awakened! That Qum in Iran and Najaf in Iraq are not only burning the night oil together but also politically rooting out surgery together.

Only the very naïve today believe that the Grand Ayatollah Sayid Ali Al-Husayni Sistani of Iraq and the Ayatollah Seyyed Ali Khamenei from Iran are under any illusions. They are aware that more than 2.5 million barrels of oil a-day that goes both to supply American, and NATO armies in Afghanistan, and send also to American, U.K. and European ports at subsidized prices. It is by tactical consent that Iraq's oil revenues are going to the reconstruction funds and to the western civil engineers that still live in the country and who are still protected, at great cost, by private western mercenaries. Understandably, because of Allah's short list, President Obama had to leave Iraq with his troops without an iron clad-deal contract that the exit of American troops does not mean that the Grand Ayatollah Sayid Ali Al-Husayni Sistani will not pull the plug on their oil shipments to their armies in Kuwait and Afghanistan, as well as to the U.S. Fifth fleet navy base in Bahrain and more importantly to American, U.K. and NATO, their countries ports at reduced current prices! The end of American troops on Iraq soil means that Iraq has its sovereignty back, and all this talk about American troops being needed to train Iraqi troops is just worthless talk to keep Iraq in the western orbit, a prospect doomed to failure.

Grand Ayatollah Sistani will not compromise his ideology nor antagonize his key Islamic Shiite coalition partners; neither does the Grand Ayatollah Sistani suffer from amnesia. He and his associates remember clearly those who were Saddam Hussein's patrons: the Western political financiers and Western arms merchants, as well as those Sunni Arab dictators and kings who'd underwritten Iraq's war effort against Iran by channeling billions of dollars to Saddam Hussein's Ba'athist regime, consciously knowing that the foot soldiers on both sides will be mostly Shiites killing Shiites! Nor have Iraqi Shiites forgotten when the American government failed (or betrayed) them after the Gulf War in 1990 by not implementing a no-fly zone over the Shiite area of southern Iraq, as they had done in the north for the Kurds. As a result, tens of thousands were killed in that rebellion, so where was the help from the West when the Shiite world needed it most?

Knowing that America needs oil to sustain its war efforts in Afghanistan, Iranian spies convinced American Iraqi puppets to exhort the fumbling American President George W. Bush to invade Iraq, get rid of Saddam Hussein, and place secular American puppets in charge of Iraq, a situation that would allow the American government access to all the oil it needed in both their war efforts in Afghanistan and

Iraq, and at home. That Operation Shock and Awe means America would now have another military base in the Middle East, one that bordered Iran and Syria. But the truth oh, humble reader, is Western greed for oil and power led to the liberation of a people who really hated them! There was no parade in downtown Bagdad for those Western armies from day one until December 14, 2011, when American forces left Iraq, in spite of the Western media hype.

In fact, the American invasion of Iraq can be described, most accurately, as a merciless mirage given to the West by those Iranian rulers who sought not revenge for the wrongs that was done to Muslims in Iraq and Iran since October 1977, but justice by Allah.

In the end, on the first day of Eid Ahah, December 30, 2006, President-for-life Saddam Hussein, a Sunni Muslim, by the will of Allah`s short list and the Iraqi Shiite majority, paid his debt at the end of a hangman`s noose for almost thirty years of despotic rule. Five years later, on December 14, 2011, U.S. President Barack Hussein Obama paid the American military and political fiasco debt at the end of the road out of Iraq by the will of Allah`s short list, and the will of the Shiite majority people because of the oppression that was imposed on them for more than fifty years of imperialist rule.

This was also the end, oh, humble reader, to the future of Western corporate oil contract plans into Iraq by the International Tax and Investment Center who no longer will they have unimpeded access into Iraq`s huge oil fields. Now because of the change in the political weather today (revenge) and the close relationship developing between Iraq and Iran (Shiite-Arabs/Shiite-Persians), the Grand Ayatollah Sistani has given his blessings for Iran to pump it`s oil through Iraq`s pipes superseding Western embargo threats against them. Also a regional summit of mutual cohesion has bear fruit in which Prime Minister Nouri Al-Maliki give China`s SINOPEC (China Petroleum and Chemical Corporation) greater access to their huge oil fields along with newer bigger contracts simply because China is more interested in energy to fuel its economy than profits to enrich its oil giants, as well as their known record of non involvement of their host`s political affairs. Allah knows best!

Indeed, Allah`s short list is getting shorter! Now it is a little late in the game in the West's war on terror and its hearts and minds war to worry about anticorruption ideals in Afghanistan, to worry about where American taxpayer money is going and that "show us the poppy fields" means that you are as lost as those Bible-toting missionaries building schools and Western engineers building roads and bridges over there. Afghanistan's Western puppet ruler, Hamid Karzai, who used to be a spy for the CIA and a consultant to the American UNOCAL corporation and who was never elected by his peers, has long realized that he is not the master of policy in his country, but the true slave of uncontrollable events both inside and beyond his country's borders. So, when news reached Karzai that Holy Qurans had been burned by American soldiers at the Bagram Air Force Base, a place long notorious for the torture and murder of prisoners of war by coalition forces, it is of no surprise that he said, "They claim they burned Qurans by mistake, but really those were Satanic acts that will never be forgiven by apologies." Just days later, after a massacre of sixteen Afghan men, women, and children by an American soldier, Sgt. Robert Bales, Karzai then announced to a world audience, "This was not the first incident, indeed it was the hundredth, the two hundredth, and five hundredth incidents. The Americans in Afghanistan are demons."

President-for-life Hamid Karzai, the appointed interim leader by the West, has been forced to endure a marathon of extended and merciless siege against him by the patient resilience of the Taliban and other Islamic resistance fighters, one that will only end in his expulsion from Afghanistan or his death, insha Allah.

So much for the longest war in America's history! A war that has seen American and coalition forces kill more civilians than their enemy Al-Qaeda, Taliban, and other Islamic resistance fighters put together! A war in which American soldiers urinate on their dead enemies; a war in which American and Western trainers don't trust Afghanistan soldiers that they are teaching for fear of a bullet in the back of the head or a "love you so much hug" from a so called suicide bomber. A war whose reality is a no-win scenario for President Obama or that President-for-life Karzai and his dysfunctional regime that depends on hundreds of billions of dollars of U.S. aid, and as well as profits almost exclusively from opium production and bribes. The truth is, only a fool believes that Karzai, the corrupt and Western-appointed president of Afghanistan, will not be found hanging from a traffic light in downtown Kabul if he wishes to remain in Afghanistan as president for life after American and NATO forces leave Afghanistan in 2014. Just like his Communist predecessor before him . . . Dr. Najibullah Ahmadzai, hanging in Ariana square, Kabul.

I'd like to be frank for a few more moments on this matter called Operation Enduring Freedom, that is, this campaign of war which cannot be sustained without Western aid, weapons, and the sacrifice of countless lives for the sake of a corrupt Afghan government that will not stand and fight on its own! The only real traffic on this Afghanistan road from Kandahar to Kabul is those Islamic ideas of that other jihadi fundamentalist Mohammed (Mullah) Omar, the spiritual leader of the Taliban commander of the faithful, may Allah bless and guide them all. I don`t care who you are or what your beliefs are; you just are not going to give 100 percent in a fight once it is known that fraud and lies is in your leadership that you are fighting for! Just ask Ahmad Wali Karzai, the half-brother of President Hamid Karzai; General Mohammad Daud Daud, the former top counter-narcotics official in the Afghan government; former Afghan president Burhanuddin Rabbani, a former Afghan president; Mullah Arsala Rahmani, a member of the High Peace Council; or Jan Mohammad Khan, special political adviser to the present Afghanistan President. In this hearts, minds, and soul war, progress is limited only by one's own faith and imagination; likewise, the Taliban, Al-Qaeda and the true Islamic resistance, the Mujahideen, are not fighting in order to accommodate the enemies of Islam. They are fighting to be victorious against the enemies of Islam, in whatever form they may take. For example, Ahmad Shah Masud, the former leader of the "Northern Alliance" who was assassinated on September 9, 2001, advocated for a democratic form of government in Afghanistan after President M. Najibullah Ahmadzai was overthrown and hanged. His error in judgment and faith is that democracy, at its core, denies the very sovereignty of Allah, much like the Communist Russians he'd fought against denied the very existence of Allah. In truth, Mr. Masud had a problem in truly understanding aqeeda, or "purity of faith." The very fact that Mr. Masud had turned his weapons against the Taliban and other Islamic resistance fighters—in other words, his own Muslim brothers who'd fought with him against the Russians invaders—he committed an act of treason unto Islam, especially since his principle reason for fighting his former comrades-in-arms was so that a future Afghan government would be democratic in its nature, one where every tribe would have equal rights and sovereignty will be placed in the hands of a tribal leader, much to the delight of the Western secular governments who were his sponsors!

Over the course of my studies, I have learned from my teachers in Saudi Arabia, *hum du Allah*, that there is no substitute for Shariah law for all the Muslim peoples of this earth.[60] *"As to those who are rebellious and wicked, their abode will be the fire: every time they wish to get away there*

---

[60]   Quran 32:20-22

from, they will be forced there into, and it will be said to them: "Taste ye the penalty of the fire, the which ye were wont to reject as false." "And indeed we will make them taste of the penalty of this life prior to the supreme penalty, in order that they may (repent) and return." "And who does more wrong than one to whom are recited the signs of his Lord, and who then turns away there from? Verily from those who transgress we shall exact (due) retribution" (Quran 32:20-22). That to invite foreign ideas, ideals and soldiers into Muslim lands on the belief that these modern viewpoints will enhance the livelihood of the people, even if this means spilling the blood of those who are Allah—fearing, is grossly misguided. With it comes, the excuse, mostly from those Muslim-in-name-only leaders, that Islam is not sufficient enough to neither provide justice and security for the minorities in Muslim lands, nor will Islam help keep the peace. In the end, though, these provocateurs are true devil's advocates, in that the end of the day they are advocating the idea of—Democracy or Communism—thus justifies the means: murder or rebellion.

The Emancipation

It may be that Allah will grant love and (friendship) between you and those whom ye (now) hold as enemies. For Allah has power over all things; And Allah is often forgiving, most merciful. Allah forbids you not, with regard to those who fight you not for (your) faith nor drive you out of your homes, from dealing kindly and justly with them: For Allah loves those who are just. Allah only forbids you, with regard to those who fight you for (your) faith, and drive you out of your homes, and support (others) in driving you out, from turning to them (for friendship and protection). It is such as turn to them (in these circumstances), that do wrong.

—Quran 60:7-9

Again, we must pause here because what needs to be said must be understood clearly—not just for those who disagree but also for those who are ignorant. Yes, hum du Allah that my Lord had made me a Jihad Salafi Muslim, and I thank Allah for all my teachers, especially my parents. I learned from my Salafi Muslim teachers at Mecca University in Saudi Arabia that you do not kill outright your leaders, even if they oppress you. I had first heard of this in the Al Haram in Mecca, but I was also made aware of this by many of my teachers and fellow scholars that the Shiite branch of Islam has different interpretation and opinions of Prophet Muhammad (sas) and follow these in

185

accordance their own book of *Hadiths*[61]. In the case of a ruler who commits murder, for Shiites the sentence is death, or imprisonment, or impeachment and/or exile (the shah of Iran Mohammad Reza Pahlavi, 1979). And (President—for—Life Saddam Hussein of Iraq, 2006). We Sunni Muslims can impeach or imprisonment or exile our leaders but have yet to have a fair trial with justice upon our leaders, even once found guilty, put them to death for the crimes of murder or treason (President for life of Egypt-Hosni Mubarak 2011).

Similarly, I must confess that not every citizen, after experiencing years of oppression in their land and witnessing the murder of family members and countless neighbors, will not always be so levelheaded and behave the way that is prescribed by their own law. I too must also confess that my forefathers living in the Americas, those who first came to these shores enslaved with no rights and remained oppressed for centuries, suffered great oppression and witness murder. Violence does beget violence, hate does beget hate, and revenge does beget revenge. But I, like my forefathers, are aware that Allah is truly merciful to those who are patient under hardship. During the time of slavery, not once did one of us in the millions ever attempt to kill any leader in Congress or Senate or any President of the United States, from George Washington to James Buchanan, thou many American presidents, senators, and congressional representatives were African-American slave owners themselves! By this time we'd been enslaved for nearly three centuries. Even in 1863, after Abraham Lincoln's Emancipation Proclamation, millions of my African-American brothers and sisters still had no rights in this land. For another hundred years after our "emancipation," we were still murdered, lynched, raped, burned, robbed and denied human rights, equal rights, justice, and due process of law, up until the Civil Rights Act became law in 1964. All of this in spite of the fact that a great majority of us, at the time of our oppression, were of the Christian faith like our masters given unto my ancestors by their masters! Yet we remained patient, and we overcame, and now a man of African descent, President Barack Obama, and his wife, the great-great granddaughter of oppress slaves, reside in the White House. Numerous members of the United States Congress are also African-American. More than four hundred years of patience has its rewards, and if asked, most American citizens, black, or white or Asian look favorably at our centuries of patience under oppression, and innately understand that justice does beget peace.

---

61   Nahjul Balagha, Speech #37

To have patience, even with a holocaust in your people's history, is a true jihad. But the horrors of a holocaust upon a people can likewise be undone by those of later generations who are only interested in the hearts of the oppressed once they gain their liberty. However, I, Muhammad Dawud, a Muslim African American, the great-great grandson of slaves here in Americas, differ from President Barack Obama, whose father came to this country as a free man and whose ancestors were never enslaved here in the Americas. President Obama's family history did not suffer a holocaust like the great majority of African Americans, yet he is an African American who understands that a great crime against humanity was perpetrated onto us as a people. In fact, it is difficult these days to imagine anyone drafting a law that denies the atrocities of slavery here in the West, for an abundance of evidence exists to support it. The prospect of anyone today or even tomorrow drafting a law that would criminalize a person who would deny the holocaust the genocide slavery of what happened to the early African Americans here in the Western world is imprudent. What might still be appraise, however, is how we as a people never became fixated on exacting revenge, but instead became the trumpeters of justice both here at home and abroad. In fact, once freed, we as a people never enslaved nor oppressed anyone here in America or anywhere else, and our leaders have always stood for truth and justice in spite of the actions of our former slave masters' descendants.

Therefore, it is my assessment and the assessment of many of my African American leaders like Dr. Ralph J. Bunche, that reconciliation fundamentalist who was awarded the Nobel Peace Prize in 1950 for his mediation in Palestine and Israel, the first African American in history to be given such an honor. In Dr. Bunche's own words, "Hearts are the strongest when they beat in response to noble ideals." In addition, "We must fight as a race for everything that makes for a better country and a better world. We are dreaming idiots and trusting fools to do anything less."

Why am I bringing Dr. Ralph J. Bunche words front and center into your world? Because, oh, humble reader, Dr. Ralph J. Bunche knew that change must start first within the hearts of the people; they the disputants themselves must want justice and peace with their neighbors unconditionally. He knew that desire for justice outside of themselves is the only way peace can be sustained for all. Yes, he did obtained signatures on armistice agreements between Israel and the Arab Muslim States in 1949. However, that unwillingness to want for others what you want for yourself in terms of justice undermined the spirit of the armistice between the Hebrew and the Arab (Muslim-Christian) people living in the Promise Land, resulting in unnecessary wars of arrogance, greed and selfishness in spite of them both having holy books from the same author, sadly till this very day!

This is our fundamental perception and viewpoint of the true reality on the ground today: "Israel at the present cannot say they are far from a generalization of the true nature of the hearts of the Hebrew people living in the Promise Land, because that golden rule applies to everyone. People deserve the government they get." For anyone to cite that the political parties in Israel are evenly divided over the main contested issues of the Palestinian demands for rights and independence, is because of the disputes between the "religious orthodox Jews", and the so-called secularist modern Jews; that this is why there is no peace or justice in the Promise Land is very naïve and is an outright lie.

For a surety it is better to ascribe the conditions and state of the hearts of the overall Hebrew people living therein. Where is that demand for peace and justice outside of themselves from their own hearts for others and their neighbors as if their very own lives depends on it? That is the fundamental question.

As we consider this. It is truly perplexing as well as frightful to me that that nation of Hebrew people whom I have no doubt also suffered a genocidal holocaust has not, as gratitude to their Lord, become the champions of human rights, equal rights, justice, and due process of law for all the people in the Middle East living in the Promise Land! In fact, it seems that their pursuit of civil and social liberties is directed only for themselves, in spite of the mercy of Jehovah ultimately had upon them when facing the oppression of an "enemy near," that Christian-in-name-only European despot Adolph Hitler. Have their hearts changed that much since their liberation from those concentration camps in 1945? It was not the Muslims, or the Arabs that expelled them from Jerusalem and destroyed their temples in the Promised Land almost two thousand years ago, or oppressed them and murdered them in the millions in Europe. And yet, how can a nation of people in whose recent memory lies those Nazi concentration camps, a people who were then they believed delivered by their Lord back home to the Promised Land, and afterward, they force another nation of people living in the same land to live in refugee camps by force of arms given to them from aboard. Broadly speaking I am thunderstruck, such arrogance, everyone with ringside tickets in the Middle East got another debut of above us only sky. This apparently was because the hearts, minds and souls of the Hebrew people could not find a way to reconciliation and justice with their own neighbors within the Promise Land?[62] *"You shall not let molest or oppress an alien, for you were once aliens yourselves in the land of Egypt"* (Ex.22:20). Also, is not the 'Tenth': *"You shall not covet your neighbor's house. You shall not covet your neighbor's wife, nor his male or female slave, nor his ox or ass, nor anything else that belongs to him."* 'Ninth': *"You shall not bear false witness against your neighbor."* 'Eighth': *"You shall not steal."* and the 'sixth Commandment': *"You shall not murder."* given unto the Hebrews from Prophet Moses valid anymore?[63] (Ex. 20:13, 15-17) Or does the end of that journey back to the Promise Land justify the means. That landscape idea of a monotheist faith never looked so disturbing and so unpromisingly unbelievable as now.

It's, what happen to that redeeming Israeli fundamentalist, Yitzhak Rabin, a Noble Peace Prize winner and prime minister of Israel, who felt the gun at his back before the bullets on November 4,1995. Who did believe in those aforementioned commandments and had the audacity of faith to make peace with his enemies, as well as had the desire to share both the Promised Land and Jerusalem with his half-brothers, that tribe of Ishmael, and that he paid for it in full with his life blood, which comes to front and center stage. We are obliged to remind our readers of this historical betrayal of trust within the ranks of the Hebrew community living in the "Promise Land" because this betrayal has affected the entire monotheistic community that was sincerely seeking justice and peace in the region. What did that Hebrew nation of people who were murdered, and oppressed in Europe do, Jehovah, in regards to amends afterward his murder by his own people? This is what really matters in this sinful world in search of justice in the eyes of the concerned monotheist fundamentalist beholders. We know all that talk of peace by these present day Hebrew leaders living in Israel is just only talk and distractions. I really do wish to see more action of those 'Hebrew grass root masses' out there with more concern for justice for others and those who claim to desire peace to act sincerely on what they say to the world stage.

I, a descendant of those who were oppressed and experienced a holocaust, I bear witness that the holocaust of a people can be undone by those who are only interested in the hearts of the oppressed after they have gain their liberty! For example, what if, after the American Civil War, in 1865, the freed slaves had decided in the millions to go

---

[62]   Ex. 22:20
[63]   Ex. 20:1-17

back home to Africa, the land of our "roots," because in spite of being free the hatred and oppression that lie at the heart of slavery here in America remained! Wars do not end racism—only justice does—and it was self-evident then that justice was not to be part of the American landscape for a long time to come. However, had our descendants embarked on an exodus back to our African homelands, back to our roots and our ancestors of old, to lands from which they were forcibly taken away from by their own murderous African neighbors in league with a European "enemy far" who was interested solely in profit and gain. Would then that brand of crusade be justified even if reclaiming these ancestral lands and property required force of arms and lead to the bloodshed of those who refused to leave the disputed territory of our ancestors? We believe our leaders and people at the time would say no! Why? Simply because the end does not justify the means, which is another thoughtful golden rule one cannot wish away regardless of era.

Alas, oh, humble reader, the reason to such a hard spiritual question and answer rest with, "Did not the hearts of those ex-slaves change for the good that was oppressed and murdered by their masters coming from afar have good gratitude towards their Lord?" Because that radical transformation of the heart is dear in the eye of the beholder. Likewise, I believe, that if it was our destiny to go back to Africa in mass after the emancipation here in America, we would have become the true champions of human rights, equal rights, justice, and due process of law, as well the leaders of non-violent revolution for all Africans to see and be inspired by. For we as a people would have remembered what it was like to be enslaved and oppress as our hearts had indeed changed for the good; the cries of mercy from human lips would never be deemed irrelevant to our ears and hearts, for "The Promised Land is for those who keep their promise to Jehovah—Allah" is true and enshrined!

Forthrightly, otherwise, we African Americans would be despised and hated by our African neighbors therein who would rightly view us returning Africans as heartless ex-slaves that was oppress who has now returned home to Africa demanding lands, property, rights and revenge!

"See, I am sending an angel before you, to guard you on the way and bring you to a place I have prepared. Be attentive to him and heed his voice. Do not rebel against him for he will not forgive you your sin. My authority resides in him. If you heed his voice and carry out all I tell you, I will be an enemy to your enemies and a foe to your foe" (Ex. 23:20-33).

"Here, then, said the lord, is the covenant I will make. Before the eyes of all your people I will work such marvels as have never been wrought in any nation anywhere on earth, so that this people among whom you live way see how awe-inspiring are the deeds which I, the Lord, will do at your side. But you, on your part, must keep the commandments I am giving you today" (Ex. 34:*10-16*).

"So, Moses returned to his people in a state of indignation and sorrow. He said: "Oh my people! Did not your lord made a handsome promise to you? Did then the promise seem to you long in coming? Or did ye desire that wrath should descend from your lord on you, and so ye broke your promise to me?" (Quran 20:85).

Alas, we as a people did not embark by the millions back to Africa but stayed right here in America and the West and became champions of civil and social liberties for all. Yet this has not been the example followed by our Hebrew brothers and sisters who had been oppress in Europe. Woe, then, to those who lose their immunity unto their enemies from their divine lord and forget or turn away from their promise to their one and only divine Lord!

Yet, it is not my interest to demonize a nation of people who have suffered. In the end, however, what truly counts is what a community of people—or, in this case, what a nation of people says and does, not what those who are oppressed think of themselves. For these same people who had suffered, under the pharaoh's oppression in Egypt, at the hands of the Babylonians in Iraq, at the hands of the Romans in Israel, at the hands of the Nazis in Europe, had their prayers answered and came to live on each occasion in the Promised Land. And each time, in my assessment, they became a great nation of people until they turned away from their promise unto their lord while living in the land divinely delivered to them and within a land that they been expelled into. Considering this, I provide you fair warning when you ask any man, "Where have you come from?" And the reply is "The Promised Land of my one and only divine Lord." Because the next fundamental question, for those who fear that one and only divine Lord, inevitably is "What is the condition of thy heart?"[64] [65]

---

[64]   Isa. 42:18-25, 56:1-8; Jer.4:14-31, 7:1-33; Ezek. 5:1-17, 6:1-14, 7:1-27; Mal. 3:16-17, Mal. 4:1-6

[65]   Quran 20:80-81,86

This is no fairy tale world that we all live in; for millennia, in fact, oppression has crippled humanity. It's only when people open their eyes to history that they grasp the rules of hope and get busy living the message of justice. Few can imagine seeing more than a third of their population murdered and not undergo a change of heart in regard to their neighbors and their Lord. Therefore, when a nation of beholden people, one who has suffered greatly, by the actions of an oppressor because of their own hearts, has undergone no change of heart in regards to justice, then it is not difficult to understand the sentiments of that hard-core Shiite fundamentalist President Mahmoud Ahmadinejad when he said, "Israel is not a legitimate entity and has no right to exist." Or when he proclaimed that "The accounts of the Jewish holocaust are myths." Or when that daring Iranian fundamentalist supreme leader, Ayatollah Seyyed Ali Khamenei, said: "This regime that is occupying Qods [Jerusalem] must be eliminated from the pages of history." In truth, the list of what both Muslims and non-Muslim have said about the oppression of the Palestine people by Israel cannot be comprised in this book simply because there is not enough room to list the sins of this apartheid regime.

Since its independence from Great Britain in 1948, virtually every nation on earth, on multiple occasions, has condemned the State of Israel for violating the human rights, equal rights, justice, and due process of law of their own neighbors: the Palestine people, the Jordanian people, the Syrian people and the Lebanese peoples. Likewise, it is shameful but not surprising the number of times America and Europe has vetoed UN resolutions brought by other third-world nations condemning the oppressive actions of Israel against the Palestine people and their neighbors.

However, being truthful does not favor those who sit and assume that Muslims have friends in Europe, oh, humble reader. There are many people who believe till this day that most Western European countries most notably Italy, Germany, Poland, France, and the Scandinavian countries are most typically in support the Palestinians and their intifada. Nevertheless, this vocal support is frankly just empty political rhetoric designed to conceal the whereabouts of their own sinful hearts in not having to worry about the Jewish problem in Europe anymore. The fact is, there is no call for international trade boycott and blockade of Israeli companies and goods from the so-called caring and humane European Union because of Israel's shameful inhuman acts of the past and present. Facing the dire economic realities the European Union did not choose the high moral ground of justice regardless of the price or profit when the issues are financial interest versus moral integrity! This fact shamefully is as well as there is no call for this same international trade boycott and blockade on Israel from these soul-out Arab leaders in the region for the same reasons which is greed.

As a religious man who wishes to be sincere to his Lord, I understand the similarities, in both spirit and campaign, between Zionism and hajj. In fact, the basic meaning of each is "homecoming"; as I came to better understand the meaning of Zionism and Hajj, I shared these religious ideas with young Jewish observers back in the spring of 2000 when I visited Hebrew University in Jerusalem. There I walked and talked with a number of rabbis and Jewish students, each of whom seemed amazed that Allah did indeed give forth, by way of Prophet Muhammad (sas), the rules to Hajj to those who wish to return home and worship their Lord. For some time we stood on the beautiful grounds of that modern university, this place where Jews both young and old walked about freely; and as the only Muslim on the campus by virtue of the American passport in my pocket, I was free to speak and so drew to myself a small crowd of Jewish listeners. I then said to that group of rabbis, Jewish students and the growing crowd of curious onlookers, that we Muslims understand and respect their right to a homecoming, one that is based in worship of that one and only divine being. However, like all homecomings, and worship, there are rules that must be abided if these same homecomings we so cherish are to be rewarded by that same divine being to whom we all pray. The example of a peaceful and accepted Zion is the same, I believe, as a peaceful and accepted hajj, only if the intention of that Zionist worshiper is sincere unto his Lord. Yes, we parleyed and volleyed back and forth with respect to the very meaning and importance of Zion and hajj in our lives; however, the central tenet is hum du Allah, as a man who has been accepted into the city of Mecca by Allah and made hajj. As a person who has made hajj four times in his life, (I believe I may speak forthrightly on this matter) one must not break any of the Commandments of Jehovah-Allah; one must respect those inhabitants who live in the cities and lands, humble himself before Allah, and my neighbors, whomever they are, as well as before those in authority and their custodians. Hum du Allah, I also lived in Mecca for four years, as a student of knowledge and a teacher of English, under those same rules. It gives me confidence to say that if the Hebrew people, knowing that they are inhabiting sacred ground, would conduct themselves with humbleness and respect for all and behave as if they were visiting Muslims to Mecca on hajj, then there would not be the need for wars between us! Likewise, if the Muslim and Christian Arabs of Palestine would have conducted themselves like Jethro, the priest of Midian and the father-in-law of Moses, and extended the hand of mercy to "those who were in exile by their Lord, because of their hearts and had suffered murder, and oppression"[66] then I believe, there would not be the need for wars between us, and the Hebrew people. Thus, the result would be the city of Jerusalem will then live up to its name (the city of peace) as a reward from Jehovah-Allah! All this arrogant talk of dividing the city who`s life`s blood is justice is only nonsense for those who want for their neighbors what they want for themselves! For the truth is, we Muslims, Christians, and Jews were oppressed in this same land by the same Imperialist mindset. Moreover, it is quite obvious that these very same Imperialists are still playing us against one another for profit and worldly gain, making us see each other as the enemy near when, in fact, we are brethren of the very same monotheist faith!

As I slowly walked along these ancient narrow cobble stone streets of old Jerusalem looking beyond the script of nostalgia and talked with both Muslim and Jewish shop owners, as well as passerby who have been living together here for countless generations, I couldn't help but realize what Jerusalem's real problem is. Despite all those holy books they are selling and being sold to people who still don't comprehend the divine significance of the streets upon which they walk. Or the mosques and temples they pray in. I believe it is because of the fear of the alternative of justice and a lack of trust amongst all its citizens therein. Yes, the issues these people with such ancient histories are facing are contentious and eternally exacerbated along with the eternal concerns of a faithful Diaspora on both sides. Yet the most promising signs of respite for the conflict in the Promised Land, the sign so many of the "faithful" that resides therein of all faiths seem to miss, is sadly simple gratitude.[67] [68]

---

[66]   Exodus ch.2 v.15-25, ch.3 v.1-4
[67]   Malachi ch.4 v.1-6; Matt. 7:12
[68]   Quran 4:36, Quran 16:90

What Worries Me

But whosoever turns away from my message, verily for him is a life narrowed down, and we shall raise him up blind on the Day of Judgment.
—Quran 20:124

Islam is a true declaration of independence for mankind from the servitude of men. It is Islam, in appealing to the reason of mankind, in of itself presents a spiritual message to mankind; it is Islam that says Allah offers freedom, opportunity and the pursuit of real happiness on this earth. It is Islam that aims to end all systems and governments which is based on the rule of men over mankind, including democracy.

With this concept of freedom, however, does not mean that Muslims can make gods of their desires. Opportunity does not mean Muslims can engage in opportunism. The pursuit of happiness does not mean Muslims accept happiness as the lone criteria in one's life. Nonetheless, it is not the true intention of Islam to force its beliefs on people, even if they are Muslims-in-name-only living in non-Muslim countries. Yes, it is those Muslims-in-name-only living in Muslim countries who must submit to the Allah-fearing, the only kind of leader acceptable in Muslim lands. Even so, the *munafiq* and those "name-only" Muslims have the freedom to accept or not accept the faith as it is. Only then, by not accepting the Islamic faith as is, you cannot rule or be a leader over true Muslims that do. You likewise have the power to leave any Muslim land in peace. Yet here on earth Islam does not operate in a vacuum; for in truth Islam is in a race with other faiths for the hearts, minds, and souls of all mankind. The sin is that so many Muslims-in-name-only abandon who they really are, an act which only perpetuates the will and determination of our natural adversaries to defeat us and our jihad.

So I ask: will we, the fundamental believers of this faith called Islam, stand by our Prophet at the finish line in Mecca and Jerusalem, or will we stand in shame with our profit in hand at the finish line of Dubai's International Racing Caravelle in the United Arab Emirates? If the answer is in Dubai counting the money this is what's worrying me, because now who's the enemy?

Alas, in July of 2009 the thought police came for me in Damascus, Syria. I had promised not to tell about it. I had promised not to tell about those thousands of Allah-fearing, good Samaritan Syrians of Damascus, Dara, Homs, Hama, Tartus, Latakia, Ras Al-Basit and Aleppo whom I had met. They did not care that I was just only a student of knowledge studying Arabic at Damascus University and teaching English at the University and private schools. What I had promised not to tell is, in truth, the real story—the only one that matters. The story of those honest merchants in Hamadeya market, Damascus, who serve you tea or coffee, with a smile as you come through the door. I had promised not to tell about that Syrian doctor thirteen years ago in Damascus, the one who, for five dollars, helped to straighten my baby daughter Khaoula's crooked legs with special shoes, hum du Allah. Or that female doctor who made house calls and helped deliver my son, Salah Eddin M. Dawud, at our home in downtown Damascus. I had promised not to tell about that school on the hill, Abu Noor, and its historic legacy in Rukn Al-Din, Damascus. Yes, I had promised not to tell about never seeing anyone sleeping in the streets of Syria; that no matter how poor they were, a roof could always be found over their heads. I too forgot to keep quiet about no one starving in the land of Sham; about our kind neighbors, who made sure my family had enough heating oil during Syria's cold winters. And that public servant who refused to accept my money to pay our electric bill. I had promise not to tell how Omayyad Mosque, like so many other Syrian mosques, is full of faithful believers. I don't care if I promised not to tell, yet I will: Of the time I met that other Good Samaritan on the bus on the road to Damascus, who'd said to me if I don't stop to help him, what will happen to him?" Then a stranger paid the fare! Then another stranger gave the Bedouin some food! Followed by cheers and smiles from us all!

Yes, it was my entire fault that the thought police wanted to deport me, at gunpoint. Yes, indeed, I had promised not to mention that Damascus is that city in the world where, for less than ten dollars a day, a man can feel like a king. Prophet Muhammad (sas) was correct when he described the soft hearts of those people in Sham. So yes, let the secret police search my home all they want, and let them take their time. For yes, I am a jihad Salafi Muslim from the West, and I shall do my time in their dungeons with those other long-bearded ones who had also promised not to say a word under threat of being deported to the West, or East, or hidden behind the sun. Allah knows best and always keeps his promises, yet this is what`s worrying me!

What worries me is not that talk of the red line by President Obama unto President for life Bashar Assad because of his use of chemical weapons upon his own citizens in their civil war with him. No. This is because I am aware that here in the Western secular nations these political leaders are saying in their hearts, "It`s a pity they all cannot lose." What worries me is that unspoken word called 'slow bullet'—"Biological Weapons" that Mr. Assad has and can use against his foreign enemies that publicly calls out red lines. Oh, humble reader, I hope you are really good at seeing details. Slow bullets does not need rockets but a die-hearted individual standing behind enemy lines with a visa and an aerosol can full of mass destruction in a crowed public arena.

What worries me now is Iran`s nuclear program and its legitimate right to develop nuclear energy. And American, European, and Israeli attempts to stop Iran from developing nuclear power is troubling. In a speech on February 13, 2012 President Mahmoud Ahmadinejad of Iran said, "All plots hatched by enemies are aimed at hindering Iran`s progress because they are fearful of our development." Indeed, I do have suspicions when nations like America, with its tens of thousands of nuclear weapons, and the U.K. and Europe, with thousands of nuclear weapons, along with Israeli and its nuclear arsenal, all protest to the world that Iran is trying to produce nuclear weapons. Yes, I have legitimate reservations about the motive of the aforementioned Western powers, after their enterprise in the Afghanistan and Iraqi war fiasco, particularly in terms of how Iran's influence helped undermine Western Coalition efforts therein. As I see it, the desire for revenge against Iran is real on the part of the West, as is the persistent and familiar claim of weapons of "mass destruction," which in simplest terms translates into the eagerness of those Western powers to attack Iran.

Don`t get me wrong. I just feel that Western intelligence has been overestimated in the spectrum of common sense far too long. After reading the new President of Iran Mr. Hassan Rouhani speech at the U.N. on September 26, 2013, of which he said basically his country will never give up the right to enrich uranium, and that this issue of nuclear weapons will be resolved, I conclude that no one can stop Iran from having a nuclear bomb if they wish to have one. What worries me is that idea concept of what is a weapon in the eyes of their enemies and their level of fear.

From my experience as a Sunni Muslim from the West living and studying in the Middle East, I feel that all Muslims of faith will face Allah's true wrath if we allow sectarianism to bring another war between Sunnis and Shiites! So then I must ask: In that they (Sunni-Muslims) will permit non-Muslims to come into their lands and air space to fight their Shiite Muslim brothers next door, thus do the leaders of the Gulf States fear Allah or a nuclear-armed Iran? Truly, if the answer is the latter, I feel Allah will punish those who did not take heed to the dangers of sectarianism, as demonstrated in Europe since their so-called Reformation a hundred years ago, as Protestants and Catholics murdered one other for a nationalistic flag on a worthless pole in two World Wars in the tens of millions! Why have we Muslims forgotten those religious wars also between Britain, France and Spain? Was it not the devil who had a parade rather than the "victors"? Why then should we Muslims give Satan another parade, on our own lands, with all these kufr cheering him on from the sidelines?[69] *"He will say: Oh my Lord! Why hast thou raised me up blind, while I had sight before?" "Allah will say: Thus didst thou, when Our signs came unto thee, disregard them: so wilt thou, this day, be disregarded"* (Quran 20:125-127).

May Allah protect the Muslims from themselves and their own hearts! What worries me greatly oh humble reader is that perilous civil war which is looming dangerously close by brought on by that military junta and their coup d'état in Egypt by general Abdul Fattah Al-SiSi on July 3, 2013, against Mr. Mohammed Morsi the first democratically elected president in the history of Egypt. Yes, it is true that the Egyptian people have the right to choose how they govern themselves like other people who live in the Arab-Muslim world. Yet, the tragedy is that this coup d'état follows a sad historic precedent of transferring national governing power not by the consensus of the majority of the people for Islamic law (Sharia), and/or, not by the consensus of the majority of the people for Democracy (power in the hands of the people—one

---

[69]   Quran 20:125-128, 16:88-89

person one vote), but by the military junta's gun and the huge chanting crowds on the streets who had lost their election freely and fairly at the ballot box not willing to be govern by the winners of that same ballot box because of the arrogance of their own hearts.

Of course, there is great feeling of outrage in Egypt by those religious Allah fearing people who had won at the ballot box freely and fairly three times in a row: the presidential elections, the parliamentary elections and then the referendum for the new Egyptian constitution which passed with more than 64 percent of the vote counted.

And of course there is a great level of jubilation amongst members of the ex-president of the Mubarak era armed forces. Like members of the Mubarak era justices of the Supreme Constitutional Court, like Mr. Adly Mansour (now acting president of Egypt, former judge). Members of the Mubarak era benefiters like Mr. Hazem El-Beblawi (now acting prime minister, the economist). Members of the Mubarak era benefiters like Mr. Mohamed Elbaradel (now acting as a liberal champion, a Noble laureate, who fled the country on August 14, 2013 to Europe, because he did not want blood on his hands); and Mr. Tamarod (now acting as the Arab anarchist—"The Rebel" movement). All of whom and many others are now coming to power by betrayal and revolt, not by the ballot box or democracy that they avow in public. Egypt has entered into the brink of civil war like Syria, this is what's worrying me.

I am sadly convinced, by reality that at the heart of this treachery and duplicity are those now—silent Western secular imperialist governments like my country America. Avowing democracy in the daytime and financing subversion at night, by way of military arms grants to despots in uniform once again. As well as, Saudi Arabia, Kuwait, and the United Arab Emirates governments in the daytime avowing Islamic principles, but at the undercover of darkness with Satan, are financing subversion in aiding those Egyptian generals with money. Who had committed treason unto Allah, and the people of Egypt, simply because of their fear of the "Muslim Brotherhood, Sharia, and justice coming to power. They the enemies near, and far, are all-determined to have their own way regardless of the outcome of a free and fair election or even the Islamic principles of their own holy books. Yet resistance always starts with a spark, not caring where the flame will rest. Thus, human tragedy can be an impetus rather than an impediment that makes a revolution necessary and a standard of justice insha Allah.

Yes, what worries me greatly is knowing that history repeats itself like those 51 people shot to death in prayer and protest on July 8, 2013, by the Egyptian republican guards similar to like what had happened in Algeria in the 1990`s which started off their civil war. Worse, more than 1,100 people shot to death in August 14, 2013, in Cairo, and at the Raba`a Adawiya Mosque in Nasr City, Cairo; are similar to the thousands dead in Homs, Syria, which started off their civil war in 2011. Certainly, oh, humble reader, the soul of a revolution answering to Allah in the dark of human arrogance is its capacity of patience and sacrifice. Thus, I endorse Imam Ibn Taymiyah idea with concern, oh, humble reader, that, "This world lives with justice and disbelief and does not live with injustice and Islam."

PART II:
The Enemy Far

Their Hearts and Minds War

I am compelled to put forth this book so that the heart, mind and soul of the world body will bebetter informed.

> *Fain would they deceive Allah and those who believe, but they only deceiving themselves, and realize it not. In their hearts is a disease and Allah has increased their disease: and grievous is the penalty they incur, because they are false to themselves. When it is said to them: "Make not mischief on the earth," they say: "Why, we only want to make peace!*
>
> —Quran 2:9-11

As a *Jihad* Salafi Muslim American who was born in London, and at twenty months old moved to the Bronx, New York with my father, an American citizen, and mother, a Jamaican citizen. I am not surprised or fooled by my country's failing ideological struggles of the twenty-first century, the hearts and minds war, or misled or disheartened by our myopic presidents and other Western politicians.

One does not have to be a mystic to correctly make the assessment that America and its European allies have lost this hearts and minds war because of their abandonment of human rights, equal rights, justice, and due process of law aboard and at home. But it saddens me greatly that the government of America, my country, currently, at its own peril, is the most egregious and hypocritical supporter of oppression, injustice, and subversion in the Muslim world and the third world!

Throughout the course of human history, men—both as individuals and as nations—have fought for power, resources, beliefs, and liberation, so as to protect their future, increase their wealth, ensure their freedom of worship, and to remain emancipated from bondage. Yet what has been gained by these noble efforts? Today President Barack Obama sits in the Oval Office of the White House sorting out unsettled debts before they achieve critical mass due to the failed governmental policies and moral shortcomings of his predecessors. Their war on terror is lost, just like our other wars on drugs, crime, poverty, AIDS, cancer, and illiteracy; these policies which have failed not only because of poor judgment and insufficient strategic planning, but because of a chronic political cowardice that for centuries has burned like wildfire throughout the offices of the ruling Western secular elite. Currently, President Obama has been "reelected" to hold that bag of more than seventeen-trillion—dollar debt and to face the grim consequences of losing their war on terror. It has become now ever more apparent that the American secular political and corporate military elite wanted a war with Afghanistan and Iraq, but America and her Western European allied nations just didn't want the war it got from Islamic fundamentalist organizations throughout the Muslim world!

Three decades ago, American policy in Afghanistan was to support the Islamic resistance in their fight against the Soviet invasion; at present, however, the Taliban, Al-Qaeda and the Mujahideen are now our enemies, thus the official standard feeble reply.

The truth is those same "freedom fighters" America had supported and armed against the Soviets— the Taliban, Al-Qaeda and the Mujahideen—found out about those greedy American arms merchants selling weapons to the Northern Alliance who was then, and still now fighting, for political gain, a civil war against their own Muslim brethren in Afghanistan. Once upon a lifetime, a people or a nation can succeed with a policy of we are allies in war then enemies in peacetime. Yet such political or social legacy in today's modern era where betrayal is explicit, hence unforgiving, this idea of deceit has a means of their own undoing! Therefore, why the big surprise on September 11, 2001?

Iraq under Saddam Hussein did the same thing; he took revenge in March 1987 when one of its American-made F-1 fighters jet fired two Exocet cruise missiles at the USS *Stark*, killing 37 American sailors and then apologizing for the "accident." I ask, then, is it a coincidence that the USS *Stark* incident happened only four months after news of the Iran-Contra Affair was first leaked to the public? Likewise, was it an accident that American Project Democracy funds raised its money by advising Israel to sell arms at bargain basement prices to Iran, who in turn used these weapons to destroy Iraqi tanks (U.S. TOW: anti-tank missiles) and shoot down Iraqi warplanes (U.S. Hawk: anti-aircraft missiles)? Frankly are you really surprised, oh, humble reader, would you really bet your life since we're all "allies" in war, that President Saddam Hussein, the so-called renowned Arab humanitarian against Iranian Shiite theocracy, accepted U.S. Secretary of Defense Caspar Weinberger's apology in the first place? Are you really surprised of the perspective pragmatism of Sunni Arab nationalist despot leaders and Shiite Iranian religious leaders when they hear the words of Mr. Henry Kissinger, the ex-Secretary of State of the United States, in regards to the war between Iraq under President-for-life Saddam Hussein and the Ayatollahs of Iran, "It's a pity they both can't lose!"

The Big Business of War

One day we will ask hell, art thou filled to the full? It will say: "Are there any more to come?

—Quran 50:30

Let's have a heart-to-heart understanding! Both America and Europe are the world's leading arms merchants. We export more tools of death, pain, anguish and misery to the Muslim world and Third World than any other single commodity sold aboard! Shamefully we sell more bombs than we sell computers, more guns than we sell TVs. We even sell more bullets than we sell computer chips! Much has been written concerning peace deals between nations, but the root of the problem in maintaining that peace lies in the huge congressional lobbying power and military financial backing these war profiteers possess. These merchants of death are highly resistant to any change in policy that threatens their profits and/or power; likewise, they benefit whether a war is just or unjust, lost or won. Whether their nation is fighting for truth or for a shadow of lies is of no concern to them! If we the believers of this Islamic faith are truly going to be successful here in the present-day secular West, the truth must be told about the big business of war and its corporate war profiteers dedicated to spilling the blood of our fellow Muslims abroad for profit and gain.

Today, we the believers are living behind enemy lines where the laws of Allah are disregarded and the laws of mankind accepted. That they have (Western political establishment) lost their moral bearing comes as a surprise only to themselves! Did not Allah, the most merciful and most graceful, provide a number of guiding voices that warned against war profiteering to nations of the emerging West? Patriots like the old guard fundamentalist Tom Paine who said, "That there are men in all countries who get their living by war and keeping up the quarrels of nations is as shocking as it is true." Or former president Dwight D. Eisenhower who on January 17, 1961, warned in his farewell address to beware the military industrial complex that threatens the best interests of our nation! Since the consequences of war are real enough, why then are the words from the people of the book not guidance enough, especially when their warnings are so convenient to read? It was my father who said to me, "If we do not live by the love we do not see, then we will live by the hate we all feel."[70]

The huge business of modern war has primarily been a rivalry of the dark side between the most powerful men in Western governments who will challenge whomever citizen to distinguish a naked photograph of a weapon of mass destruction from any other weapon of death. Along with the most powerful of men in the Western armament industry who will challenge whomever national to distinguish a naked prostitute from any other politician of protest!

In particular, since the day of President John F. Kennedy's assassination on November 22, 1963, I believe neither American political party, whether it is Democratic or Republican has spoken with an intuitive understanding of the language of the people they are supposed to represent and likewise defend. Sadly, today's politicians do not exist for the sake of the welfare of the people but for the sake of their powerful political patrons, most notably those in the arms industry. Nowadays the decision-makers are the billionaire mega-donors funneling their dark money into political super-PACs and blue chip corporations with multi-million dollar lobbying budgets called American Security Council. It is they primarily, not the politicians, who decides how dangerous Russia or China, Iran or North Korea, Afghanistan or Pakistan, Syria or Iraq really is to their vested interests.

Yes, that incestuous affair between Western governments and the big business of war may as well be called live and let die.

Yet how many times have we heard from our elected leaders in the West that the spoils of war are democracy? Likewise, how many times, in the middle of the night, has that little voice inside your head telling you that democracy doesn't need a bayonet? Most often, in most any endeavor, the truth is that nothing builds stature like success. Only

---

[70] My father, Mr. Constant P. Hickson

where's the success, or even the hints of democracy, as a result of the wars in Vietnam, Afghanistan and Iraq? The dilemma facing the West after 9-11 is how to respond to Islamic fundamentalism, most notably Al-Qaeda, who has had enough of Western imperialism. If Western governments were sincere, instead of deploying arms merchants then soldiers they should had sent full brigades of Peace Corps volunteers—whose creed is "Live, learn, and work with a community overseas"—into Afghanistan after Soviet troops were defeated by the very same Islamic resistance fighters that is now fighting the west. Instead, former presidents George H W Bush sr. and Bill Clinton could had worked with the ISI, Pakistan's intelligence agency, as well as Saudi religious leaders to support those Taliban, Al-Qaeda, and the Mujahideen fighters, not just the Northern Alliance, all of whom were allies in war against the communist Russians.

Western powers should have made all interested parties understand that civil war in Afghanistan was not an option. "Allies in war cannot be enemies in peace time!" That there would be neither funds nor arms available for one Afghan group to use against another, as this would only increase the hatred and distrust amongst those former allies who'd together defeated the Soviets. One honest Afghan summit between Western and Muslim leaders when President George H W Bush sr. and Bill Clinton was still in office may very well have helped prevent the September 11 attacks as well as the subsequent war on terror and its implications for Western powers and Muslims worldwide! A long-term vision for Afghanistan that took into account the advice from Allah-fearing Muslims from both North American and Europe would have gone a long way toward establishing peace and justice in that war-ravaged country. Why then were all mainstream Muslim leaders opinions and viewpoints ignored here at home in the media and aboard as a policy?

If the goal is justice and the method is peace, then a recipe for successful foreign policy would be to pair up the Peace Corps with UNICEF (United Nations Children's Fund) and get "allies in war" to listen to one another and thus change the course of lives in peacetime. Yet it was only Western governments and India that feared the rise of an Islamic government under Sharia law in Afghanistan, one making huge profits from an oil and gas pipeline running through it from Turkmenistan's Caspian Sea heading east through Afghanistan then south into Pakistan. For this scenario was as much a threat as a Communist Afghan government reaping those same huge profits and thus benefitting the Soviets up north. Accordingly, the Russians are now having the last laugh, as they watch that coalition of Western powers entrapped by the same imperialist policies originally designed to defeat their communist invasion of 1980! Allah knows best!

Ask any Muslim overseas, "Who is the greatest threat to world peace?" and they will not hesitate to tell you those Western merchants of death! So who are they these self-interest dogs of war? They are, Bechtel, Fluor, Parsons, Shaw Group, Dyncorp International, Blackwater, Triple Canopy, The Louis Berger Group, Halliburton and their subsidiary Kellogg, Evergreen Security, Brown and Root, and The Rendon Group. Leading the war profiteers scramble for spoils of war, and success to riches is Mr. Joe Lopez—senior V.P. Gov. Ops Kellogg, Brown and Root. Mr. Thomas W. Rabaut—president and CEO plus Dir. United Defense Ind. The largest share holder "The Carlyle Group." Mr. Jay Garner—President Sy. Coleman—Ex-Viceroy of Iraq. Mr. Vance D. Coffman—Chairman and CEO Lockheed Martin-The worlds #1 Military contractor who makes U-2, Sr-71 spy planes, F-16`s, drones. Mr. Philip M. Condit—Chairman and CEO Boeing—smart bombs F-15`s, Apache Helicopters, Joint Direct Attack Munitions (JDAM). Mr. Daniel P. Burnham-Chairman and CEO of Raytheon: which means, "Light from the Gods." Bunker Buster Bombs, Tomahawk missiles, Gbu-28, Tow, Maverick, Javelin, land attack cruise missiles. Mr. Ronald Sugar, CEO President Northrop Grumman—B2 bombers, Airborne Warning and Control Systems (AWACS) also Alq-15 jamming. Mr. Nicholas D. Chabraja-Chairman and CEO General Dynamics-F-16`s Abrams Tanks, and Trident Subs. Mr. George David-Chairman and CEO United Technologies-Sikorsky, Blackhawk, and Comanche Helicopters. General Carl E. Vuono-President of Military Professionals Resources Incorporated-Teaching the art of war-a cozy club of top shelf mercenaries, all so called retired Brass, rumor has it they educate murder and subversion. Mr. Paul V. Lombardi-President and CEO Dyncorp, rumor has it a rent a cop business (Mercenaries) in Afghanistan, Iraq, and Colombia!

So who are the top ten 2012 arms exporter nations of the world? For their records, and public eye . . . United States-$8.76 billion; Russia-$8.00 billion; China $1.78 billion; Ukraine-$1.34 billion; Germany-$1.19 billion; France-$1.14 billion; Britain-$847 million; Italy-$847 million; Netherlands-$760 million and Spain-$720million!

And who are the top ten 2012 United States arms buyers of the world? On paper . . . South Korea-$980 million; United Arab Emirates-$801 million; Turkey-$772 million; Australia-$634 million; Afghanistan-$469million; Britain-$450million; Saudi Arabia-$425 million; Morocco-$416 million; Taiwan-$412 million; Iraq-$316million;

and Israel`s total amount is subsidize in secret by the U.S. congress and paid for by U.S. taxpayers.

As they see beyond the moment of reality, human beings are, in the sight of arms merchant's approximations, living bags of clay mix with brine. Such a profitable witch's brew laced with irony and enchanting ideals of life in the view point of the merchant of death that must be kept in mind at all times. Yet it is universal and not the wise to win contracts and count your money when your proxies lose wars and count the values in this modern era of revenge.

Yes, this Western secular world is wired for war today greater now than at any time in its history. But that trend of winning every battle but lose every war it gets involve in has an insane price. We the people, currently, are witnessing and realizing that that democratic vote is becoming meaningless because our nationalistic majorities are defending their national interest, which is in a conflict with a silent moral minority, whose conscience just will not step out of the way! That global economic stagnation since the 2008 housing crash has truly hurt and weakened the Western secular support for a democracy that needs a bayonet in its foreign policy and usury in its domestic banking policies!

Now that the idea of convergence of Western, and Eastern civilizations has come of age, it is those in the Islamic resurgence that has the upper hand on a spiritual high ground against Western cowboy diplomacy, and drone invasions. In this new era of smart phones and instant social media, the, we the people, and we the believers are beginning to see and feel those strategic insights in this imperfect world with its ugly truths that the big business of war campaign is bankrupting the economies of the Western world. As well as stirring up permanent hatred towards the Western world from the Muslim and third-world aspect! So it`s only a matter of time, or the next 9-11 from our outlook, as we the religious believers are concern, when their western inner demons will stop running around with the bloody batons looking for just the right amount of evil to hand them off to.

Yes, it is worth the wait, patience—there is no doubt in my mind that the business of war is hellish and as chaos grows, must be won at all costs. The ferocity of genius is the ability to recognize the solution before the obvious. There is a bad karma, a true reckoning of consequences, I believe, in selling death and pain which is a cruel and an immoral practice for any nation that claims to be a civilize peaceful society knowing that the earth is becoming a village. No one person I believe can bankrupt this big business of war, which is meant to be a profound compliment for those persons or those jihadis waiting in the wings.

The Kafir Community

Oh ye who believe! Take not my enemies and yours as friends or protectors, offering them your love, though they have rejected the truth that has come to you, and have on the contrary driven out the prophet and your selves from your homes, simply because ye believe in Allah your Lord! If ye have come out to strive in my way and to seek my good pleasure, take them not as friends, holding secret converse of love and friendship with them: For I know full well all that ye conceal and all that ye reveal. And any of you that does this has strayed from the straight path.

—Quran 60:1-2

It seems like just yesterday that I had gotten off that red double-decker bus and walked down those green garden streets of Whitechapel, East London, UK, coming home to my apartment in East London Mosque from a Kensington Town hall meeting in July 2004. The guest speaker there was that Egyptian scholarly fundamentalist Sheikh Yusuf Al-Qarardawi. He is quite known in the Muslim world as a moderate Sunni scholar, yet the political weather here in the West particularly here in Europe has changed for the worst in light of the worsening war situations in Afghanistan and Iraq! As anticipated, in the mind's eye of the kafir (plural of unbeliever-unbelievers) he seems to be the reflection of the mainstream Sunni Muslim world in revolt not willing to submit to a Western new world order! Therefore, I knew what he had to say was very important and made it my business to hurry and be there.

Yes, Sheikh Yusuf Al-Qarardawi does have a mission of why he is here in London undoubtedly. Publicly, his idea and fatwa that "suicide bombings" are justified "Martyrdom Operations" in times of oppression and foreign occupation did not go well here with many politicians who stood and voted for war and many unbelievers who has families overseas fighting in two Muslim countries! (Afghanistan and Iraq) Along with his belief that Muslim women have the right to wear headscarf (hijab) where ever she is regardless of country. This made it even more difficult for those who wish Muslim women to assimilate into the kafir communities. Avowing homosexuality is a sin like a disease did not win him a lot of applauses in this Western domestic secular audiences; be that as it may, during his visit to London he talked mainly about the simple principals of Islam it`s benefits, and it`s contributions to mankind.

I was glad to see and meet him in person, yet the way he walked and talked, I can tell he was not at ease in being here in London. The Sheikh was indeed carrying a lot of responsibilities and had a lot on his mind. The Western media hype was very repellent in my opinion, very hostile towards the visiting sheikh, because of not only his religious Islamic fatwa's in the past in regards to how Muslims should view the actions of the Western secular Democratic ideals but as well as Western secular nations invasions of Muslim countries under pretexts of lies.

Furthermore, he said, "Muslims should recall the invasions of Muslim countries by non-Muslim forces as hostile and that those who call themselves civilians and who work beside Western occupied soldiers in the oppression of the Muslim people therein are not innocent civilians and can be treated like enemy soldiers!"

I had always believe that there is always an era that truth stood the test of time consistently! Yet, sometimes free speech isn`t obvious to everyone! Once upon a time, you did love what you heard and what you didn`t agree with, but needed to know about it anyway in regards to who`s telling the truth. Hours after hearing the historic speech by Sheikh Al-Quaradawi had passed here in London the most civilize city in Europe I believe, where crime is a minimum, social graces a maximum, health care for all without the stress of payment, and a people who honestly really loves each other`s company. The police even walk the streets without guns they carry only their honor. Yet that idea of confronting an awakening Islamic agenda with a renewed awareness by today`s Western politicians who has drag their nations to war is truly gone with the wind because of the political cowardice and greed. This sense of dread became obvious to me at each step I made homeward bound. I felt deep down in my heart that disputed religious call for reason has fallen on deaf ears, and a great opportunity for constructive dialogue between the secular and Islamic civilizations had been ignored by these leaders here in Europe.

Yet what a beautifully green metropolitan city London truly is to had been such a host. My home away from home! Full of enchanting people hormonally in tuned with the life they have been given. However, Allah knows it is very important to be keen on separating truth from patriotic imperialist chatter. Sheikh Al-Qarardawi did his part in delivering the message. Hearing free speech doesn't give you shelter from that reality storm that's right around the corner from where you live and work, so I quicken my pace and muttered a few prayers. Free speech means the gauntlet is in your hands! All that talk you hear throughout town about "denunciation of killing innocent people" and "any act of violence which makes innocent people a victim is not allowed" is just talk and worthless media hype to a person who is conscious and aware of the realities of this dynamic rainbow world. Are you innocent, or are you collateral? The answer then is that they the people are abetting a wrong cause in reality, and knowingly in spite of the truth, which lies before them unanswered. Are not the people responsible for their own government! Then, why the denial of the dire situation and fear of the alternatives that is confronting such human beings of comforts? Do they wish to be rehabilitated or remain as enemies?

As I silently walk down these beautiful streets of Whitechapel, East London, towards East London Mosque, where I live, I pondered in my mind's eye the ramifications of that right of "having your say" so imbedded in this modern society, would this act, and idea not open the doors of awareness for those unbelievers, those kafir, who do not wish to oppress anyone who love "justice," and are deeply disillusioned because of their leaders' actions? Will this opportunity to speak out make a change? Yet, where's that traction of the change of hearts? Where is that demand for a change of policy as well as for justice?

Yes, it seems like only yesterday that ideal trend of free speech, in this kufr community, in this midst of war and global uncertainty perhaps may hold some hope for justice and peace be taken to heart.

Yet sometimes free speech isn't so obvious a benefit—in fact, a bitter pill—especially if the host citizens are viewing and listening to a renowned Islamic scholar talking to them about how Islam can improve their lives as well as a good contribution to their spiritual well-being. But it is apparent to all that their guest is exiled at this time from his own home country for decades, forbidden to give this very same speech or any speech for that matter to his own countrymen by his own government his own despot that rule the land promised to them because of the hearts of his own people!

Indeed, I am sure, it was self-evident to the Islamic scholar standing here in this beautiful free green city called London giving his free speech knowing that his host's government is a supporter of the invited guest despot president Hosni Mubarak. They, the British government, are a true supporter of the oppression upon the invited guest's peoples by way of arms and finance that horribly effects tens of millions of his people; this fact does not go unnoticed by him, I am certain, in spite of the welcome mat given to the Muslim scholar and hope given to him by the domestic Muslim people of this country.

Yes, sometimes free speech is not so obvious for people with spiritual and intellectual development disabilities. Try as best as you can the right words of wisdom, they will not appreciate those words, only the wise will heed so it seems. Sheikh Yusuf Al-Quaradawi came to the United Kingdom, I believe, in spite of the kufr public misperceptions to tell the government therein to "let my people go" with phenomenal rhythmic acuity and grace! Yes, it does seem like only yesterday when shepherds first challenge the accepted awesome routine of seeing beyond the hype.

It was only a fortnight ago it seems that I gotten off that metropolitan shuttle bus with my family and walked over to Masjid Ansar As-Sunnah, in downtown Paterson, New Jersey here at 63 Washington St. United States of America. What a relief it is to step into such a Masjid and listen to Imam Hamza Abdual Salam speak freely on that Friday Juma service day. He talked about the Islamic way forward in these troubled social-economic times and that ability of seeing beyond the hope, thus modeling our lives according to the authentic teachings of the prophet Muhammad (sas) and his righteous companions. Yes, you feel welcomed at the door; I kid you not. Like in Newark, Camden, and Trenton and other New Jersey cities deep in poverty, Masjid Ansar As-Sunnah is surrounded by legions of homeless and poor, drug addicts, and those who seemly gave up on life and hope. Yet this humble island Masjid, is filled with many young African Americans and multi-cultural minorities yearning for a spiritual difference in their lives, those who are tired of living for the city.

Imam Hamza Abdual Salam, an astute African American Salafi Imam who's aim is to guide his faithful congregation of Muslim believers through these challenging crisis here at home in America that we are all facing, with the pure faith of Islam, is now undergoing an uphill jihad fight of his own. Trying to inspire faith on those who are at the brink of social destitute, and keeping the Masjid from being foreclosed upon.

Yes, every time I step into these simple Masjids like these here in urban America a true lighthouse to the ignorant and poor where the atmosphere of welcome is refreshing, I tend to remember that contrast of those numerous multi-million dollar Mosques (museums) here in America and in the Middle East. Many with their corrupt business men and princes in tow, they who are nothing but wolves in men clothing when it is time to embrace or give in charity, what say`s jihad. We`re nothing but dust making a fuss, chasing after nothing real, so they think in their hearts. That`s why the poor, we`re on our own here behind enemy lines truthfully I feel. Yet, nevertheless, Allah (swa) is enough.

In retrospect, if our unbelieving adversaries have neglectfully lost their moral bearings here in these Western lands that we all call home, then truly it is an act of sheer folly for the believers living here to lose our moral compass. *"Oh, you who believe, obey Allah and obey the messenger (Muhammad) (sas), and those in authority from amongst you . . . If you differ in anything amongst yourselves, refer it to Allah and his messenger, if you believe in Allah and in the last day. That is better and more suitable for final determination. Have you seen those hypocrites who claim that they believe in that which was sent down to you and that which was sent before you and they wish for judgment (in their disputes), to refer to the tagbut (false judges) while they have been told to reject them? But shaytan (devil) wishes to lead them astray. When it is said to them: Come to what Allah has sent down to the messenger, you will see the hypocrites turn away from you with aversion."*[71]

When we fundamentalists say "believers," we are not talking about those who come to Western lands to assimilate into the *kafir* communities. Neither are we talking about political refugees or asylum-seekers who travel to non-Muslim lands in a state of war with Islam. Those nations that, for example who are in a state of war with Islam are every non-Muslim country that invaded with soldiers and/ or invaded with missionaries, merchants, and mercenaries into Afghanistan and Iraq against the will of its people therein. Refuge must be sought amongst Allah-fearing believers first. Hum du Allah, there are fifty-two Muslim countries on this earth from which to choose. One, who is truly Allah-fearing, does not travel from the Muslim country of his or her birth or citizenship to seek refuge in a kufr country, unless

---

[71] Kufr: Unbeliever/Kafir: Unbelievers – Quran 2:8-20, 4:97-100

the goal is jihad for the mercy of Allah. That one has come to the secular West or pagan East, to help Muslims overcome, by good efforts and deeds, the actions of the unbelievers. Hadith: (narrated by Abu Dawood 2645 and Al-Tirmidhi 1604 and the women 4780 narrated from Jarir ibn Abdullah). As of now, we the believers in the Islamic faith do not have the social, economic, and political power in the secular West to legislate into law the Sharia; in fact, in many cases we do not even have autonomy over our own communities. Despite this, our goals in these lands are clear, and our mission is noble behind the enemy lines of the *kufr*.

America and Western Europe represent the cutting-edge frontier of Islam, with a population of nearly thirty million Muslims. Today, in these *kafir* lands, we the believers are confidently overcoming an array of obstacles. American and European governments have rarely, if ever, considered the interests of their Muslim citizenry, and the influence of Muslim leaders in regards to foreign policy in Muslim countries has been virtually nonexistent. With the exception of U.S. Congressmen Keith Ellision of Minnesota, Muslim communities have no other government representative that speaks on their behalf. Likewise, the clear view points of Muslims in the United States, UK, and Europe, toward their governmental domestic civil policies, has only hardened with suspicion. As of today, thanks to the United States, UK`s and Europe`s war on terror, the rendition programs, Patriot Act, Homeland Security, The Terrorism Bill, The Terrorism Act, the repel of habeas corpus, torture, and secret detention centers accepted in Sweden, UK, Bosnia, Italy, Macedonia, Germany (Ramstein), Poland, Romania (Timisoaba), Spain, Turkey, Cyprus, Azerbaijan (Szymany), and Guantanamo Bay Cuba. As well as secret detention prisons on U.S. warships like USS *Bataan,* USS *Peleliu,* and USS *Asshland.* Would we Jihad Salafi fundamentalist living here in the West be wrong in saying that there is a serious outstanding credibility gap, which is profound, between minority citizens of the desired faith of Islam and the ethnic cleansing policies of our Western secular governments?

Since the fall of the last caliphate, Muslims have lived in America and Western Europe as successful traders, businessmen, doctors, artists, engineers, and craftsmen; yet mainstream Muslims have still not triumphed in the realm of political leadership or governance. Though it is not forbidden for a Muslim man to work or study in non-Muslim lands, but when he has earned sufficiently or has completed his course of study he should return back to his Muslim country to share his wealth and his knowledge. The Muslim man is forbidden to travel to non-Muslim lands and make his stay there permanent with intentions to assimilate himself or herself into the non-Muslim society unless, as mentioned before, he or she is in jihad for the mercy of Allah and their intention is to help transform the adopted nation into a Muslim land! The question to be asked then is as a Muslim, what are your true intentions in seeking Allah`s bounty on this earth? For this is the first thing to be considered at the onset of any ideological struggle.

It is fair to ask oneself sincerely, before others ask themselves sincerely, what`s the use of having that one divine one in your life if you have to run for your life for some hope, justice, opportunity, and freedom outside from that one divine one`s eminent domain? Behold thus the quagmire of the true vanities. Can not the Muslim take a stand in their divine one`s eminent domain and realize their dream with dignity? Seeing that forlorn treasure hunt is in obvious conflict with one`s loyalty to one`s faith, just how far does one have to travel before you are mugged by reality?

Freedom does not mean Muslims can make their desires, ambitions, and their longing to be free from tyranny their God. For it is arrogant and ignorant to believe you can find liberty in the lands of an enemy far, such thinking which demonstrates the deficiency of a people`s intuitive understanding of both their own faith and the true meaning of liberation. Any Muslim who travels to America or Western Europe so that he or she can attain civil liberties is an outright disgrace and insult to themselves as a person of faith. Words which I speak with a heavy heart knowing this to be true after more than eighteen years proselytizing—to both Muslims and non-Muslims, and to all classes of people—in America, UK, Europe, the Arab world and Pakistan, the beautiful faith of Islam. Know your enemy is extremely important in life in these days of ideological warfare. Bringing a message to both non-believer and non-Muslim alike that Islam is a true declaration of independence of mankind from the servitude of men, yet you could not achieve freedom, peace, and justice in that Promise Land of your Lord, speaks volumes about themselves and their lord.

But the reality is that millions of Muslims, some of them with their Qurans in tow, had to run for their liberty, and in many cases their lives, to the nations of the West, seeking that which they were not willing to take a stand for, or fight and die to the last for. At the same time, those *kafir* living in their own lands, enjoying their civil liberties and their freedoms, in their most inner hearts are saying to those Muslims who come to the West from the oppression of their own despots, because of their own hearts, "Where is that God of yours, or is this the forsaken lot before us?" It is well understood by the kafir that those who are oppressed vote with their feet; however, Americans and

Western Europeans have a deep philosophical objection to foreigners demanding civil liberties that they themselves didn't fight for in their home countries, an attitude which mars the hope of any national cohesion in Western secular lands.

Opportunity does not mean Muslims engage in opportunism, particularly those Muslims coming to the West with intentions to assimilate their faith and identity into a secular and pluralistic society whose goal as a people is to remain in this society permanently and to be governed by it for personal gain and citizenship! How truly naïve is it to believe that your redeeming quality, your saving grace is more business as usual, that you are successful in the sight of Allah because of your material wealth (Quran 11:116-8).

So who are these shameless renegade opportunists amongst us in these secular lands of the West, who will call themselves by their nationality or ethnic group first then perhaps their faith afterwards? For example, I am a Muslim African-American not an African-American Muslim because my faith comes first, and foremost. We are Muslims of British nationality, not British Muslims. We are Muslims of European nationality, not European Muslims. Not only can you tell their true stripe by how they name themselves when they arrive on Western shores but also by the names they call their organizations when they assemble within our lands. They are, for example, the American Muslim Council (AMC), a group that calls itself "a non-profit organization for Islamic causes and a political movement for the civil rights and justice for all Americans."

For the record, the AMC goes on to say that, "they support American government action against world terrorism and reaffirms its condemnation of the terrorist attacks of 9-11-2001 against our country." Likewise, the AMC commended President George W. Bush's leadership in reaffirming that the war on terror was being waged against terrorists, not against the Afghan people, Muslims or Islam. Moreover, the AMC commended President Bush for his statement that the American military campaign would take measures to protect the civilian population of Afghanistan, and that the A.M.C. is "particularly grateful for President Bush Jr.`s compassion and humanitarian efforts for the Afghan people and fully supports his efforts to deal with the causes of terrorism. We support our brave men and women who are fighting to protect us from terrorism."

However, the AMC, and its leadership, is clearly hypocritical. For example, on October 8,

2001, Mr. Aly Abuzaakouk, the executive director of the AMC's media department, said, "I think if we were outside this country, we can say, 'Oh, Allah, destroy America, but once we are here our mission in this country is to change it. There is no way for Muslims to be violent in America—no way. We have other means to do it. You can be violent anywhere else but in America." Similarly, on December 29, 1996, Abdurahman Alamoudi, the founder of the AMC, spoke to the Islamic Association of Palestine and said, "We are all supporters of Hamas. I am also a supporter of Hezbollah." Much the same, on June 27, 2002, Eric Vickers, the former executive director of the AMC, said that Al-Qaeda was "involved in a resistance movement."

President George H. W. Bush and President Bill Clinton as well as President George W. Bush selected, trained, and certified Muslim imams as chaplains for the U.S. military from the American Muslim Council with Abdurahman Alamoudi's knowledge. This is a true violation of Islamic hadiths and Muslim principals. *"The Commander in Chief of a Muslim in battle can only be a Muslim."* It was Mr. Alamoudi who presented the first Imam in the U.S. Army with the newest insignia, a silver crescent and moon to Army Captain Abdul Muhammad commissioning service in 1993. It was Mr. Alamoudi who help created the American Muslim Armed Forces and Veterans Affairs Council in 1991 to certify Muslim chaplains hired by the U.S. military. But what was the AMC conviction on American Muslim communities facing the U.S. government? "As long as the war on terrorism exists, the U.S. government is not going to cease profiling Muslims, having selective INS [Immigration and Naturalization Service] registrations, spying on Mosques and Muslims, detaining Muslims, raiding Muslim organizations and businesses, bringing fishing expedition criminal indictments, etc. (former executive dir. Eric Vickers January 31, 2005). The new AMC response to Imams in America on how to deal with the FBI: "We call upon you to demonstrate mass criticism and activism against the new FBI policy, which directs FBI field offices nationwide to conduct an inventory of Mosques and Muslims as part of their charge to develop demographic profiles of their regions to combat possible terrorism." The AMC executive dir. Eric Vickers memorandum to Imams January 28, 2003.

Ironically, Mr. Abdurahman Alamoudi is now in a Federal Prison serving a twenty three year sentence for planning to kill then-Crown Prince Abdullah of Saudi Arabia, who is now King Abdullah bin Abdul Aziz Al-Saud on behalf of Moammar Gaddafi, the ex-leader of Libya!

Can a nation of people who call themselves Muslims and who are not on a jihad actually migrate to non-Muslim lands and lead the believers there towards the true goal of autonomy over our own communities and to eventual governorship of these countries under Islamic laws, thereby becoming an Islamic state? The ultimate victory! We the believers of this Islamic faith, who are indigenous to these secular Western countries, must affirm no! Those who call themselves Muslims who migrate into non-Muslim lands or nations for the sole purpose of seeking economical gain therein and/or political power within cannot lead us to that ultimate victory. Just how could such people be our fortress, our refuge in these lands? Just because they have the *money* to build the necessary mosques, Islamic schools and centers, just because they endorse a kufr organization of power like what the AMC did, do they think they can buy their authority over us? Do they think with their kufr political influence and organizational support they can coerce their way into authority over us? Yet for every Muslim who flees their homeland with a heavy purse, there is rarely one word in their organizational or corporate charter that speaks of gaining autonomy over our communities here in the secular West, indicating at the very least that they have the aspiration that they have the will to live under the law of their propose faith of Islam and let come what may, Hum du Allah! Surely you have been misinformed that we fundamental believers of this Islamic faith who are indigenous to these Western secular lands shall abandon our birthright that power to legislate in our lands by way of politic, intrigue and if necessary by force of arms the Sharia law. Nor shall we abandon our birthright as indigenous host to lead this noble jihad for Sharia in our lands or to thus, abdicate our rights to those that flee dictators, despots, tyrants and presidents for life in their own Muslim home countries seeking political and/or economic gain.

Whether we are discussing the secular West or the Muslim East, the same wisdom applies: you cannot run with the lions and the hyenas together! At the end of the day, with all of the fault lines in this geopolitical world with its ongoing ideological warfare, Islam looms on the periphery of America and Western Europe, a reality that grows increasingly more dangerous as time marches onward because of the conflicts of ongoing human interests and faiths. Just because you forget that you are living behind enemy lines, this does not mean your enemy forgets who you really are and that standard or principle by which a person is judged.

You cannot run to the land of your enemy far because of the oppression of your enemy near and not be seriously compromised. We Muslims living here in the West must deal with reality of that ideological warfare or reality will deal with us. It is not in the interest of the secular democratic West to allow an Islamic revival within its borders. Likewise, a secular Western government will not tolerate a domestic Islamic political party whose aim is to establish Sharia law for the purposes of obtaining power for governorship without threat of civil war!

I personally believe that many Muslim communities and leaders today are not capable of performing the necessary jihad within the borders of the secular Western nations in which they reside simply because they are foreigners and ignorant of the ways and customs of these lands. For many in these lands their main interest is simply survival. Likewise, many Muslims feel compromised, both in their need to be lawful citizens but also for the lack of a noble agenda of where do we go from here now that they are here in somebody else's Promised Land. The fact that you have fled from that muezzin's call in the East, to that statue, the Statue of Liberty, in the West, cannot be ignored by non-Muslims. You can preach all you want about Allah who is unseen, but it is they (kafir) who have justice; amongst themselves that is witness. Sincerely, I know that there are many imams and Muslim community leaders who are conscious of the importance of such a noble jihad and its ramifications here in the secular West, but the pragmatic truth is that mosques and Muslim communities that are purposely ethnically divided because of their own ignorance, are just worship museums for the kafir to view. If you stand there listing to their alibis of why they are here in this country outside of a jihad for the mercy of Allah and to their leap from their Promise Lands, it is they that will take the very taste of jihad right out of your mouth!

But the kafir is not succeeding in this hearts, minds and souls war despite the hype; and they know it even with the support of local Muslims who are in name only! Why? (Quran 7:51).

Your Hearts Reflects
Your Freedom

O my servants who believe! Truly, spacious is my earth: Therefore serve ye me . . . And me alone!

—Quran 29:56

Both the imams and the Muslim leader's native to the beauties and richness of this secular West know that justice is what gives society order! So what is it about Islam that can be added to the systems of Western justice so as to make all citizens better human beings with the knowledge that they are here on this earth not just to breath the air and enjoy the fruits of its bounties, but with a higher purpose in serving their lord with gratitude? Raison d'être says that an oppressed man from the East preaching about Allah before free unbelieving people of the secular West is only insulting his own intelligence. For the way your hearts reflects your freedom is easy to understand if you were born free and raised in the West. The cause of the problem before us all is the hearts of the people under oppression by decree from their lord living in the East in the lands of the prophets not implementing what is in their own holy books into their very own lives. Thus, in the mind`s eye of those Western secular free people with their full civil rights standing there listening to a man from the Middle East, talking about the goodness of that divine one, upholding a monotheist faith, and is aware of the realities in the Middle East, truthfully this conversation is really too hard to fathom, too much to swallow as truth what says believable. *"Or do those in whose hearts is a disease, think that Allah will not bring to light all their rancor?"* (Quran 47:29). Logically one could reason the cause is the faith of the people itself. But in fact it is the hearts of the people themselves. Therefore, it is true your heart does reflect your freedom.

Simply migrating to kafir lands that have justice and civil liberties amongst themselves does not change your spiritual conditions or your heart. The problem is not solely a land diseased with hearts of arrogance, hate, selfishness, greed, injustice, love of power, paganism, fear, secularism, nationalism and lewdness. The problem is that the people in those Eastern lands have forgotten the promises they once made to Allah, liken to Jehovah by a Hebrew people before them! And it's not just the hearts of those afflicted people spreading these diseases worldwide, but also those unable to resolve both their problems with themselves, and with their Lord whereas the people here in the secular West has put aside divine laws in the public arena and hope to resolve their social problems with themselves with manmade ideas of justice that suits their desires. Consequently, the indigenous Western Muslim leader who has enjoyed the justice and the liberties of his country must possess a vision of ultimate victory, one that makes his countrymen realize that Islam can bring them all to a higher degree of human accomplishment and achievement provided that they possess a gram amount of faith. Hum du Allah, our helmets, shields and compasses will manifest through our faith in action, our exclusive fear of Allah, the remembrance of our purpose as Muslims, and our depth of persuasion towards those who are seeking the truth is all we need.

Yet, there is simply not enough cohesion amongst all Muslims who are religious here in America and/or in Europe for us to all work in tangent, so that our divine and collective force will choose the man who best understands our nation's practices and customs so that this secular society can see by our example that the problem is the people's hearts not the monotheist faith itself. A leader who innately understands that Quranic principle of "We must change the conditions of our own hearts," so that our Lord will, in his mercy change our condition here in this land we call home! (Quran 8:53).

Oh, humble reader, when I first read the Quran, I was nineteen years old at Howard University. It was interesting reading but I was also aware that hundreds of millions of people that are Muslims who are living in lands that are corrupt, whose leaders are also oppressive. Did not their hearts reflect their freedom? Of course it did. So I was not alone with my hopeless heart. I was nineteen years old a poor black man enrolled at Howard University in my nation's capital, Washington DC the most powerful and richest city on earth, yet in truth Howard University is an island of hope surround by a sea of black hopelessness, and white corruption. Our pitiful black leaders are the walking dead; black discrimination and black unemployment are the reality. Does not my faith in Christianity reflect my freedom? Did not my heart in Christianity reflect my freedom? Did not my ancestors take on the religion of their slave masters under oppression? The answer to all was yes! So what good is a monotheist faith if one's oppressors also share the same faith?

In my mind's eye, what is the evident dominant culture all around me at the time? The cure for more and better freedom was not religion but the pursuit of materialistic ideals. Did not the secular leaders of my faith at the time till this day collaborated with the corrupted capitalistic system here in America? Of course they did. Does my faith in these materialistic ideals reflect my freedom? The answer again is yes! I had no faith in this capitalistic society, I knew I was just a nigger to a great majority of my countrymen, my dreams meant nothing even if I had some pennies in my pocket and a smile on my black face. Living in a space between appearance and reality, I did not love; in fact, I hated what's looking back at me here in the ghetto. Even a blind man can see the difference between Washington DC (northwest and southeast, a black ghetto) and Washington DC Georgetown (a white prosperous neighborhood) even to this day. Washington DC is a repulsive segregated city then and now like so many American cities. My people are dying slowly everywhere I looked in my country by design and me with them by design. Walking in this culture of exploitation heading nowhere, I then knew who my enemy was. Did my faith in America reflect my freedom? The answer once again was yes. Now in hindsight I realize I must cherish my mistakes and never allow an external force to decide the internal value of oneself, which was the first crime of my life. But I shall never forget that portrait of my world, I was a young black man who had lost faith in the religion of his oppressors and hope for the future, reflecting just a heart full of dreams of opportunity, and nightmares of reality. Yes it is true, everybody got a hungry heart, everybody got a hungry heart . . .

Therefore, your heart reflects your freedom regardless of your nationality and regardless of your race, regardless of time, and regardless of oppression. This was my first lesson in Islam.

Like light to the blind, that pursuit of happiness does not mean that Muslims accept happiness as the criteria for success in their own lives. Our understanding of kader (fate), simply does not allow for it. This is one of the many truths about Islam that can be very difficult to grasp, especially during stressful times in one's life. A truth compounded by the reality that mankind is not divine, but mortal and that we all will someday die. But it's how we are going to die that is important! This relates to the tangible reality of being both dependent upon, and at the full mercy of a divine creator, one whom, by his own definition, cannot be understood by human description, and by whose design has already determined the life of every human being that has ever lived or will live, a creator that knows the choices we all will make before we are even conscious of our existence through whose mercy we're given volition over our lives, and yet needs neither worship nor anything else from its creation. A divine being that only demands gratitude in spite of what may befall us in our lives is something to ponder about. That divine one who endows us all with a fate we cannot outrun or hide from. That divine one who endows us all with a faith that will reflect our freedom depending on our hearts.

If you are not willing to fight to the death for the Islamic creed in your home country, then your kader is Diaspora. Those people with Muslim names whose motivation is the pursuit of happiness—yes, they are creatures of comforts. They long for a life of ease on this earth, their allegiance lying with whomsoever can guarantee them peace and happiness. The very thought that they themselves will have to fight— perhaps to the death—an Islamic jihad for the pursuit of happiness is not even in their vocabulary. Their creed is not kader, but free will. But for those believers who come to the secular West for the mercy and pleasure of Allah in jihad, we welcome you in our struggles and sacrifice, knowing Allah's promise is true. For whomever Allah guides, none can mislead, and whomever Allah leaves astray, none can guide aright.

Of utmost importance here in the West—even more so than in the East—is for true believers to choose wisely into their ranks those who call themselves Muslims. Simply because here in the West, live the puppeteers of those very same despots of the East! Yes, this is the land of the colonialist, the birthplace of the imperialist, the home of the oppressor in spite of their genius.

One way a nation of monotheistic peoples can transcend the challenges of living in the secular West is for believers to be innovative in our forward thinking and creative ideas, yet not in our faith. If our faith, ideas and policies cannot withstand the light of an open and free debate on a true level field of issues then in reality our faith, ideas and policies cannot be truly sustained. In an ever evolving world of hopes and dreams, ideas and aspirations, the great majority of people anywhere demand more than just the bread and butter issues of the working poor and the economic concerns of the middle class. Thus, most urgent is the need to engage the hearts, minds and souls in the pluralistic and secular West and to inspire a powerful message of how Islam can better both the individual hearts as well as the hearts of society in which they live.

For me personally, justice brings creditability to the Islamic faith when Muslim people demands freedom and justice in their lands wherever because the creed of their faith demands it. It's then living with despots in whatever land never looks real particularly if you say sovereignty belongs in the hands of the divine one only. Just how do you expect that humble reader or the world to know that there is a divine being up there somewhere if we the believing fundamentalist down right here are not ready to commit ourselves completely our way of Islamic life anywhere on this earth regardless of the pagan, secular, democratic or Communist environment we my live in? When the humble slave servant appeals with an open heart to his creator that divine one becomes evident, it would then be self-evident and apparent that our faith of Islam reflects our freedom and that creed of justice is imbedded in it to such a degree that we are willing to fight and die for it against whomever.

By broadening our audience we Muslims can create the opportunity to engage people on a massive scale, focusing on the issues that won't go away, that which is being hidden in plain sight, as well as understanding the consequences of not living by the truth of "In God We Trust." For as mentioned, not only can Islam can make you a better person Islam can make this a better country. It is only a matter of attitude, aspiration, and patience, and the mercy of Allah upon our jihad.

Sure it is going to be a long war of hearts, minds, and souls, a struggle that will vex and frustrate the unbelievers as well as believers. Putting forth this idea, that contribution that Islam can benefit our Western societies thus turning the hearts of the people therein to be more just to others outside of themselves is worth the struggle.

If a blind black fundamentalist like Ray Charles can first win the "heart" of the state of Georgia then travel the country and unchain the hearts of white America, then we the Muslim believers of the West need to open our eyes and expand our collective faith, much in the same way that the Million-man March in Washington DC changed the African-American perception of reality. So I say to you the whole world been suing for justice and peace for ages. It's time we start turning skeptics into believers by being the solutions to their very needs! Islam is within our reach here in America and in the West. How many states in America can we win over by engaging the public, by being outspoken, by taking a stand in the streets, and fearlessly presenting to all people Allah as the true source of our common wealth in this land?

As that pop-star fundamentalist Michael Jackson and others once sang, "We are the world. We are the children. It's time to make a better place, so let's start giving." Yes, if that moon-walker who told us about "The Man in the Mirror," if he in all his brilliance and sincerity along with the work of so many others in the music world can get their message out to an ever-broadening audience, then why can't we fundamentalists—we who've received from our Lord a book which illuminates true success in this life—raise the bar, and become more outspoken in how our faith in that Divine One can make each man and woman a better person and make each country a better nation. Our job is to turn those divine words "In God We Trust" into reality in people's hearts.

Yes, your heart does reflect your freedom. My only gripe is you cannot be half a jihadist and a half beggar unto mammon. If people should see you walking down those streets and you start to smile, you start to shine every time you venture unto that field of mammon. Then one look at you and jihad is no longer a mystery, relished. They just do not simply walk on by, because not all people are incoherent. Anyone who has a lion's heart knows that faith is the composer of one's freedom. An Islamic faith is a faith that is thinking out loud when Allah is enquiring on his subject state of heart and welfare, therefore separating winners from losers!

Yes, I had no doubt in my heart that your heart, oh, humble reader, reflects your freedom. If you fear for your life in the land that you are standing in because of the lack of liberty and justice, as well as the lack of freedom, then why are you standing there telling me and the world you are a Muslim, or a Jew, or a Christian for that matter, and not take a stand, and do something about it? There is something about that man in the mirror, that can make that change of your heart so that it may reflect your faith and enhance your freedom who will not sit still, if you just let it be so.

Dying For Love

One does not live by bread alone, but by the very word that comes forth from the mouth of God.

—Bible, Matt. 4:4

We all know what should be like navigating through our own closet. We somehow get caught up in our own red tape on how to say and do the right thing to ourselves and others.

Some of us adrift within our own promenade while others protract into characteristic doctrines of Murphy's law because of the ambiguity of this life. I, the great-great grandson of ex-slaves into Americas on both my father and mother side from Africa, am guilty of thought crime.

Which thought crime? The thought crime of attempt suicide! I had the gall to complain to God all mighty about the ambiguity of my life and all life on April 11, 1981. Yes, the audacity of trying to step out early on God's date-due note has its price. Therefore, God sent me to a prison for seven years where I met some of the best friends and the best human beings I ever met in my life at the time. Thus certainly confirms there is a world invisible, with a light of its own; many may consider this as a merit of its mercy for those tired of being afraid of being alive. By the time Ramadan came by in April 1987, I was already a Muslim, I had found Allah in the dark, and in heart and spirit, freer and happier than at any time in my life, in spite of being in prison. My life was even better then when I was out there than outside these walls walking the streets in America looking for hope in that seems like hell on earth, yet Allah (swa) knows best. I was freer than hundreds of millions of my own countrymen outside of these walls of this prison, this fact I shall remember till the day I die. That`s how I know God did indeed bless America, and how America made me become a better Muslim, such an inconvenient truth and an ironic signature of this modern age!

That`s why "beware what you pray for" is very important early in life; to understand a picture is worth a thousand words is true but a prayer is worth a lifetime if it is accepted should be ingrained in the heart at an early age. Yes, one simple ideal image can speak volumes unto the ignorant masses but one simple sincere prayer that`s positively answered can help a person understand his lord, himself, and his enemy if he or she has the patience. For example, *"On no soul doth Allah place a burden greater than it can bear. It gets every good that it earns, and it suffers every ill that it earns. [Pray]: 'Our lord! Condemn us not if we forget or fall into error; our Lord! Lay not on us a burden like that which thou did lay on those before us; Our lord! Lay not on us a burden greater than we have strength to bear. Blot out our sins, And grant us forgiveness, Have mercy on us. Thou art our protector; help us against those who stand against faith"* (Quran 2:286).

For those of us here in the West that is religiously inclined in our resistance, we must see the big picture in order to achieve the stated goals of our jihad. It is true I went to Howard University because I wanted to be an engineer, or a businessman, perhaps enroll in the ROTC program (Reserve Officers Training Corps), military. I felt at the time I could benefit myself, my family, and my community. Consequently this was a burden I placed on myself I could not bear. The why became apparent if I was only more patient with my lord! Therefore, my prayers to be successful at Howard University was indeed achieved, thou Allah most merciful preferred I learn more about humanities and undertake a journey that became infinitely more harrowing and rewarding than I had anticipated before my patience and/or tethered date due note runs out.

However, not everybody`s perception of spiritual bankruptcy because of their view of the present ambiguity in their lives ends in a favorable good reckoning from their lord! What`s really going viral in the commonwealth of mankind for generations is that growing virtual invisibility of hopelessness! For example, that cherished Christian fundamentalist Mother Teresa said, "The greatest disease in the West today is not tuberculosis or leprosy; it is being unwanted, unloved, and uncared for. We can cure physical diseases with medicine; but the only cure for loneliness, despair, and hopelessness is love. There are many in the world who are dying for a piece of bread, but there are many more dying for a little love. The poverty in the West is a different kind of poverty; it is not only a poverty of loneliness but also of spirituality. There is a hunger for love as there is a hunger for God."

Similarly, it was Malcolm X, the cherished Muslim fundamentalist, who said, "Who`s to blame for the hate that hate begets?" Even so, in today's world dominated by the secular West cultural ideals and its baby boomer generation holding these countries` top leadership roles, have men and women leading the world today learned to avoid the dire mistakes of their predecessors? "We Fundamentalists" believe not. In fact, the true legacy of the secular West since the end of World War II, is defined by an endless wave of wars, greed, corruption, injustice, and scandals. Including the cold war, the Korean War, the fiasco Vietnam War, the nuclear arms race, the conflict over civil rights in America, the apartheid in South Africa, and apartheid in Zionist Israel, the savings and loan bank scandals, corporatization and globalization, that demand-supply Drug war, the huge increase in alcoholism, the September 11 attacks, the fiasco wars in Iraq and Afghanistan, to name but a few. For the real inconvenient truth is that socially, economically, and politically, the secular West and its democratic systems have egregiously continuously failed the people!

Therefore in this era of ideological warfare, the alleged crime of suicide deserves your attention. One doesn't need to be a born-again political ambulance chaser to realize that the act of intentionally murdering oneself is becoming more and more fashionable when the rainbow isn`t enough and your reach doesn`t exceed your needs. But what to do when one lives in poverty amongst countless others cast into similar circumstances? What do you do when your dreams are not fulfilled and you are bankrupted by reality? When that dream mate, that dream parent, that dream sibling, that dream job, home, or friend, has vanished? When you find yourself living in what so often seems like the absurd enterprise of life? One does not need to stand there grieving among the dead in the coroner`s office to be aware of the growing human epidemic of self-destruction here in the democratic secular Western world with its capitalistic heart, where money talks and everything else walks.

Out of control? Of course, it is, for a long time; that human scale of self-violence has been the gospel anatomy of human failures for ages!

The World Health Organization (WHO) states that approximately one million people will take their own lives every year. Simply put, every forty seconds a human being in this modern era dies of a self-inflicted wound brought on by poverty, loneliness, distress, and a pronounced spiritual vacancy. Was it not that rejected Jewish fundamentalist prophet Jesus of Nazareth who said, "Man does not live by bread alone?"[72] Yes, most of us are living in denial, yet the battleground is all around us, a literal mine field devoid of hope and trip wired with despair. However, in the secular democratic West the facts are clear: Suicides greatly outnumber homicides by a great multitude of times. Homicides in America in 2010 totaled 13,636 people; and Homicides in Europe, both eastern and western is 23,400 people in 2010. In 2010, the number of suicides in America is 38,364 according to the Center for Disease Control and Prevention and American Association of Suicidology. It is greater than all the homicides of America and all of Europe combined and then some. In 2013, the suicide rate has peaked over 40,000 nationally. Suicide is now the fourth most common cause of death, behind cancer, heart disease and unintentional injury such as drowning even surpassing fatal car crashes!

Dr. Gudjon Magnusson from the World Health Organization (WHO), a director for Europe in charge of Mental Health, told the Society (guardian.co.uk) in Helsinki, Finland, that "Europe needs to lose it's shameful record." He also said, "There are 873,000 people who commit suicide worldwide and there are 163,000 people who commit suicide in Europe. In addition there is probably ten to fifteen times that number of attempted suicides!"

Because I am still a fan, I can still remember somewhere over the rainbow back in June 22, the year 1969, back when my family was still living in the Bronx, New York City, and my younger brother Clive and I were driving with our father going on about town coming home late one weekend night on the West Side Highway. On the radio, the Beatles had just finished singing "I Want to Hold Your Hand" and "All You Need Is Love" when the rhythm of our sky-blue Buick was cut short by the announcement that Judy Garland was dead from an apparent suicide!

With the news, I turned to my father and said, "Why didn't she just click her heels and say, 'There's no place like home'?" And my father said, "She's not alone. Not everybody's home has love under its roof!"

Like Judy Garland's final exit indicates, the rate of suicides in the secular West continues to grow. Stricken by their lot in life, by the

---

[72]   Matt. 4:4

false promises of a system of opportunity and a spirituality that has failed them, thousands of people destroy themselves and the lives of their loved ones every day. Yes, it is an inconvenient truth that the consequences of a failed domestic policies are the death chimes of hundreds of thousands of people whose hopes and dreams have gone unnoticed and unfulfilled. "We Fundamentalists" believe that this domestic institutional neglect is part of a policy of social, cultural, and mental conditioning predicated solely on the agnostic idea of the "survival of the fittest!" You may ask how can this be in such a modern era of our times that when millions of our neighbors are in such desperate spiritual need the answer to them is denial of the problems they are faced with? They are deemed just not fit enough, so ignore and move on. And, if so, what has been gained in making the positive change today here in this secular Western world?

When we look at the annals of American and Western and Eastern Europe today, the truth is millions of their citizens are living in a suicidal twilight zone, with more than 40,000 known dead by their own hand just in America every year and 163,000 known dead in Europe every year and growing. Now, with the help of our modern-day life insurance industries, many people are "worth more dead than alive" in these times of economic and social hardship. In many cases, the American dream consists these days of platitudes about achieving success, but only words themselves and a bank account in the black cannot truly sustain the social fabric of any nation! The reality is millions of people feel unwanted, unloved, and uncared for, a spiritual condition that is truly toxic to any society. In spite of all the hype about freedom, justice and the power of the dollar or euro, the central tenet of the secular and capitalist West is "Show me the Money." Yes, we the people are free to speak, but there is no real dialogue on these issues; between the citizenry, secular faiths, and the governments we have. Likewise, what is impressed upon ordinary people—from the young, to the middle-aged, to our seniors—engaged in social media and networking on sites such as Google, Yahoo, Face-book, Twitter, and YouTube is the acceptability of consumerism, idle gossip, and pornography, while religion is treated as a last-place oddity. Nowadays the people of the West do not have to run from despots and tyrants, but they are running away from each other! As such, if we refuse to listen to one another, then how can our hopes, ambitions and dreams possibly enrich the society as a whole? What should had been said in this past presidential election year, the lines coming from all the candidates worthless mouths should not be about more and better jobs and less taxes, but about more and better trust amongst ourselves and less unnecessary drama in our world! For those of us who want so much from that divine one whom we trust in heaven, strange that we give so little time to our fellow human beings right here on earth. As parents, I know we are carrying a lot more drama and social weight unnecessarily in this so-called modern social era, so this heart-to-heart talk is really overdue and critical.

I ask of you: do you really have to travel far to discover what will it take to make the dreams, hopes and aspirations come true in this land of the free, and home of the brave. Just open your hearts and eyes and declare what are we going to do with our time here now that the lord has thrown that gauntlet at the feet of the Muslims, Christians, and Hebrews here in the West.

Now, that we have found our lord here in the land of broken dreams and heartache. Our test is how to embrace one another and to help someone else touch what they are dreaming of; otherwise, those outside the house of prophet Abraham, as well as those still searching within, will continue to ask Allah, their Yahweh, their God, of what good their lives are for! Is this life, just meant to be a struggle, survival of the fittest, then the cold grave? As we considering this, it's easier to imagine what Mr. George Harrison, that musical fundamentalist ex-Beatle, means, when he sang "My Sweet Lord" that "I really want to see you." Is Mr. Harrison suggesting that, in the end, to face the one who gave purpose about oneself in this life in regards to ones lord is more relaxing and more rewarding than the music of the times?

As we the believers walk these lands of liberty, freedom and justice, we call out daily to our Lord for guidance, to help by way of example, to fasten the seatbelts during these turbulent times, and to remind us all that the lifejacket lies truly above our prayers. To those we've embraced, we'll stand by you; and if you wish to stray from the path in pursuit of bliss and happiness, may you always know there is always a safe spiritual port in which to moor!

In truth, however, we shouldn't be having this conversation. Have you ever listened to a Muslim praying? A Christian praising? Or, for that matter, a Jew chanting the Torah? It is no secret that we are all living in this benighted era because we all have not collectively put our backs together and come to understand that so long as we love each other more than our enemies hate us, we shall always win, insha Allah. We can have all the freedom, liberty, and justice we desire; but if we do not have a common spirituality, that unconditional will to want for others what we want for ourselves, then suicides will be more fashionable and the lessons thereof ignored. That idea to continue to intentionally murder ourselves in this "promised land" of broken dreams will not be stopped by today's governmental hype and social-cultural scarecrows, but by a new voice of compassionate spiritual attitude of hope reaching out to others unconditionally.

Yes, there comes the moment in all our lives when we will get off that self-made treadmill and assess our purpose in life. Yes, indeed even for those who are merely spectators, those hidden prisoners of conscience the word is getting out what most people think of suicide as a solitary act, one that affects a single person, and/or stranger is over. Indeed, after the massacre of twenty second-graders and six school staff members at Sandy Hook Elementary school in Newtown, Connecticut, on December 14, 2012, it's that lack of fundamental chemistry of love within the home and the denial of domestic violence in society which is still being ignored to our peril. The problem is the firearm; as far as these cowardly politicians and conceited Western secular corporate media is concerned, they wish to portray the problem is the gun. Such a devious political spin who's aim was to disarm the people in general by their own government by taking advantage of such tragic events must be noted. The answer is how we view ourselves as a people and how the mentally ill all around us are cared for! Consequently, the great majority of people in this secular society took God out of the classrooms and God out of their lives in public and at home. Then, wonder why, thoughtlessly, why there is so much violence in the public arena and so much domestic violence at home? Where is the compassion, the love, and the hope we all should be saying to ourselves?

Where's that gift of insight and care? A month before Mr. Aaron Alexis, an African American, who went on his murderous rampage of shooting up the Washington DC Navy Yard on September 16, 2013, killing twelve people and injuring another dozen people who was his co-workers, thereafter; was shot to death by police. Lo and behold, just two days later the public found out it was he who called the police in Rhode Island New York, to complain that he had to change hotels three times because, he was being pursued by three people, keeping him awake at night by sending vibrations through the walls! He said they had a microwave machine and he heard voices speaking to him through the walls, floors, and ceilings of which he shot a bullet up into." Poor Mr. Alexis also told the police that he was a Navy Yard contractor in DC and twice that month he sought treatment from the veterans affairs Department hospital for psychiatric issues. What did his concerned doctors do for Mr. Alexis other than increase his anti depressant pill Trazodone, and send him on his way is a good question in regards to how we treat people who have serious mental health problems.

Why there is so much mass and serial killing and then suicide by the accused in public and in our schools and universities in such a hideous and merciless way? Why? Why not! The "devil loves a vacuum" and is aware that the public arena and schools reflect the community and homes that they serve; thus, that is his domain. The merit of sanctity is no myth to the wise! We fundamentalists have to be frank about this sad and heartbreaking issue; please just name that true God-fearing religious school, university, and home that had a mass killing amongst themselves and suicide in it to me here in America or in Europe. May it be Muslim, Christian or Jewish!

Thus, the consequences of suicide go far beyond the shooter or the noose, or the pill-overdose; in fact, with each of these acts, countless family members, friends, coworkers—even absolute strangers—are likewise murdered and/or killed as a result of such acts of desperation and hopelessness. Most importantly, the suicide murder leaves more children without parents and more parents without children than today's homicide throughout the world, yet this fact is ignored by today's governmental social media that shamefully feels this is not fit to print and expose and address.

Simply talking about peace, love, and soul is most often not enough of a safety net these days. Sometimes it's who's that soul mate of yours is when you are riding that *Soul Train* together in life, if you have one at all. Just ask that African American entrepreneur pioneer fundamentalist Mr. Don Cornelius what I am saying is true or not; one can have what one wishes for in life and the fame, but are you happy about where those tracks are leading to in life off stage? That is the lingering iconic question. Personally I am just deeply saddened by too many losses of such men or even women like Ms. Phyllis Hyman by their own hands, whose death note reads, "I'm tired. I'm tired. Those of you that I love know who you are. May God bless you."

Those amongst us who don't have to worry about the rent, the food bill, the electric bill nor the lack of success and fame are strangely enough taking the back door out of our lives! Those that helped inspire the dreams and hopes in other people's lives are running out on empathy for themselves? That is strange. What neighborhood in the African American community that he could not lean his gray head

on somebody`s shoulder without a fuss who is from the old school who
does have much reason for hope to share? More than anything she
looked liked a beautiful woman grimly in need of love in the prime
of her life. Perhaps he was just an ordinary man entrapped in an
extraordinary circumstance like everybody else. Perhaps she was just an
ordinary woman starved of . . .

Abortion

Kill not your children for fear of want; we shall provide sustenance
for them as well as for you. Verily the killing of them is a great sin.
—Quran 17:31

Perhaps all women are ordinary people who at times entrapped in extraordinary circumstances unlike everybody else, that they are regular people who have to make hard decisions in serious moments of their lives like everybody else does. So now that this is understood, why don`t we everybody else not make a federal problem for the women of our lands and let them resolve their extraordinary circumstances like ordinary people without everybody else having to pay for it!

On the subject of abortion, the West's secular media and its public opinion polls of dubious statistics flat-out lie. Here in the West true public opinion on the issue of abortion is not fully known because it does not suit the interests of those in power to allow ordinary people to make an informed spiritual decision on the issue. We the believers understand there are consequences when any life is unjustly ended. Especially the life of an unborn human fetus that has only just begun to live that does not threaten the life and health of its mother!

Personally, I don't believe it to be a failing for a woman of modest means and facing the serious consequences of an accidental pregnancy, to make the wrong decision to have an abortion out of ignorance, even when her unborn child is not a danger to her health. I am not talking about a woman of the monotheist faith and/or married woman in general, but a woman who is ignorant to the word of God. Here in regard to the issue of abortion and abortion rights, I am in agreement with many other scholars that an individual's right to privacy is essential to any civilized society and must be respected. Where we are in disagreement with the secular Western world or Communist world is whether or not abortions can be funded with public money and that belief that life starts at the time of conception.

Whatever two people do under the boardwalk down by the sea, or behind closed doors where nobody can see, is their own business, so long as the actions of both partners are consensual is the law of these lands. Instead, the real question we must confront as concerned citizens, no matter if we live in the East or the West, is whether or not our faith in scientific validation should overshadow our collective spiritual wisdom. Thus, it is simply wrong to force any citizen morally opposed to abortion to pay taxes that fund hospitals and clinics that perform the procedure in the land.

Roe v. Wade, the United States Supreme Court's landmark 1973 decision, helped pave the way for the benighted era in which we are living; for by and large the West has failed to confront the most profound yet basic humanitarian issues. Since *Roe v. Wade*, the United States Center for Disease Control and Prevention estimates approximately fifty million American human fetuses have been aborted since 1973. They were murdered rather than orphaned, in America, but why should ordinary citizens be forced to pay the bill for an abortion that does not threaten the life of the mother is the central question? Our culture's understanding of the sanctity of life has radically changed over the years, particularly in the terms of women whose faith was always paramount. For it was Mary, the mother of Prophet Jesus, a Jewish woman who'd guarded her chastity, yet was informed by her Lord of glad tidings of a son named Jesus.[73] Yet Mary, her lord and her nation of people knew that there was no father to this son named Jesus.[74] Notwithstanding, Mary, mother of Prophet Jesus, did not seek out an abortion in spite of what her lord had announced to her. Still she had the volition to do as she pleased and not carry the unborn child to full term, knowing there was no father to this child, yet her faith overshadowed both her reason and the wisdom of her land. Likewise, Allah says, *"Kill not your children for fear of poverty. We provide for them and for you. Surely, the killing of them is a great sin."*[75] Similarly, in

---

[73] Quran 66:12
[74] Quran 19:28-37
[75] Quran 17:31

regards to rape or incest and the child does not threaten the life of the mother, Prophet Muhammad (sas) asked, "*What crime did the child commit?*" (Hadith: Al-Bukhari)

Surely, for many here in the secular West and Communist East, where scriptural reasoning is often blinded, the fetus is simply just a lump of flesh and blood. Be that as it may, taking into account life's apparent realities, so many people define themselves by consumerism, and whatever latest trends and fashion there are, this ruling popular culture that our secular and or socialist society today has embraced, we've concluded, that of utmost importance is not religion in one's life, but the challenges of being a human being exercising free will without regard to karma in today's media driven-world. The critics, in my humble opinion, who do not harbor that idea of life beginning at conception this is frankly too much a leap of faith for them. Indeed, for many, it is a vexing question to ask if the fetus is simply a vessel for the soul to enclose itself in human form, thus an impossibility to think about heaven for many when the voices of the bird in hand says death and taxes. Life at conception? Between a certain past and an uncertain future, of the billions of people that make up the human race, most wish to live a second life beyond the grave; the others just wish to stay alive and in good health, with some meaningful hope here on this earth without paying alimony.

Allah? Jehovah? God? The fact that billions of people believe in a divine intelligence beyond themselves and this material plane certainly doesn't make it true. However, the fact that thousands of different societies have independently come to embrace the spiritual notion of monotheist belief does require one to pause. Only how does a nation of people overcome the despondency that sets in when a women's bond between unborn child turns to hopelessness and that sacred moment of motherhood turns to dread? Who now must carry for nine months and give birth to an unwanted child? Life at conception? Not all women have faith; for many it's how do I survive a life with an unwanted child?

Despite this persistent fear and dilemma, the fact is millions of children born in the West and East, have lived their early lives in orphanages; and over time, and with guidance and love, many of these children have become both fine citizens and great contributors to society. As such, the media must tell the public more of the stories of these unwanted children. If we wish people to value their lives and each other more dearly, more of today's newspaper and magazine bylines should feature people who encourage the values of hope and love. If we wish mothers to value their unborn children more dearly, then we the believers must be determined to touch the hearts of our neighbors and assert that generational murder cannot be sustained! Yes, at one time the Hippocratic Oath—"to do no harm"—meant something; in turn, one of the great evils of the ages I believe is when a public servant oath`s no longer means anything. Similarly, one of the greatest crimes against humanity in Western and Communist societies lies in the murdering of their unborn children (infanticide). Yet the greatest affront to humanity is to say to the world that Islam is denying girls the right to education on Western terms. Hearing this, thus in the minds of religious fundamentalists would say in response to the accusers, "They seem to care about the rights of children that are born but when the issue is those millions of children who are unborn those children have no rights regardless of gender? Such a hypocrisy of the hearts. I must state this publicly with concern, why this is regarded a different issue and concern as if the believers are blind to the truth!"

Many nights I lay awake, thinking, yes, I am troubled about these moral issues that put me at odds over at my job working as a volunteer over at the Urban League in Englewood, New Jersey in the spring of 2011 whose staff and management was publicly "pro choice" in their agenda. Except me a supporter of "pro life" in my creed, so we parted ways sadly in spite of their integrity in other business and social affairs. I am aware today that one needs both a powerful voice and a strong pen to back the kind of change that resonate truth, hope, and love. Yes, it is a crime when millions of unborn children are put to death and you and I have to pay the bill. Yes, it is a crime when mainstream society knows that abortion is a miscarriage of justice, yet their only solution is to ask what a poor woman will do with an unwanted child? But what if that poor woman's moral code is different from our own? Yes, it is even a poor woman's right to choose, but responsibility must come with that decision (Quran 17:32). It is time we as a people stop living in denial and taking the last word from cowardly politicians in regards to the practice of infanticide in our society. For we are well aware that preventing people from discussing diverse opinions only brings about ignorance, resentment, anger, and hate!

Motown

To be alive is to feel the soul.

—Muhammad Dawud

The great challenges of our time demand that we all feel that soul outside our own. Someday is today; hence, only people without any talent or vision who thinks this creative life we are all experiencing is all about money, sex, and power is both stunning and ominous. The challenges the poor and middle class that must overcome now in today's world are greater than ever before. In ghettos all over the secular West one can see stacks of bleached-out dreams and bone-dry hope littering the neon-lit streets corners. I never saw the truth in the American dream; just the same, I've had to endure the journey demanded by my Lord. Yes, we all endure—as a family, as a people—so may Allah bless my parents and my country!

As a child, I did not know how poor my family was because in my Bronx neighborhood we were all poor. Black, white, Asian and Hispanic—in the 1960s and 70s we were all chasing that shadow called opportunity. Though there were people selling death in the form of heroin to anybody who wanted an easy lift and a moment of no frustration from their lot in life, but it was Motown truthfully that was really a hard competition to beat, who was also selling a mixture of fury, hope, and love uncut. It was Mr. Berry Gordy, that daring African American fundamentalist who knew how to take a mundane moment and make it livable and real, who gave my neighborhood "The Miracles" to anybody who wanted to "Shop

Around," and there were many people who truly needed that moment of deliverance and gratitude to savor which those songs provided.

In those emerald cities across America—with their millions of "hopeful" addicts trying to earn a decent living, keeping some meaning in their lives and all the while praying for a better tomorrow—truly it was Motown that trustworthy novacain for the African American people in the 1960s, 70s and 80s when so many just couldn't bear the pain of living the American dream any longer!

Looking out westward from my secret lair, that fourth-floor window of our apartment on 1818 Prospect Avenue gave me the bird's-eye view of the people and the world I inherited as a child in the Bronx, New York. My family (mother, and younger brothers Clive and Sherod) stayed away from and was saved from that depression-era nightmares and blues by taking our novacain early in the mornings. Yes, it was by listening to the radio before 'Corn Flakes' and/or buttered pancakes that mom would make, it's that novacain which goes a long way in setting the right perception, the right tone. As the sun rises, Diana Ross & The Supremes entered our humble home live and, never minding who's right or wrong, sang "Love Child" (born in poverty); thus, life wasn't a stranger anymore! "Someday We'll Be Together" tidied up our small world as a family! As the world turns, I remember those innocent days back when the "Four Tops" crooned "Reach Out I'll Be There"; they genuinely resurrected from the dead that idea of a man's love and faithfulness to his family for a few moments! "Can't Help My Self (Sugar Pie, Honey Bunch)" helped me comprehend the depth of love at the age of eight! These were the sound tracks of our early lives that helped triumph the day's rays.

Yet, it was Mr. Lou Rawls, that gospel-rooted fundamentalist who comes to my mind when he sang "I rather drink muddy waters and lay down and sleep in a hollow log" it was he I believe who understood the life challenges we the African American was facing without breaking a sweat or panic, in all this confusion and racism of how to make ends meet in this land of the American dream. Singing "Lady Love" spilled the beans about how a man can win the heart of any woman that looks his way! He was truly a three-dimensional artist who understood what was going on in this heart, mind, and soul war; yes, he was the one who put his money and time where his mouth was for the United Negro College Fund. That's why that song "At Last" was so successful because thousands of my poor African American young brothers and sisters knew what it means to get that scholarship to study in a college or university here in America without selling out your soul for it.

You just knew deep down in your heart that Gladys Knight and the Pips gave up the recipe and save you all that heartache of an odyssey of how to truly keep that man, when she chanted, "If I was your Woman . . . you will have no other woman!" But if you wish to get to the "The Nitty Gritty" and stay out of the devils dragnet and his charms because people are people, then we tune into the Temptations when they sang "Just My Imagination (Running Away With Me)" when those moments of unfulfilled dreams and expectations came again and again.

I was indeed blessed, oh, humble reader, now that I stop to think about it, living here in America at the right time and place, being influenced by everything from the street life urban scenes that was all around me to what life had to offer every step of the way, to that hidden era of trying to live inside the culture of the Fifth Dimension with their song "Let The Sunshine In" to dealing with that new lifestyle of the Jackson 5`s "The Love You Save." I just want to say 'thank you all' for help bringing in those best human moments of my life.

Today I have no doubt that millions of my fellow African Americans, together as well as tens of millions of poor and middle-class Americans, yearn again for that trustworthy novacain that is risk free. That inspirational live human voice of positive passion and meaningful conversation and your world momentarily becomes a peaceful, loving, and quieter place to endure is truly not amongst the grass roots anymore!

Yes, those yesterdays are gone. That positive grass root passion of meaningful conversation that can bring out the human dynamic spirit thus given rise to a passionate voice, which can return the compliment of life in a song, is, alas, falling in the social ratings against the street-level juvenile rap, trash hip-hop, alcohol, cocaine, heroin, and suicide by design!

Oh, humble reader, the essential trustworthy novacaine voice that is risk free has been push to the rear and made out of fashion. Since it`s no longer deemed suitable by the sorcerers culture of the dominant social elite, the current demand today is cheap chatter and fast rant! Living the now in a space between an "appearance" and "reality," without that essential trustworthy novocaine voice, we are just dangerously attracting I believe, the wrong kind of karma in our social lives! Essentially do you love or hate what`s looking back all around at you? This important human constitutional musical moment of clarity is being ignored at a price; this non-resonance era and getting all dressed up with no real place to go is suicidal.

Back in the day, you can body surf the crowd, and reach a Quincy Jones "Razzamatazz" and/or a Barry White "Love Theme" and stay sane until the next paycheck. Yes, you can rationalize all you want, but we are now being smothered to death from breathing in all this drama of being a commodity pop of corporate systems of power in spite of our earnest struggles to achieve social and economic liberation in our lives. Attempting to "live within the truth" midway through the day not just "within one's means" is why human songbirds matter in this creative and extraordinary lives we inherited and experiencing.

Everything is Permissible

If the truth had been in accord with their desires truly the heavens and the earth, and all beings therein would have been in confusion and corruption! Nay, we have sent them their admonition, but they turn away from their admonition.

—Quran 23:71

What keeps me up at night is that the words of one Russian novelist may have merit. It was Fyodor Dostoyevsky, that chilly fundamentalist who noted that, "if God did not exist then everything is permissible." The notion of our lives without the commandments of a Divine being to be feared and obeyed is an important viewpoint to consider. But will human value laws (secularism) give way to the law of the "survival of the fittest" heralding the consequences which might be worse than that alien animal kingdom`s masterpiece of that merciless insect kingdom law of "friend or foe." Why? Too often so-called modern civilization has thrown away that essential purpose of human life and that we humans did not bestowed individual life and the soul that comes with it. I believe this is simply because as human beings we have a great capacity for selfishness, greed, and most notably destruction, both of our own species and to the other creatures of the earth, over which we are the stewards. Yes, there are times when one must be a rationalist; for if the idea of a Divine Being is removed from the human mind, we lose that essential element of sanctity in our lives. Correspondingly, the moral value of human life will be diminished as we become predatory and descend to the law of survival of the fittest, thus heralding a new reality in our lives featuring the seven deadly sins—pride, greed, lust, anger, envy, gluttony and sloth—on a global scale never before witness. "Just don`t get caught" will then be the gospel of the times!

It would be naïve, however, simply because I do not agree, to ignore an idea held by hundreds of millions of people. But just look around: If Allah, Jehovah, God did not exist then everything would indeed be permissible, and don`t get caught the golden rule. Yes, we all begin our lives as if we are awakening from an infinitely long and timeless sleep. The survival of our fledgling consciousness depends, against all odds, on a perfect conjunction of parenting, purpose, and luck. Even so, in this world there is more than what meets the eye, other than every day you keep waking up until one day you die. So let`s call a spade a spade and argue that if, in fact, life is this way—if indeed everything is permissible in our world—how much more difficult is it then for one to achieve humility? To acknowledge the obvious that the soul is our truly vital dimension, our bodies is merely how the soul clothes itself! Yet my sense is that to ignore all this means trouble.

My analysis, oh, humble reader, is that this Western and Eastern world is full of financial insecurity amongst a vast majority of the people who are trapped in this political, social and economical turmoil. To add this idea and law to the people "that everything is permissible" where human values base on desires is a world were sanctity is a myth, and this indication means this is a very dangerous world!

My perception of such a crisis world that is full of fools, nuclear weapons, and biological weapons is a people prying into evil from curiosity. Following their desires, and lusts without shame, pussy can pull a boat a golden rule that cannot be ignored is troubling. As humanity passes the seven-billion mark, and still having a great callous attitude toward the opinions and suffering of others; whose creed is "everything is permissible, show me the money, money talks, and don`t get caught" shall forecast the rule of money, and power, upholding societies that is apt to be patient with the evils they witness all around them. Behind the scenes, however, whether at the home front or workplace or on the sidewalk, trust will never stand a chance!

The "end justify the means" polices of this day precede "everything is permissible"; so if you are like the 3 billion people out there who are in some way or form in a Monotheist jihad against people therein who refuses to sincerely contribute to the elucidation of truth, and justice, then it is about time you be a part of the future while you still can!

Homosexuality

Thou shall not lie with mankind, as with womankind: It is an abomination!

—Lev. 18:22

If a man also lie with mankind as he lies with a woman both of them have committed an abomination: they shall surely be put to death, their blood shall be upon them.

—Lev. 20:13

We also sent Lut (Lot): He said to his people: Do ye commit lewdness such as no people in creation ever committed before you? For ye practice your lust on men in preference to women: ye are indeed a people transgressing beyond bounds and his people gave no answer but this: they said: "drive them out of our city, these are indeed men who want to be clean and pure!

—Quran 7:80-84

If you are willing to spend ages painting your life, then at the very least be merciful to yourself and put that life in a frame of good light.

I still remember the time when that dude walked by with such flare your breath was taken away. He didn`t care! Something in the way he wore that dress you just knew this act was no dare. For Flip Wilson, that shameless American fundamentalist comedian, the world was his stage. Yes, I remember those days we as a family, along with millions of others, laughed till our kidneys hurt. Except my father, of course, who at times sat stone faced a fan of Reverend Leroy who would only mutter, "You're right; the devil made you do it." For Ms. Geraldine Jones's implied message, one running across both urban and rural African American communities against our trusted social and religious grapevine was that homosexuality is an acceptable lifestyle choice.

I was a child of twelve when my father reminded me about that Lord's Prayer, that my mother taught me, not to be led into temptation. My father was an austere religious black man with both American and Caribbean roots, so there was no confusion when my Father explained to me, in a Jehovah-fearing way, that homosexuality was a lifestyle choice of the heart and mind, one that was unacceptable to Jehovah. It was my Father, who told me I was the fourth generation born free in the West, and that we as a black people had been denied our human rights. Our fore-fathers and mothers were kidnapped, beaten, raped, and enslaved by barbarous Europeans and greedy African kings. My father told me we were from those lost African tribes betrayed. Choosing his words carefully, he explained, with deep care, that this was not a world in which to wait, or beg, for change. This life of ours is a struggle like everyone else's, but we as a people will have to struggle more than others.

In his humble and matter-of-fact tone, he went on to say that since there is enough blood in the ground of our people to fill Yankee Stadium, the best way in life to remember the holocaust of our forbearers is to maintain a good character in your life, that I should always remember our humble beginnings as a people, for this can help a man hold on to his good character, and that those who can remember their humble beginnings under stressful times have a fair advantage over others.

My father went on to say that homosexuality is a state of mind; the cause is a moral disorder, and the effect is a moral disease, a sin. Life here in America is very difficult for the black man, he said, so why make life here even more difficult by being led into temptation and following your lust? Then he gave my right ear a light tug, smiled, and said, "Never forget it is not an easy life to be a black man here in America or anywhere else for that matter, so, never throw away your self-respect!"

For those who knocks and pause, reason tells us life is short, that not everybody can take it all in. So please do not misunderstand Islam, or Judaism, or even Christianity for that matter. If you wish the true intentions of the Divine One in regard to homosexuality then simply turn to the book of Leviticus, chapter 18, verse 22. The last word resting with the divine one is the key to life! Who dares to have the last word in your life, oh, humble reader? That is really the question one must consider!

Hey, son of dust, you got a lifetime to decide which whispers onstage or offstage in this world is in true rebellion to your very own soul that much is true. But are you going to be merciful to yourself and put yourself in a frame of good light? That is also the question. So beware that trial by fire: once everything is accepted permissible, then in such a case prophet Lut (Lot) is just superstition, your prayer just walked away to obscurity, the whole holy books is just a dead letter on nothing here gate!

How telling that the African Anglican church has become the mainmast of their denomination by rejecting homosexuality as an acceptable lifestyle choice. The primate of Nigeria, Archbishop Peter Akinola, said in a statement, "There is no longer any hope therefore for a unified communion. If we fail to act, we risk leading millions of people away from the faith revealed in the Holy Scriptures; and also, even more seriously, we face the real possibility of denying our savior, the Lord Jesus Christ." He went on to say, "We want unity (with the American and European Anglican church) but not at the cost of relegating Christ to the position of another wise teacher who can be obeyed or disobeyed. We earnestly desire the healing of our beloved communion, but not at the cost of rewriting the Bible to accommodate the latest cultural trend. We have arrived at a cross roads; it is for us, the moment of truth." The archbishop went to say, "Schism can only be avoided in the unlikely event that those churches which tolerate homosexual clergy and same-sex blessings change their ways. Repentance and reversal by these North American provinces may yet save our communion." In response to this, I must truly say, from my heart, that this is a God-fearing man struggling with an appropriate response to his Christian brethren gone astray over which side best represents the true ideals of Christianity in the face of the conflict over how to preserve the dignity of the faith.

All faiths have their insurgency, and we Muslims too have been tested by our Lord to see where our hearts lie.[76] *"But those who break the covenant of Allah, after having plighted their word thereto, and cut asunder those things which Allah has commanded to be joined, and work mischief in the land;—on them is the curse; for them is the terrible home!"* (Quran 13:25). Doesn't it seem odd that the Archbishop of

---

[76]   Quran 13:25

Canterbury, Dr. Rowan Williams, the titular head of the worldwide Anglican Communion, would cross an unsupportable line into moral depravity by making the church more inclusive of homosexuality contrary to the clear teachings of scripture? Yet the true motives of this same Archbishop of Canterbury—a position which not elected by his peers, but shamefully appointed by his secular government, regardless of party—are mysterious. However, the 2003 ordination of Gene Robinson, a homosexual, to bishop by the American Anglican church exposed itself to true debacle, humiliation, and ridicule, not to mention utter disregard for Leviticus 20:13 *"As a result, they have no excuse; for although they knew God they did not accord him glory as God or give thanks. Instead, they became vain in their reasoning, and their senseless minds were darkened. While claiming to be wise, they became fools and exchanged the glory of the immortal God for the likeness of an image of mortal man or of birds or of four legged animals or of snakes. Therefore, God handed them over to impurity through the lusts of their hearts for the mutual degradation of their bodies . . . Therefore, God handed them over to degrading passions, their females exchanged natural relations for unnatural, and the males likewise gave up natural relations with females and burned with lust for one another. Males did shameful things with males and thus received in their own persons the due penalty for their perversity . . ."* Rom. 1:21-32. Despite the obscenity of Robinson's appointment, it is indicative of the mind-set of many in a secular democracy, where the politically correct decision is the proper decision, scriptural reasoning be damned!

I sincerely believe every person has the "right" to choose his or hers preferred lifestyle, but I also say to you this divinely granted volition of lifestyle has its consequences. So is there any truth to the whispers that Dr. Rowan Williams, the Archbishop of Canterbury traded truth for unity at the Lambeth conference? Perhaps the Archbishop possessed *The Truce of God*, a book in which he has written to give him the authority he needed on this issue, though, personally, I would like to see this *Truce of God*. Authentic new scriptural revelation is something to pay great heed to, not to scoff at.

Though I too abhor divorce, the ever-present shrill of that whispering campaign of "I told you so" got a boost when that homosexual Anglican bishop Gene Robinson said publicly: "I always wanted to be a "June bride." This is the same Anglican bishop who had divorce his wife and children to go live with and marry another man!

Prophet Muhammad (sas) said, "Once you lose your shame, do as you wish!" and "Allah curses men who wears clothing of the women and women who wears clothing of the men!"

To be fair and not wishing to exacerbate a fallen Christian fig leaf, I do remember a Mr. Kissinger, my Boy Scout master back in 1972. Mr. Kissinger was a natural leader, a European American in his fifties who stood about six foot five and possessed a distinct air of self-confidence. You didn't have to ask if he was a veteran. You could tell by his stride and mannerism; thus from his guidance, my brother Clive and I earned a number of merit badges.

Mr. Kissinger taught twenty-one young scouts not just how to earn a merit badge for swimming, he taught us how to be lifesavers. He also taught us never to panic in the woods if we ever got lost, a perfect metaphor to understand if you wish to see the forest from the trees. For it is true that entertaining alternative viewpoints in this jungle called life enables a man to better choose the correct path amongst the many trails. Yes, it was that Boy Scout master, Mr. Kissinger who lived on Roosevelt Street off Glenwood Avenue in Teaneck, New Jersey, who sat around the bonfire we built together on a cold November night in the backwoods of Pennsylvania, making sure we all knew our Boy Scout oath by heart:

"On my honor I will do my best, to do my duty to God and my country and to obey the scout law, to help other people at all times, to keep myself physically strong, mentally awake, and morally straight."

Indeed, how strange how few men today realize the importance of promise made unto one's Lord! It was fresh evenings like these in those dark Pennsylvania backwoods that made me reflect, anchored me when I've been at my ends, just living by the hour. To remember to "always be prepared" isn't a bad motto to live by; it's also the high moral ground that counts. So it's instructive to look at the June 28, 2000 Supreme Court case of *the Boy Scouts of America vs. Dale*, argued on the basic principle of freedom of association, where the court ruled it reasonable to exclude a person from membership of a group when "the presence of that person affects in a significant way the group's ability to advocate public or private viewpoints." Secular governments and likeminded organizations have always been known to intrude into the internal affairs of private groups—for example, by forcing a group to accept a member it does not desire, such as in the *Boy Scouts of America vs. Dale*. So, why the anxiety as far as the archbishop of Canterbury, Dr. Rowan Williams, is concerned?

Perhaps, it is knowing that not all shepherds are saviors; the creator of the heavens and the earth created me to be a man. I choose to remain that way in fear of him, in spite of the cultures conjured around me. My father was right. It is not an easy thing to be a man and say no to your lower desires! To say no and not live by your passions and lusts! Yes, my father was right. God does not create abominations for that abomination to turn to its lord and say, "I am thus because of your will! No!" Men and women are thus because of their own desires, given their own volition, given to them by their own Lord so he may judge their own hearts! Yet not everybody had a father nearby in their lives to warn firmly about those afflictions in life that may come their way! Yet not everybody in life will take heed their creed of faith that`s there to warn firmly about those trials by fire in life that`s sure to come their way.

Alas today, in this secular Western world, where human values rules supreme. Jehovah gets the blame in that their belief that homosexuality and lesbianism is a decree by their lord from their lord in their DNA that they had no choice in the matter of their life style so they plea! Yesterday, in former times Yahweh also got the blame! *"But after them there followed a posterity who missed prayers and followed after lusts, soon, then, will they face destruction, except those who repent and believe, and work righteousness: for these will enter the garden and will not be wronged in the least"* Quran 19:59-60.

That War On Drugs

All that talk about the war on drugs is just rhetorical brilliance. You can surely see everything clearly from behind these enemy lines where Mr. Booze is king if you wish to know the truth.

When the unrelenting struggle of the daily grind sets neighbor against neighbor, Mr. Booze is there, incessant in his thirst to please. Yet the primary question remains: why has the human thirst for alcohol persisted for millenniums despite a yearly human death toll in the millions? The World Health Origination (WHO) on their "Global Status Report on Alcohol and Health" says that 2.5 million people worldwide die annually from alcohol-related deaths. Of which 320,000 young people die annually between the ages fifteen to twenty-nine from alcohol-related deaths. The National Council on Alcoholism and Drug Dependence says that 6.2% of all males and 1.1% of all females die of alcohol-related deaths in America annually.

But I could not help but wonder at this time and moment and say honestly to myself where this entire scourge would lead us to as a people? Yes, it is a fact that alcohol has successfully helped quench the spiritual thirst of the secular Western and Communist worlds for centuries. For every whispered blessing over wine, celebratory toast, and champagne cork popped to greet those in the world's winners circles, alcohol has brought about the ruin of men, women, families, communities, tribes and even entire nations.

Yet we must not be greedy with our desire to want every blessing for ourselves. We must share the blessings of our mutual Lord with all people of the book and recognize the potential social destruction we all face both, in the East, and here in the West. Yes, we are all allies in this particular jihad; for if we did not then Mr. Booze would pit us against each other. We the believers must hear that noble trumpet call. We must be that Southern Comfort, that *Book of Common Prayer* for each other. We cannot hope to be spectators and expect to succeed, for that power of suggestion which resonates in the hearts of men, now equates with the perils of free will.

But what can be done about this scourge? Yes, what shall we do? Foremost, we must be willing to look objectively at the grass roots of our society. Western as well as Eastern societies are in a deathly denial when it comes to alcohol, the number one killer drug facing humanity. Yet their governments have totally surrendered when it comes to war on alcohol. Instead, a majority of governments have decided to join in on the human scourge by legalizing it and taxing it rather than hoping to abolish it all together. Secondly, getting Christians to throw their bottles of beer, wine, liquor to the pigs will be easy once they see Muslims expand their Islamic law beyond Mecca and Medina and into every Muslim city and homes. Thirdly, Jews and pagan enterprisers would be less inclined to invest money in Mr. Booze once they see the light of brotherly love in the mosques and temples shining brighter than the neon from the pubs. For us, the believers, why should we think that abstinence for all is not our business? For us, helping the kufr get rid of ladies` nights and happy hour would bring about the best of consequences, brothers cleansing the wounds of brothers, sisters uplifting the chastity of sisters. Yet the kufr must see this scourge for themselves and act on it wholesomely.

It is true. We must be prudent, to not merely throw stones into the well that quenches a human thirst to the neglect of a spiritual thirst. For the obituaries in our homes and communities are truly a breathless tale of heartache, and misery and can no longer be accepted as the norm in the secular West. Since no matter our creed we are all investors on the larger scale, the affordable truth is that we are facing a runaway crisis of spiritual health, for which the only practical remedy is to legalize all drugs! Why? For at its heart, what we have is not a "law and order" problem but a "public health" problem and a "demand and supply" problem predicated on a spiritual vacuity. But is today`s society willing to confront the dangers of challenging the alcohol and tobacco industries? Or perhaps it is easier to deal with the international drug cartels only and cash in with the governmental hype? How do you fight a war when the adversary rests inside the hearts of hundreds of millions of peoples whose sin is the need to escape momentarily from their daily grind of their lives? Please don't expect help or relief from those elected political cowards of the ruling Western secular elite and/or the United Nations Commission on Narcotic Drugs, whose only plan of action adopted in Vienna in 2009, which basically fleeces their taxpayers of billions of dollars and euro's on a futility war that can have no end. Meanwhile, ever since, millions of people have overdosed, millions have been imprisoned, millions more have become addicts, millions of families have been destroyed, and billions of dollars and euro's have been made for the few hundreds. What has been accomplished?

Till now I still happily remember that summer tranquil evening back in 1976, when my girl and I were circling down Manhattan's Eastside highway, listening to Petula Clark's "Downtown" on the stereo as we headed into the heart of the city that never sleeps. Faith in those days was in short supply, so we lived for weekend nights like this one, for in it lay the true mantel of happy hour as we happily cruised down the neon streets of Chinatown into Greenwich Village, digesting a fine Chinese meal and sweet conversation. For I was dedicated then to the golden rule of not running out of money, soft ideas, and blissful action when you are with your girl.

We parked my 1969 canary yellow Camaro on East Third Street and made our way to the Blue Note, the famous jazz club. This is one of the few places you end up sparkling when you get caught between the moon and New York City. We were ready to wash away the daily grind with a mellow nightcap evening of music in the ripe darkness of the moment. Soon I was nursing my ice cold Budweiser, the "King of Beers," though I was bearing witness to a greater truth, one which began manifesting in my breast right then. As we sipped our beers and listened to the rhyme and music of the live band, I noticed the Anheuser-Busch posters featuring the "Great Kings of Africa" on the walls. It was then I realized that Mr. Booze was exploiting our noble roots in order to maximize profits. But this was a brilliant stroke of marketing coming at the economic expense of millions of minorities mis-educated by the American public school system and who was unaware of our noble past. Looking at those posters, I realized that we as a people were like tropical plants: we were cultivated in the Western world to serve the special interest of our masters. Truly, "*Winds can wake up the dead*," as Eric D. Walrond, that fundamentalist Harlem renaissance writer once wrote. And I agree with Alex Haley, the author of *Roots,* and coauthor of *The Autobiography of Malcolm X,* how Budweiser, the king of beers, awakened the consciousness of so many African-Americans back in 1975 in regards to who we are as a people before that holocaust, before that Middle Passage, like no other American public library or public high school could ever have done. That journey from kings and queens to slaves to niggers to kings and queens again is an acknowledgement of the depths and brilliance of jihad, and of the understanding that "Allah will not change the conditions of a people until the people change the conditions of their own hearts."

Whichever drug they may use against us—alcohol, heroin, cigarettes, cocaine, or pills—they are all webs to catch the wayfarer. Still there are those audacious enough to believe that this isn't merely a demand-and-supply problem. All our lives we've heard the mantra: Raise the age limit and tax the hell out of it, then let the Drug Enforcement Agency (DEA) and the Bureau of Alcohol, Tobacco, Firearms (ATF) deal with the problem. But as today's policies to support the continued fighting of a "drug war" paid for with taxpayers money, policy makers continue to ignore the cause of the problem, which is demand. And making sense of this demand is endemic to implementing their secular-minded policies. Likewise, today's Western media mostly refuses to confront the reasons for the massive demand for drugs in our society. Those in power realize the wisdom of not giving voice to those that possess the moral high ground, lest the lifestyle, influence, and profits of the power elite be threatened. Thus, as far as the believers are concern, it is our responsibility to transform drug policy from a law-and-order problem to a public health problem. Why is that demand for drugs is so high in our community in the first place.

How many fatwas must be written to remind the world that the true sanctity of human life is not a monopoly of today's Western secular thought. There is nothing as barebones and sobering as DOA: (dead on arrival) when it comes to the loved ones we all hold dear. Go ask Jimi Hendrix over at the Greenwood Memorial Park in Renton, Washington, about the wreaked carnage of Mr. Booze. Or if you think Billie Holiday cannot help you out the back door of any pub, then perhaps Barbara Payton can help you "Kiss Tomorrow Goodbye." Just go ask John Belushi about that mix of heroin and cocaine; or stay overnight for breakfast with Paula Yates, perhaps listening to David Ruffin sing "My Girl" and you will know it's time to let go. Clearly, it was no lie when Whitney Houston sang "Saving All My Love for You." In retrospect, when that boy next door, Cory "Don't stop Believing" Monteith, died from a lethal combination of alcohol and heroin and Amy Winehouse who sang "Rehab" died of alcohol overdose, we must wonder about that culture for whom all that narration was for and why didn`t those somebody's out there know that the goal was to get her and others rehabilitated not to just listen to them sing about it or run away from it! You tell me how many rich or poor, white or black, Philip Seymour Hoffman`s out there in our streets or in their homes are we all going to stumble across with syringes still in their arms, before our society say`s enough! It`s rehab express for all, till they sober up!

It`s true. Prohibition has been tried in America, Europe, and Middle East (hotels and casinos) and failed. Yet it`s we the people who possess that urge that won`t go away, so there's nothing here to win. Instead of inspecting illegal aliens and "wrong" ideas, it`s time to start walking through the shifting currents of desires in our own neighborhoods, sorting out citizens who are really free yet who only want to get higher and higher until they're able to buy that special place of their own. That War on drugs? Who's fooling whom? What happen to the draft of the Salvation Army? Where`s that full embrace of the temperance movement`s full aspirations? Nobody knows how to sing in the prohibition national committee in those church quires in the land? A quid pro quo deal couldn`t be revived and had by those upcoming knights of Labor Unions? Is there really something here to win? Yes, prohibition has been tried in America already, and it failed. Why? Was it because no one looked NAACP way? Is there no one in the committee that knows how to smoke a peace pipe over at the bureau of Indian Affairs? Nobody to show them the money to those wealthy scoundrel media magnates at the time to help keep the lid on for safe keeping till journeys end, till the nation sober up?

War on Drugs? Who`s fooling who, in all that cheap talk about the war on drugs in Latin America, when the truth of the matter is there is no need to send Western paramilitary troops and agents into Latin America to fight the people therein if we look at our own selves here north of the Rio Grande and in Europe, and find out why we the people have such a demand for these drugs that ordinary people will gladly pay for the high, whatever the price? Who's the enemy: the one who demands, or the one who supplies? Economics 101 taught me at Howard University more than thirty years ago if there is no demand, there is no supply; if there is no supply, demand is still present. What is it about our life`s daily grind that we have placed ourselves into that we need such remedy?

There`s hell to pay in this life if you don`t know how to throw an anchor into heaven! No matter if we came to this land as pilgrims, on slave ships, or through Ellis Island, it's the devil's due to believe the fare will be cheap, the journey easy. In this battle for the hearts, minds, and souls of our fellow countrymen, there's nothing here to save except lives from a lifetime of addiction. On this issue of drugs, we as a human race face a humanitarian crisis, one that challenges both people of faith and those of reason to redefine the scourge of illegal and legal drugs as a public health problem that warrants Abbey and/or rehab time, rather than a law-and-order problem that mandates jail time, which in the end does not resolve the primary issue of that demand, that need for a high or buzz in one's life. This heartbreak policy of chasing after the supply is only filling up our prisons in the millions with the poor minorities more than half of whom are drug addicts themselves that got families to raise. Those hopeless enterprising young drug dealers that got bills to pay, and no meaningful job career in sight that can awaken a dream. Along with no end to the cure to the delight of big business in the alcohol and cigarette industry. On the other hand, is this something to do for the law enforcement agencies in our land to earn their paychecks off the misery of the addicted? Oh, humble reader on a higher plain, if there is no change in our demand for drugs, guess who is going to pay for all this futility fiasco.

Half Your Faith

O mankind! Reverence your guardian lord, who created you from a single person, created of like nature his mate, from them scattered countless men and women. Fear Allah, through whom you demand your mutual rights and reverence the wombs [that bore you], for Allah ever watches over you!

—Quran 4:1

You can rest assured one soul at a time a moral journey is based on the notion that something doesn't come from nothing! Personally speaking, after more than seventeen years of marriage to a wonderful wife, I must honestly say that if a man cannot bring out that little girl in his wife, he is not much of a man. Prophet Muhammad (sas) said, "The best of you men are those who treat their wives well." I cannot thank Allah enough for helping a man like me, with only dreams to bargain with walk away from Fez, Morocco, with a beautiful bride. I can testify that wherever you hang your hat to always make sure you have plenty of room for the imagination of that girl in your life. Truly one's wife is the sugar, spice, and everything nice, the one whose laughter can help ease the troubles and anguish in a man`s life.

Prophet Muhammad (sas) also said: "Your wife is half your faith." Having a love not based on cash flow but on faith, natural affinity and understanding, I can testify that soul mates are diamonds in the rough—we polish each other with our karma. You know what I am saying is the truth if you found one in your life. Soul mates are the safe havens in that pursuit of happiness together on this earth. What a shame that not enough men know how to be that loving husband, that understanding father that cares. So many millions of my generation here in America has forgotten those lost episodes, the values of *The Honeymooners, I Love Lucy, Father Knows Best, My Three Sons, Stanford and Son, The Andy Griffith Show, Chico and the Man,* and *All in the Family*. These shows helped push an essential ugly truth about America in the eyes of African Americans. That we men in the Western world, take our wives too much for granted!

That art and idea of starting a family of your own with that girl with love and pray for the blessings from Allah or Jehovah that our ventures will be fruitful and that idea of marriage will be sustained by his grace is going down in these Western secular culture ratings. I say this with a sad heart knowing there is not one primetime TV show today that focus on the important aspect of family values like the above mention shows of the past, or even can hold a spiritual family message like *Little House on the Prairie*. What the people are getting today is fast-food junk comedy, cops and robbers, and a cheap non-moral shows, with a material world staring a broken family whom you never wish to meet, on center stage singing a worthless message.

Islam and Judaism, I believe, makes Muslim men and Jewish men focus on the idea more firmly in their lives that a wife is a true test of their manhood, responsibility, and maturity!

Contrary to Western secular media reports, in all my years of travels to Muslim countries, I had not experience Muslim men therein being abusive to their wives and daughters. As a matter of fact, Muslim men, whether they are rich or poor, regard women as a reflection of themselves and a prize that has been given unto them from their lord as a test!

It's that Islamic and orthodox Jewish social family viewpoint that matters regardless of time or place; thus, chastity and modesty goes a long way and cuts both ways for men and as well as for women at the home front. However, having lived in both secular and monotheist societies with and without a wife by my side, I have become aware of the fact that men in general from rich countries tend to shower their wives a lot with gifts but not with their time! And I also notice that men from poorer countries tend to cherish their wives a lot but not so much their wife's opinions!

So would Islam make a positive contribution towards the life of women here in America or in the Western secular world? I would say yes because Islam would make husbands more committed to be greater family orientated in their lives and be more responsible towards their children! And at times very importantly we Muslim men and families are less prone to drugs like alcohol, which is forbidden in our faith.

It is true that the rights and responsibilities of women are equal to those of men, but they are not necessarily identical. We are compatible in the sight of our lord and have different roles to play in contributions to our families and societies as a whole! This difference should be understandable because we men and women are different in our psychological, physiological, and spiritual make up of who we are and what our purpose in life is!

Our sacred holy Quran and the history of early Muslims bear witness to the fact that women are considered as vital to life as men!

In the social aspect of our lives together as Muslims, girls and women have as much right to education as boys and men do. A Muslim woman has the right to accept or reject marriage proposals, and her consent to marriage is a prerequisite to the validity of the marriage contract. Islam grants women equal rights to contract, to enterprise, to earn and possess business independently. It is Islam that says, girls and women can have a share of inheritance, that they cannot be disinherited! It is Islam that says women are exempt from all financial liabilities; thus as a wife, a woman is entitled to demand of her prospective husband a suitable dowry that will be her own. And is entitled to complete provision and total maintenance by her husband! She does not have to work or share with her husband the family expenses. As a daughter or sister, she is entitled also to security and provision by the father and brother respectively. Those Western and Communist governmental and corporate media images of Muslim women as ignorant, oppressed, and uneducated because of their faith are but propaganda. All a sincere person have to do is stand at the doors of abortion hospitals, and clinics doors inside these countries, in the secular West, and Communist East that misinforms, and inquire thereof to the women about the quality of love of their partners.

It was inevitable, oh, humble reader, that I got the word to come and visit Sheikh Ibn Baaz at his office in Taif, Saudi Arabia in the spring of 1996. So on an early April weekend I shored up my courage and made that two-hour taxi trip up those reddish mountains from Mecca to Taif trying to connect the dots of what I have done wrong. I knew that my grades were low and my Arabic still wasn`t all that great. Yet on the way up, I did take the time to notice those beautiful early desert blossoms that scented the air, which helped calm my fears, and those hawks high on the wing, screaming their opinions of human intrusions in their lives. These people in Taif were the descendents of a people who almost stoned Prophet Muhammad (sas) to death. And he replied to an angle not to have the mountains come down and destroy the people because of their unbelief, saying perhaps in some latter generations maybe someone there in the community will become Muslim. Patience—every time I come near these red mountains, I am reminded of the awesome power of patience.

Upon entering the sheikh's office with a dear Saudi friend of mine who lives in Taif all his life and who's profession is a doctor, Sheikh ibn Baazs came straight to the point. He asked me how old I was? I bowed my head and said I was thirty-eight. Then he said to me why have I not gotten married? I said, "Allah knows best. I cannot afford to." Then that smile came again, that right hand rising up to pull his reddish gray goatee in thought. At that moment, Sheikh Ibn Baazs said, Prophet Muhammad (sas) said, "Your wife is half your faith!" Subsequently the Sheikh turned to his secretary and said, "Give this man ten thousand durhams ($2,350) as a dowry for his wife and five thousand durhams ($1,270) so he can bring her here to live with him as travel expensive." I was totally surprised by the depth of concern a Muslim scholar has for his students and his followers in faith. Truly not all men are created equally! Wanting for your brother in faith what you want for yourself in life is a high bar. Till this day, every now and then, every time I look at my wife and three children I remember that blind Sheikh's smile and words. Yes, a man's wife is half his faith; she will test him his faithfulness to his lord and his devotion to his creed. So beware. Choose well that girl that will mirror your commitment and trust.

The heart of every forward operating base is the home; this is the true state of being of the God-fearing family. For ages, however, women of the secular world have been assaulted by all of the soap opera and Hollywood images, that any girl's lifetime dream is to love and be loved by that someone special. Unfortunately, this myth does not materialize for the majority of women in secular societies. In spite of making more money, having more rights, justice, and due process of law, the status of women living in the secular West has truly been getting worse especially when it comes to family values, drugs, suicide, health care, crime, abortions and education! Yet what have we Western men done to reverse this trend? Because of the smallness of our own hearts, we've mentally abused our wives and children here in the West because we men are unable to learn how to resolve our disputes in a dignified way out of the public view within the creed of our faith. Since the Stone Age, we men have been dancing in the moonlight, standing by our gods in amusement and fear. At the same time we've been dancing around the fire, ignoring our families, unjustifiably celebrating our good fortune and the demise of our enemies. Yet through all this, what has been gained in the physical and spiritual livelihood of our women, our mothers, wives and daughters? Are they happy sharing their lives with you?

Yes, at this moment, without a doubt, the heart of every forward operating base is the home front. Indeed this is the prize in every battleground country to be secure at home. That fundamental pillar of the family is the women in the home under the roof of the loving and protecting husband.

So it is not a conspiracy theory when one`s enemies ponder schemes and portrays negative images of division between husband and wife, between father and son, between mother and daughter, between families of different social religious groups and their pagan neighbors, and between families of the same social religious group and their apostate secular governments.

Yet all is fair in love and war! And religious civil wars are the worst threat I believe to any family trying to endure life. They are indeed bloody, heartless, without pity, and at times without mercy. The best news one can hear any day without a doubt is that your enemy is engage in a religious civil war with itself and that the men and the women are fighting each other within their communities.

All praise is due to Allah, there are thousands of women enrolled with the Mujahideen, Al-Qaeda, and the Taliban who realize the threats all around them and unto their families. Frankly, there is not enough space in this book to put their official life stories of why they joined, and fight and in many cases sacrifice their lives against those who are apostates and against those who are oppressors towards the faith of Islam in and outside of their countries. Quite simply, Islam does not discriminate when it comes to jihad or education simply because the smarter and wiser the fighter, the better the chances of success in life.

But that underhand odyssey of undermining the building blocks and pillars of one`s enemy`s society by enrolling the women and children against each other is not new, oh, humble reader, as these ideological warfare mentalities continues to grow and worsen between the Islamic Monotheist faith and secular and pagan faiths. Nowadays, most of the times that`s how it looks like in this hearts, minds and souls war: Muslim women and children strapped with ideas, guns and bombs focusing on whom can they kill in this era of oppression. Pagan and secular Western women strapped with subversion ideas and ideals, invading Muslim countries backed by guns and bombs of their invading armed forces looking for the weak-minded and rebellious woman, knowing that a house that is divided cannot stand. Western predator drones circling high above focusing on whole Muslim families assembling out in the open including women and children as targets so that they can get that possible insurgent to kill then call it oops . . . collateral damage with impunity. Indeed spectators do have a reason to wonder why it`s so important for a secular government with Muslim names only and their desire to close down those madrassas and force an Islamic puritan community to have secular—oriented schools, teachers, books and programs against their will.

Yes, female education is important in any society; yet the key idea to understand is who is choosing the books, the teachers, the program, and who has the last word when it comes to the direction of these classrooms and children in the communities! This is where the problem lies in this media-hype world stage of women`s rights, faith, and education. Islam has been greatly stereotyped by the Western secular corporate media that, orthodox or not, they say Islam discriminates against women when it comes to education. Secularist with Muslim names and secularist worldwide are using women in Muslim countries like Ms. Malala Yousafzai from Mingora, Pakistan, who was shot in the head in October 2012 by the Taliban. The truth of the matter is she was shot not because she wanted education for girls and women—no, this is not the truth. She was shot because she and her family sided with the secular Pakistani military government, with their ongoing civil war in the northern mountainous district of Swat and in the North-West Frontier Province (NWFP) in which the puritan majority of Islamic peoples who are living there are demanding, and fighting for greater autonomy in their lands against their own secular corrupt government. They are fighting against Pakistan`s Paramilitary Frontier Corps, which is trying to indoctrinate their ideology of Secular military rule over the people. They the Muslim puritan majority in Swat and in NWFP are also fighting against American agents (CIA) who are using drones to kill whole families if needs be if they can get a single rebel insurgent (resistance). And the Muslim puritans are as well fighting foreign soldiers like United States Special Operations Command (SOCOM) who are using ideological warfare to indoctrinate with their propaganda of divide and conquer on one hand and killing the hearts of whole communities with money and books in their lands in their civil war quest for Sharia law, justice and self-rule.

What`s happening in Pakistan is a religious civil war. I know this to be true because I was there in that beautiful country of Islamic hope where men, women and children are fighting side by side, against other men, women, and children who has turned secularist, who has apostate their faith called Islam. I was there visiting the hospitals and saw female doctors and nurses tending to those who were sick and ill. I was there standing in those madrassas looking at female and male teachers teaching those Muslim children about Allah. Yes, I am a witness of those Muslim puritans who refuses to take Allah out of the classrooms and out of the public arena. Yes, I am a witness to those doctors, teachers, leaders and nurses who refuse to take a bow when someone praises them for saving a life. And yes, there are times when there is a war, one does not leave half his faith at home.

Yes, indeed education is very important in any society; and the key ingredient is who is choosing the books, teachers, and programs. We Fundamentalists know it`s who has the last word in the classrooms and on the children in the community that will decide the course of history of that tribe of people or nation. Therefore, it came as no surprise to me—or to the believers for that matter—that on April 6, 2013, the American diplomat Ms. Anne Smedinghoff was killed, the second one within a year, in Qalat, the provincial capital of Zabul, Afghanistan. She and five other Americans were killed as they were in an armed convoy accompanying that corrupt provincial governor, Mr. Mohammad A. Naseri; they were on their way to a local school ceremony inauguration with the intention to donate books to students there! If ignorance is bliss, then what is arrogance but mis-education? Who in today`s world would think but an imperialist, would believe but a colonialist, that it is OK to support with arms, guns, money, and books a foreign religious civil war where brother fight against his own brother for profit and political gain? Then invade that same country when their corrupt proxy loses the civil war because now his enemies attack you since you aided his own brother against brother (Vietnam) (Afghanistan) (Iraq) (Pakistan).

It is never a surprise to us fundamentalists when colonialist call the people therein insurgents not (resistance) when they fight them and the corrupt government which they empowered to rule over them against their will, conclusively cannot be sustained and falls simply because of that golden rule, "the longer the war, the larger the lies" (Vietnam-Afghanistan-Iraq). Subsequently, in the eyes of the imperialist it is the fault of the so-called suicide car bomber, and that so-called suicide bomber wearing an explosive vest who greeted Ms. Anne Smedinghoff and company along the way to their school. Is it really they the insurgents (resistance) who committed such an daring and terrorist act when he or she hears that their enemy is coming to take a bow, who has paid and built their schools; selected their teachers; chosen their programs; and now wishes to donate books of mis-education to one`s own children in their own country!

Yes, education is very important in any society, and women are in the cockpit of every revolution; so the key ingredient is who is choosing the books, schools and program right. We Fundamentalists do know it`s who has the last word in the classroom and on the children in the community that will decide the course of history of that tribe of people or nation. Therefore, it came as no surprise to me, and the believers to learn that on February 3, 2010, Staff Sergeant first class David J. Hartman and Staff Sergeant first class Matthew S. Sluss-Tiller, both of the Ninety-sixth and Ninety-fifth Civil Affairs Battalion (Airborne), and Staff Sergeant Mark A. Stets, of the Eight Psychological Operations Battalion (Airborne) Fourth Psychological Operations Group (Airborne)—all from (SOCOM)—were killed in Dir, Pakistan (NWFP). It was by a roadside bomb waiting for them as they were driving in a five car armed convoy in their attempt to attend the nearby inauguration of a girl school therein and take a bow, which had been renovated with United States Humanitarian Assistance dollars. These American soldiers were part of a "Special Warfare Training Group" along with U.S. female soldiers; their primary task is to engage the female population in an objective area. Their focus is on basic human behavior, Islamic principles, regional culture and women. (SOCOM) is part of an American military "Ideological Warfare" culture support program, whose aim is to ultimately degrade and defeat so-called violent extremist organizations and their ideologies overseas.

What saddens me greatly was that a few of my humble Muslim brothers and I less than twenty years earlier had taken that same lovely scenic and rocky country road up into that same town of Dir, Pakistan, and was met by cheerful, simple people who knew how to entertain guest with roasted lamb, chicken, rice, bread, milk and honey. Who fear Allah only, till this very day! We also visited the schools there met the smiling teachers who introduce me to happy, healthy, joyful children who were glad to meet Muslims from America, Europe, and South Africa bearing good news, candy, and toys. Allah knows best.

So I ask of you, oh, humble reader, frankly, who has the last word? If indeed half your faith is your wife, then how much of a remainder is your children?

Long Live the King

I am not writing this book for the purpose of making a tirade of the American dream. For millions that American dream is real and noble. Yet the past is a parable of today's times. Nevertheless, because of the smallness of the understandings of the corporate elite in our geopolitical realities, hundreds of millions of people have been denied the opportunity to live that dream; in fact, for many it has become an American nightmare of unnecessary poverty, corruption, secularism, racism, as well as too many foreign wars of folly.

Being frank leaves no room for shyness in what must be now a vibrant, thoughtful and, consciously provoking word from the heart. At the present time my government is man-slaughtering our future customers here at home because of their greed, conceit and ignorance. My advantage, only Allah knows, I feel, that the real issues of this era is who has the last word in these Western secular democratic lands that we believers live in which for now is under the control of the corporate elite.

Therefore, we the believers have to do more than just get out the vote here in our lands, we have to win the hearts, minds, and souls of a great majority of our countrymen by our own individual efforts, without the aid of the corporate media that's in our lands simply because they are complicit with the corrupt powers that be. When people face great suffering in their own society by their fellow countrymen for profit and gain, and feel it is imposed upon them by their racist rulers for the love of more money and power, then like the past it's what's "behind your name?" That's what matters when you live behind enemy lines.

For instance, when the Reverend Samuel Billy Kyles says, "Crucifixions have to be witness," I believed then as now because I too was a witness that a King can be murdered because of what's behind his name.

Where do we begin? Making Allah the true and only executive branch here in the secular West will not be easy! The reality is that we Muslims living in the West must learn from the hardships of our African American neighbors, who have faced countless instances of prejudice and racism from the domestic majority. We see the most notable of these in Dr. Martin Luther King Jr., that African American Christian fundamentalist during the Civil Rights Movement of the 1950's and 60's. Despite how we so often see Dr. King portrayed on television today, the American and European media at the time was no ally of the Nobel Peace Prize winner or his Southern Christian Leadership Conference. We native Muslims of America were not fooled by the fallacies put forth by Max Robinson, the African American television anchor-man, who was forced by his masters in the established order and corporate media to portray the false image of integration, integrity and justice in America at the time. That corporate media plan of misdirection and mis-education by way of not addressing to the domestic, and world audience what needs to be said about the real mission and message to his fellow African Americans in what they needed to hear did not go unnoticed by all! Those alive today who remember and/or marched with Dr. King aren't fooled by the change of the political weather. Dr. King, the man, was hated by almost every major American media outlet, as well as the FBI and military intelligence till the last seconds of his epic life because he inspired a populist backlash, which challenged the moral integrity of the entire nation! Yes, without Dr. King and other African American martyrs, that other African American fundamentalist poet, Gil Scott-Heron, would have been truly ignored in his warnings to us all that "the revolution will not be televised."

After the assassination of Dr. Martin Luther King Jr. it is strange that the Southern Christian Leadership Conference, once full of such great potential, failed to reorganize under another leader with the same faith and vigor and forge ahead knowing that the jihad for civil liberties and social justice must be paid in blood. Why wasn't a man who had a personality and vision like Mr. Medgar Evers, that black pragmatic martyr fundamentalist from Mississippi, given the reins of the movement? We Muslims living in the West have taken notice of how the Poor Peoples March being planned for early summer of 1968 just before Dr. King's murder never came about because of the lack of leadership, cohesion, and courage within the SCLC. Perhaps bearing witness to the crucifixion of another "king" would have been too much to bear? But if I randomly ask one thousand or five thousand or even one hundred thousand African-Americans today who heads the SCLC now, do you really think 50 would know who? Such ignorance and mis-education underscores the words of Dr. Ralph Bunche, that other African American fundamentalist and Nobel Peace Prize winner, who warned that democracy must be color blind for it to work. Yes, it is addictive these rules of this old ideological warfare, you must never try to ask or allow the enemy corporate media to show the dangers associated with any positive homegrown resistance movement. It`s just not in their interest. At the time they on one hand trying to present the African American liberation movement in the struggling 1950`s, 1960`s, and 1970`s in the most innocuous manner possible, and in the other hand till this day a war by innuendo. Putting our legacy, and struggles into the hands of professional governmental liars and corrupt corporate media who have their own special interests at heart is suicide of the ignorant that are oppressed to say the least, a plan for failure, if you wish to say the truth. This is why we Muslims believe we will be treated in the same manner in spite of our so-called freedoms here in the West. That enemy near hasn`t changed their stripes, just the landscape.

Till this day I still remember the last public benediction Dr. Martin L. King Jr. gave at Mason Temple in Memphis, Tennessee, on April 3, 1968, and not just the last ten seconds, that "I've been to the Mountain Top" section of the speech. No. Dr. King`s speech on April 3, 1968, a day before he was assassinated, was not about how he`d been to the mountain top, or how he would like to live a long life, or how he had seen the "Promised Land" and that we as a people will together make it there. Neither was it about "not fearing any man" or having "seen the glory of the coming of the Lord." Instead the true focus of Dr. King`s speech was not about himself, which was the true aim of his enemies, but about *"Verily we have created man into toil and struggle"* (Quran 90:4).

"Thank you very kindly, my friends. As I listened to Ralph Abernathy in his eloquent and generous introduction and then thought about myself, I wondered who he was talking about. It`s always good to have your closest friend and associate say something good about you. And Ralph is the best friend that I have in the world.

As you know, if I were standing at the beginning of time, with the possibility of general and panoramic view of the whole human history up to now, and the Almighty said to me. "Martin Luther King Jr., which age would you like to live in? I would take my mental flight by Egypt though, or rather across the Red Sea, though the wilderness on toward the promised land. And in spite of its magnificence, I wouldn't stop there. I would move on by Greece, and take my mind to Mount Olympus. And I would see Plato, Aristotle, Socrates, Euripides and Aristophanes assembled around the Parthenon as they discussed the great and eternal issues of reality.

But I wouldn't stop there. I would go on, even to the great heyday of the Roman Empire. And I would see developments around there, through various emperors and leaders. But I wouldn't stop there. I would even come up to the day of the Renaissance, and get a quick picture of all that the Renaissance did for the cultural and esthetic life of man. But I wouldn't stop there. I would even go by the way that the man for whom I'm named had his habitat. And I would watch Martin Luther as he tacked his ninety-five theses on the door at the church in Wittenberg.

But I wouldn't stop there. I would come on up even to 1863, and watch a vacillating president by the name of Abraham Lincoln finally come to the conclusion that he had to sign the Emancipation Proclamation. But I wouldn't stop there. I would even come up to the early thirties, and see a man grappling with the problems of the bankruptcy of his nation. And come with an eloquent cry that we have nothing to fear but fear itself.

But I wouldn't stop there. Strangely enough. I would turn to the Almighty, and say. "If you allow me to live just a few years in the second half of the twentieth century, I will be happy." Now that's a strange statement to make, because the world is all messed up. The nation is sick. Trouble is in the land. Confusion is all around. That's a strange statement. But I know, somehow, that only when it is dark enough, can you see the stars. And I see God working in this period of the twentieth century in a way that men, in some strange way, are responding—something is happening in our world. The masses of people are rising up. And wherever they are assembled today, whether they are in Johannesburg, South Africa; Nairobi Kenya; Accra, Ghana; New York City; Atlanta, Jackson, Mississippi; or Tennessee—the cry is always the same "We want to be free."

And another reason that I'm happy to live in this period is that we have been forced to a point where we're going to have to grapple with the problems that men have been trying to grapple with through history, but the demand didn't force them to do it. Survival demands that we grapple with them. Men, for years now, have been talking about war and peace. But now, no longer can they just talk about it. It is no longer a choice between violence and nonviolence in this world; it's nonviolence or nonexistence.

That is where we are today. And also in the human rights revolution, if something isn't done, and in a hurry, to bring the colored peoples of the world out of their long years of poverty, their long years of hurt and neglect, the whole world is doomed. Now, I'm just happy that God has allowed me to live in this period, to see what is unfolding. And I'm happy that He's allowed me to be in Memphis.

I can remember, I can remember when Negroes were just going around as Ralph has said, so often, scratching where they didn't itch, and laughing when they were not ticked. But that day is all over. We mean business now, and we are determined to gain our rightful place in God's world.

And that's all this whole thing is about. We aren't engaged in any negative protest and in any negative arguments with anybody. We are saying that we are determined to be men. We are determined to be people. We are saying that we are God's children. And that we don't have to live like we are forced to live.

Now, what does all this mean in this great period of history? It means that we've got to stay together. We've got to stay together and maintain unity. You know, whenever Pharaoh wanted to prolong the period of slavery in Egypt, he had a favorite, favorite formula for doing it. What was that? He keep the slaves fighting among themselves. But whenever the slaves get together, something happens in Pharaoh's court, and he cannot hold the slaves in slavery. When the slaves get together, that's the beginning of getting out of slavery. Now let us maintain unity.

Secondly, let us keep the issues where they are. The issue is injustice. The issue is the refusal of Memphis to be fair and honest in its dealings with its public servants, who happen to be sanitation workers. Now we've got to keep attention on that. That's always the problem with a little violence. You know what happened the other day, and the press dealt only with the window breaking. I read the articles. They very seldom got around to mentioning the fact that one thousand three hundred sanitation workers were on strike, and that Memphis is not being fair to them, and that Mayor Loeb is in dire need of a doctor. They didn't get around to that.

Now we're going to march again, and we've got to march again, in order to put the issue where it is supposed to be. And force everybody to see that there are thirteen hundred of God`s children here suffering, sometimes going hungry, going through dark and dreary nights wondering how this thing is going to come out. That`s the issue. And we`ve got to say to the nation: we know it`s coming out. For when people get caught up with that which is right and they are willing to sacrifice for it, there is no stopping point short of victory.

We aren't going to let any mace stop us. We are masters in our nonviolent movement in disarming police forces: they don`t know what to do, I`ve seen them so often. I remember Birmingham, Alabama, when we were in that majestic struggle there we would move out of the 16th Street Baptist Church day after day: by the hundreds we would move out. And Bull Connor would tell them to send the dogs forth and they did come; but we just went before the dogs singing. "Ain`t gonna let nobody turn me around." Bull Connor next would say, "Turn the fire hoses on." And as I say to you the other night, Bull Connor didn't know history. He knew a kind of physics that somehow didn`t relate to the transphysics that we knew about. And that was the fact that there was a certain kind of fire that no water could put out. And we went before the fire hoses; we had known water. If we were Baptist or some other denomination, we had been immersed. If we were Methodist, and some others, we had been sprinkled, but we knew water.

That couldn't stop us And we just went on before the dogs and we would look at them: and we`d go on before the water hoses and we would look at it, and we`d just go on singing "Over my head I see freedom in the air." And then we would be thrown in the paddy wagons, and sometimes we were stacked in there like sardines in a can. And they would throw us in, and old Bull would say, "Take them off," and they did: and we would just go in the paddy wagon singing, "We Shall Overcome." And every now and then we`d get in the jail, and we`d see the jailers looking through the windows being moved by our prayers, and being moved by our words and our songs. And there was a power there which Bull Connor couldn't adjust to; and so we ended up transforming Bull into a steer, and we won our struggle in Birmingham.

Now we`ve got to go on to Memphis just like that. I call upon you to be with us Monday. Now about injunctions: We have an injunction and we`re going into court tomorrow morning to fight this illegal, unconstitutional injunction. All we say to America is "Be true to what you say on paper." If I lived in China or even Russia, or any totalitarian country, maybe I could understand the denial of certain basic First Amendment privileges, because they hadn`t committed themselves to that over there. But somewhere I read of the freedom of assembly. Somewhere I read of the freedom of speech. Somewhere I read of the press. Somewhere I read that the greatness of America is the right to protest for right. And so just as I say, we aren't going to let any injunction turn us around. We are going on.

We need all of you. And you know what's beautiful to me, is to see all of these ministers of the Gospel. It's a marvelous picture. Who is it that is supposed to articulate the longings and aspirations of the people more than the preacher? Somehow the preacher must be an Amos, and say, "Let justice roll down like waters and righteousness like a mighty stream." Somehow, the preacher must say with Jesus, "The spirit of the Lord is upon me, because he hath anointed me to deal with the problem of the poor."

And I want to commend the preachers, under the leadership of these noble men: James Lawson, one who has been in this struggle for many years; he's been to jail for struggling; but he's still going on, fighting fights of his people. Rev. Ralph Jackson, Bill Kiles; I could go right on down the list, but time will not permit. But I want to thank them all. And I want you to thank them, because so often, preachers aren't concerned about anything but themselves. And I'm always happy to see a relevant ministry.

It's all right to talk about "long white robes over yonder," in all of its symbolism. But ultimately people want some suits and dresses and shoes to wear down here. It's all right to talk about "streets flowing with milk and honey," but God has commanded us to be concerned about the slums down here, and his children who cannot eat three square meals a day. It's all right to talk about the new Jerusalem, but one day, God's preachers must talk about New York, the new Atlanta, the new Philadelphia, the new Los Angeles, the new Memphis, Tennessee. This is what we have to do.

Now the other thing we'll have to do is this: Always anchor our external direct action with the power of economic withdrawal. Now, we are poor people, individually, we are poor when you compare us with white society in America. We are poor. Never stop and forget that collectively, that means all of us together, collectively we are richer than all the nations in the world, with the exception of nine. Did you ever think of that? After you leave the United States, Soviet Russia, Great Britain, West Germany, France, and I could name the others, the Negro collectively is richer than most nations of the world. We have an annual income of more than thirty billion dollars a year, which is more than all of the exports of the United States, and more than the national budget of Canada. Did you know that? That's power right there, if we know how to pool it.

We don`t have to argue with anybody. We don`t have to curse and go around acting bad with our words. We don`t need any bricks and bottles, we don`t need any Molotov cocktails, we just need to go around to those stores, and to those massive industries in our country, and say, God sent us here, to say to you that you`re not treating his children right. And we`ve come by here to ask you to make the first item on your agenda fair treatment, where God`s children are concerned. Now. If you are not prepared to do that, we do have an agenda that we must follow. And our agenda calls for withdrawing economic support from you."

And so, as a result of this, we are asking you tonight, to go out and tell your neighbors not to buy Coca-Cola in Memphis. Go by and tell them not to buy Sealtest milk. Tell them not to buy, what is the other bread? Wonder bread. And what is the other bread company. Jesse? Tell them not to buy Hart`s bread. As Jesse Jackson has said, up to now, only the garbage men have been feeling pain; now we must kind of redistribute the pain. We are choosing these companies because they haven`t been fair in their hiring policies; and we are choosing them because they can begin the process of saying, they are going to support the needs and the rights of these men who are on strike. And then they can move on downtown and tell Mayor Loeb to do what is right.

But not only that, we`ve got to strengthen black institutions. I call upon you to take your money out of the banks downtown and deposit your money in Tri-State Bank, we want a "Bank-in" movement in Memphis. So go by the savings and loan association. I`m not asking you something we don`t do ourselves at S.C.L.C. Judge Hooks and others will tell you that we have an account here in the savings and loan association from the Southern Christian Leadership Conference. We`ve just telling you to follow what we`ve been doing. Put your money there. You have six or seven black insurance companies in Memphis. Take out your insurance there. We want to have an "insurance-in."

Now these are some practical things we can do. We begin the process of building a greater economic base. And at the same time, we are putting pressure where it really hurts. I ask you to follow through here.

Now, let me say as I move to my conclusion that we`ve got to give ourselves to this struggle until the end. Nothing would be more tragic than to stop at this point, in Memphis. We`ve got to see it through. And when we have our march, you need to be there. Be concerned about your brother. You may not be on strike. But either we go up together, or we go down together.

Let us develop a kind of dangerous unselfishness. One day a man came to Jesus; and he wanted to raise some questions about some vital matters in life. At points, he wanted to trick Jesus, and show him that he knew a little more than Jesus knew, and through this, throw him off base. Now that question could have easily ended up in a philosophical and theological debate. But Jesus immediately pulled that question from mid-air, and placed it on a dangerous curve between Jerusalem and Jericho. And he talked about a certain man, who fell among thieves. You remember that a Levite and a priest passed by on the other side. They didn`t stop to help him! And finally a man of another race came by. He got down from his beast, decided not to be compassionate by proxy. But with him, administering first aid, and helped the man in need. Jesus ended up saying, this was the good man, this was the great man, because he had the capacity to project the "I" into the "thou," and be concerned about his brother. Now you know, we use our imagination a great deal to try to determine why the priest and the Levite didn`t stop. At times we say they were busy going to church meetings, ecclesiastical gathering and they had to get on down to Jerusalem so they wouldn`t be late for their meeting. At other times we would speculate that there was a religious law that "One who was engaged in religious ceremonials was not to touch a human body twenty four hours before the ceremony." And every now and then we begin to wonder whether maybe they were not going down to Jerusalem, or down to Jericho, rather to organize a "Jericho Road Improvement Association." That's a possibility. Maybe they felt that it was better to deal with the problem from the causal root, rather than to get bogged down with an individual effort.

But I`m going to tell you what my imagination tells me. It`s possible that these men were afraid. You see, the Jericho road is a dangerous road. I remember when Mrs. King and I were first in Jerusalem. We rented a car and drove from Jerusalem down to Jericho. And as soon as we got on that road, I said to my wife, "I can see why Jesus used this as a setting for his parable." It`s a winding, meandering road. It`s really conducive for ambushing. You start out in Jerusalem, which is about 1200 miles, or rather 1200feet above sea level. And by the time you get down to Jericho, fifteen or twenty minutes later, you`re about 2200 feet below sea level. That`s a dangerous road. In the days of Jesus it came to be known as the "Bloody Pass." As you know, it`s possible that the priest and the Levite looked the other over that man on the ground was merely faking. And he was acting like he had been robbed and hurt, in order to seize them over there, lure them there for quick and easy seizure. And so the first question that the Levite asked was, "If I stop to help this man, what would happen to me?" But then the good

Samaritan came by. And he reversed the question: "If I do not stop to help this man, what will happen to him?"

That's the question before you tonight. Not, "If I stop to help the sanitation workers, what will happen to all of the hours that I usually spend in my office every day and every week as a pastor?" The question is not, "If I stop to help this man in need, what will happen to me?" "If I do not stop to help the sanitation workers, what will happen to them?" That's the question.

Let us rise up tonight with a greater readiness. Let us stand with a greater determination. And let us move on in these powerful days, these days of challenge to make America what it ought to be. We have an opportunity to make America a better nation. And I want to thank God, once more, for allowing me to be here with you.

You know, several years ago, I was in New York City autographing the first book that I had written. And while sitting there autographing books, a demented black woman came up. The only question I heard from her was, "Are you Martin Luther King?" And I was looking down writing, and said yes. And the next minute I felt something beating on my chest. Before I knew it I had been stabbed by this demented woman. I was rushed to Harlem Hospital. It was a dark Saturday afternoon. And that blade had gone through, and the X-rays revealed that the tip of the blade was on the edge of my aorta, the main artery. And once that's punctured, you drown in your own blood, that's the end of you.

It came out in *The New York Times* the next morning, that if I had sneezed, I would have died. Well, about four days later, they allowed me, after the operation, after chest had been opened, and the blade had been taken out, to move around in the wheel chair in the hospital. They allowed me to read some of the mail that came in, and from all over the States, and the world, kind letters came in. I read a few, but one of them I will never forget. I had received a visit and a letter from the Governor of New York, but I've forgotten what the letter said. But there was another letter that came from a little girl, a young girl who was a student at the White Plains High School. And I looked at that letter, and I'll never forget it. It said simply, "Dear Dr. King: I am a ninth grade student at the White Plains High School." She said, "While it should not matter, I would like to mention that I am a white girl. I read in the paper of your misfortune, and of your suffering. And I read that if you had sneezed, you would have died. And I'm simply writing you to say that I'm so happy that that you didn't sneeze."

And I want to say tonight, I want to say that I am happy that I didn't sneeze. Because if I had sneezed, I wouldn't have been around here in 1960, when students all over the south started sitting-in at lunch counters. And I knew that as they were sitting in, they were standing up for the best in the American dream. And taking the whole nation back to those great wells of democracy which were dug deep by the founding fathers in the Declaration of Independence and the Constitution. If I had sneezed, I wouldn`t have been around in 1962, when Negroes in Albany, Georgia, decided to straighten their backs up. And whenever men and women straighten their backs up, they are going somewhere, because a man can`t ride your back unless it is bent. If I had sneezed, I wouldn`t have been here in 1963, when the black of Birmingham, Alabama, aroused the conscience of this nation, and brought into being the Civil Rights Bill. If I had sneezed, I wouldn`t have been down in Selma, Alabama, been in Memphis to see the community rally around those brothers and sisters who are suffering. I`m so happy that I didn`t sneeze.

And they were telling me, now it doesn`t matter now. It really doesn`t matter what happens now. I left Atlanta this morning, and as we got started on the plane, there were six of us, the pilot said over the public address system, We are sorry for the delay, but we have Dr. Martin Luther King on the plane. And to be sure that all of the bags were checked, and to be sure that nothing would be wrong with the plane, we had to check out everything carefully. And we`ve had the plane protected and guarded all night." And then I got to Memphis. And some began to say the threats, or talk about the threats that are out. What would happen to me from some of our sick white brothers?

Well, I don`t know what will happen now. We`ve got some difficult days ahead. But it doesn`t matter with me now. Because I`ve been to the mountaintop. And I don`t mind. Like anybody. I would like to live a long life. Longevity has its place. But I`m not concerned about that now. I just want to do God`s will. And He`s allowed me to go up to the mountain. And I`ve looked over. And I`ve seen the promised land. I may not get there with you. But I want you to know tonight, that we, as a people, will get to the promised land. And I`m happy tonight! I`m not worried about anything. I`m not fearing any man! Mine eyes have seen the glory of the coming of the Lord."

For many African Americans living in the era of the civil rights movement, those days were truly an enlightened age. Yet for some of us that era are most clearly defined by Dr. King's assassination on April 4, 1968, the day which effectively ended social justice in America; for Dr. King understood both the true goals of his people and how to apply the proper methods so that these goals can be sustained.

"Always anchor your external direct action with the power of economic withdrawal" was a long-lasting prime time words to the wise." Yet very few African American leaders today put these words to action. Yes, racism in America can only be confronted with a call of unity and unselfishness, together with the power of economic withdrawal tactics envisioned by Dr. King, so why the hesitation when the obstacles that confront us all can be faced with victory? We the decedents of slaves after more than one hundred years of so-called emancipation, we had a king who knew what`s behind his name and who fully appreciate the value and significance of what`s behind the slave names of his people.

But obviously only the bold and the malefactors knew of such truth and consequences of having such a king—a lesson learned by only a few, unfortunately, for not appreciating and protecting your King who knows the true goals of his people and how to apply the right methods so that our goals can be sustained here in America.

The renewed surge in social injustice attacks by the enemy far should have been no surprise. Political acrimony was getting more frequent and bitter. President Lyndon Johnson will not run again for public office, that ripple effect of a Vietnam War of folly abroad coming home to roost!

That spontaneous uprising called the Tet Offensive in January 1968 did indeed hasten the end of the war in Vietnam, but millions more Vietnamese had to suffer before the conflict was officially "over." Likewise, that spontaneous uprising known as the "Memphis Injustice Offensive," by those in the underground both began and ended on April 4, 1968, with Dr. King's assassination. Subsequently, millions more died slowly under continued oppression of injustice; and tens of millions of African-Americans continued to suffer under racism, thus symbolizing the dehumanization of those who are economically, socially, and politically enslaved by those who wish greedily to hold on to power.

Perhaps that`s why it`s no myth why that red-flamed fundamentalist (Satan) decided to start a parade on that bright early morning of April 5, 1968, a day my brother Clive and some of our classmates of PS 90 in the Bronx will never forget. We called it the "devil's parade." We were all just children then. I was ten years old, just a kid, unaware of the degree of the previous day's crucifixion and critical events as I, and millions of others walked to our schools across the nation and were greeted by our white, black, Hispanic, and Asian teachers with worried looks and a body language that betrayed their anxiety. In my classroom sitting behind me near the window a girl my same age and black like me, she sat crying, holding a newspaper whose front page read "The

King is Dead." Knowing how impressionable we were, our teacher, with her nervous white hands, took the newspaper away from the girl. But it was too late. We understood that our King was gone. We had a King!?

I believe now since then that there is an enrichment factor in every nation and tribe of people, ebony, ivory and all those cedar hues in between. That enrichment factor is there for a reason. Some people say's the Id always remembers Dr. Seuss rhyme: "The time has come." That jigsaw puzzle, that idler wheel, began to crystallize. We had a King! The cry was joined by shouts by half the students in the classroom of fourth-graders; "We had a King." This was truly the first true awaking moment in my life! Afterward half the classroom of thirty-five students were crying, and within half an hour the bell rang and all of us, a thousand students ages eight to ten, one-third black, one-third Hispanic, and one-third white, all in a crying rage, "We had a King" not just a president of America—were marshaled to the huge cafeteria where for two hours we all sat and watched the principal who tried to vainly explain what the hell is going on. What we saw was a white man trembling in fear of the unknown, and the hearts of the people outside our school walls. Until finally he dismissed us to our first field trip in the nationwide devil's parade, where outside PS 90 in the Bronx New York, it was standing room only to watch "the best and finest" run for their lives.

Not to be outdone; by Dr. King's April 3 benediction, that Red flamed fundamentalist was still giving his own public benediction of incitement, which started on April 4, 1968, a raging filibuster of a public benediction that went national. He was illustrating to that real Supreme Court upstairs, the merits of his own case: *"Allah said: Oh Satan. What is your reason for not being among those who prostrate themselves? Satan said: I am not one to prostrate myself to man, whom thou didst create from sounding clay, from mud molded into shape"* (Quran 15:26-42).

It was truly a very ubiquitous event. We couldn't go back home the way we came because Sheridan Avenue was in full retreat. A mass of people of all hues were rioting by the thousands—neighbors, strangers, teens, adults, young, old, were all raging in the streets with unmerciful malice. Some were even trying to kill each other. I stood there huddling in front of the school with my brother Clive and a few of our classmates, surrounded by this sea of rage. Not knowing what to do, we ran two blocks east toward PS 22, the neighborhood junior high school, and tried to navigate our way through the angry crowd; but this was impossible. We watched in horror as white teachers and white students ran a gauntlet of clubs and knives. The roar of the crowd was deafening; Grant Avenue had surrendered unconditionally. A moment later we turned back and headed south, but in vain. Sherman Avenue had been overrun by angry gangs, as the police attempted to hold the line near the Bronx criminal courthouse on East 161st Street. Grocery stores who cashed in a lot on people's IOU's on Morris Avenue were being destroyed. Police in four-man patrols roamed everywhere and gunshots rang out from rooftop snipers.

Finally, our small group ran west to the Grand Concourse on 163rd Street, only to be greeted by the roar of tens of thousands of people, though empty Yankee Stadium was five blocks away. Because of so many abandoned cars, traffic was at a standstill in both directions, as far as our eyes could see. From All-Hallows School up to Fordham Road, the real traffic problem was the stampede of people in every direction. The police were besieged, firemen were overwhelmed by both fire and stone throwers, and the sounds of sirens of all kinds were being muffled by the moans of the injured and the cry's of the "King is Dead." Even, Taft High School in the Bronx, across the street from where we live on 1368 Sheridan Avenue, like so many other minority schools in the nation, it had been taken over by its own black students. Their rage exquisitely visualized, that brick in the wall nakedly heartfelt, you can hear that roar from those demanding invisible black students five blocks away "Long live the King!" That deception of democracy in the form of our obelisks government standing on racism and oppression now self-evident in this human earthquake brought on by broken promises and a true lack of social justice had finally gone public. And even now, in my mind's eye, as those protesters flooded into the streets on the day after Dr. King's murder, I can see that this chaos was intentional, planned by a government that was fearful of those spoken words of action by a king on April 3. Yes, that immoral intelligence is just as deceitful then as they are more so now; like the edge of shadows it is they the oligarchy that are real in spite of having a black man living in the White House in Washington DC, talking about change!

Simon Says

Moses called all the elders of Israel and said to them: "Go and procure lambs for your families, and slaughter them as Passover victims. Then take a bunch of hyssop and dipping it in the blood that is in the basin, sprinkle the lintel and the two door posts with this blood." But none of you shall go outdoors until morning. For the lord will go by, striking down the Egyptians. Seeing the blood on the lintel and the two door posts, the Lord will pass over that door and not let that the destroyer come into your houses to strike you down."

—Torah, Ex. 12:21-33

In spite of living in an age of Internet, Face book, Twitter and YouTube, the dark realities of injustice, racism, oppression, as well as the crippling limitations on free speech and the right to freely assemble are all of serious concern. I am well aware that there are those that believe the relationship between faith and reason should remain separate but equal in these so called modern times. But just remember whatever Eleazar Ben Simon—that Hebrew fundamentalist from Galilee almost two thousand years ago, with his back inside that holy temple wall in Jerusalem—says, you do. That`s if you wish to win against the pagan and secularist siege occurring here in the West.

All three monotheist Abrahamic faiths tells us of a sentient being named Satan who possesses a hatred for humanity (*Job1:6-12*), (*Matt.4:1-11*), (*Quran 15:26-44*). Yet, how different are we really are from him in terms of arrogance, he of fire and we of clay? Yes, we are the consumers in this tree of life who persist in our selfishness; even

in these times of great oppression, we as monotheist faiths to our loss
have yet to develop a kind of dangerous thorn of unselfishness amongst
ourselves in times of trials of evil. Good enough, believers cannot be
only discreet when marking their doors with the blood of lambs,
in defiance of the despot's wrath in these so-called modern times.
Yet is there, anywhere in our holy books, a more stunning contempt
for injustice? [77] Such an open dedication, anywhere in the world,
regardless of political season, such a bloody sign towards oppression
with conviction and purpose is impossible to dispute. This warning
taken up by today's hopelessness against oppression is truly capable of
producing an arresting moment of human clarity globally, in any era.
Of course there are other stunning feats of contempt of injustice in
our holy books for those who are wise and seeking the mercy of that
divine one. For in truth we don't have to argue, curse, or spread evil
with our words; we don't need guns, knives, stones or bombs. Better
to read more about slavery in those holy pages, about those people
with nothing to lose but the rags on their backs. For me, the past is
never dead. For me, you do not just read about Prophet Moses; you
take heed about Prophet Moses. You just don't read about Prophet
Joseph; you pay heed about Prophet Joseph. You don't just read about
war; you construe heed about Prophet Joshua. For the lessons we
Muslims believers must take to heart is that after more than 400 years
of oppression African Americans still have to fight our way through
hell on earth to be free from our slave masters. Did Prophet Jesus stand
silently before them, or did he say about those Pharisees, "Do as they
say but not as they do"?

Until I flew East at the age of thirty-two, I believed that America was
more of an idea than a place per se, a storm of ideas and a tornado
of ideals. For "In God we Trust" answered the prayers of the enslaved,
not the enslaver. Furthermore, those enslaved must still follow, with
extreme prejudice, and obey their God, Yahweh, Allah's prophets
or kings. Ultimately we the believers must register those prophets
and kings amongst ourselves and protect them before our enemies
register them amongst themselves and destroy them! Today it is no
longer fashionable to be discriminating against those of different
color of skin, faith, or ethnic group. Still secular nations of both the
West and East continue to discriminate against those of a different
faith in a manner much deeper than the hue of one's skin. Literally,

---

[77]   Ex. 12:21-33

a common misconception has been spread that Islam and Sharia law are incompatible with cultures in the secular West or East. Yet I truly believe Islam has much to contribute to this secular Western society, and perhaps the greater sin is that Muslims in the secular world are not doing enough to combat this misconception.

Life can never be considered normal for us faithful Muslims living in the secular West. As such, we must be arbiters of our own destiny. For the true jihad work that must be done, this is a humanitarian work in the defense of those who are in despair and are yearning. An earnest jihad says we cannot wait for the understanding of our fellow non-Muslim citizens; for only fool's wait for the suspicions, prejudices, and racism of others to wane. Islam has an agenda before it; thus, an Islamic resistance movement must take shape here in the secular West, with membership consisting of a network of trained professionals working in cohesion at brigade strengths. Yes we must have our own partisans, and let the trenches be our mosques, our universities and libraries, our courts and town halls, and yes even in the living rooms of our own homes. From the shadows, the eyes of the West will be watching to see if we can muster the will, while the eyes of the East will be watching if we can muster the courage to match our faith.

At the present time, with more than ten million Muslims living here in America who must never forget what the Roman army did to those believers defending the Holy Temple in Jerusalem and at Masada, in Israel, almost two thousand years ago simply because history has a way of repeating itself. "Render to Caesar what belongs to Caesar and render to Jehovah what belongs to Jehovah" is a golden rule which one cannot avoid living in a land ruled by pagans, secularist, and atheist. Caesar is going to always want more, so let him take more or leave the land. If one cannot leave the land then have patience. With patience, hand over to Caesar all you have knowing that Jehovah is a—jealous God. Inevitably, that merciful Jehovah will not share his slave-servant with anybody! Eventually, Jehovah will respond to Caesar until there is nothing left!

Thousands of Hebrew slaves—some in chains, others in linked roped fetters about their arms and necks—were marched at the point of Roman spears and swords through the mercilessly hot desert. Most of them didn't even understand what was happening, these Roman citizen Jews who believed themselves safe sitting on the sidelines as spectators while the temple in Jerusalem burned and their kinsmen— those Pharisees, Sadducees, and Sicariis—spilled each other's blood and the blood of their true enemies, the pagan Romans, in defeat. What a sight to behold! Thousands of old Jewish men, women and children in rags these forsaken ones whom nobody will pay a Roman silver Denarius coin for at the slave market in Tartus, marched bitterly onward. Cornered, the slaves were marched in front of Masada, before a group of free Hebrews led by that fundamentalist of conscience, Eleazar Ben Ya'ir, who immediately recognized the Roman's strategy of protecting themselves by marching behind their slaves. Those free Hebrew fundamentalists then had to decide either to rain their arrows, spears, and stones upon their enslaved loved ones below before they could battle the Romans or to embrace suicide and avoid becoming slaves themselves.

The question is then what would you do if that Roman battering ram was using your own people as human shields, and your only choices are kill them all and or die fighting with sword in hand until death, or commit suicide or be enslaved?

For me, I believe what my teachers in Mecca, Saudi Arabia, have told me: "That there is an enrichment factor in every nation and tribe of people for a reason. Yet not everybody is going to claim that birthright"! Truly, oppression is worse than death. So when your Simon says regardless of era- just do it!

What`s Going On?

Can a nation of people who call themselves Muslims on a jihad achieve their goal of governorship of the nations of the secular West and thus create an Islamic state under Islamic law? If you believe so, then buckle on your armor and shout it out.[78] For either we as a people stay relevant in our creed, united before humanity, or we disappear amongst a sea of batons, tear gas and bullets, because our focus determines our destiny.

Surely you are free to question my faith, my patriotism and my politics.

For many American and European Muslims, this is the land of Goshen where oaths are given to whichever pharaoh, Caesar, or king rules the land into which they have wandered. As long as they receive some promise of opportunity and justice from the kufr, they are the willing slaves. One of the most common misconceptions in these modern times is to think that history doesn't repeat itself. In fact, these modern-day pharaohs, Caesars, and kufr rulers, like their pagan Roman brethren in the shadow of Masada past, will march behind today's slaves I believe with Muslim names those creatures of comforts, and head directly toward us, their true enemy, in an effort to build a rampart against the believers. Nonetheless, many enslaved economically and socially will just continue to march blindly onward anyway until we with the help of Allah enlighten them or destroy them!

---

[78]   Quran 20:8

Yes, we just had to go through this life experience come what may as a people of color. It's true we shall overcome, even more so then in April 4, 1968, in spite of having an African American president in the White House. Why? What's behind the name of Barack H. Obama? Yes, this is a historic era and he is still in the field and relevant to the present and future. However, there is a difference between a king who believes his sovereign is divine and a president whose creed is sovereignty is to "all the people"!

Just the other day, for the absence of Coca-Cola, Wonder bread, and certain brands of milk, as well as patronizing our own banks and insurance companies nationwide, I believe this is truly a small price for us African Americans lead by a king to pay. For we as a people would be investing in our future legacy, boycotting domestic organizations that do not have our interest in getting rid of discrimination on job employment and/or sales marketing; as well as becoming more economically and politically aware of our powers. But once that king was murdered, the reality was no real shout from the trenches in the form of new leadership passionately keeping alive those polices of that king, which must go forward; only then the meaning of those words "Long live the king" is in earnest for those who are wise!

Yes, we fundamental believers remember those shouts of panic and anger in times before, "They made a scarecrow of our King," "We are surrounded and doomed," "Worship the man but do not put into practice his ideas if you value your life!" Then they that noble inner circle fled for their lives in their bickering and acts of disunity to become mayors of cities of their oppressors and an ambassador of an oppressor nation of their own people unto the United Nations in New York, United States America.

"What's going on?" was on the lips of millions of those of us who really cared looking at those social and economic brutalities which lies ahead of a leaderless nation of oppress people.

Did they send out the call in earnest of that Poor People's March for the millions to assemble and march on Washington DC in the summer of 1968 after Dr. King's assassination in spite of the fear, anguish and sorrow? Did they see it through? Of course not!

What's going on? We lost our leadership of our race, and there was none to step forward to rally the cause. This was a true bitter experience that I acknowledge with my generation as a child, a teenager, and an adult.

Regional economic boycotts and/or national economic boycotts that will help strengthen our goals here in this country was hardly an insight under the new wave of individualism by a leaderless people, seeded by a campaign by our local master enemies who had their own interest at heart.

A national holiday for Dr. Martin L. King was the call!

Oh? Has racism, oppression, drug addiction, alcoholism, suicides, single-parent homes, AIDS, black-on-black crime, poverty, social injustice and massive unemployment taken a holiday since those dark days of April 4, 1968 till now, in spite of have having Mr. Barack H. Obama as president of the United States talking about change?

What`s going on? All you got to do is look at the state of affirmative Action that was before the Supreme Court in America 2013. Where is that full court campaign to protect our legacy? The very reason why America had an affirmative Action in the land in the first place is effectively and efficiently forgotten. By those who not only are African Americans in name only but also by the ignorance of our own grass roots who thinks that affirmative Action is an injustice to those who suffer no legacy of oppression or social injustice at all here in America!

Please, oh, humble reader; it is my intent to be as forthcoming as possible. Let`s be frank at least to ourselves, do you really think Dr. King would had accepted such an honor of a national holiday in his name if resurrected and seeing the current state of his people here and now?

Seeing beyond the moment, we fundamentalists know it was more than a famine of humanity that the true Hebrew and the true African American leaders have left behind; in fact, it was a hell on earth for all because only a few today know the taste of unselfish sacrifice or the fruit of jihad! Of utmost importance today is how we fundamentalists can avoid fighting and killing our own people in the millions because of their own lack of faith and becoming creatures of comforts here in the secular West. How can we stay united, protect our families, and keep the sell-outs at bay all the while achieving and sustaining our goals in spite of that pagan-battering ram behind millions of our people forcing our own people blindly onward, economically enslaved and politically ignorant? This is the prayer of the believers and of that strong future leader who knows what`s behind his name and your name!

Once awakened, there is no need to pause. Make it your drink this space called life. Only then we'll have no doubt when answering Marvin Gaye, that black pearl fundamentalist, when he asks the question, "What`s going on?" Mr. Gaye who said publicly before he released his famous record that he "wanted to write songs that would reach the souls of people [and] make them look at what was happening in the world." It is that very definition of news and that very definition of solutions that's making the awakening of the 1960's to the present day opposed to the damning view before us all! For what really is going on, thanks to those nuclear weapons that supposedly "won" World War II, is that we human beings are still living in an era that have the power to turn our enemies to ashes in the hundreds of millions which is nothing but a sad chronicle of death for all. What state of peace, and peace of mind, has been gained now that tens of thousands of nuclear weapons are aimed at our neighbors all over this earth? Is humanity any safer now because of a nation of people, murdered by the reality of their own fear, ignorance and denial?

Atom bomb, hydrogen bomb, neutron bomb—really, what's the difference? For the truth of these days of rage is that injustice makes a world full of terrorists. That the true suicide bombers are those mad men in military uniforms here at home, full of conceit and whose collapse of true courage have given rise to a nation of people led by fear willing to wash the day away. Oh, Gracious Majesty, will our journey come to an end because of the smallness of our politics and the singularity of our vision? Oh, Gracious Majesty, when will we the believers of "In God We Trust" dare to imagine and aspire to everything that is noble in jihad? If others here in these lands of the secular West do not wish to drink this space called life, please then give us the patience to lead both those within our faith and outside our own creed to sweet waters. Oh, Gracious Majesty, why have we not listened to words of General Omar Bradley, that fundamentalist of a five-star American general, when he said, "We have grasped the mystery of the atom and rejected the Sermon on the Mount. Ours is a world of nuclear giants and ethical infants. We know more about war than we know about peace, more about killing than we know about living"?

Pull back some more curtain. Don't be shy; in the secular West, justice allows one's soul to breathe freely. And without that key ingredient, the anxiety becomes more than a living hell. It's like meeting the Divine One you had denied. Much like the best coffee comes from the best beans, the best justice comes from the best hearts! As we fear less, now is the time to understand more. We seek refuge in Allah (swa) from the evil of our bad deeds and ourselves. Whomever Allah guides is truly guided and whomever Allah leaves to stray no one can guide. A nuclear weapon-free world and the age of more justice on the earth was two of the first five prayers I made in the Al Haram in Mecca back in the fall of 1992. On my first night in that beautiful house of Allah (swa), by his mercy I received a whispered reply in response to my prayer about nuclear weapons: "Is it not the finger that pulls the trigger and that all the triggers on earth could not pull one finger?" I then asked about how we are defining ourselves here in the West. And out of the clear desert air, I received a second whispered reply that said, "Justice is the true product of your humanity."

What's going on? The postmortem of the September 11, 2001 verdict was as clear then as it is now, after more than thirteen years. Have the hearts of the people changed here at home? Now is the time to understand more as we fear less. Justice or is it just us? Oh, humble readers, beware the short list because the unthinkable can come to past again! We are the top arms merchants of the world. Thus being the number one arms merchants of the world has its consequences in this global village that getting smaller! So why would nineteen human beings commando those commercial airlines, and in spite of the pleas of mercy, the enemy always remembers oppression? If history is to continue as the victor's justice, then beware those who inhabit New York City. The accepted hidden agenda is that the American government and the military industry affiliated with it are not interested in promoting peace, especially when its primary export is weaponry. Just walk around Wall Street in downtown Manhattan and it is difficult not to notice the hideous promises made by a business arena prospering under a foreign policy based on terror and greed. A culture where the Security and Exchange Commission permits an industry whose central focus is to sell pain and death—the same pain and death that came home to roost on September 11, 2001, at our own World Trade Center. But were these events an omen to be ignored and scorned because of the stripe of their own hearts?

Currently, there's tens of millions of people in the secular West trying their best to get rich off other peoples blood, a grotesque symptom of a larger social, political, and spiritual disease. For an ever-growing contingent of "we the people" has failed to learn the lessons carried forward from a dark past, bearing witness but remaining silent in the face of the painful death and oppression of almost a million people in the Islamic and the developing Third World every year since those days of Vietnam.

Take a closer look don't be afraid; pull back that curtain some more. That FDA-approved patient labeling says you can get dizzy, faint, have a stroke or heart attack, even die; just do not take that blue pill call justice if your desire is being number one international arms merchant of the world and international peace composer of the world at the same time. It`s a prescription for disaster! For the love of money or a fist full of dollars, this war on terror here at home is a loser and a grotesque symptom of our larger social and political disease of the heart!

Each time you want a refill, just remember—oh yes, Mr. Alfred Adler, that "life tasks" fundamentalist who said, "It`s always easier to fight for one`s principles than to live up to them."

However, for years now after the fallout of 9-11-01, many people here at home are saying, "who`s to stop the will of the American people, or any democratic government that chooses of their own free will to export billions of dollars of arms, guns, bullets, pain, suffering, death, and tools of oppression if they wish to do so unto the world global market anyway?" Fanatics?

So here we are at Ground Zero, at the intersection of Liberty Street and Church Street, in Manhattan, New York City, which stands the symbolic heart of a nation that is beyond the pale of reason, home to a people beyond the pale of mercy. Presently, the so-called Freedom Tower, or One World Trade Center, is currently under construction. To this I wish to now give in advance my deepest sympathies to those whom I truly feel will soon lose their loved ones again at Ground Zero—the world's biggest bull's-eye. Sheikh Omar Abdel Rahman`s fatwa is still valid in the hearts, minds and souls of millions of Muslims worldwide. So why didn't the American people demand first to know *why* a bomb exploded under the World Trade Center on February 26, 1993, an event that could have killed thousands of people then? To ask not why, the cause, but rather who, the individuals, is to deny the religious, political and social realities of the world we all live in, as well as the true magnitude of the consequences that we all face if these realities continue to be ignored. For it is frightening how truly oblivious most of my fellow Americans are when it comes to self-interest—from the haughtiness military to corporate media types, to the top 1%, to all those people of the secular West who are trying to get rich even if others have to die trying to live a humble life, pay the rent, the food bill, and raise their families in their own countries. Objectively, not all people want straight answers to tough questions; but what disturbs me is the fashionable political spin put on these issues, that successful-icon social buzz, and that out-of-sight-out-of-mind moral silence that`s going around and around. So when will the living dead awaken here in "the land of the free and the home of the brave"? Only Allah knows? Why hasn't my beloved country learned from the experiences of its dark past; or is it always just business as usual, show me the money, come what may? Is this the proper way to define ourselves on the world stage as the most powerful and influential country on earth? To this day there`s a sign over Ground Zero that says "We will never forget," but is this a promise for justice unto the Divine One for reform, or an oath of revenge? Oh, countrymen, we must mend our politics and principles, stop our current practices of piracy for the mercy of that divine one. Why? Because Islam has Samsons too!

Just what are those issues and unsettled accounts that will not die, that are so purposely unmoored from the concerns of ordinary people here in the West? Take fear of a Divine One out of the equation and the act of humility becomes that much harder, as does the peripheral vision required to see the open doors everywhere amongst us. Yes, President Barack Obama is the man forced to hold the bag of debt, the man forced to pay the price of losing two wars he inherited; but can he be the one to deliver the bag of true justice without firing a shot or sending a drone? Yet wasn't Obama awarded a Nobel Peace Prize before he or his government had even accomplished any measure of peace anywhere on the planet? Hence where`s the peace? What`s going on? A Nobel Peace Prize for being the first African-American President of the United States is an insult. You know that, and I know that! Or was this award given solely as a quid pro quo? Especially on a promise to pull American troops out of Afghanistan and Iraq, while still supporting these countries' corrupt leaders that were elected into office through elections fraught with outright fraud and vote rigging? So where`s the peace? What`s going on? Is this is how President Obama`s idea of protecting democratic ideals and promoting peaceful tolerance works? What`s really going on?

The courage of one's convictions means nothing if our leaders lack the will to engage with those who oppose them for political and religious reasons! In this world village that's getting smaller by the day, making peace with your enemies, not just your friends, is wise and requires true courage. Like most guerrilla wars, this conflict—the war on terror versus the heart, mind, and soul war—will be won by the side who offers the most illuminating ideas and enlightened principles to the global body. As far as I am aware of, therein lays the genus of our human species. But just what are the terms of this jihad fundamentalist Osama Bin Laden, and his ideological descendants demanding? In truth, their demands are quite clear for ages for those who wanted the facts:

1. To remove of all American bases and Western military forces from all Muslim countries

2. To establishment of Islamic Law in every Muslim country.
3. To stand up to the capitalists and imperialists secular American and European West as well as to those Communist States and affirm the dignity of the Islamic peoples.
4. To unify all Muslim countries into a single Islamic state and caliphate.
5. To stop secular Western countries from favoring Israel in its conflict with the Palestinians.
6. To end the financial and military support by Western and Communist nations of Muslim-in-name-only dictators and despots in Muslim lands.
7. To acknowledge that Allah did bless America, but not exclusively, not only.

Politics and religion each provide an accepted social mission that cannot be ignored if the core goal is justice and the method is jihad.[79] President Barack Obama's order to kill Osama bin Laden occurred on May 1, 2011; however, in my opinion and in the enlightened opinions of many others, it is a great mistake when a man of Osama bin Laden's caliber is killed unarmed. America and secular Western Europe, as well as the communist states, have been fighting Islamic revolutionaries for more than a century. Killing the individual resistance leader does not end the war; only killing the ideas and ideals of that resistance leader ends the war. Killing individual oppressive leaders and their countrymen does not end the war; only again killing their ideas and ideals would. So I ask, has Al-Qaeda surrendered since the killing of bin Laden in May 2, 2011? No! Because its foundation rests on accepted Islamic revolutionary ideas and ideals, and Osama Bin Laden was a Muslim revolutionary whose ideas for ending oppression and ideals on how to achieve victory has been accepted by millions of Muslims who want an end to oppression and despots. Likewise, there has never been an Islamic leader, warrior, or politician, that died in jihad against the oppressors of Islam who was not then been replaced by those that follow the ideology of the one martyred. Muslim martyrs cast long shadows! If President Obama had ignored his myopic advisors who wanted revenge and gave the command to deliver Bin Laden alive to him at Camp David in order to have an engagement of minds and a path to peace and justice thus ending this "War of Terror" that they are in, then the whole world would have believed on May 3, 2011, that

---

[79] Quran 42:39-42

justice, not revenge, had been served. All imaginings aside, thus a Noble Peace Prize well deserved in advance!

Oh, humble reader, in a world full of ideas, injustice makes the world full of terrorist! Sheikh Ayman Al-Zawhiri is now the leader of Al-Qaeda because adversity remembers injustice and oppression, thus, constantly considers actions of bold possibilities. All supposes aside, this so-called war on terror will not end with a bullet, a bomb, or by military means; it will only end with unconditional proposals of justice, where each side is both willing and courageous enough to look beyond the rhetoric! Yes, this war will end when both sides can look beyond the components of peace and into the sustainability of justice.

What's going on? We are now living in a period of transition of human history where humanity possesses the power to annihilate themselves in spite of their noble creeds. Since we are all witness to the unlawful deceptions made for both material gain and the accumulation of power over nations in the developing and Islamic world, revenge is inevitable, as it has been over the course of humankind's tormented history. The civilian population here in the West has itself become a hostage, not only to the capitalists and their war profiteer allies, but also to the fear of our own governmental policies that they have instilled into us, which is the mistruths they propagate about acting in our best interest rather than in the interests of the ruling elite!

What's going on? One needs no spyglass to understand the ways of these secular Western globalists; all you have to do is follow the trail of money and pain. Most notably, the International Monetary Fund (IMF) that paves a path of destruction for the World Bank (WB) by coercing poor, developing countries to usuriously restructure their economies by giving Western corporations easy access to that nation's resources. These foreign western corporations then work to remove worker protections like strong unions and national health care programs. Next they flood the host nation's markets with cheap imports, undermining domestic markets at home. Only when the host nation starts to experience rising unemployment, deficit spending, paralyzing strikes, a civil service in revolt, and a devaluated national currency, does its so-called international benefactors order them to slash social spending, so that to ensure that the original patrons, the IMF and the WB, continue to get returns on their investment. Seduced by promises of more jobs and modernity, these powerless nations make easy prey for "free" trade and globalization.

Thanks to our dedication to the "pursuit of happiness," America's own blue-chip bankers, arms merchants, and corporate elite have, in their greed, begun to enact their golden swindles upon their own countrymen. As we the people who are stakeholders who had placed our bets on the American Dream, we have been sold short by the men in those fancy boardrooms, those pirates on the Forbes list laughing all the way to their offshore bank accounts. Meanwhile, there's a black man sitting in the Oval Office of the White House holding a $17 trillion in debt, with an annual interest payment topping $700 billion, a sum which is often paid not by taxation but by printing more money! Of course, President Obama hears those drums approaching; likewise, we hope President Obama has the good sense to realize that if he truly wishes to save America from economic ruin, then the days of mortgaging the future of the American people to pay for foolish ventures—both domestic and foreign—must end. We as a nation of people must confront that ideological differences between the poor, the working poor, the middle class and the one percent pulling the strings of the corporate and political elite with their media and propaganda machine. This way, we the people have a chance of learning the real truth and achieving true justice.

Nonetheless, whether or not President Obama hears those drums, the U.S. needs to deal with a new emerging reality. The purposely forgotten four trillion dollar costs of this war on terror all have their consequences. Moreover, not everybody is going to accept blood money out there. Still surprisingly, President Obama and other leaders of the secular West expect "green zones" of stability right here at home, even as Obama himself said, "The single biggest threat to U.S. security both short term, medium term and long term, would be the possibility of a terrorist organization obtaining a nuclear weapon." The President went on to say, "If there was ever a detonation in New York City, or London, or Johannesburg, the ramifications economically, politically, and from a security perspective would be devastating. We know that organizations like Al-Qaeda are in the process of trying to secure nuclear weapons or other weapons of mass destructions, and would have no compunction in using them."

In contrast to our Cold War conflict with the Soviets, today's geopolitical realities present no guarantee of restraint of a mutually assured destruction (MAD) if any private organization ever obtained a nuclear device or other weapons of mass destruction. The even more inconvenient truth is that when dealing with a patient and resourceful enemy that sees glory in martyrdom, retribution is only a matter of time. For in spite of the West's fear of a fundamentalist Islamic resistance group successfully obtaining—or constructing—a nuclear weapon, the likelihood of this scenario becoming reality is overwhelmingly real. Just imagine the power of a nuclear weapon-backed demand that all American and other Western troops leave not only Afghanistan but all Muslim countries immediately? Unconditionally! Imagine a sworn enemy who had been oppress military, imperially, whose despots was on our pay roll, now their patience has now come to an end, whose idea of political correctness is finding another word for dead? The naked truth is one of no-fly zones in the East being replaced by no-walk zones in the West, due to radioactive fallout or a weapon of mass destruction explosion, a reality that might only be avoided by delivering justice before the Arab Spring becomes a runway for revenge.

What`s going on? Making a livelihood off people`s pain, suffering and death does have its price! Underscoring that there`s no hostile intent for a nation of people to be killed by reality because of their own arrogance, conceit and denial. Has the hearts of my countrymen here in the secular West change since 9-11-2001 in regards to the issues of oppression, injustice and the support of despots overseas? We believe not.

Now given that thought crime of facing unpleasant citizenship responsibilities here in the West. It presently takes today in our modern era about three minutes or so to decipher on the news channel without sound which Muslim city is burning? Tyre, Beirut, Gaza, Sidon, Baghdad, Ramadi, Falluja, Basra, Karbala, Mosul, Najaf, Kabul, Kandahar, Damascus, Mogadiscio.

The question is, will this change only come once the citizens of Los Angeles, Chicago, New York, London, Paris, Rome, Madrid, and Moscow are cowering in their underground shelters while their homes, churches, schools and factories, all burn in hellish flames above them as well?

The fact remains that once we liberate the minds of the youth of all nations and let them see their common ground, their potentials, as well as the strength that lies in their unity, humankind will no longer have to worry about wars of folly and threat of mass destruction because the youth know it is they who will be on the front lines. Yes, it is easier to both talk and listen to one other in a rooftop garden than in a fallout shelter, so we the believers of this monotheistic faith have every reason to be distraught given the prospects of war today. By neglecting to negotiate, we all lose more than those material things burning on the ground floor. Likewise, how foolish to pretend that President Obama`s leadership can truly effect change, that by some chance a black man burdened by a $17 trillion debt and beholden to an array of special interests would actually succeed in negotiating with individuals who both hold weapons of mass destruction and operate on a promise made unto that divine one. Now is the time for reconciliation while we still have the time. Once the enemies of the secular West with memories of oppression and blood debts to honor, feel it is time to cash in, it is my intuition that mercy will be a foreign word. Reconciliation, however, is useless unless it comes with that idea of justice outside of ourselves!

The true challenges humankind faces in this era means the survival of our species here on earth, so we must be just to each other unconditionally. The time has passed for these so-called leaders with their historical summits that changes nothing, with their watered-down demonstrations of peace that have inflicted untold damage to the dignity of mankind, with their refusal to sit down and actually talk peace and justice with their enemies; and to truly see the injustice suffered by others. Leaders who erroneously believe that they are immune to retaliation and retribution because of the arms they possess are only deceiving themselves and their followers. Such shameful reliance on military options drains the spirit of humanity, ignores our common humble origins, and misconstrues true human purpose here on earth.

What's going on?

That raid upon those people living in Mumbai (Bombay), India, in November 26-29, 2008, with 164 people dead is a consequent of what's happening to the Muslim people in Srinagar, Kashmir, India, from 1947 to the present day. Thousands of Muslim people had died fighting in Kashmir and are still oppress demanding independence from Indian rule. Yet where's that strong international call for change and justice?

Real freedom seems too compromised without real justice these days; too many game changer ideas are ignored by the corporate Western media, thus those oppressed sitting in dungeons surrounded by millions above who refuses to take action waiting for the commercials!

Call it what you want. It is only a matter of time hopefully, before presidents, kings, prime ministers, dictators, revolutionist, jihadist, and so called fanatics meet at the same table as equal individuals with a cause and who's concerns for justice will be heard unconditionally!

What's going on? The Arab Spring has been successful, because on the street level people are building the capacity to network with their neighbors and produce change for a better tomorrow through positive engagement with their countrymen. As we have seen with the incipient Occupy movement, it is only a matter of time before the Arab Spring arrives here in the West; in fact, the signs are all around that the growing poor and working class are ready to revolt against the corrupt corporatocracy epitomized by the media and banking industries. The question is will we, the human community, wait for the establishment's official inquest of fraud to be read? Must "We the people" be forced to filter out the lies that have been forced upon us as truth?

In a world full of ideas, if secular democracy doesn`t deliver the social justice it has promised for all here in the West, and if these same democracies fail to end their imperialist enterprises worldwide, then inevitably there will be revolt here at home in the West followed by the world stage that will stop buying or selling oil for dollars or euro's tomorrow!

The Free Press

Oh ye who believe! If a wicked person comes to you with any news, ascertain the truth, lest ye harm people unwittingly, and afterwards become full of repentance for what ye have done.

—Quran 49:6

Ideas are how this world works; however, the public can no longer tolerate a media that only reports the symptoms of the effect while ignoring the causes of a problem. The awakened public can no longer tolerate conflicts of interest in the news media, the newspeak George Orwell writes about in *1984,* which William James, that thoughtful fundamentalist, reiterated when he said, "There is no worse lie than the truth misunderstood by those who hear it."

Those concerned must beware that, yes, the First Amendment of the United States "forbids Congress to make any law prohibiting the freedom of religion or abridging freedom of speech, freedom of expression, and freedom of assembly"; but when today's rich billionaires and powerful media conglomerates together wear a mask called the free press, they threaten our rights of citizenship under the First Amendment. These media conglomerates abridge freedom of speech by not airing the messages essential to the public interest simply because this might not be in their own best interest. This conflict of interest, which most notably resides in the news media of the secular West, relegates the notion of a "free press" as a true oxymoron, for it is certainly neither independent nor unbiased. Owned by wealthy, powerful corporate interests, today's press cannot be seen as anything other than tools of propaganda. Truthful dissemination of information is both vital and essential to our pluralistic society by unabashedly informing the general public, as well as providing it with alternative ideas and viewpoints. So, where are those anti-trust laws in regards our corporate media here in America? Are they also too big to fail? Without question, the media industry here in West needs serious reforms.

A new era has dawned upon humankind today. The so-called public enemy has turned into the enemy combatant with a weapon of mass destruction and a cause, hence the passion for which will not die under the force of oppression. It`s a different forest out here now that the rabbit has the power to kill in mass. Thus, today's Western media, a true oligarchy representative, have a grave problem coming to terms with a patient enemy within its own borders, thus the complicit and obvious rollback in civil liberties by their corrupted kinsmen in government because of fear. Today it is a known fact that the top six media conglomerates control nearly everything we in the secular West gossip about, watch, hear and read. These multinational propaganda machines, are run by some of the wealthiest white men of the secular West: J.R. Immelt of General Electric (NBC), who presided over $147 billion in revenue in 2011; Robert Iger of the Walt Disney Corporation, with its $40 billion in 2011 revenue; News Corporation under Rupert Murdoch with 2011 revenues of $33 billion; Jeffrey Bewkes, who as CEO of Time Warner oversaw $27 billion in 2011 revenues; CEO Phillipe Dauman of Viacom with 2011 revenues of $15 billion; and Leslie Moonves, the CEO of CBS, revenues in 2011 were $6.5 billion.

These corporate ministries of media propaganda are not an independent press, nor are they dedicated to public service; instead they are entities interested solely in profit and patrons to misinformation, rather than being agents of honest discourse, a voice for the masses, and the so-called fourth estate of democracy. As controllers of information, that most essential of all commodities, these corporate media conglomerates are, arguably, the planet's most powerful special interest, regulating the images we see, the ideas we hear, and the products we buy. Rarely do we see any true investigative journalism in today's media; rather, the news has become show business, a slick and for-profit version of Orwellian "newspeak," rather than a vehicle for informing the public about the important issues of the day.

Today`s Western media fails to reflect the true ethnic and cultural diversity of its population, which is self-evident in the way these organizations choose what is and what is not fit to broadcast and print. Not only are the people on the streets and in their homes being subjected to conflicts of interest, but conflicts of race, faith, culture, and wealth. Ms. Amy Alexander, the African American journalist, describes in her book *Uncovering Race*, the troubling lens through which ethnic minorities in America are so often viewed by a predominantly white journalism corps. The result of which has been urban riots, segregated suburbia, the decay of civil liberties, lack of concern for the poor, a surge of racism, the imbalance of crime and punishment, and the ever-growing class divide. Finding much to carp at others, and much to ignore in themselves. Rarely will the media report on that individual making a positive change in his or her community, or cover the passion so often seen in a town hall meetings demanding social change, lower taxes, the end to wild spending spree by public officials of tax payers hard-earned money, and better public services to address the problems at hand. Because there is, no millions of advertising dollars are to be made featuring basic fundamental stories like these.

Seeing beyond the moment, I freely acknowledge it's frightening the scale of damage the Western media has wreaked upon the society it's supposed to be defending. Today's press is no watchdog for truth or justice but rather a co-conspirator in a game rigged against the interests of we the people; in fact, to be honestly frank about it, it is we who are paying for the views of the rich and powerful to be trumpeted over those of all others. But what can be done about this . . . ? Implementing those antitrust laws would help bring truth from the rich shadows of ideological greed. Certainly the break-up of these media monopolies by nonpartisan governmental and independent public oversight would be a good start, but can this ever be accomplished considering the adversaries' vast power and resources? In truth, one cannot be calm, cool, and embraced a detached thinking that this will all sort itself out because in reality, hopefully, this all depends on the will of the people, and their refusal to be oppressed and misinformed any longer. So why should those of us who believe in one divine being allow ourselves to think that we need the authorization, or even the endorsement, of that Western media oligarchy to validate our jihad? Their opinions and interests have already been heard and summarily rejected. For those of us who truly believe in the words, "In God We Trust" know that when the information coming from a culture starts to sound fraudulent, when its prisons are full of the poor, veterans and minorities, when its rich keep getting richer, the poor, poorer, then it's time to sincerely question the heart of the message, the hearts of those people who bring us these messages of misinformation and the hearts of those people who owns those printing presses.

What's shocking, oh, humble reader, in this new age of information is that flagrant abuse of the universal right to free speech! So I thank Allah for blessing me with good parents and teachers for teaching me that a person should first examine one's own intentions then speak from your heart that matter you wish to convey unto others. For example:

There are no fatwa's that I ever heard of against free speech in any Muslim country I ever lived in for the more than 14 years of my life when I was there. You are free to speak like everywhere else on this neglectful earth amongst the unequal's calling for something new, old, or just something inspirational that would unlock that hidden potential in people. Yet you pay in full the consequences of what you say; the practical realities of this world, this life we live in! The conventional wisdom is that the burden of truth is falling increasingly heavily on the poor.

However, it's those rich Western secular media conglomerates that wish to pay the consequences of their slander and libel unto others not now but later on, perfidiously, preferably in a Western so called civilize out-of-court, out-of-sight, settlement. As they cut against the grain of enlightenment, their world is their own reflection and their own ideals suit their own self-interest.

Let's keep the issues where they are. I believe that image, that secular cultural idea of lampooning and using satire on sacred beliefs on monotheist prophets as an advertisement of modern civilize free speech in this awakening Western world and onto the world stage, contains the seeds of their own destruction. For example, *"Keep thy tongue from evil, and thy lips from speaking guile."* (Torah, Ps. 34:14) and: *"Those who slander such of the believers as give themselves freely to deeds of charity, as well as such as can find nothing to give except the fruits of their labor and throw ridicule on them, Allah will throw back their ridicule on them: and they shall have a grievous penalty. Whether thou ask for their forgiveness, or not, their sin is unforgivable: If thou ask seventy times for their forgiveness, Allah will not forgive them: because they have rejected Allah and his apostle: and Allah guides not those who are perversely rebellious."* (Quran 9:79-80) as well as: *"A slanderer going about with calumnies; habitually hindering all good, transgressing beyond bounds, deep in sin; violent and cruel, with all that, base-born; because he possesses wealth and numerous sons, when to him are rehearsed our signs, "tales of the ancients" he cries! Soon shall we brand on the snout!* (Quran 68:11-16)

What`s worrying me, oh, humble reader, is that with all the enlightening and enchanting ideas here in the Western cultural revolution to read about to talk about and to be aware of, it`s still customary to read and hear the gossip of those Western publishers and executive editors acclaiming slander and libel as part of free speech! Yes, indeed, Google was asked by the Obama`s administration days before September 11, 2012, to remove the Prophet Muhammad (sas) libelous film *Innocence of Muslims* from You Tube which Google owns, but they refused citing the U.S. First Amendment!

Yes, there are no fatwa`s against free speech. You just pay in full the consequences of what you say! These Western slanderous and libelous events, which was ignored by many Western politicians and corporate media was defended by free speech, which had preceded these ignominious state of affairs in the Middle East are still simmering in the hearts of the Islamic world. Reading between the lines for many, the Western world was indeed reckoned by that heralding fundamentalist Ayatullah Ruhollah Khomeini who did wrote out a fatwa for the death of the author Salman Rushdie because of his slander of God-fearing Prophets in his book *The Satanic Verses* in 1989. Now Mr. Rushdie needs bodyguards for the rest of his life, yet that is no guarantee against a jihadi who wishes to still cash him in.

So it came as no surprise that that Dutch filmmaker Theo Van Gogh was force to pay in full the consequence of what he said and thus was killed because his film, which libeled the Muslim faith and it`s people in 2004, only highlighted the high importance the value of one`s "word" by people who up hold the integrity and honor of monotheist prophets regardless of where they are living on this earth.

When the Holy Quran was defiled by American guards oppressing and torturing Muslim prisoners at the Guantanamo Bay prison in Cuba starting fatal riots in the Muslim world in 2005; this was not a good example of humanities a country like ours would portray trying to win that heart and mind war. As well as that Denmark Newspaper "Jyllands Posten" that had libeled Prophet Muhammad starting fatal riots and burning of Denmark embassy in the Muslim lands in 2005, this did not help relations between America and Islam also Europe and Islam by far indeed. These provocative chronicle ideals of intolerance in fact can only fuel the fire of hate and revenge.

And who does more wrong with a lie than that American filmmaker Sam Bacile which is most likely a pseudonym name, subsequently is imprisoned once again on parole violations in America because of his film *Innocence of Muslims?* This film outraged the Muslim world, and thus acts of retribution; resulting in the deaths of the American

Ambassador to Libya Mr. J. Christopher Stevens along with his three consulate workers with him in Benghazi, Libya on September 11, 2012. Any one can say this is all a sequence of unnecessary provocations by those few in the Western world as well, one can say, with no doubt, an overreaction of anger, by those in the Muslim world. Yet it`s that image in the Western culture that says it has a free right to slander and/or libel religious people and religious ideals regardless of who they are!

Mr. Ekmeleddin Ihsanoglu the Secretary General of the Organization of Islamic Cooperation (OIC), said on this issue in September, 2012, "The international community should come out of hiding from behind the excuse of freedom of expression." The fact is OIC has been for years calling for an international code of conduct for world media and social media to disallow dissemination of incitement material world wide at the United Nations, yet nothing still has been enacted! Those countries that has been quietly hiding behind the scenes holding up the barriers against an international code of conduct for world media and social media at the UN are in fact America and European nations.

Presently, this social and religious tinderbox of words and outrageous cartoons images between civilizations that is secular and religious in their constitution cannot be allowed to continue for the sake of human dignity. The rules are simple respect, and tolerance! This was a true measure of progress in the Dark Ages and shall be, whether mankind likes it or not, a true measure of survival in this ongoing era of human revolution of information in today`s heralding thirst for truth. The trend that is now before us all of how different civilization changes the way people look speak and read about each other must be a positive one for the benefit of all mankind. How we as human beings view and react to strange civilizations that`s all around us with different beliefs, ideas, and customs, will be crucial to the future prospect of mankind here on earth.

As I stated before, there is no fatwas against free speech anywhere in the Islamic world. You only pay in full the consequences of what you say! One has to beware and understand that responsibility of what you say comes with free speech in the East. I am a believer that people should have free access to modern global media platforms worldwide. Yet it is an illusion to believe that what an individual or corporate media say and portrays to the world stage has no effect on the viewing world audience. Many Western countries have laws explicitly forbidding slander and libel towards individuals but not towards religious ideals. Thus, humanity must mind the gap. The so-called free Western secular press is not bounded by monotheistic religious sanctity in regards to the facts. And a theocracy-minded people who are in a jihad removing salt from seawater is not bounded by secular's sanctity of freedoms. But this obvious gap does not mean acquiring truth in this social world of vested interest is in vain. Being respectful and being tolerant of others precedes the news is wisdom.

Oh, humble reader, when push comes to shove, only a fool believes human bones have nothing to say! Contemplating the local obituary here at home, a true surrealism on paper; the fact is we are all ambassadors of our nations when we travel abroad and at the very mercy of our host in regards to what our countrymen say or do back at home! From the very beginning; the mystery of how Ambassador J. Christopher Stevens and his three other consulate workers that died with him was known in this hearts, mind and soul war. But the American political-weather preferred denial. They all died because their countrymen back at home showed no signs of outrage at the insult and libel of their host religious beliefs. No throngs of secular minded people on the streets in the West avowing that this affair had abused their privilege and rights by slandering and libeling their neighbor's faith abroad and at home. No scathing rebuts to be seen by the major secular Western corporate media channels. No one who is somebody but Obama and Muslim leaders on the phone demanding and calling for respect and tolerance, yet who knew about the effects of such libel and slander will do to all those ambassadors and citizens of theirs abroad now that the damage of *Innocence of Muslims* has been done? No one strong enough, with the will to dare pull the plug on Google, and Western media on humane principles of respect and tolerance!

Yet what is really worrying me, seeing beyond the moment at hand, is that scheme expresses by the American corporate media and political elite, in their portraying of this sad event that happen in Benghazi, Libya to our ambassador Mr. J. Christopher Stevens and his three consulate workers with him. Denying that their deaths were due to the broadcast of the insult and libel of Islam and Prophet Muhammad (sas) by Google and Western media *"Innocence of Muslims"*, standing on freedom of speech! They portrayed instead the lie that their deaths were a revenge and retaliation by Islamic forces on the eleventh anniversary of 9-11-01! Not the throng of angry demonstrating Muslim citizens, who lived nearby the consulate, who were tired of the insults on their faith. Therefore, indeed, what Mr. William James said, is correct: "There is no worse lie than the truth misunderstood by those who hear it!"

Justice and Islam

Thus, says God, the lord, who created the heavens and stretched them out, who spreads out the earth with its crops, who breath to its people and spirit to those who walk on it: I, the lord, have called you for the victory of justice, I have grasped you by the hand; I formed you, and set you as a covenant of the people, a light for the nations, to open the eyes of the blind, to bring out prisoners from confinement, and from the dungeon, those who live in darkness.

—Isa.42:5-7

Oh ye who believe! Stand out firmly for justice, as witness to Allah, even as against yourselves, or your parents, or your kin, and whether it be against rich or poor: For Allah can best protect both. Follow not the lusts of your hearts, lest ye swerve, and if ye distort justice or decline to do justice, verily Allah is well acquainted with all that ye do.

—Quran 4:135

Justice will live as long as the human soul has the desire for it. Thus, direct dialogue with an enemy is better than posturing for time with tongues of intermediaries of proxy whose sole interest is self-glorification, not compassionated by deeds of justice! This idea cuts both ways, for the criteria of the Muslims, here in the West is the achievement of justice. My Allah-fearing teachers in Saudi Arabia have told me justice is the prize. Similarly, it was that genius but misunderstood fundamentalist Imam ibn Taymiyah who said, "Who holds the achievement of justice in a state as most fundamental is deserving of Allah`s support, even for a nation of disbelievers. The land of justice is the land of Islam. In this life, people`s situations uphold when justice prevails in their society, even if they fall into various kinds of sins. However, people`s situations do not uphold when injustice and the lack of rights prevail in their society. That is why, the saying goes, Allah upholds a state established on justice, even if it were a nation of disbelievers, even if it were a nation of Muslims. But the other saying also goes: this world lives with justice and disbelief and does not live with injustice and Islam."

The necessary consequence of jihad is always justice. This is how we define ourselves as Muslims. Every acceptable nation of people has been ruled with justice, and though many have been affiliated with Islamic law, most have been ruled with both ideologies and customs foreign to the faith that Allah revealed. Likewise, many millions of Muslims have fled to the secular West, only to be subjected by to foreign ideologies and a denial of justice in their new lands (Europe). For the land of justice *is* the land of Islam. So when we do not abide by and/or implement the laws that Allah has revealed by the Sharia, then we must also pay the price of Islamophobia here in the West as well as the price of abandoning our Muslim lands to injustice given to the Muslim people by Allah. The belief is widespread amongst many hundreds of millions of nonbelievers that Muslims have come to the West to run away from themselves as a people of faith and to enjoy those Western hard-fought liberties and justice—that by doing so, they have voted with their feet the extinction of their faith. Yet to truly consider why a nation of people had run away from the land given to them by their one divine being is disconcerting. For to maintain the hope, the believers and people therein need only to be just to themselves, as your heart does reflect your freedom!

So what does Islam have to offer that can benefit the unbelievers here in the West? Don't get me wrong. People who are not believers in our faith are not stupid; it's just that Islam and justice are not shown in the Western media as reflections of each other, a gross misrepresentation of our faith to the world stage. Yet if we can only first learn to be just to ourselves, then perhaps we the believers can save these unbelievers in the West from their hellish circle of wars of folly, corruption, and hopelessness.

Though I am not perfect, my own story—I who was born a Christian in the East End of London, who immigrated to the Bronx in 1960 as a child by a Christian father who was an American citizen who thought he can run away from the racist Jim Crow laws in America, to Europe then he realize the bigotry was just as bad there, came back to New York to rise his family. I attended Howard University in Washington DC in 1978 surrounded by racism and oppression of my people; was sent to prison in Butner, North Carolina, and became a Muslim; was a few years later in 1993 accepted and studied at Mecca University in Saudi Arabia on a scholarship from the people of Saudi Arabia so as to learn more about my faith and be dynamic. I also made hajj four times, hum du Allah. I did not receive a scholarship from my own countrymen so as to learn more and be a beneficial and productive member of my secular society except in prison. Thus, I am a sincere testament to the gateway that opened for me by the mercy of my lord.

Yet, perhaps it is you, oh, humble reader of this book, who may be more endowed than me to understand the dire circumstances of the world today. What would you have me say otherwise? Here behind enemy lines justice hangs by a mere prayer, so truly it is time to bring a new dimension into our system, and call upon the one divine Lord for help, protection, strength, knowledge, guidance and wisdom. For we are surrounded by enemies near and far, a situation we did inherit to test our own hearts, yet we did not create ourselves, or our souls. We did not ask to be here on this earth despite our presence here being an invitation to behold truth. The divine one who placed you here on this earth has made it known to you, through his prophets, of the laws to live by so that you will not go astray. Obedience is the supreme fundamental law. If we as a nation of believers wish to be successful here in the West, then Islam and justice must be accepted as a true reflection of each other, not because we are free to utter these words to ourselves, and to others. But because both our neighbors, strangers, and ourselves may utter them without fear and say this is the truth.

Islam means peace; Muslim means one who submits to the will of Allah. Therefore, peace can only be achieved on this earth by justice. Humankind, I believe will not be able to sustain itself on this earth unless it is just both to itself and its neighbors. America, the UK, Europe, and other secular nations of the West are masters in promoting the illusions of justice; as such, the fight for believers here in the secular West is not for our lives and the acquisition of material things, but to see the justice of that second jihad becomes a reality. In this land of opportunism, there are millions of ideas being put forward; so then we, the believers, must be our own trumpeters. We must nurture our own media if we truly wish for the good word to reach all the people without bias. We must invest in each other, nurture good shepherds who walk the talk in regard to how Islam can bring a nation of pluralistic and tolerant people together to forge an identity representing a new and positive era for humanity. No man, or, nation, or faith is an island, in this era of struggle; this earth is a quilt of humanity, all of whom, both the believers and the nonbelievers, will be held to account on judgment day.

To this, I ask: how long will the believers keep relying on justice from the kufr and the munafiq to cover the cost of their lack of faith? By whose justice will we roll back the ghettos and lift the growing ranks out of the grips of poverty, crime, addiction and despair? By whose justice will we build our own courts on? By whose justice will we establish our own law's on?

So what does Islam have to offer that can benefit the unbelievers living here in the West? Is it truly that idea that peace only works with the motivation of justice first? All this political and media-hype talk about peace treaties and Oslo peace talks is really just wasteful talk if people and their own leaders are not talking about justice for their adversaries! These political leaders that we have in suit and tie—I truly wish they stop bodysurfing the masses for sovereignty and political correctness! If there is no justice there is no peace—this is the golden rule. Thus, our world we can all live in is a world of justice and unbelief whether we all like it or not.

Miseducation

Let not the believers take for friends or helpers unbelievers rather than
believers: If any do that, in nothing will there be help from Allah:
Except by way of precaution, that ye may guard yourself from them.
But Allah cautions you to remember himself, for the final goal is to
Allah.

—Quran 3:28

Today's world is split into two kinds of peoples: those who have money
and power and everybody else with their fantasies. Invariably the ruling
elite inevitably lead by focusing on the sensational and misdirection,
while ignoring the troubling underlying dynamics of the essentials in
life of the common people.

Contrary to this mindful reality, today we Muslims in these western
secular societies have less than 7 percent of Muslim youths in America,
the UK, and Europe attending full-time private Muslim schools. Is
this not, an indictment against ourselves as believers of our faith on
the very way in which we are educating our youths? Why, I ask, have
the great majority of Muslim parents living in the West chosen to
send their children to secular public and Christian schools rather
than build their own schools with their own hands and their own
money? If it really is only a matter of the high tuition of most private
Muslim schools, where then are the Muslim charities that will help
the poorer families amongst the believers to raise the needed funds
to educate the children of their own faith? For generations wealthy
Jewish communities here in the secular West have assisted their poorer

brethren in educating their children in their own schools rather than be a witness against themselves watching them go to secular public or Christian schools. It`s just I shall never forget my friend, that old sheikh from Sudan, Abdul Majed, black as a plum and just as wrinkly. Who gave me laments for the living; and what he had said to me on this issue of education was, "Lions don`t send their children to hyena school or to snake school or to crocodile school or to zebra school. They send their children to lion schools so they will learn how to be lions and be just to each other!" You think that brick in the wall isn`t there? Who then I must ask is eclipsing whom as a nation of people here in the West so that the good or iniquity may come into this world? How truly naïve a great majority of Muslims are here in the kafir West, believing that their western educational orientation and lifestyle is compatible with Muslim scripture and lifestyle. That idea of salvation can only be attained by a master's degree or a PhD or full acceptance of kufr culture, is truly a showcase of mis-education, for ambitions such as these matches with neither history nor current realities.

Along these lines, I clearly remember back thirty-five years ago, to the time I was a Howard University student participating in a discussion in an English 101 class about Dr. Carter G. Woodson, that controversial yet visionary African American fundamentalist and his book titled *The Mis-Education of the Negro*. As I sat in that classroom with other students at age 19, I slowly came to the realization that the mission to uplift myself with that American dream was a lie. For me presently, despite the election of President Obama, Dr. Woodson's fundamental analysis was truly accurate when he said, "We as a people of color are nominally free but economically enslaved."

Because no one likes the smell of their own blood wasted. It was at Howard University that made me appreciate that African educator fundamentalist Mrs. Mary Mc Leod Bethune, and what she had to struggle through in promoting education for young people of color by building schools so that people of color can overcome the hazards of living that American dream many years ago and that we as a people of color can prove our worth in spite of Jim Crow beliefs all around us.

Yet the greater reality is of today`s deterioration—that we, the people of color, are doomed by the millions to poverty, servitude, drugs, urban sharecropping and crime, our goals, skills, and potentials as a tribe of people still a forlorn hope. Can I be any more explicit than to say that our most talented 10 percent is being trained to serve the dominant social order? This legacy cannot be sustained unto the next generation. How truly disturbing that in spite of millions of college diplomas, master's degrees, and PhDs, thousands of millionaires,

Hollywood awards and pop stars, our suffering as a people has not abated; in fact, it can be argued that it has gotten worse. Simply because we have not been educated in a way that makes us aware of our purpose, mission, goals and methods that will both enrich us and guide us as a people. We are not educated as a tribe of people working in cohesion with our talented tenth in understanding and appreciating that trial of middle passage that holocaust from Africa to these Western shores in chains and rags. Instead, we have been trained in the millions to blindly serve others. In today's market environment we the African American people commute to work, rather than working smartly from our homes and communities to enrich our own neighborhoods making them green zones of fulfillment. Each day we leave our ghettos, our urban and suburban worlds, for the sake of a paycheck and the hope of advancing our careers. It's the talk of the cities and towns here in the West—that we as a people of color have not been educated to huddle together easily and come forth with a plan of action. Unlike the ways we've been educated for teamwork on the football field or the basketball court, we as a people have not been educated to know the importance of huddling together and emerge with a plan of action in our own social, economic, and professional arenas independently. So do those commuting to jobs that enrich communities other than their own really believe their actions have no consequences? Won't they take heed the peril of "serving others as a tribe of people until we can serve ourselves"? That this is a strategy that carries a great deal of risk of retaliation; called riot.

Nearly 80 years after Dr. Carter's *Mis-Education of the Negro* was first published; 58 years after the Supreme Court's *Brown v. Board of Education* decision, 142 years after the passage of the Fifteenth Amendment by Congress, and 48 years after the Civil Rights Act became law, five years after President Obama became president and reelected, today's African-Americans, as a community, remain horrifyingly unable to see the benefits of employing one another within our own communities, unable to sustain our own livelihoods and institutions independent of government aid, and, worst of all, unable to envision the merits of boycott as well as patronizing ourselves within our own habitable zones, in spite of having that determined fundamentalist Ms. Rosa Parks who had refuse to sit at the back of the bus because she is "black," as an example of boycott and way forward in understanding that you don't compromise dignity for dollars! Similarly, in my own relentless pursuit of jihad, I too have come to realize as truth what Frederick Douglass, that ex-slave fundamentalist, meant when he said, "It is vain that we talk of being men if we do not do the work of men! We must become valuable to society in other departments of industry than those servile ones from which we are rapidly being excluded. We must show that we can do as well as them. Society is a hardhearted affair. With it the helpless may expect no higher dignity than that of paupers. The individual must lay society under obligation to him or society will honor him only as a stranger and sojourner."

My faith tells me that my Muslim brothers and sisters are confronting a looming struggle which is similar to the one African Americans and other minorities have faced here in the secular West. Surrounded by a sea of enemies representing powerful special interests of different hues and class, Muslims today are at a crossroads much like African Americans were in April 1968. So then, the question is, do we the Muslim communities possess the will to follow our prophet and be led unconditionally by a leader of our own with a plan and knowledge of the customs and way of this pluralistic Western secular society through unity and faith to that Promised Land, or will we remain a sleeping, faceless, rudderless tribe of individuals slaving to the grind in our selfish and materialistic society of ours like others before us?

The making of today's modern-day slave by the modern-day slaver is a no-win way for a society to succeed and prosper. As a people of color born free—we as a nation, a race, that adheres to a creed of a monotheist faith have a heritage of our own to safeguard against a dominant social order whose goals is to indoctrinate our youth, robbing them of self-confidence, self-awareness, and self-respect. Why then should we let the corporatocracy, and the ruling elite control our most precious resource; our youth? All you got to do is look at the hip-hop gait of the accepted black culture of our youth in these modern Western times with their pants sagging, their self-confidence dragging, their self-awareness flagging, and their self-respect lagging! Mr. Russell Simmons, that African American entrepreneur known as the godfather of hip-hop, cofounding Def-Jam, is under great criticism from many conscious African American leaders today, for promoting a culture of debauchery and not uplifting our children. He has responded on August 24, 2013, to his critics on CNN; he said, "It's important to let our youth tell the truth as they see it" and "I cannot tell the poets what to say." Oh, humble reader, we believe Mr. Russell Simmons is complicit in the promotion of decadence aimed at the African American youth of this country for profit and gain. We fundamentalist believe if what you have to say desecrates the character of the individual who speaks the truth as they see it,

words which echoes the soul then what kind of poet are you, a Pied
Piper? In contrast, Mr. Russell Means, that Native American Indian
fundamentalist with the feathers in his hat, was right when he told the
world to "always remember that you are the ancestors of those unborn."

We know the cause of the problem is the condition of the hearts
of the people. Thus Dr Carter G. Woodson was correct in saying that
"Education is a process or system that imparts the dominant values,
principles and beliefs of a given society." Now, whose values then
are dominant here in the secular West? Mr. Woodson likewise said,
"Training is the process of learning skills such as reading writing and
computation. The mere imparting of information is not education.
The effort must result in making that person think and do for
themselves. Because of what we see of ourselves often influences
what we do about ourselves, the role of education in controlling our
thoughts and actions is more important. When you control a man`s
thinking you do not have to worry about his actions. You do not have
to tell him not to stand here or go yonder. He will find his proper
place and stay in it. You do not need to send him to the back door.
He will go without being told. In fact, if there is no back door, he will
cut one for his special benefit. His education makes it necessary."
Truly it is a sin, I believe, to look and not see the wrong, to hear the
call but only for prayer! Yes, we as a people are still on the menu in
spite of having a President Obama in the White House, and in spite of
that congressional black caucus in the U.S. Congress. So the question
is, what have we, the nation's people of color, gained in terms of
a national revival? Why nearly one million of us in some part of the
correctional prison system and/or on parole rather than enrolled in
this country's colleges and universities? What are we as a community,
as a nation of people, doing to correct such a damning legacy? Sadly,
the pragmatic truth is that we have been trained to believe that we are
not our brothers' keepers when he has risen or fallen, whether it be by
folly, fortune, or fate.

Yes, of course, there is a reason that no one wants our children
when we as a nation of African American people attempt to educate
them and fail. Fifty years of busing our children into communities
outside our own, thinking there will be a change ignoring that central
problem which lies within our own homes does has a high social
price. As we consider this dialogue gravely, how can anybody expect a
nation of people who cannot educate their own children to educate
anybody else's? Bill Cosby, that dauntless fundamentalist, was roundly
criticized when he said, "Lower economic people are not parenting
and are failing the civil rights movement by not holding up their end

of the deal." But is he not right? Is it not true that middle-class African
American family with two loving parents, and achiever children under
one roof, as depicted on *The Cosby Show,* for years, really just a TV
fantasy to a great majority of millions of African American people who
are poor or middle class, living with just one loving parent under one
roof if they are lucky, then and even more so today? Of course it is a
fantasy because of our own hearts and the lack of love, faith, and true
leadership!

With over 70 percent of our children that are born out of wedlock,
and millions not even knowing where their fathers are, our nation's
people of color are facing a self-inflicted genocide. Being a willing slave
to fashion and carnality is worse than being a slave to oppression to any
man or nation; yet we as a people of color lack the presence of mind
to forswear individualism, as well as lewdness, and cleanse ourselves of
the greed, and glitter of this world. Yes, we are free to speak, free to
vote, and free to march for more than forty-five years now. But no real
change has occurred because collectively, as a single tribe of people, we
do not think for ourselves, act in our own best interest, or listen to each
other enough to act in making any real difference in our communities!
When the United Negro College Fund says, "a mind is a terrible
thing to waste," then we as a people should be giving more to them
than patronizing designer clothing companies and the liquor industry
because of simple birthright principles and deep historical legacies that
we have.

The national unemployment rate is currently 6.3 percent, but for
African-Americans it's more than seventeen percent. For black-teens
the rate climbs to more than forty five percent, and overall there are
millions who have given up looking for jobs and are not even counted
in these statistics. Both President Obama and Education Secretary Arne
Duncan know that just two thousand of the nation's twenty thousand
high schools produces half of all dropouts nationwide, and that
grievously almost fifty percent of black children attend one of these
dropout factories.

Perhaps President Obama should pay a visit to America's most
notorious prisons, those institutions where a disproportionate
number of black youth mostly are receiving their real education, and
give his inspiring speeches about "change." Yes, we as a people are a
minority in America's universities and colleges, but a majority in its
prisons. So when Mr. Jason Riley of *The Wall Street Journal* writes that
when "African Americans are thirteen percent of the population, but
comprise thirty-eight percent of prison or jail inmates in the U.S . . .
and [when] blacks commit fifty—two percent of all murders and make

up forty-nine percent of all murder victims, of which ninety percent of them are murdered by other blacks." Then, I believe it`s not the Tea Party or the KKK that's the problem! The problem is not being more self-aware in mass, not being more socially attuned. It`s a fact that forty-five percent of all the people in American prisons are in there for drug-related crimes of which seventy percent are minorities. It`s a shameful fact that there is no other country in the world in which a person is serving a life sentence without parole for a crime committed before the age of eighteen, so says Mr. Alison Parker the director of the United States programs for Human Rights Watch. He also says that there are more than two thousand-five hundred juveniles offenders serving sentences of life without parole here in America, of which almost half are minorities who are in a sea of 2.3 million people already in our prisons. "Change?" Yes, Mr. President Obama, we need some change right now—enough of the talk of change because that ripple effect of abasement, ignorance, and hopelessness is changing the course of tens of millions of African American lives that is now being discovered in the slush pile called slim chance! When more than seventy percent of black children are born to single black women, and millions of those same children are living in poverty and abusing drugs, it becomes even more essential to ask when we will truly become our brothers` and sisters' keepers and tell these politicians they can keep the change!

I have been asking myself lately from the very depths of my heart, is that new Jewish Chicago mayor Mr. Rahm Emanuel correct in closing fifty schools that are nothing but dropout factories in areas that is full of menacing homicide statists and neighborhoods that are alarmingly crime ridden, which is predominantly African American, of Chicago`s southern and western side?

Is this really racism when a white Jewish mayor with a billion-dollar deficit in his city school budget says no more funding to "majority-black schools" with their "majority-black faculties members" who have undoubtedly failed to inspire and educate their own ethnic people because of the lack of ethics?

To be frank, what a shameful legacy this is that a Jewish mayor today is addressing and correcting a problem called infanticide within our own neighborhoods when we had before an African American mayor Mr. Harold Washington who had grew up in Bronzeville, Chicago, and saw the same urban decay within our communities. Yet, we as a people of color lived in denial to the dangers that is all around us and did nothing substantial to save our own children.

I have been asking myself lately from the very depths of my heart, is President Obama really in tuned to the African American community when he said on July 19, 2013 "Trayvon Martin could have been him thirty-five years ago"? Is he really conscious about the realities of racism here in America? Is he really conscious about the true realities that African American youths are killing each other by a great multitude of times, greater than any other race killing them? So why is he, President Obama, and other African American leaders not addressing this important issue firmly to our own communities and make that necessary social change a priority in his administration? A president refusing to play by the rules of denial, with the experience of race, culture and history, that person of color, who is sincere to himself, must say enough; and accept the fact that the true cause of this bloodshed is illegal (heroin-cocaine-marijuana) and legal (alcohol) drug related crimes within our communities. As well as, abandonment, of basic family values, by African American fathers in our society! Our mostly African American unemployed, uneducated urban youths are in a turf warfare battle with other African American gangs and Hispanic gangs competing with each other to sell all kinds of drugs in their neighborhoods to make a hopeful living for themselves and their families.

Oh, humble reader, I hope you don`t mind if I put down in words what we fundamentalists see in that light box trending in all around us because these are the dire moments that mark your life. This is the time that you come face-to-face with yourself sternly and address this important issue before us all. No one is surprised about this idea concept we in the African American community have when people outside of our race harm us and kill us we should take note and object loudly and publicly for change. But when the issue is lack of awareness, disunity and cruel violence between ourselves as a people we remain lethargic and torpid as well in total denial of what`s happening within our very homes and in our subjugated communities. What`s really going on is that with each life it touches, we as a race of people have been trained and indoctrinated to racial profiling ourselves to our ruin. This is what matters yet in spite of our legacy does this indoctrinated cultural of self-hate deserve to exist?

Yes, indeed, there are moments in this life that mark your storms of life, and there are times that I too had to come face-to-face with myself when I was living the now regardless of eras. So on an early Monday twilight evening March 26, 1979, on Elm Street, Washington DC, in front of Carver Hall at Howard University, I did heard two shots rang out. I turned and looked out my dorm window and saw a fellow student stumbled back into our dorm lobby from the streets. Alarmed I step out into the hallway and shouted out the alarm that someone has been shot. We all ran down the stairs and was shocked by the sight of a fellow student laying flat on his back in great pain; he was shot through both of his legs.

But in spite of his pain, he told us our fellow student friend Blaine is really hurt bad and is still in his car. So a large group of brothers rushed out of the dorm doors looking for Blaine's car. However, I was frozen at the door not out of fear but of a six sense of certainty of death looking out into the dark horrible night. I wanted to remember brother Blaine Pitts who was 20 years old from Dover, Delaware as he was, a handsome always smiling young black man and easy to get along with, who lived just two doors down from me in Carver Hall, he had a dream like all of us living off hope.

The brothers quickly found Blaine slumped down in his car on the driver's side on the corner of Elm St. withering in agony of death; he had been shot through the arm and into the heart. Oh, humble reader, please abide with me just a little longer because time is unique in a dreadful way on this issue of African American's killing each other in cold blood is of the essence. For this lesson of how to live in a sea of hopelessness is dire. Yes, hope is wired to the soul. So I just could not move, I just stared into the cold dark hopeless night, there is nothing I could do. Seriously, hope is wired to the soul; thus, it took a few months for the police to find that African American soul without hope who would murder another African American, a human being with some hope just for his watch. This is what's time it is in an urban sea full of black hopelessness till this day. Nothings change.

That black young man about twenty five years old who was without hope in his own life who stole a gun and then stole a life full of some hope was sentence to forty five years to life without hope. Till this day I will never forget . . . who the enemy was . . . all you got to do is follow the pain, I simply followed the same pain into the same prison less than three hellish years later without hope.

Till this day I will never forget that first African American principal at Teaneck High School. His name was Mr. Joe White. This was the school I graduated from back in 1976. I meet with him for the first time in his office at the high school and requested addressing the class body of 2002 about Islam, which was on about the first week of October of 2001. I felt he fervently declined my request out of fear. I was then very disappointed because Teaneck High School had a history of students who had graduated and years later came back and address to the student body of what they have experience or accomplished, and I felt very sadden at the time that he did not think what I overcame and did was important enough for the class to know about. Thou African Americans are only 12 percent of the town's population but we are almost 35 percent of the student body and faculty. So when on June of 2006 I was informed that Mr. Joe White, the Teaneck High School's first black principal, was arrested and imprisoned for official misconduct, endangering the welfare of a child, and possession of child pornography and had to resigned from his job. I knew we as African American people have not truly risen in spite of the positions, degrees, money, fame, and power we have accomplish in our lives. We forget to easily to be our brother's keepers and up hold basic moral values just so we can make it financially in our lives.

Sure, it is true when people say, "It takes more than food to make a meal" in retrospect "It takes more than knowledge to make a teacher." The initial crime of our life I feel as educators is not being able to see that valuable potential of any student that comes before him or her. Fair enough, when I was living and studying in Mecca as well as teaching English at Mecca University, I was blessed in meeting an old merchant Sheikh whose name was Theka (confidence). Who likes to think of himself as an oracle of an old era. He once said to me, "A teacher is a person who carries away that doubt of fulfillment, and who understands that knowledge is justified true belief."

With this in mind, for decades we African American educators here at home, have been down loading training, to make a fervency of enlightenment within our communities, But it is going to take a lot more than hope to get through all that virus of doubt; consequently, we have obviously failed to huddle amongst ourselves and carry away those doubts of fulfillment within our own communities!

It is often a thankless job being a part of an Islamic resistance movement admonishing one's countrymen to always be prepared. Being one who earns his living sacrificing for a noble and just cause as a Salafi Muslim from the West, I see the history and struggle of my African American brothers and sisters as one of the golden rules to remember by heart. Like what happens when your king or prophet's last words to you as a people tells you to do something and you don't do it because of whatever! For what's the use of having a God in your life if you hesitate to make that sacrifice, or even risk your life, for that noble cause, after bearing witness yourself how one of your own noble leaders had laid down his life for the very same cause? You don't fight for a holiday in his name; instead you fight for the fulfillment of his name, for the justice he championed for against so many diminishing social returns here in America nowadays. Let's make one thing clear: You automatically become an insurgent in their view point if you fight against government corruption, predatory bank loans that target minorities, mis-education, corporate greed and massive poverty with benign neglect. You earn this distinction of title called resistance movement only through action as in team working in cohesion, thereby treating the disease rather than it's symptoms. The task is daunting I kid you not.

Today I am a jihad Salafi Muslim American, but I can still remember those days of my youth as a Christian African American believing in that mis-education as gospel. I had tried to measure the heavens and solve the mysteries of my own universe right here on earth living in America, cursing and despairing the real realities of being a trained black man. Please don't be brainwashed into thinking that the big bang is indisputable truth and that our world came from "nothing." The real "big bang" means a bullet is heading your way or you can't pay the rent, or buy food to feed your family. All that talk of how we came from nothing really just means that science hasn't yet identified or cloned the human soul. Likewise, I never did quite buy Charles Darwin's ideas on evolution, when all the evidence one needs for the existence of that "divine beneficence" requires just one honest look into the mirror.

Presently, fundamental Islam is challenging this age-old concepts of true social progress, and mis-education, contrary to what has been put forth by the secular governments of the West in alliance with Judeo-Christian ideologies, both of whom believe they hold the monopoly on accepted values. The truth is, democracy does present both a challenge and an opportunity for us believers who practice forbearance; for true competition is no handicap in this hearts, minds, and soul war, where youthful dissidents believe divine law can overcome and defeat their secular laws. Where youthful dissidents who believe that sovereignty must be placed into that divine trust not into the public trust. Once Wall Street is liberated from corruption, once those streets really are cleaned, what laws will the people then trust? Once we are known as a people who are just, both to themselves and to their neighbors, as a people that demands just governance, then the question remains: Can a union of believers win the trust of the majority who are not of the same creed of faith to govern effectively and efficiently? We must be prepared to say to our kinsmen: try it our way. We the people of monotheist faith all know that ideals fade when compared to the boundaries of justice and the margins of grim reality. Still we are confident that mixing religion with justice and politics is worth fighting for if your motto really is "In God we trust."

All too often Western secular governments ignore the "cause" of the problem, because our politicians` indulging in the obsession of power and fame. How long then will the idea that "greed is good" be accepted as inspiration for us all? Is it because of Mr. Adam Smith`s book *The Wealth of Nations* says so? As hostage citizens here in the nations of the secular West, do we realize that our governments are ignoring this single greatest threat to the very lives of their citizenry? One thing is ominously clear: ballot referendums that place tougher regulations and provide more oversight on social injustice, banking, and defense industries have gone nowhere. Yes, President Eisenhower warned us fifty years ago of the threat of the military-industrial complex; yet in these modern times, with tens of millions of people out of work and struggling for a living wage, the American dream is now being achieved only by the greediest in the rat race. Why hasn't our beloved country learned from the dark experiences of its past, and continues to persist with an agenda of "business as usual"?

In order to survive the multiple crises we face, both here in America specifically and in the secular West in general, we must first remind ourselves, as well as our neighbors, of the Garden of Eden and its tree of knowledge of good and evil. For from its fruit comes our power to choose (volition), a divinely given right. But what are most troubling are the choices that have been made, and without any of the awareness or concern of the consequences of walking a blind path base on greed and self-interest.

We believe the true futility of mis-education and making estimates on the true ascent of the very nature of mankind today rest without seriously considering the very nature of his trusted chariots. Thanks to those evil geniuses hard at work burning that night oil, the best car on earth today is a M1A2 Abrams main battle tank not the Cadillac CTS-V. The top sea captains graduate from military naval academies. Thus, the most trusted ships on the high seas are American aircraft carriers like the USS *Abraham Lincoln,* rather than a luxury liner like the *Queen Elizabeth II.* The best pilots fly the best planes like the B2 stealth bomber not a 747-LCF Dream Lifter commercial airliner. The best-built rocket is not the Space Shuttle that can be ready to launch within four to six months of the command to fire, and carry eight human beings to explore the heavens above—oh no, but the Minuteman-3, a thirty-seven-ton mobile intercontinental ballistic missile that carries three nuclear warheads each, of which are more than a hundred times more powerful than the Hiroshima bomb, and that it can hit and ash a four-mile radius any target on earth within 250 yards, a weapon that can be launched within a minute of the command to fire! Simply put, despite our material, medical successes, and scientific advancement, today`s Western societies are on a self-defeating path once the cutting edge of our technology is being used to create products whose sole purpose is to kill people wholesale. Likewise, we have no reason to ever expect any kind of spiritual altruism from such lucrative Western industries and those corporate individuals who owns them, whereby they would undertake a more humanitarian business model simply because of their mis-education of the reality of the world we live in.

So just how do you clean up this mess, this scourge here in the secular West? Perhaps, knowing that not every nation deserves to be safe helps! Though millions of American and European Muslims remain in denial and continue to assimilate themselves into a pagan culture where rights and liberties have been limited because of the oppression and the blowback of hate their hands had sent forth before them. This mission may be all beyond salvage of the believers of this monotheist faith, only Allah knows, perhaps it is best to save ourselves, and our families from the fire that is to come. Is it mis-education knowing that the leadership of the secular West have failed to abide by a central tenet of our faith? That golden rule, "To want for others what you want for yourself!" This problem, my Muslim brothers and sisters and all those who are God-fearing, transcends the ongoing violence both here at home and throughout the world. A belief that say`s we will not be limited by our own lack of nerve of being humane to others. In their so-called war on terror," Muslim charities and organizations throughout the West have been shut down with millions of dollars in zakat[80] seized. Thousands of Muslims from the West have been placed under rendition, where they are arrested, detained, tortured and interrogated for countless hours, days or even months about their religious beliefs and political views. As such, it is clear that the laws today places limits on our freedom; in fact the conventional wisdom in reality is we are free as their law will allow.

How do we clean up this mess? The aim must be justice; due process of law still has not been fully reinstated since the Patriot Act became law in 2001because of hype and fear. Despite President

---

[80]   Charity

Obama's promising talk of being a global peacemaker, the fact remains that social justice and civil liberties here in America as well as in Europe continue to be under attack.

The secular West's understanding of the realities of Islam where sovereignty is with Allah only is both irresponsible and dangerous; thus, we the faithful have a moral obligation to change this. As we see it, the West's idea of social progress is measured by how fast Muslims become secular within its borders, yet we beg you to bear in mind that, individuals are sovereign in a true democracy; the government only maintains a just and authentic power by delegating measures of that power with free individuals. True Muslim people of this country and everywhere else place their sovereignty with Allah only, that divine one. Yet when we stand in the West, we stand in a sea of mis-education, a people who had placed their sovereignty into their own hands is a very strange place indeed. Mankind is not perfect this is self-evident. The choice we have today is simple; who shall we allow to lead us, that imperfect person here on earth, or that perfect divine one above who put us here on earth in the first place? Muslim leaders and Muslim writers of such who are true to their creed are obliged at some point in time in helping our people realize that civil disobedience can be justified in this so-called secular democracy based on mis-education. Therefore, any truly free individual may elect to stand apart from the domain of law and express their right to disobey. For as citizens here in the West we hold a basic tacit consent that permits disobedience, even revolution. One of the ways to hold those 1 percent status quo keepers and political clowns accountable if their democratic governments breaches their side of the contract in the form of mismanagement and/or corruption in these secular lands is then to view the duty to obey the law is a matter of situation and degree, by reason that human sovereignty is imperfect. Thus, once classes of peoples are no longer fully enfranchised members of a society, then consequently these same people are no longer fully bound by its laws.

If a class of people are not fully enfranchised members of a society because of a collative punishment plan seeded by a Western secular governmental failure on that war on terror plan, then consequently we the believers of the Islamic faith as citizens thereof are not fully bounded by its laws. Neither are we to accept the given idea of mis-education that we are free under this situation as the law will allow!

Piggy Banks

If you lend money to one of your poor neighbors among my people, you shall not act like an extortioner towards him by demanding interest from him.

—Torah, Ex. 22:24

When one of your fellow countrymen is reduced to poverty and is unable to hold out beside you, extend to him the privileges of an alien or a tenant, so that he may continue to live with you. Do not exact interest from your countryman either in money or in kind, but out of fear of God let him live with you. You are to lend him neither money at interest nor food at a profit. I, the Lord, am your God, who brought you out of the land of Egypt to give you the land of Canaan and to be your God.

—Torah, Lev. 25:35-38

Those who devour usury will not stand except as stands one whom the evil one by his touch hath driven to madness. That is because they say: "Trade is like usury," But Allah hath permitted trade and forbidden usury. Those who after receiving direction from their Lord, desist, shall be pardoned for the past; their case is for Allah to judge; But those who repeat the offence are companions of the fire: they will abide therein forever." "Allah will deprive usury of all blessing, but will give increase for deeds of charity: For he loves not creatures ungrateful and wicked.

—Quran 2:275-276

We believers of the fundamentals of our faith know it is quite apparent that these words are dear so please beware and have no fear.

There are tens of millions of people in the U.S. and Western Europe who are literally one month away from living on the streets. Sadly, millions have given up hope of ever owning their own homes. Worse still, millions of families, many of limited financial means, have endured the heart-wrenching nightmare of having their homes foreclosed on them! One of the roles governments of the secular West have traditionally undertaken has been to oversee and regulate a mostly privately-owned banking sector as a means of directing the country's pace of economic growth. The U.S. Federal Reserve directs the banks to lend out money on cheap credit in good times and then, in lean times, restrict the volume of new loans in order to prevent an overheating of the economy. Simply put, these institutions, which so many people hold in such high esteem, are brazen and unrepentant usurers who have helped destroy the lives of tens of millions of families with their house-of-cards values!

Look, I am not one of those zealots who demands perfection from others. However, there are far too many people who are too busy watching daytime soap opera, boozing, chasing women, minding other people's business and making Ponzi-schemed money to have any clue about the serious decisions their leaders are making in their name! As such, at present, nations do not follow God; they act as if they are God! Consequently the best way to rob a bank is to own one, such are the true confederates! In the preface to his code of law, that Babylonian King Hammurabi states: "I Hammurabi the exalted king, who fear God, to bring about the rule of righteousness in the land." Hammurabi's code goes on to say that no advanced society can survive without competent banks and bankers. For example, he writes, "If the debtor has neither money nor crop, the creditor must not refuse goods"; likewise, "If the debtor's crop failed, payment was deferred and no interest could be charge for that year."[81] Oh, humble reader, you don't have to be blessed to heed. Just keep in mind that moral compass: "Ex. 22:25 or "Leviticus 25:35-37 and Deuteronomy 23:20-21. Or when the word drew high unto Jerusalem: Matthew ch.21:12-13 and Matthew 25:24-30. Or, when it came to pass: Quran 2:275-280 or Quran 3:130 or Quran 4:161 and Quran 30:39. America's post-cold war domestic policy is no longer focused on containing the spread of Communism,

---

[81]   Mr. Charles F. Horne Ph.D. The Code of King Hammurabi, 1915 Yale Law School

or preventing Asian, Hispanic, and African-Americans from becoming integrated members of our capitalist system; the concern amongst secular politicians and their brethren in the banking industry is the rise of "Islamic banking" here in the West.

Just how do you create a city, a town, a community without sorrow, offering investment strategies tailored to meet the needs of its people? Well, "In God we trust" cannot be just mere words we say to each other in our homes, temples, and on our currency; yet in our national, and international Western commerce "usury" is the golden rule! Simply, the Western banking industry idea of success is making a profit whether their clients is successful in their enterprise investments or not! The Western banking industry base on usury is not willing to be a wholesome partnership with their clients as long as the title deed is in their pockets of the clients and the value in question has not shrunken. Thus, as far as Wall Street is concerned, today's foreclosure schemes is just pulling the thorn out of the lion's paw and keeping his rawhide.

An Islamic bank means you have a business partner who has a percentage of capital of investment towards whatever your business adventure is. An Islamic banker is a financial advisor who's interest is the success of the business. If the business is successful then they and their client both share the profits. If the business is not successful then they and their client both share the loss.

But when a people has toiled in hell on earth for a long time, trying to tell those same people that good business without usury and that demand for justice for your opponent is fundamental on earth is at hand is a difficult sell. Oftentimes in such cases, when we the believers talk of Sharia law and or Islamic banking, we become the enemy combatants in their eyes, for our words of admonishment and acts of violence seemed both extreme and unnecessarily judgmental. Nevertheless, hundreds of millions of people, of all stripes, have invested divine authority into their secular leaders and in the end felt betrayed and disgusted by their brutal realities of love of money and power. Only where have these expressions of democracy and acceptable usury gotten them? Better to give that authority to leaders who are more God fearing; perhaps then that era of peace and justice will arrive, for it's the social contract between the people and their government that matters most of all.

A national conceit can be a devastating curse, one to keep hidden at all costs. Conceit that bases its supposed superiority on race and ethnicity, rather than standing on faith and values, are particularly destructive. For example, here in the secular West our nation is the guiding force for many allegiances of organizations, both public and private, whereby many different religious affiliations are grouped together. But the opposite is true in Islam, where faith is the unifying principle under which both nations and organizations associate. The consequences are profound, and alarming, but not surprising in this clash of worldviews, where the market-driven West subscribes to the doctrine of profit and loss, while our faith-based system obeys a doctrine of prophet or hell. Ultimately, the question of compatibility remains, and thus rests inside the hearts of all the people.

Since our noble jihad envisions a pure monotheist community living in a pluralist society, then winning the confidence of the people in the secular West must be worth more to them and us than what their money can buy. We, the believing fundamentalists, for the mercy of Allah, must first sincerely confront and then bridge this crisis of trust and cultural and religious incompatibility with our neighbors. The most obvious misconception between religions within the same monotheistic faith is that we do not all worship the same God, so we allow the devil's advocates to put aside our faith and let our diversity impede our mutual goals as peoples. We, the fundamental believers of our monotheist faith, reject this secular concept of separation, because we all worship for the same needs. As such, our jihad here in the West must do the unprecedented: make visible those invisible people alienated by poverty and polarized by class, race, and faith. Likewise, we must be revealing to all people of our global village the true merits of mutual tolerance and work against the Islamophobia created by Western governments which enables the ruling elite to continue their ongoing enterprises of economic oppression. Our respective faiths will not impede our mutual goals as nations of diverse peoples; in fact, it will only strengthen these goals of a people that wish good will upon all.

Personally speaking, I wasn't there behind the crime scenes, but it's just a gut feeling I have. All those graffiti that are written on those bank walls couldn't all be lies. Like, "Bernard Madoff is not the only one." By the numbers it's all scandalous, "selling fish in the sea." Government regulators have seized and/or shut down more than 320 fish in the sea banks since 2007. Debut times have gotten so bad with foreclosures that today's real business are in firms who buy debut and take you to court. If you look closely at that vanishing American dream, do I need an eyewitness to say to the working poor on unlivable minimum wage and underwater middle class, that once upon a not very long time ago America was the land of the radiant future. At the present time and juncture one doesn't need to remind one's fellow countrymen and citizens that seventeen-trillion-dollar debt, pleas for lower taxes, less governmental spending, more federal oversight over conglomerate monopolies, and an end to banking syndicate usury Ponzi schemes is a justified plea that's being heard by no one. But it's now about a government, our government that lives within its means. To put it another way, about the ability of all of us who are living here in this blessed land we all call home to realize our dreams and opportunities behind enemy lines by starting to patronize our own independent Islamic banks within our communities and keep away from all others. Trying to persuade this secular government to do the right thing in regards to banking is just a waste of your time.

Secular Western societies are facing a banking humanitarian crisis that is unprecedented. For America to say it never saw it coming is a lie. Now that more than ten million Americans have stopped paying their mortgages on their homes since 2007, and hundreds of millions of Americans have become disillusioned with an Obama administration that has been far too worried about protecting heartless corrupt banks that were "too big to fail" than protecting homeowners facing those robo-signed foreclosure notices, amid the despair of knowing they've been swindled by those who used the American dream as bait! Where's that relief in action to those millions of families, and I am not talking about Advil! Now that those "too big to fail" banks received their governmental golden—parachutes, who will be the next victim of the American dream bait? Who will be the next family whose lives will fall into disarray and indigence because of voodoo economics? As Samuel F. Miller, that fundamentalist of a Supreme Court Justice, wrote in 1874 for the majority, in *loan association v. Topeka:* "Today with one hand the power of the government on the property of the citizen, and with the other to bestow it upon favored individuals to aid private enterprises and build up private fortunes, is none the less a robbery because it is done under the forms of law and is called taxation."

One doesn't need to be a Sherlock Holmes, or a Dick Tracy, to comprehend that the best way to rob a bank is to own one. Or see the consequences surrounding the millions of deaths of those who aspire for that American Dream. Many lifeless examples have been found nationwide, in suburban neighborhoods amidst the trimmed bushes and manicured lawns. In pawnshops and used car lots across the country lies the missing jewelry and unaffordable cars, bygone imprimaturs of wealth and status, harbingers of continuing economic distress and symptomatic of our larger political disease. The body hanging from the noose in the attic is overwhelming evidence that the most important thing to them is not their faith, or their dreams, but the material costs of being a human being today. Just don't let them set you on fire is my personal vibe to you. An era of belated postmortem has now arrived giving us all total recall to when corporate and financial banking exploitation preys upon the ill informed and unwary and is continuously looking for more substantial returns on its investment at your expense!

Two glaring examples of which is Fannie Mae and Freddie Mac, two once-renowned institutions to which people who craved a home of their own rushed into with the hope of fleeing the epidemic of poverty. Now tens of millions of people rue the day they fell prey to Fannie and Freddie's usury. Caught in the crossfire of a foreclosure maelstrom are millions of the working poor, minorities, the young middle class, and first-time home buyers, all of whom were simply jettisoned by Fannie Mae and Freddie Mac en masse to the banker's fleecing machine, as subprime mortgage-backed securities which became too much of a high risk currency to bear. In short, because of indulging in massive speculation and conflict of interest, the ability of Fannie and Freddie to finance such an essential part of the American dream—home ownership—didn't match their mission. So why did so many Americans trust these government agencies? The truth is that we the people—the underpaid, overworked, and fed-up—believed we were in good hands, suckered by a guarantee of hope by our own country.

In addition to Fannie Mae and Freddie Mac, the list of financial institutions that, in the name of greed, have manipulated a rotten system, is long indeed. Executives at Morgan Stanley have plead guilty to mortgage real estate fraud; likewise, a suit launched by the Securities and Exchange Commission found Goldman Sachs guilty of mortgage fraud. Unabashedly, Bank of America has presided over more foreclosures on homeowners and small business than any other single American banking institution in American history and is being sued for mortgage fraud by the Attorneys General of both Arizona and Nevada. J.P. Morgan Chase has used robo-signing to expedite their foreclosures while Citigroup lied to investors about $40 billion in subprime exposures, and HSBC is suspected of laundering drug money for the Mexican Cartels. That faceless Lehman Brothers repo—105 accounting fraud in the millions of dollars in which nobody goes to jail is real! As well as: "Now your money not only tastes better, it is better" is the alibi and thanks of giving so much pain to someone else that Enron-fraud scam.

On the other hand, that noisy unemployed Occupied Wall Street protester living in a tent in a nearby park downtown is arrested and goes to jail for trespassing. This brings to mind the words of that forthright fundamentalist Mr. Victor Hugo who said, "There is always more misery in the lower class than there is humanity in the upper class."

In short, sadly, the more the secular West continues to rely on deceitful usury economic practices to grow and enrich itself, the more our political leadership is complicit in the overall corruption. Take, for example, that so-called bipartisan Financial Crisis Inquiry Commission hearings set up by the U.S. Congress in December 2010 to inquire about the financial fraud, abuse, and regulatory failures, which in the end accomplished little. It was truthfully an inquiry commission designed to bore you to death about where have the money gone to. Is it really so difficult to know exactly how many banks and corporate conglomerates need to be regulated, with their trillions of dollars worth of derivative bets and collateralized debt obligations? Not enough underpaid bureaucrats to keep track of the racketeers, the syndicate credit card pirate companies, and corrupt bankers, all of whom without having even the most remote concept of the hardship they continue to wreak upon their countrymen with their usury and greed, which is undermining the very fabric of our financial stability here in the West.

As always, the heart of the problem always seems to rest in kings, presidents and prime ministers refusing to ask themselves "Who am I?" and citizens, therein refusing to say to themselves in the mirror, "This must end today!" In this day and age, why are people facing predatory loans from governmental guarantee funds targeting lower income borrowers and first-time home buyers seduced by that great "American Dream," baited into taking loans that normal consumers realistically could not afford to pay in their lifetimes? The real truth is that these usurious practices were highly lucrative for sub-prime lenders with their fat fees yet little regard for their customers. So much for a government guarantee designated to keep hope alive for millions, when it's placed right in the hands of secular shamans in snake suits, smiling as they spin that Wall Street`s roulette wheel.

The real challenge facing our leaders today rests not in thinking about whom to rescue, but what to do with a population that now finds itself a hostage in this economic and social atmosphere of debt and fear because of a lack of a moral compass. Thus, so many are condemned to scavenge for anything resembling the American Dream yet, the hard question now is what can there be done for these people who are now in a helpless position of homelessness. President Obama, holding that $17 trillion bag of debt, pledged on his 2012 State of the Union "that the wealthy play by the same rules as ordinary Americans," daring his detractors to "call this class warfare all you want . . . [only] most Americans would call that common sense."

To this day, what's helping me keep it real because I am still a fan is that I can still remember back forty-five years ago, watching *It's a Wonderful Life* as a child in front of my family's black and white TV on Christmas Day with my mother and brothers. The movie starring that sainted actor fundamentalist Mr. James Stewart which suggested that, "social graces is that chain on that anchor thrown into heaven." It's a pity you don't hear more about those good Samaritans and God-fearing nonprofit charities that's being overwhelmed by the current deluge of voodoo economics and usury. With millions homeless, and one in five Americans on food stamps like myself included, our social services are inundated with the task of providing some meaningful hope to those millions down and out. Yes, it's a pity you don't hear more people nowadays talking—either in public, or in private—of this being a "wonderful life." This is simply because America is no longer a place but an "idea," an idea that fails to go along with the media hype understanding that a wonderful life can be achieved for all under its present social capitalistic trickle down economical usury plan, which is simply not possible under the present conditions of today's economic corruption. Why? Because Allah (swa) will not change the conditions of a people until the people change the conditions of their own hearts. Until an entire culture obligates itself to the concept of wanting for others what we want for ourselves, it's then we shall have that change of circumstance we all been hoping for in our lives. Only then, the people shall attain the success they truly desire. For this is the secret of enduring success, and to this I ask, what is the condition of your own heart?

The Heavens are Not Empty

Even now, behold, my witness is in heaven, and my spokesman is on high.
—Torah, Job 16:19

Can a man hide in secret without my seeing him? Says the lord. Do I not fill both heaven and earth? Says the lord.
—Torah, Jer. 23:24

To the righteous soul will be said: "O (thou) soul" In complete rest and satisfaction! "Come back thou to thy lord," Well pleased (thyself), and well pleasing unto him! "Enter thou, then, among my devotees!" "Yea, enter thou my heaven!
—Quran 89:27-30

Yes, the heavens are not empty, so how long are we the God, Jehovah, Allah-fearing people living amongst the ignorant going to wait and allow our neighbors to be spiritually foreclosed upon and thrown into the streets because they dared to dream a dream you heard and read about?

That Trinity Baptist Church over there on 259 Passaic Street in Hackensack, New Jersey, is where I got my first job after eighteen years of preaching, studying Arabic and Islam overseas in Muslim and in non Muslim countries. I was greatly overjoyed that I was working with a serious religious nonprofit group that really cared about others that was next door to my hometown Teaneck, New Jersey.

Their mission was aiding and helping the homeless, the poor, and people addicted to illegal and legal drugs and those people who are just release from prison and/on parole in which we gave those needed clothes to wear, shoes and a smile to lighten their burdens uplifting their hope. The Christian management there called this place "hope." This was the best and first job I had coming from overseas, however I was disappointed that my own Muslim community in my nearby hometown was alien to these important spiritual values and key potentials, which a religious community regardless of faith simply cannot ignore. Up until now, because of their focus on themselves they live in a bubble outside the American frontier of street-level aspirations for social change.

So far so good is what I keep telling myself, even though I knew my health was waning back in the fall of 2010. I am in good hands; the heavens are not empty. My homeless family is sleeping in my best friend Elijah Muhammad basement home. Five months later Social Services put us all in a nice hotel for two months. Then, when my health really waned on me because of a large tumor in my head, and I needed surgery over at New York University hospital, (NYU), my government picked up the tab and made sure that my family had enough food stamps to buy our needed food and some cash to buy the soaps and the bureaucracies of this life.

"I am in good hands; the heavens are not empty is the only idea worth holding on to nowadays. Seeing that I was flat on my back, my country paid the rent now more than two years and gave my family full health insurance, "family care." This is how I know Allah did indeed bless America. We're all in good hands as far as I can see it. Just walk into any large market here in America and look what's available on those shelves ready to be consume, don't take my word for it, just look at all those countries like I did who have to worry about the rain not haunting them anymore because of their record of injustice. Just look at what's on those shelves ready to be consumed overseas in Africa or in Asia. It's only then you will understand that price of justice towards ourselves is a great bargain. Yet it is strange being back home with my family after being away overseas for eighteen years, my country has changed for the worst. I feel I am not the only one on recovery. There is a slow waning climate of fear and uncertainty in the land that has not still went away in spite of the time of long ago crisis.

In spite of all this, there is no place like home. I was greatly distressed that my own hometown Muslim community Dar Al-Islah did not develop into an active Community Center of Bergen County that they loudly proclaimed to be after I first started being a part of their Muslim community some twenty-five years ago. Their creed is to be a guiding light of Islam to people of this community and to our neighbors, and to teach the faith of Islam to our children and help inspire those who wish to learn more about our faith.

But the true realities is a divided Muslim community of Asian (Pakistani and Indian) Muslims who send their children to the weekend school in the Mosque here in Teaneck on Sundays and the minority group Arabs in the same community who send their children to a different weekend school in the same Mosque but on Saturdays. Such is the case; our diverse Muslim races here do not mix well together socially, even outside of the Mosque's Bergen County community events. The membership is about two thousand, which consist mostly of Asians, Arabs, and some African Muslims. Only a hand few Muslim African American brothers and sisters do attend regularly.

Frankly, over the years, yes, Hum du Allah, our Muslim community has grown but not bonded, the inconvenient truth is that growth is coming from new Muslims from overseas coming on board with their naiveté of this country, language problems and harboring racial prejudice. Not by the real hard work of proselytizing their American neighbors who are non Muslims who live next door to the Mosque and who live near to them at their own homes, jobs and business. This is not how you make tomorrow happen in a positive way that will help make the awakening of all hearts and minds here in our mix community of faiths a fruitful blessing.

The proof is self-evident, over twenty-five years that I know of this Muslim community, less than a handful of our close neighbors had visited our Mosque under invitation and came back on their own initiative to hear more of what we Muslims have to say. Depressingly, perhaps once every four or six months will pass when somebody or a stranger stands up in the Mosque and declare their intentions to take a vow becoming a Muslim. Sorrowfully, after a few weeks, they do not come back either. There is not so much of an inquiry or even a note of concern from many of the so-called elders and leaders of this community, who are foreign to these lands to say where is that phone number somewhere of such a person, or even who will be that somebody to visit and/or call and say hello, how are you doing, how is your family, what's happening? Social bonding within a religious community is very important and promotes fellowship that is needed in these times of national uncertainty. Just the other day as our juma (Friday prayer services) was ending I looked around the huge prayer room and saw no new or old native faces who had declared their faith to be a Muslim in our Mosque. It's an inconvenient truth that they're proselytizing to themselves is their ironic comedy of success.

I am well aware that I must be patient with these new Muslims who come to these western secular shores. I don't know all what's in their hearts or their true intentions in coming here to these Western lands of my forefathers. But what I do know is that many old ideas have to change if we as a Muslim community as a whole wish to move forward in a positive way; otherwise, our own neighbors will rightfully believe that Islam is a faith for foreigners, not for them or their children.

It is time those believers of our faith who act on their faith with their hands, and feet, not those Muslims who see but only talk about the issues that we all face, and definitely not those Muslims who only pray and confess about the issues that we all face and then walk away, but believers who admit that that welcome mat at the door of our Mosque does not exist and is willing to do something about it because the heavens are not empty. We as believers of this faith called Islam will be held to account of what did we do with our time here in this secular and pagan lands. Did we do our utmost in spreading the awareness of what is Islam really is so that the people living here in these lands can bear witness to the truth of our faith for the mercy of Allah now that we are here in these un-Islamic lands, or are we here for enjoyment and ease in life?

The heavens are not empty, so why should I pretend my life otherwise? Patience—yes, they have Muslim names but no real sustainable Islamic agenda. Strange, yes, it is strange that our Muslim community have a lot of doctors, engineers, and business professionals who have an eye for making usury money, and inviting over politicians come voting time; but they have no will or vision to work with me or the like-minded to labor with the grass roots of this secular society for the mercy of Allah with the goal of focusing on people's needs. That way we can win their hearts. Nor, do the leadership of this Muslim community invite native Imams to these lands, and/or sit down with me working in cohesion who are native to these lands and talk to this community we are in and give a sermon on Fridays on how to better the cultural and religious bonds of this society and get that important message of Islam out to all the people in a way that will bring about a positive response and save some souls.

Yet why have I allowed myself to be a part of this Muslim community here in Teaneck, New Jersey, even when I know they are unfocused in faith and unbalanced in their actions? Straightforwardly, I know I must be patient and not run away from the creed of my faith simply because of the myopic weakness of faith of others, and the feeble actions of my Muslim communities leadership.

Since the heavens are not empty, we all have to face our mutual challenges together and if needs be throw that anchor into heaven. At the present, there are only a few hard-core Islamic public relations campaigning for the hearts, minds and souls of the grass roots of America here. So I must start out on my own working with those few who believe and is willing to act. Winning the confidence and hope of a people in this secular society for the mercy of Allah is going to be hard work and I am going to need a lot of trustworthy support, yet from where I really just do not know?

Truthfully there are only a few believing Muslims here that is willing to work with me in making visible those invisible people in our Bergen County or next door in Passaic County N.J. or in Newark N.J. that are alienated by poverty and polarized by class, race and faith. Realistically I am still recovering health wise from surgery now twenty-four months. I just do not have the strength or the funds to start out on my own and build my own Muslim community that shall, I believe will answer the needs of the people in light of what Islam can do for those who are seeking true guidance in their lives in such a land as this.

Undoubtedly I am aware of that austerity lie; what's coming to light is that my secular Western pluralist society is facing an enormous economic and humanitarian crisis that is unprecedented in our American history which is looming before us all. "Years of widening income inequality and the lingering effects of the financial crisis had frayed the country's social fabric and undermined American's belief in opportunity." So says U.S. president B. Obama, on July 27, 2013.

Basically America's seventeen-trillion dollar debt and the growing divide between the "have mores and the have not's" is going to hamper the fundamental delivery of life's essentials, one of which is called hope for a better future. Social Services, Medicare and Social Security today are under financial threat and will face hard choice cuts real soon. People's pension funds are no longer safe and presently and quietly under attack by state, city, and corporate intentional bankruptcies.

These looming scenarios affects us all and will have wounding effects on the lives of hundreds of millions of Americans who are already struggling and stress out as it is. Thus, Islam here in America has to join with Christians and Jewish relief organizations and contribute more than just talk and chatter about the why and the how we as a nation of people must move forward, but also be that active positive contribution in the lives of people in need all around us. Those days of leaving the door open and the light on for those who are looking for guidance is not sufficient or practical. We the people, are in desperate times now together, whether we like it or not, it is time to dismantle those social barricades, clearly illegal drug use is growing, suicides is getting more common, homeless families are growing, hope for a better tomorrow is waning and the fear of poverty is becoming more real in the lives of millions of people. This is where that creative idea class is heading to those who act on those words of "In God we Trust." This is the time for full active participation in our communities helping those in need regardless of our faiths. In this way, when our countrymen who are looking for a solution that excites hope for a better tomorrow they can say with certainty that the heavens are not empty because of the examples of those Muslims, Christians, and Jewish peoples out there reaching out to each other, and to those outside of their faiths in spite of the culture clash of our modern-day austerity plans, the callous hearts, and politricks that's going on all around us.

Ideas

O ye who believe! If you fear Allah, he will grant you a criterion (to judge between right and wrong), remove from you (all) evil (that may afflict) you, and forgive you: For Allah is the lord of grace unbounded.

—Quran 8:29

It wasn't entirely a surprise then, when I made up my mind a long time ago in Mecca, that the frontlines of the heart, mind, and soul war of which I have been speaking about may happen anywhere and at anytime, undertaken by anyone who desires to stand up and fight with his hands, fight with his words, fight with his pen, and prayers and march all together—with jihad in their pockets if need be. Those believers of this monotheist faith who are ready to be carried off to prison, or even the grave, against those barbed wire barriers of social injustice, due process of law abuse, human rights violations and the denial of equal rights for all. Hum du Allah, today more and more people are standing up and being counted demanding more than a cloud of their own, not surprisingly most notably in the West.

It was that hammer-and-sickle fundamentalist, Joseph Stalin who once said, "Ideas are more powerful than guns." Who, may I ask, can deny the gravity of such words? Because of the smallness in the mentality of our media, we the believers are not fooled by Western propaganda. Similarly, those who were denied life, liberty, and the pursuit of happiness across the Americas, found fruit and stood by the ideas of that Cuban socialist fundamentalist Fidel Castro, who once famously said, "History will absolve me." Who but a few could have imagined how long a revolutionary person like Castro would remain in power, especially after his imprisonment in 1953? Rejecting any plea bargain with the Batista court, Mr. Castro published his demands through a manifesto he wrote in matchboxes in prison. Those details of the five revolutionary laws he wished the world to see were the following:

1. The reinstatement of the 1940 Cuban Constitution
2. The reformation of land rights
3. The right of industrial workers to a 30 percent share of company profits
4. The right of sugar workers to receive 55 percent share of company profits
5. The confiscation of holdings of those found guilty of fraud under previous administrative powers.

Truly, those children of the Cuban bourgeois and propertied classes in exile today across North and South America sincerely wish to their god that it were they and not their fathers who had received such a generous manifesto in favor of the disenfranchised Cuban poor. This way they would all have human rights and equal rights and be still living in Cuba owning still some of their lands, homes and property; thou not all the good lands and property for themselves only. That idea matter of justice on such a historic island has its own rewards once (the have mores) and (the have nots) realize it is in their interest to work together and where to look when it comes to their own future together.

As one Tropicana fundamentalist wanes in Latin America many waxed.

"I am the legitimate President of Mexico," so says Mr. Lopez Obrador to his constituencies. This, even I, to this very day many years later, I don't doubt it. But sadly or luckily, Allah knows best; a rare popular uprising has been put on hold or stolen. Yes, this is quite a memorable notice to protesters of all stripes who refuse to be somebody's fool and an adherent to blind justice, not to forget that other idea of that fundamentalist Joseph Stalin who also said, "It is enough that the people know there was an election. The people who cast the votes decide nothing. The people who count the votes decide everything." Please look closer, because the numbers contradict accepted wisdom; yes, it would be naïve to assume that the elite of

Mexico, a country with more millionaires than Germany, would wish to change the status quo of not doing the right thing towards their very own disenfranchised people. The very idea that the Christian religious right for the mercy of God would demand the rich to invest more of their wealth into the lives of their poorer neighbors at home so that their compatriots do not have to leave their own country seeking opportunity is an inconvenient annoyance. Therefore, in these times of geopolitical turmoil, Mexico's legitimate fight for the political and economic emancipation of its people continues to be a long and sobering jihad. The truth is I believe all evidence do suggests that Mr. Lopez Obrador is the legitimate President of Mexico, and that he did not count what says guarded the votes.

1. "I fight against poverty and injustice the rich can look after themselves" (Hugo Chavez, president of Venezuela).
2. "The worst enemy of humanity is U.S. capitalism. That is what provokes uprisings like our own, a rebellion against a neoliberal model, which is the representation of a savage capitalism. If the entire world does not acknowledge this reality that the national states are not providing even minimally for health, education and nourishment, then each day the most fundamental human rights are being violated." (Evo Morales), president of Bolivia.

The streets where I come from here in the West—that lodge this idea example of organize imperialism, oh, humble reader—does offer a metaphor: "Crime does not pay." Mafia bosses indebted to their syndicates and similarly Western political leaders indebted to their corporatocracy all started out as masters of the subtle form of seduction, coercion and deceit. However, over time, the ones who make it to the top of their game take to wearing impeccably expensive tailored suits and wrap themselves for all to see as examples of modern society with the air of respectability.

Yet sadly, behind all this Western cultural idea of idolized national patina is a trail of human suffering and blood, especially when so-called debtors and or nation debtors refuse to submit, pay or cash in their sovereignty. In reality, the economic hit men move in behind offers that should not have been refused in their minds eye. Likewise the special ops people (assassins) move in behind economic hit men's offers of governmental collusion of the Muslim and Third-world countries that should not as well had been refused and rejected.

I find this to be an offensive irony that supposedly good people who are representative of my country do bad things; therefore, it is entirely understandable why my moral philosophy is in tuned with Mr. William James, that forgotten American philosophical fundamentalist in his hated but well understood literature piece: "A certain blindness in human beings as an inability to adopt a sympathetic and sensible point of view toward those who seem distant, alien, and even unintelligible. The pro-imperialists have dehumanized and objectified foreigners thereby rendering their humanity and especially their individually invisible."

Hence, it is hardly surprising to me that corporate economic hit men preceded America`s C.I.A. then special ops who are skilled in subversion of foreign governments and assassinations of foreign government leaders to suit their own vested interest. That epic idea power struggle between my country America and Muslim and Third-world nations is based upon the unkindness of so-called civilize nations not wanting for other nations what it desires for itself. Such soul-searching and hard—talking debate that rages about why we have that Western apathy towards those nations of peoples who are our neighbors with the same needs as ourselves but are poorer, different in ethnic race, and who worship a different economic god is long overdue since the start of this twenty-first century!

There is no need to sketch here the life of that business consultant fundamentalist Mr. John Perkins. All you have to do is read his troubling book called *Confessions of an Economic Hit Man*. Consequently you will recognize that some people have to leave home to realize the true nature of their civilize homeland. Yet we as Americans are not outraged enough to demand a change starting with ourselves in terms of how we relate with our neighbors affairs in terms of trade and sovereignty.

In many ways; blind men of genius stumbling over humanities comes to my worried mind, oh, humble reader, as our true status in today`s worlds affairs; much of their imaginations of justice had long ago shriveled with their eyes, which is closer to reality than today`s challenging ideas that are changing the world we live in which is increasingly being ignored. It is a particularly irksome thing to me to observe those who stand upon a different mental basis to oneself and realize the great fear of my Western cankerous civilization to that ageless idea that politics are subsidiary to religion is truly astounding. I plainly ask of you, who has the courage to press that idea globally to make windows into nations hearts and secret agendas so that there will be no boundaries of faith in lockstep with justice walking the path of reason for the benefit of all?

Because politricks, is what Western political leaders do when metaphysics is ignored from reality, there are many proven effective ways to reduce the success of revolutions in the lives of the people in Muslim and Third-world nations whose ideas run counter to the authority of the Western secular world. For them the secular West, doing nothing is not one of them. All an inquisitive person has to do is ask President Mohamed Morsi of Egypt who is undergoing that spiritual isolation by means of kidnap by those who wish to live less keenly than their fellow compatriots and their raging tragedy of their own incommunicable appreciation of that Islamic lifestyle. So they (mutineers) harkens to words of discontent and treason by tales of subversion from foreign agents who play the "Kermit Roosevelt Card," the grandson of former President Theodore Roosevelt, that successful CIA spy whose job was to win over influential opposition parties and very important people by corruption through monetary bribes and extortion in foreign countries! While you are digesting this troubling significance. Please, bear in mind the fates of President Salvador Allende from Chile and his "International Socialist Movement ideas"; President Jacobo Arbenz from Guatemala and his "land reform program ideas"; President Jaime Roldos from Ecuador and his "firm support of human rights and universal justice ideas"; Mr. Omar Torrijos from Panama, as head of state who "negotiated the Torrijos-Carter Treaties over the Panama Canal and his idea of transferring of its sovereignty to Panama"; Prime Minister Mohammad Mosaddegh from Iran, democratically elected and his "nationalization ideas of his countries oil reserves"; Prime Minister Patrice E. Lumumba from the Republic of the Congo, who was democratically elected and his "nationalization ideas of his countries natural rescores and his full emancipation ideas for his people from Europe and America"; as well as President Hugo Chavez from Venezuela and his ideas of "nationalization orders of his counties oil reserves plus his Socialist movement actions in regards to his nations poor."

Now here's the bribe: I wonder how many men in Latin America will it take to die in order to sustain those ideas of that liberator fundamentalist Mr. Simon Boliver before it is too late. I also wonder how many men in the Middle East will it take to die in order to sustain those ideas of that author (*Milestones*) and Islamic thinker and activist fundamentalist Mr. Sayyid Qutb before it is also too late.

It's always a gamble speaking of human dignity, but I still remember that day in the Fall of 1979 when that civil rights fundamentalist Mr. Andrew Young, the first African American ambassador to the United Nations, was forced to resign because he dared to bring forth that idea to speak to the Palestine Liberation Organization without permission because they the (PLO) had yet to publicly state that "Israel has a right to exist." Young's unjustified resignation thirty-five years ago helped prove to both me and many others here in America that our government lacked the maturity of dialogue and the will to engage for the sake of justice on many numbers of critical global issues! This is a sad truth that endures until today despite an African American president in the White House who seems sympathetic to such concerns yet unwilling or unable to act on that idea of justice in the Middle East in regards to Hamas. In an imperfect world, diplomacy should matter not perceptions.

The desire for freedom and those people who march and advocate for it both here in America and in Europe should seize on the freedom agenda in the Muslim world (Arab Spring), Latin world (revolution), and the Third World (emancipation). In many ways the ideological warfare of the past has burst, and we are watching the emergence of an unstoppable worldwide youth revolution. As always, hope is wired to the soul, and today's ideas of justice and freedom are being spread globally by Twitter and Face book. It's these powerful weapons for real change, moving at the speed of demand, that will change warped values, correct historical errors, and cure the poison of prejudice in our lands. This is a surely new period a new era to behold. The youthful crowds who felt they were not included in the equation of life are back in the streets and the denied predictable forces of fundamental real change is featured bare-chested for all to see and ponder—that idea of social justice, that idea of how to differ amongst ourselves, that idea of ballot box and that idea of Islam. Now is the time for we the believers to face these resident evils here at home just like the millions gathering again in Cairo in Tahrir Square and the millions around Raba`a Adawiya Mosque in Nasr City Cairo, Egypt. Yes, we the people, our time-bearing silent human witness to the oppressions here in the West and East are over. Yes, we fundamentalists do believe in global trade that is fair, competitive, and beneficial to the entire world body rather than at the expense of human dignity and human suffering as well as respecting human rights for all.

In addition to those merchant-of-death arms industry, we also need to beware of those political indoctrination commissars known as Washington think tanks. These elite players have been instrumental in losing the West's global heart's and mind's war, while also failing to truthfully inform the American and European public about that unwinnable war on terror. These advocates of the supposed "free press" and other Western "liberties" were expected to provide innovative and unbiased analysis in order to promote global freedom, prosperity, and security. Sadly, these groups were key figures behind the nationalistic wave of manipulation and propaganda that overwhelmed the American psyche before and after 9/11. These same people and organizations that gave their audiences an earful of lies mixed with half-truths about American and Western enemies. The same organizations of misinformation in their promotion of unjust wars and wars of folly since the end of World War II through the dark days of the Cold War and Vietnam till Afghanistan and Iraq wars where we have won every battle but lost every war are alarmingly unashamed! The short list of these so-called nonpartisan purveyors of misinformation in this modern era includes the following:

1. Heritage Foundation
2. Brooking Institution
3. American Enterprise Institute
4. Center For American Progress
5. National Endowment
6. International Republican Institute
7. Livingston Group
8. SITE Institute
9. The National Democratic Institute
10. Freedom House
11. Hudson Institute
12. CATO Institute
13. Institute for Liberty and Democracy

Because our progress in life is limited only by our dedication to justice, taking a stand against Orwellian ideological warfare is essential. Everywhere we turn these day's governmental propagandists are working hand-in-hand with political ideologues in order to misinform the public on both domestic and foreign policies because of their own vested conflict of interests. Their ideas, however, have neither maintained domestic tranquility or kept the nation out of unjust wars of folly for the last sixty-four years. Thus, it falls on us, the discriminating people of all Abrahamic faiths, to engage all proposals of merit and debate all consequences instead of merely choosing that path of least resistance and the accepted ways of old national pride. A good first step would be the breakup of the monopoly of information those corporate elites hold here in the West. That resulting power showdown between those have mores, that report ice floes instead of icebergs, those nationalist that report icebergs instead of ice floes, and corporate media reporting insurgences instead of the resistance to oppression, will stand before us all to see clearly that this is an epic battle of ideas of propaganda verses ideas of emancipation though we all may wear different ideas and hats, we are all walking this path simultaneously and each sharing equally the same sky. Just as we fundamentalists can't walk a straight path without an absolute creed of faith that both upholds justice and lives by it, we the people can't walk in a straight path without an absolute reference like the U.S. Constitution to uphold justice and ensure it. Otherwise, we will all just continue to perpetuate the blaze that surrounds the world today.

Yes, those concrete blast walls surrounding our major government buildings do present a grievous symbol for our times. As James Madison, the fourth president of the United States and constitutional fundamentalist, once said, "If tyranny and oppression come to this land, it will be in the guise of fighting a foreign enemy." So on a refreshing early September bright cool beautiful fall day of 2013, I journeyed around with my wife and three children about down-town New York City Manhattan at high noon. We wanted to just shop around and follow the crowd and give ourselves some airtime. From what I can see, I must truthfully say there is still an atmosphere of fear and suspicion that still lingers the streets, which now have eyes amid the tall marble and glass buildings and chest-high polish Cadillac's.

In spite of the great bargains for sale, that fear agency business of terror is still running strong in the heart of New York City. For the life of me, I try to ignore the hard and suspicious stares upon me as best as I can knowing that golden rule is still valid, which says, "Lions don't cut their mane." It's a pity that so many of my countrymen in suite and tie just don't see the double talk or those in Levi's jeans don't feel the political weather of contradictions of the heart that's all around them. Faintly, it's that shepherd with an agenda, progressing, dealing with matters that's being ignored because of their fear. Once thought safe, nonetheless, badges and passwords are indeed a pain but now a norm. Much of today's financial commodity markets is still base on their clients flavor of fear. Now it's time to rethink your bonds, but I realize I alone cannot change this atmosphere of greed even if I try, it would be just an excuse by them to place me behind the sun. Just look around Lower New York City, Manhattan, yourself, and the country for that matter—at the jackbooted police officers and bomb-sniffing dogs stalking port authority bus terminals and Grand Central-Pen Central

Stations, at alert soldiers in uniform with M-16 rifles at all major airports, the private security guards demanding IDs at key business landmarks and communication centers. What a real nuisance these Homeland Security agents are, using microwaves to scan through the clothing of people walking in downtown crowds. A total menace these baited entrapment offers by the dark hearted FBI and Homeland Security agents that are being given to Muslim Americans to entrap them and their neighbors as well as to get us to spy on each other for them for a instant U.S. green card and/or a promise cash reward profit. Yet all this effort is still no guarantee because of that golden rule "not all nations deserve to be safe." Truly, President James Madison's words seem more than just prophetic.

Therefore, we walked the earth some more uptown along Broadway then over to Fifth Avenue, we strolled with the humble masse of people to the Metropolitan Museum of Art on East Central Park, finding more exquisite displays to fathom. Yes, this is a great place to be human. Captured by the green swathe of nature we pioneered in with the peaceful crowd on the paths going with the flow past strawberry-field, then alongside West Central Park enjoying the view and contrast of people. With each step we take, I notice that under-siege mentality drifted farther away behind us. Our appetite for wonder still intact, we as a family then continued to follow that cosmopolitan passage into Harlem where real people worry about their communal and spiritual social element in their lives, not only just about their struggles of the rent and the price of food. Allah has indeed bless this country! Of this fact, there's no doubt in my mind as we walked these humble streets of Harlem whose soul is still on ice, that we Americans or whatever you wish to call us still don't have an articulate spokesman of the third kind who is willing to address the issues at hand and giving all its citizens therein breathing space to reclaim their true way of life without oppressing others or be intimidated by a stop-and-frisk policy of fear, is a wonderment of hope. In spite of the historic evasions, the common Americans still hold on to decency, good enterprise, honesty, integrity and God. So then, who will call the country back to the values they cherished?

Eventually the cover story will be that our leaders can no longer buy the silence of a people under oppression, despite the measures of our Western oligarchy world has undertaken to keep them enslaved. It's that fear of retribution that makes us here in the West no safer now than we were yesterday. Is it likewise any wonder why the majority of our global philosophies are being re-evaluated by today's youth, in both the West and the East? A vast youthful energized demographic idea is growing, that deeply believes that, "what the previous generations before us couldn't achieve, we can accomplish." Who wishes sincerely to turn the tide away from individualism and selfish materialism by shining a light into the darkness of these confusing times, with a purpose of awakening a culture that wants to change that idea of how we see ourselves!

When I was a young man attending Howard University in Washington DC, I was looking for a friend or even just somebody black like me, with maturity of mind, who was aware of the gravity of the situation here in our country in regards to family, jobs, scholarships, education, careers goals and leadership skills. No matter how much I gave voice to the issues of social justice and equal rights, I was still just a faceless black youth who was poor and angry, who could not find a living wage job to sustain himself and his education at Howard University. Torn between hope and pragmatism, facing reality and the color of my face, it was impossible to convince myself that we as a people were not being overlooked in spite of the blood already in the ground. But exactly what do you expect from the reality of street life in America in the mid 1970's, a reality that has hardly changed for the better after more than 35 years? Then like now, Howard University is an island surrounded by sea of African-American youthful poverty, hopelessness and crime; a place where the ideas of justice, human rights, and due process of law are events spoken of in the classrooms and then forgotten under the normal circumstances of life in American streets. "Never again" means that we *have* understood the painful lessons; otherwise, that democratic idea which millions of our youth are being told of which is worth fighting for exists in name only.

That idea of Islam in America means I did not have to beg corrupt usury banks for a loan so I can continue onward my education that would had benefited my society in the long run economically! Islam in America means I didn't have to steal food to live; thus, a black young man like myself did not have to go to prison with millions of others and get my education there. Islam in America means once you get accepted into a University or college in America you will be given a free scholarship to study towards whatever degree you wish because a mind is a terrible thing to waste and the investment of that individual can only benefit their community as a knowledgeable, productive member of that society. Islam in America does not say, "show me the money" as paramount in regards to the poor in terms of education! This means students who graduate from these universities and colleges are not burden with tens of thousands of dollars of debt in addition to looking for a job once they have completed their degrees. I was there in many Muslim poor countries where students who were poor are accepted into Universities and Colleges and they did not had to pay for their tuition after they completed their degrees. The tuition was paid for gladly by way of taxes and social contribution of that knowledgeable student unto society that invested in him and her. No more, this capitalistic myopic idea of "Will this Pay?" Islam in America means the end of wars of folly; the war is right here at home being just to each other. Islam in America means the end of that idea of racism and segregation for profit and gain. Islam in America means the end of poverty here in America. Islam in America means the end of alcoholism where millions of people can stop looking into a bottle to get some relief in their lives. There will be no more issuing licenses of bars here in America, it`s time for a freeze on issuing liquor licenses. We have enough bars selling alcohol; the real issue in this modern era is that demand for alcohol in our social community. Islam in America means the drug war is over. If you want an artificial high in your life, then the focus is why you need such a drug stimulus in your life in the first place! The focus on this "war on drugs" should be addressing that demand for something out side of oneself so you can satisfy your life! Islam in America means that idea of suicide is no longer fashionable when our reach does not exceed our needs. The humane objective question now is what are you reaching "for" and what are your true needs? Islam in America means ideas are truly more powerful than guns, so what are those ideas that you have that can contribute positively to our society that can defeat any armory? Islam in America means when you step outside your home you don`t leave your faith behind at the door step of your home or temple just so you and your neighbors of different faiths can get along and live peacefully together in an open public arena. You take that monotheist faith with you and make it work for you as a contribution to society. Islam in America means the end of that idea of faith called Secularism as a so-called modern civilize substitute of a monotheistic faith in a civilize pluralistic society because of the fear of one branch of a monotheistic faith may oppress another faith that is non monotheistic or vice versa.

Ideas reminds us all of a danger we can`t ignore simply because ideas is that makes this world work. So if you got the guts to do some real soul searching when Johnny came marching home from Iraq war and Afghanistan war in the hundreds of thousands they like those in the Vietnam war who brought home the bitter lessons of fighting an unjust war of folly and greed, their desires will no longer be ignored. "Never again" means they did understood the *lessons*, like you must not support one brother against another in a civil war throughout the world for profit and gain was known on the American streets but ignored and not spoken of in our corrupt corporate media and adventurous military to our overall peril (Vietnam-Afghanistan-Iraq).

We are now facing the consequence once again of not respecting the sovereignty of nations when they say they will not extradite people from their nation who retaliate against us whom we believe have committed crimes in America because we had supported a civil war in their lands (Afghanistan); in retrospect these actions was in retaliation for the oppression we caused on others in their pursuit of justice and liberty no matter how heinous we feel it is!

What do we do when we as a nation of democratic people do when we are faced with a situation of global revenge coming our way especially if the side that Western Secular nations who had been supporting as proxy, loses their war and its leader (Ahmad Monsur) is assassinated on 9-9-01. Because it was not enough to kill the rebel leader as far as the Islamic resistance was concern, no, they wanted pain for pain against the Western arms merchant of the world who sold Ahmad Monsur the guns to fight against them, thus 9-11-01. Now as in the case of Afghanistan people seeking revenge, we the Western people seeking revenge because of their revenge, thus ending up sending an army invasion unto them instead of a posse hunt for justice starting with ourselves! In the case of Iraq, an outright greed for oil to fuel armies overseas in Afghanistan and pay for adventurism in the world, thinking everybody in the world crave this idea to live like us and be saved by us. This is a wrong idea! Indeed, I bear witness of that moral bankruptcy in that troubled crusade lead by myopic Western presidents and arrogant Western prime ministers and fought by the ignorant Western youth, wondering where is that change after all this effort, blood, pain, and death? Such daunting revelations of folly have been monstrous, and the reactions of atonement by ex-president George W. Bush, his administration and patrons, fierce in our heartland no matter how hard you look for someone to pay the bill to admit mistake and responsibility, the conclusion is surrealistic. How is this war going to end? Our nation's polices was not innocent abroad or at home; those milestones challenges of balancing revolutionary ideals of liberty and freedom without a true and just crusade on justice and human rights here at the home front are suicidal. We the people here in the west are only fooling ourselves and murdering our future customers of trade out of arrogance; thus our democracy that millions of our youth are told is worth fighting for exists in name only.

For the same reasons, America's youth protested against the Vietnam War, where millions demanded that their voices be heard. It really won't matter if our younger generations come to see themselves as "all of us," if they no longer wish to remain ignorant of the idea which imposes drastic measures that prioritized stability and security over justice and values. For the youth always know it will be they who will be the ones on the front lines bleeding; yet knowing there are millions of like-minded souls out there, marchers of all shades fashioning a culture of worldwide protest, brings with it a palpable strength.

In this day and age, it seems that you are only fooling yourself to think that there doesn`t seems to be much malice in the world. When the evidence reveals that there is simply not enough common sense to conduct the intricate affairs of an insincere civilization. Yes, I can bear witness to how those youthful roars of protest broke my own barrier of fear in times when victory seemed unattainable. As a child in the late sixties and early seventies, many times I skipped out of that brick in the wall Bronx public school PS-90, and (All-Hallows, Christ the King,-Christian schools) jumped the D train heading downtown to West Central Park Manhattan and saw protesters marching on New York City, unafraid of all the rubber bullets flying, of the police and National Guardsmen with their clubs and tear gas. Those young protesters boldly resolved not go back to their homes like sheep, choosing instead to stand their ground and shout for peace. Yet despite the urgings of that idea reformation fundamentalist John Lennon, telling the world to "give peace a chance," and Bob Dylan, Joan Baez, as well as numerous others all helping to shatter the official mask of social illusion in both their time and now, I ask of you, oh, humble reader, what have "we the people" attained for our seventeen-trillion dollar debt?

Is it then unreasonable to ask how long since the last large demonstrations we had here in America or in Europe condemning the same antiquated polices of relying on military forces to achieve social, economic, and political objectives? As well as ideas that prioritize stability and security over justice and values. Then why aren't the lies that led to 6,000 plus dead U.S. soldiers, in addition to tens of thousands of wounded enough for the masses to say "Never Again" and mean it?

President Obama in his 2012 State of the Union address said, "No one built this country on their own. This nation is great because we built it together. This nation is great because we worked as a team. This nation is great because we got each other`s back." This was indeed a bold speech in terms of reawakening the purpose of the American people and their sense of unity. Yet still I must ask: How do we cover each other's backs when you know he`s wrong? What doctrine do you invoke when you are only patriotic to the truth? As a Salafi Muslim American now living in America who speaks on the condition of nonanonymity because of the hypocrisy and double talk of the establishment of my land, I insist we be frank with one another, because time is short, and economic warfare on the home front has replaced the foreign wars of folly we've borne witness to in Vietnam, Afghanistan, and Iraq. Just who do you think pays this recent bill of four trillion dollars wars lost by folly, Martians?

As a matter of fact, for the young at the vanguard of any uprising who loath the unnecessary war paint the grim evidence is that we look at liberty and freedom from a Western secular scavenger-hunt perspective. Stop wanting it for others overseas, do we have liberty and freedom right here at home? Since human error is everyone`s business, never again affirmation shout-out is "what do you want? Justice! When do you want it? Now! I don`t have your back when I know your wrong! Not for that cardinal sin of murder, plunder, rape, imperialism, and misinformation. So please don't wave that flag in my face. Because I had closely watched my generation and the generation ahead of me struggle to come of age and empower itself. I am or if you wish, the generation behind me not fooled in coming to terms with the fashionable reasons of blaming it on the political bogeymen. That grand strategy of putting our money where our mouth is, is not in proportion in using the vote, civil disobedience, nonviolence, boycott, and noncooperation. Or even putting our money where our life interest is in a collective way in order to achieve our social, economic, political, and religious aspirations in a sustainable manner. All that talk of democracy, sovereignty in the hands of the people, yet our hearts are remembered for what we do next! We the people fill out those 1040-tax forms faithfully, and pay to those clowns that`s running our country like a circus because of our own hearts. That handful of bold ideas which defines our noble character here in the West; keeps walking away ominously. That debt of hard economic warfare against those power elites with their super PACs must be paid because that challenge of balancing revolutionary ideals with bread-and-butter issues leaves no room for deathless prose in the forum or in the streets. Those plutocratic have mores elites of the American and Western World Order will not go down easy; they are well aware that preserving the disorder and the asphyxiation of their dissent smothers the initiative of the aspiring poor and humiliates the routine life of the youth, simply because there is money to be made off misery.

From the carnivorous jungles of Vietnam, we knew this is not the way to live. From the zest of Hollywood to off Broadway, we knew this is not the way to liberation. From the illusions of that Supreme Court in Washington, DC, we knew eventually justice fell into the interest of those modern feudal lords and urban plantation masters. It`s during these times in my life I am aware that what this "Occupied Wall Street" protest is all about; "this subservience of arrogance" is what finally clinched the deal for all this turmoil living behind the enemies lines so that the youthful all of us can understand all the interpretations of the virtues, and vices of their homelands in a more ideological worldview and a balanced realistic way. The very words of that Chicago`s Mayor Richard Daley at the Democratic convention of the summer of 1968 in Chicago, is an historical reminder of what all of us are facing. When his police force beat up peaceful youthful demonstrators in the thousands that were against the Vietnam War in Chicago and the corrupt establishment, he said, "Gentlemen, get the thing straight once and for all; the policeman isn`t there to create disorder. The policeman is there to preserve disorder."

I thank Allah (swa) that I was in Hyde Park London on a cloudy but festive day in March 2004 with three hundred thousand other protesters of all faiths and hues, ready to march to Trafalgar Square for peace in Iraq, Afghanistan, and everywhere else on earth. Allah knows I was suspicious of the character of the march, mostly because of two highly disturbing, yet noticeable, Western phenomena. The first, Allah knows best, was that many amongst us merely just watched leeringly from within the stores, from the sidelines, and from mansion windows along the path of the marchers. The second, Allah knows best, is that, in reality, we were all doing the moonwalk, walking backwards while appearing to walk forward! For in truth, despite the earnestness of our demands, peace will only be achieved through a change in morality, sincerity, justice, and sincere economics. We the people were not marching to demand that not one drop of Iraq's oil enter our home ports to heat our own homes, fuel our cars, buses, planes, and trains; we were declaring, out loud, that the war in Iraq is wrong; yet the oil wealth coming from that country, into our own, had been obtained by illegal means—by deceit, theft, and murder, against the wishes and will of the Iraqi people. This fact we all knew was true, yet we the people marching and shouting for all the world to hear and see still allowed our leaders to take the oil anyway quietly and discreetly, with the aim of selling it to the people (us) for profit and gain!

That idea to murder people at night then sell their wares in the daytime is truly a thing horrible and an uncivilized act. Truthfully, we should not had betray the hearts of the Iraqi people by purchasing the blood-soaked wares of their lands that was for sale in the markets of the West and say that we the people are innocent of what our governments are doing in our name! Thus, that accusation by those Muslim resistance forces that's all around, underground, and watching—"blood for oil," holds merit, a true insult to the very creed of democracy, justice, and humanity which we suppose to be standing for, marching for! Yet it's that state of mind set of today's modern Western civilization and media programming that embraced the imperial greed, which at times is truly profound to me and other Muslim fundamentalists that this Western empire has come to this!

During the march, I spoke to several homegrown British reporters with their camera crews, as well as members of the Muslim Council of Britain (MCB), Muslim Association of Britain (MAB), and the British Muslim Forum (BMF) along the way. Therefore, I asked of them what was clearly on the minds of Eastern Muslim fundamentalists, viewing this march from near, and afar that are being called terrorist. In their eyes, the question was, is this march just a fantasy of naïve and obtuse-minded Westerners wishing for peace, yet not willing to reconcile their nations unjust policies of oppression toward Muslim lands? From the looks on those reporters white faces, it seemed as if they knew the true answer already; thus, I doubted my words or tape video will be socially or politically acceptable for advertisement. Similarly, those Muslim citizens of the UK did as well understood the majorities' distinct cultural mind-set; sadly they were not the only ones who seemed to implicitly understand the difference between merely talking about peace and undertaking the hard measures necessary to actually achieve it with justice. This war, and shouts of peace, is truly a racket!

For in truth, Allah knows best, the people marching to Trafalgar Square that day were relying on empty words of peace to cover the heavy cost of injustice, a true showcase of inhumanity and non-sacrifice. In truth, we fundamentalists know that actions speak louder than words of protest, no matter if they are written or spoken with true intent. Unfortunately, the people of the West wanted peace, but they are unwilling to make the sacrifices necessary to achieve it like (self-boycotting the oil) and incapable in marshaling the moral authority over their own leaders (impeachment) to sustain it! Just the right amount of wrong will *do*. Does such guile have no limits? Not when it comes to PR so it seems. Hitherto, this is a part of a sad undoing of so-called civilized nations in the shadow of dark events here in the secular democratic West. Exotic, truly exotic in spite of our greed and genius, if the sun would only sneeze then what would we all do?

Just like you, I walked down those crowded London streets on that spring-like afternoon. I studied the many exotic faces around me, and began to ponder the idea how a divine pessimistic observer might believe that life seldom becomes intelligent and intelligent civilizations do not endure because of the ever increasing complexity of life all around it. Yet a divine optimistic observer might believe that life arises to all challenges when justice reigns and thus assists mature civilizations in becoming intelligent. We all know, and Allah (swa) is a true witness over the global community, what path we all must take if we truly desire an end to these wars that they would have been ended yesterday. All the people have to do is throw an anchor into the fountain of justice, and act on that "In God we trust." Please, oh, humble reader, don't let anybody neither fool you nor esteem it as better to be a pawn and pay the rent or mortgage, whereas to ignore those coincidences of life in our realm over which we all have full control of.

In these days of uncertainty and economic stagnation, the needs and desires of the common man in America as well as in Europe are being ignored. The economic warfare here at home, from Main Street to Wall Street, is far more formidable than the jungles of Vietnam, the high mountains of Afghanistan, or the hot desert plains of Iraq. When both the U.S. Chamber of Commerce and the Securities Exchange Commission ease regulations so that the rich can become even more richer, its then we know these times in which we are living are far from normal. In fact, the S.E.C. has granted Wall Street institutions and big banking corporations guilty of fraud nearly 350 waivers of penalties over the last ten years.[82]

When you're on a mission to rescue the dried-out dreams in your own country, preaching a gospel of economic justice is essential. Our democratic secular capitalist economics here at home is not based on

---

[82]   *New York Times* Feb. 3, 2012

social justice but on usury and greed. Depression, disaffection and despair are the prevailing dogmas of our era. Since troubled societies always blame their plight on enemies both real and imaginary, the warnings issued by the youth should be taken at face value. When our youth work, save, gamble, slave, make love, buy, sell, and horde, invest, revolt, build, unite, vote, kill, and pay taxes, the bottom line is to become fluent in the language of economics here at home. But not all youth in our Western secular societies are endowed with such keen language skills of economics and economic boycott. From their point of view, there's something fundamentally wrong with the system and the economy based upon greed. Our capitalist economics here at home is not based on social justice; it is based on outright greed and the devil gets the hindmost. This is that inconvenient truth which has marred the whole script that the consciousness of our youth of today is now demanding from us "Yesterday people" who said never again, that dignity of life which can only be achieved by demanding rules based on social justice. Otherwise we are just organizing these social failures base on greed to be replaced with avariciousness! Yes, trust is ruthless behind enemy lines.

Considering the times in which we are living, do you really believe that that Divine Being will not hold a nation of people to account until after the grave? For the inconvenient truth is we are not doing enough of what is divinely expected of us. Since the start of the twenty-first century, we the people have not been innovative enough in developing ourselves more humanly so as to create a truly worthy legacy of well-being living in a civilize era of human history. At times I feel much of the fault lies with us Muslims living in America and Europe. For in truth, we are too concerned with the many corrupting faces of Western dogmatism and its hidden authoritarianism in secular robes. As Muslims, by our creed of faith, our mission to please our Lord Allah, is to bring light to the people here in the West. Instead, too many of our eyes are focused on the material things instead of understanding that life in this world is merely a passing through a door to the next. The fundamental law of both the Torah and the Quran holds that sovereignty belongs to Allah only. As Prophet Jesus, that walking-on-water fundamentalist, said, "A man can only have one master."

So then, is it not too audacious to suggest that today's secular Christian churches and secular Jewish synagogues have failed to measure up to today's challenges and have only led the Western culture down a road of greater spiritual ignorance, arrogance, and misinformation? Is it not a bitter truth that the most powerful and affluent nations on earth is frankly incapable of sustaining a just democracy because of their greed. One that likewise provides its fundamentalist religious citizenry the right to establish a justice-based theocracy if that is what the ballot box decides it needs?

Back in April 2008, during President Obama's first election campaign for presidency, that Christian preacher fundamentalist Reverend Jeremiah Wright who was pushed under the political bus for having told America: "Whatsoever you sow, that you also shall reap. You cannot do terrorism on other people and expect them never to come back to you." I pray that president Obama has his ears on the streets, eyes to the sky. Call it what you want, but there is a palpable undercurrent of distaste and distrust of this government, especially concerning the issues of faith, and the justness of the wars it undertakes. For example: when President Obama stated: "We do not consider ourselves a Christian Nation or a Jewish Nation or a Muslim Nation, we consider ourselves a nation of citizens who are bound by ideals and a set of values." Personally, that state of belief is weird, it`s always a wise move to let that divine one to take a bow. The question now, before the people is whose ideals and whose set of values are we the people going to follow outside the Monotheist faith?

Those secularists who wish to segregate the dignity of moral concerns from all old laws making people feel more exposed like their idea that loyalty to the state is not necessarily in conflict with loyalty to one's faith we submit to you the ill wind blowing. How to fight the usury wars that are lost down in Wall Street and having to fight the imperialist wars that are also lost overseas are amongst the many ingredients of a gathering perfect storm upon this land that ignores a moral compass!

It's a given, those Western gatekeepers who are called You tube, Twitter, Facebook, Internet, CNN, and the BBC are some of the deadly weapons of today`s open societies. Therefore, it is inevitable in the wake of a world full of alienable rights the weapons of media will be taken up by those who are appealing for allegiance and competing for influence. They who believe their rights comes from that divine one, not from the state. They who believes they are created by that divine one, not created by the state. They who believes sincerely the state justifies itself by securing those divine-given inalienable rights by promoting and defending them only. Consequently such a fundamental collision of interest between that medium of ideological information claimed by civil societies on both sides is worth the effort if you look and listen deeply enough into that counter attack from the world of hurt and despair. Seeing the world from their perspective, you will understand that there are some facts of life that are certain. Because fundamental collisions of interest is inevitable after their emancipation in the Islamic and Third world in the wake of political, social, and economic reform, it's that understanding that media is a two-way street that has smart fearless crossroads. Upholding free speech includes designing the perfect jihad with relevant ideas. What makes this landscape here on earth so remarkable is the presence of all these visual ideas all around us within reach of our hearts. The question then is what's your contribution?

That Stateless Government

*Mischief has appeared on land and sea because of the meed that the
hands of men have earned; That Allah may give them a taste of some
of their deeds: in order that they may turn back from evil.*

—Quran 30:41

Losing on both fronts on this war on terror is bad enough, but to have
one's own citizens fight their own government because of the wrongs
it is committing is a sign of a reassessment of today's Western social
fabric. Many people here in the West—particularly those who disagree
with those who are in a hearts, minds and soul war—is that justice is
neither blind, nor deaf, and especially not mute. Justice is a two-way
street. Therefore, it seems, unjustifiably, that under the laws of war,
citizenship has been deemed irrelevant. You need not be telepathic
to understand, what that U.S. Attorney General Eric Holder said
as he spoke in March 2012 at Northwestern University Law School,
"The legal right to kill U.S. citizens overseas without benefit of a
trial was based on Congressional authorization to use all necessary
and appropriate force against the perpetrators of 9-11-2001 or those
who helped them and the president's power to protect the nation
from any imminent threat of violent attack." However, that October
2011 American drone attack in Yemen—which killed Abdulrahman
Al-Awlaki, the sixteen-year-old son of Anwar Al-Awlaki—now offers
a frightening preview of targeted killings of Americans without due
process of law. This act of killing a Muslim American teenager, who
traveled to Yemen, and who was paying his respects in praying at his

father's grave, by his own government, has been condemned by a unified Muslim-American community here in America as an insult to a sacred religious right, despite the relative silence of the Western media on this issue. In response, John Brennan, a senior White House counter-terrorism adviser, said on April 30, 2012 that "these targeted strikes are legal . . . [and] [w]hen considering lethal force we ask ourselves whether the individual poses a significant threat to U.S. interests." Please, oh, humble reader, and ponder this idea about significant threat? Since when does an American teenager warrants a death sentence because he wishes to visit the grave of his father with a prayer anywhere on this earth justify significant threat to U.S. interests?

Losing the war on terror on the home front means that the United States Foreign Intelligence Surveillance Act (FISA) and Court (FISC) authorize by a nervous Congress is a [secret court who's hearings are closed to the public and records are not available to the accused to refute] are now working in worried overtime. Their goals and methods are fulfilling governmental rubberstamp requests for surveillance warrants and/or death warrants against American suspects whom they feel pose a terrorist threat without requiring judicial review or public oversight! Today the (FISA) and the (FISC) is now working a tense overtime together with the National Counterterrorism Center (NCTC); their real mission is how to fight a war against a stateless enemy that has no borders when you are running out of truths? Yes, in that hopeless hunt for the source of that so-called dark human creativity[83] demanding rights, assassination is permissible with neither due process of law nor judicial review, even when conducting military operations on suspected enemy combatants. The so-called civilized concept of "if you are going to make a case for capital punishment then you must have valid presentable evidence supporting it," now appears to be over within all branches of security in the United States government. We are now bearing witness to Banana Republic—type laws here at home, with the creation of military tribunals to try so-called terror "suspects" away from the public eye after they have been tortured, shunning their moral standards out of fear of defeat—a not—guilty verdict by a jury of his peers. Thus, we inherit a system that our shameful elected leaders believe to be the only way to fight a stateless enemy, such a conflict these politicians and war profiteers have brought upon themselves and their nation.

---

[83]   Quran 55:7-9

I have learned from many Sheikhs from all over the Muslim world that what really is important is not what knowledge a person has, but rather how much wisdom, based on that knowledge he or she puts into practice. No one can sincerely deny that humanity is living in precarious times without precedent. Yet I cannot speak on behalf of justice of why Sheikh Anwar Al-Awlaki should be murdered by his own government, simply because of the speeches he gave in a Muslim country declared to be on the front lines. But I will say this: if Sheikh Al-Awlaki were standing in an American court of law, he would not be facing a death sentence if found guilty of those same charges brought legally to a judge and jury of his peers. So is it treason if a Muslim American speaks the truth about his country's nefarious actions? Is it treason when a Muslim American imam declares that if his fellow Americans citizens are abetting its soldiers in an unjust war of oppression upon Muslim people and their countries, that they are not innocent civilians but as equally guilty as their government and military? Is it treason if Muslims hear statements from an American imam and attack Westerners because they know that imam's words are the truth? Just where is the evidence by the way, that says Sheikh Al-Awlaki ever ordered his listeners to kill anybody? And I'm not talking about hearsay evidence, but authentic evidence of a conspiracy to commit murder? I can't speak on behalf of Sheikh Anwar Al-Awlaki; but under our First Amendment he had the constitutional right, as an American, to speak, and to answer these charges.

How this war on terror ends truly depends on both the people and their leaders being earnest with themselves and with each other. This war on terror obviously won't end while we have whole nations of intolerant people living in labyrinthine worlds of denial, starved of information yet in need of justice, comfort and peace. This war on terror won't end with a bullet in the heart or brain or by a lethal drone attack or by supporting some group in their civil war with their brethren. Since everyone can identify with a fragrant of hell, blowing up people who call themselves innocent civilians yet who abets injustice will only make matters worse I feel, it's time to talk the issues with our adversary humanely, and resolve our problems, not just kicking the can down the road in anger. The solution to this war on terror is a jihad unto itself; a prayer that one's government never escapes its borders to spread its iniquities onto others must be considered deeply. It is, likewise, a prayer that we Muslims living behind enemy lines will be granted more time to change the hearts of our neighbors and countrymen by that stateless government based on a monotheist faith before the next attack does come because it is inevitable judging from the hearts of my countrymen. Yes, for me—an imam born in the West, whose culture is likewise Western, but whose life is committed to justice—this solution is an uphill battle. Yes, my country is at war with a stateless enemy, one that equates fundamentalist religion with terrorism. I am also aware that this stateless enemy—one that is patient with its retribution, and that views terrorism as a consequence in the fight against oppression—is in many ways superior and will eventually overcome. I am well aware that I have been labeled as a radical Islamist in spite of Title VI of the 1964 Civil Rights Act and the 1987 Civil Rights Restoration Act. That says it is illegal to discriminate against anyone because of their race, religion, sex, or national origin. Yet here we are, living an Islamic lifestyle deemed unacceptable by the Judeo-Christian majority with respect to the social, economic and political standard of secular life and its measures of justice. Yet here we are, Muslims living in a country that has lost two unsustainable wars against an Islamic resistance. In which more American soldiers who had volunteer and enrolled and was sent to fight in Afghanistan and Iraqi wars have committed suicide therein and at home, more than those who had died fighting in Afghanistan and Iraq therein and came home in spite of the mission accomplish media hype! Saying we told you so about that karma just doesn`t cut it anymore in the real turmoil of life. Yes, here we are . . . bearing witness to the perilous default position of our neighbors and compatriots who are ignoring the deadly seriousness of unjust wars coming home to roost! Yet just one generation ago, we the people said never again.

The solution? Time has come for us fundamentalist of this monotheist faith to become the policy masters here in the West and no longer accept a back seat in the corridors of power of these secular governments. For the truth is, the hearts of my countrymen still have not changed; the West will inevitably see more 9-11-01`s because of the meed of their own hearts and hands. I fear that no matter how many planes are crashed into buildings in these lands, no matter how many tens of thousands of civilians are killed in the process, the people in the West will not change their hearts when it comes to the oppression and injustice of others. Sadly, no matter how many bombs exploding in trains, buses, and cars in our cities, killings tens of thousands of civilians who abets injustice, no matter how much blood is shed, we the people of the West will remain enslaved to the interests of the power elites in our own countries and hostage to the "unforeseeable and uncontrollable events" from which they claim to be protecting us from!

Understandably, if history is to be taken as a golden rule, an ill omen, it wasn't the "innocent" German citizens that surrendered after the fire bombings of Berlin, Hamburg and Dresden. Likewise, it wasn't the "innocent" Japanese people that surrendered after the atomic bombs dropped on Hiroshima and Nagasaki. In both instances, it was that power elite that surrendered unconditionally, but only when they saw that there was nobody else to hide behind! History is full of men, women and children who have fought onward, often, to the death of all because they believed that they stood for truth and the high moral ground.

Let's be frank about that human spirit that dwells in the hearts of mankind since we came this far in our pursuit of truth and justice. Did those people who believe that they were innocent and oppressed who died in the millions in Stalingrad, Leningrad and other Russian cities by the hands of the Nazis surrendered? Of course not! Did those millions of Chinese people likewise surrendered under Japanese oppression! Of course not! So why would anyone think a stateless enemy based on an Islamic monotheist faith would surrender under secular (pagan) and/or Communist (atheist) oppression? Thus, without both a spiritual and a political reawakening of our own compatriots by their own countrymen who understand the true nature of the dangers of fighting a monotheist stateless enemy without borders, we the people therein of the West are doomed because of our own hearts and imperialism. Thus, we are at the mercy of our enemies at their time and choosing! Contrary to what most believe, we the people here in the secular West are not innocent civilians, but rather the abettors of our leaders' arrogant, greedy, and deceitful actions. We are coconspirators in lockstep with the fight to maintain our empire, who together will tumble over the nationalist precipice with our eyes wide open if there is no change of heart real soon! For it is only a matter of time before a stateless government without borders, much like the one the West faces in its "war on terror," obtains a nuclear weapon or any other weapon of mass destruction either by theft, design, black-market, or via a third party that seeks revenge, justice, or favor! The question to ask oneself then is how will all this end?"

The truth is, we the Islamic fundamentalists here in the West must find the way to our countrymen's hearts and make that change, not just be the solution to it. But as with any heart surgery, however, time is not on our side, though I cannot ignore the words of many of my Muslim brothers sincere in faith who are saying, are we really, trying to save lives whom Allah wishes to destroy? Are our efforts fruitless beyond the state of salvage in the eye of that divine beholder? Truthfully, I don't know how much of a respite we have against that stateless government and/or Allah's fury, but it is Allah (swa) that has the last word on this matter so we the believers must do our part and ignore the repercussions that are sure to come and get the word out called justice promptly.

How will all this end now that Muslims of Western citizenship are openly preaching to all who will listen, for government agencies to stop spying on them in their mosques, work places and homes? Now that the fear of fundamentalist Islam here at home is so great that Muslims are the only people being tortured by their own governments in order to get information? How will it end now that Muslims are losing fear of their own oppressive Western governments? I can attest there will be more Sheikh Anwar Al-Awlakis to come, so the question is, where exactly are the lies in their speech? In fighting a war against a secular democratic enemy that tortures and water boards people, uses beatings here at home, and fires cruise missiles from drones abroad, will they surrender? Of course not! In fighting a war with a stateless religious enemy, the body count is irrelevant, because the only justification they need is one whisper that the enemy is unjust and an imperialist; such a voice will be lethally echoed to hundreds of millions of listeners. This is why recruitment is overflowing in the Muslim world. Yet when the inexplicable does happen, the political and military leaders of the Secular West will for sure all point fingers to a terrorist culprit outside of themselves.

Stating the obvious truth can indeed turn the human tide about something that must be said, understood, and done! "We do not all worship the same God, but we all worship for the same needs!" so said Sheikh Muhammad Ibn Saleh Al-Uthaymeen that Salafi Fundamentalist from Saudi Arabia! Under growing pressure from many Muslims born, raised, and/or citizens living in non-Muslim lands in the secular West who consider themselves mainstream Muslims, the question at the time was what will be the best decisions and actions of those of us indigenous Muslim people of these lands and what path we shall take now that we have burned our boats and decided to stay here in this secular Western lands and spread the word of Islam for the mercy of Allah? It was Sheikh Muhammad Ibn Saleh Al-Uthaymeen, may Allah bless him with heaven, who addressed this heavy and important question and said during a tele link on July 28, 2000, to an audience in the city of Birmingham, UK, "I invite you to have respect for those who have the right that they should be respected, those between whom there is an agreement [of protection] for you. For the land in which you are living is such that there is an agreement between you and them. If this were not the case, they would have killed you or expelled you. So preserve this agreement, and do not prove treacherous to it, since treachery is a sign of the hypocrites, and it is not the way of the believers. And that is authentically reported from the prophet Muhammad (sas) that he said, 'Whoever kills one who is under an agreement of protection will not smell the fragrance of Paradise.'"

Today, oh, humble reader, the underlying question for those of us indigenous Muslims and Muslim Western citizens living in non-Muslim lands under an agreement of protection (civil rights) is what to do with those Western nation governments that we live in that is unjustly practicing piracy as a foreign policy upon Muslim people living in Muslim countries. Is such an agreement (civil rights) from them these non-Muslims governments worthless respite null and void? Can a non-Muslim government be trusted to fulfill the civil rights to its Muslim minority citizens at home? The same non-Muslim country that declares an unjustified war on Muslims overseas base on greed? Are we Muslims really safe living here with our families in the secular West, thinking that their word is bond, should this be our only peace of mind, or, our true battle plan on the forefront behind enemies lines is a reformation of our neighbors hearts and keeping our powder dry. Yet our Muslim brethren fighting for liberty and justice under secular and communist rulers overseas, against those who are but proxies to Western and Communist states are their cries in vain to our ears. The issues and conflicts cannot be ignored by us, the people lives and blood therein are not expendable in our eyes but a barometer of our success or failure here in the West! The jugular vein of these Western and Communist states is within reach for those of us who live here behind the enemy lines; this we feel, must be known by our enemies here if we must consider what had happen in the past to the rights of foreign citizens and their treatment living in these same countries during World War I and II, should we be deceived about their word being a true bond.

I am of the opinion with many Muslim scholars sitting in the East not living behind enemy lines that if Allah wishes to destroy once again the lives of our Western countrymen en masse because of the wrongs that they have committed that would be the easy. Yet my heart tells me the hard part is the procedure of an emergency defibrillator nationwide. It will be useless upon a nation of people whose hearts have not changed toward reconciliation but revenge! Promises by non-Muslim nations that go to war against Muslim people in their home countries first by proxy then outright lies followed by invasions for reasons of imperialist greed, should they be trusted? Honestly, oh humble reader, we are here now, the hearts of our countrymen is the only thing we the believers have to go by! Frankly, the people therein call themselves a democracy, yet it is obvious that they the people do not have the will or the power to stand up to their own governmental elite and say never again when it comes to foreign adventurism of unjust wars and mean it! In other words, they the main stream Western people in spite of their liberties, and rights are mentally enslaved to their own civil servants as in the East because of their own hearts.

Thanks to the internet, what`s *making* this landscape so remarkable thus far was the presence of Sheikh Anwar Al-Awlaki`s mind over Major Nidal Malik Hasan and millions of other Muslim Americans and Muslim Europeans who are fine-tuning into the jihad networks worldwide with a passion, thus tired of waiting in the wings. Yes, thanks to the Internet, one does not have to be a clairvoyant to have a very close encounter with an Islamic fundamentalist sheikh anywhere in the world who knows what he is talking about when it comes to putting on a uniform outside of your faith!

Yet did not those treasonous persons in the American Muslim Armed Forces and Veterans Affairs Council know about Prophet Muhammad (sas) words of warning about not joining into any army or militia if that army or militia commander in chief` is not a Muslim? Of course they did and are aware of our prophet's words! Yet sadly, dying the death of a kufr if they should die in any battle enlisted in a kufr army or militia is not a problem for those Muslims by name only in Western secular lands. A Muslim pledging his or her allegiance to a military leader of their own nationality who is not of their own faith only demonstrates one`s owns arrogance, and ignorance towards a divine being Allah, (Quran 1:6-7). Did they not, those so-called American, British, and European Muslims who enrolled in their countries military know about and read about Prophet Muhammad`s (sas) last sermon when he said in a accepted hadif just before he died "Beware of nationalism, nationalism is poison." (Al-Bukhari). But what is also intuitive is what Prophet Jesus said to those Pharisees and Herodians was a lesson forgotten also by tens of millions of Jews and Christians till this very day at a bloody price but not a lesson lost to the pagans to their credit who wish to rule with secularism over those who where ignorant of their own faith to their demise! For example: *"Tell us, then, what is your opinion: Is it lawful to pay the census tax to Caesar or not? Knowing their malice, Jesus said, "Why are you testing me, you hypocrites?" "Show me the coin that pays the census tax." "Then they handed him the Roman coin. He said to them, "Whose image is this and whose inscription?" "They replied, "Caesar`s." At that he said to them, "Then repay to Caesar what belongs to Caesar and to God what belongs to God." When they heard this they were amazed, and leaving him they went away"* (Matt. 22:17-22).

In our opinion, only a fool believes he can serve two sovereigns. Such imbeciles actually believe in this era of enormous possibilities that one can violate an allegiance to a divine being and give his allegiance to a state, which believes and acts itself as a sole sovereign and still thinks everything is OK. Additionally where are those so-called guiding and demanding voices of those leading imams here in these secular Western lands impeding the very idea of our Muslim youth enrolling in the military of their lands who's commander in chief is not a Muslim, whether it is here in America or anywhere else in the world regardless of their own nationality? Shame on them, may Allah punish them for remaining silent on this important issue! What is strange forty-five years ago at the height of that Vietnam fiasco, no Muslim African American I ever heard of who was worth his salt enrolled into the U.S. military even if he was drafted. No, not just because of what that "float like a butterfly sting like a bee" fundamentalist Muhammad Ali said about the Vietnam War, "Got nothing against no Viet-cong. No Vietnamese ever called me a Nigger" or "So now I have to make a decision. Step into a billion dollars and denounce my people, or step into poverty and teach them the truth. Damn the money! Damn the heavyweight championship. Damn the white people. Damn everything. I will die before I sell out my people for the white man's money."

It was the embodiment of it all. Oh, humble reader, I believe that those Muslims at the time and era despised the very idea and publicly condemn any Muslim of this land or any land to join any organization lead by any unbeliever by putting himself in a position where he will have to take a person's life against the laws of Islam and against the example of our prophet Muhammad (sas). I thank Allah there are still millions of Muslims here today in America and elsewhere that knows and remembers what I am saying is true. Our alibi then was not conscientious objectors but people who are truly Allah fearing, regardless of the political weather, culture, or fashion of the times. Yet why I am bringing this issue forward to your attention, oh, humble reader?

Tragic as it was, there is no doubt in my mind that Dr. Major Nidal Malik Hasan who killed thirteen people and wounded twenty-nine other people over at Fort Hood, Texas, wanted to be a fighter for a true patriotic cause. He wanted to be a doctor to help heal the wounds of war, a man who religiously and ideologically wanted out of the U.S. Army, who did not wanted any more to be affiliated with his military colleagues whom he believes did unto Muslim people unspeakable things in the name of a faith that is not his own, with total obedience without question or regard for an earthly sovereign that he believes is unjust! He was an army major psychiatrist who heard first hand confessions, statements, and crimes at his desk, committed by American troops who were on a tour of duty in Afghanistan and Iraq. Wrestling between conflicts of faith and country, Dr. Major Nidal Malik Hasan wanted an end to the talk therapy campaign at his door of American troops who he believed wanted to clear their conscience of murder, torture, rape, and kidnapping with nationalistic patriotic salvation therapy. As quiet as the American media wanted it to be he also demanded unto his superiors that patients in his programs face prosecutions for war crime charges based on statements they made to him during psychiatric sessions with him. Those gallant fools, who should had known that trust is ruthless. He would also tell to all that would listen that he was a solider of Allah. Those business cards that Dr. Major Nidal Malik Hasan was giving out to people and soldiers on the bases he was working on and even on base at Fort Hood Texas boldly read "Soldier of Allah."

In a stroke of genius, the U.S. army ordered his deployment to Afghanistan on November 28, 2009. You can call it insubordination, oh, humble reader, but it's those unforeseen ambushes as quick as "Allah is the Greatest." Life is short, and not everybody can take it all in! You tell me who loves to fight and kill for lies? Friendly fire? Terrorism? Is there a justification for such a man who realizes whom his real sovereign Lord is after giving an oath of allegiance to an earthly state sovereign in ignorance? Yes, they where troops who was going to Afghanistan and Iraq to participate in the murder of Muslims in wars that is unjustified as well as already lost. Yes, he could had walked away from it all here behind enemy lines, got on a plane, and joined the Islamic resistance on the front lines, and pity those who paid tickets to fight and murder people for lies and/or participate in the murder of their own people of faith for falsehood. But as far as Sheikh Anwar Al-Awlaki is concern, pity those soldiers of Allah who will pay for tickets to go fight on the front lines when they are standing therein behind enemy lines. That pragmatic truth is Dr. Major Nidal Malik Hasan had a choice to make; he did wanted to be a fighter for a true patriotic cause! He did received wrongful guidance from his imams living behind enemy lines, they who are living for a life of ease dreaming of U.S. citizenship and acceptance of the kufr way of life. Thinking critically, and living faithfully, he knew, he became aware of, as time marched onward and the confessions of American soldiers that mounted on his desk that came home from the front lines in Muslim countries piled higher and higher, that he was wearing the wrong uniform if he truly wanted to be a fighter for a true patriotic cause, a "soldier of Allah." Yes, indeed, he did tell his superiors in the army he wanted out of the U.S. military; they did refused his request! Allah is merciful, who gave him life and guidance, and no state government on earth can start life for anyone or guide anyone astray whom Allah guides. In the eye of the divine one, did Dr. Malik Hasan commit murder and treason? In the eye of the American government did Dr. Malik Hasan commit murder and treason? Oh, humble reader of this book, in my opinion the answer is, in who`s court will he be found innocent or guilty: the one here on earth or the one that matters the most up in heaven.

On August 28, 2013, Dr. Malik Hasan was found guilty of murder and sentence to death by U.S. court marshal. Beware: Islam is not a secular faith, which is more than just words in of itself!

Officially, a stranger—let`s call him Sam for the sake of simplicity—entered a public park called Hyde Park Speakers Corner in London, UK. And he was seemingly amazed at the sheer magnitude of speakers available therein. With a bewildered look on his face, he approached me while I was giving an open public lecture on social justice; he raised his hand and said to me, "I want a faith for all reasons and seasons." I looked at that man in the large inquisitive crowd deeply and told him to embrace Islam. To the dismay of some people in the crowd and to the cheer of others, he said in reply he shall seriously consider it and will read the holy Quran. But it was his follow-up question that drew the crowd closer with earnest on such a lovely spring Sunday April morning of 2010. Sam said with a loud Brooklyn accent, "Would I condemn that Christmas Day bomber Umar Farour Abdulmutallah and the Times Square bomber Faisal Shahzad?" I said to Sam and the listening crowd, "No, I shall not condemn them. If you came this far on such a fair day, then you can all come a little bit closer, and I will tell you why. Trust is ruthless, which is more than just words in of itself for nations who`s creed is in God we trust. If you got the faith to do some real soul searching, then pushing back the darkness on this war on terror that's coming home to roost has its price. I don`t believe it`s a failing or a fault if you imagine there is a heaven to go to and a hell to fall in. But it is a serious and outstanding fact that jihad is just in vogue for show and wear for millions daydreaming fear. On the other hand, that jihad is a true bearing for a revolutionary struggle upward for those who have perception, insight, and faith overcoming tremendous daily obstacles within these kufr lands with confidence and awareness. I am not going to stand here before you and justify their actions. No, I am not. "Yet I am aware and at liberty to tell you all it is a tribute to the consequences of a people here in the West who fail to inspire themselves and demand justice for all people not just for themselves." It`s not my secret to keep, in all this ideological warfare that's going around like the flu, that nobody who is somebody is not demanding that not one drop of oil from Iraq shall enter American or European ports to warm our homes and to drive our industries as well as our cars yet at the same time we want the peace but not at the inconvenience of our lives! We want that justice but not at the inconvenience of our wealth. Yes, it`s not my secret to keep in all this ideological warfare hype that`s floating around like the plague, that nobody who is somebody`s ambassador is not demanding an arms embargo to the allied dictators and despots in the Middle East. Or for that matter an arms embargo to "Russian" allied dictators and despots in the Middle East as well (Syria). That an appeal for war crimes has been put on political hold in the United Nations against Western leaders because of their unjust acts of war and aggression upon the Muslim people, the act of funding their civil wars in Somalia, Sudan, Afghanistan, Pakistan, Iraq, and Yemen; where brother fights brother, but in their Western secular hearts it`s a policy of, "it`s a pity they all cannot lose." Those false accusations of the Muslim people of Iraq unto the United Nations that their government had weapons of mass destruction, justifying their invasion and the resulting deaths of more than a quarter of a million people; shall not be forgotten. That African marionette Mr. Kofi Annan who was the United Nations Secretary General at the time said on September 16, 2004, "From our point of view and from the charter point of view the war (Iraq) was illegal."

Don`t let anybody fool you into a state of stupor. Of course these signs of the times is depressing, it is suppose to be depressing. Americans and Europeans were trapped in a mire of two foreign Muslim conflicts with no plan B and hundreds of thousands are dead and millions seeking revenge! The Americans are spending twenty-five million dollars an hour, the British are spending more than two million pounds an hour, and the Europeans are spending up their national interest per second over there what could have been spent right here at home addressing dire outstanding domestic affairs. Wasting young people`s lives hopelessly on unjust wars for profit and gain is cruel, devastating and could cripple the aspirations and dreams of one`s youthful generation beyond recovery.

Yes, it's tragic that our secular Western leaders are politically unwilling to engage in a dialogue with their enemies; such a stance, considering we are talking about civilizations that truly cherishes freedom and liberty to the point of inconvenience. It is these ideals that is truly making life here in the West so much more brutal and harsh than it needs to be. Tragically, in this war on terror we have refused to confront our darker selves and sincerely asked why they are fighting us. Yet have we the people made a change of heart since 9-11-01, or 10-7-01, or 3-19-03 or 3-12-04 or 7-7-05?

What good karma can there be awaiting, by having to ignore the dire implications of these events just so we can remain a first-class number one arms merchant nation with just enough security to do as it pleases. Must we now wait for those charred bodies in the thousands and the forever broken lives lie before us before we in the West understand the magnitude of what being a victim is all about? Truly, it's not that difficult to look honestly into the mirror and understand that either we are all collateral damage or we are all innocent victims! Quite frankly after two world wars, a cold war, Vietnam war, the leading secular democratic Western nations are now at war with the most poorest but mineral rich Muslim nations of the world. In the not long ago past these same Muslim people would dream of hijacking planes, fly them to Western airports, and achieve liberty and freedom in their lives from their own despots because of their own hearts. Today with the growing high rate of blood-vendetta, many Muslim believers through-out the Muslim world dream of flying hijack-Western planes full of Western people into Western buildings full of the same people who abets injustice, and call themselves innocent. Allah is my witness, within one generation, people who have a claim of oppression and want liberty and freedom from Western nations are now flying with bombs in their underwear and bombs in their shoes in planes. Likewise, in spite of living in a land with liberty and freedom, there should be no happy new year for those nations who practice imperialism on Muslim people, this was the mindset of Mr. Faisal Shahzad who attempted a car bombing at New York Times Square on May 1, 2010.

So please don't fool yourself into believing or imagine it a favor from God, that that so-called suicide bomber doesn't love death more than you love life. That value of life imagined by that so-called suicide bomber is less than his enemies. Neither is it safe to assume that that so-called suicide bomber hates life more than you hate death. Or ponder that value of life or death imagined by that so-called suicide bomber or that so-called innocent victim—is it greater than his or her enemies standing before their lord to judge on the matter at hand? Yet this is not the main issue. Is it not better to understand the truth and cause about why Muslim people are becoming bombers and fighting secular Western and Communist interest in the first place? Therefore, before we jump to western media-driven conclusions and condemn another's willingness to die alongside their enemies and face judgment before that divine being altogether, would it not be wiser to reassess the definition of sinful behavior and innocents. When billions of exquisite, intelligent beings are fighting every day to preserve their humanity, their sanity, their dignity, is it not fair to ask why such unnecessary drama? Better still, I believe, to listen to the words of that $E=mc2$ fundamentalist Albert Einstein, who said, "Nothing will end wars unless the people themselves refuse to go to war." Wise words from a man whose work made possible the technology behind some of today's most destructive weaponry and the very essence of a trump card for millions who dare to believe in their unstoppable future."

An example of the fundamental quandary of the West's war effort here at home can be seen through the words and actions of Long Island congressman Mr. Peter King, chairman of the House Homeland and Security Committee. Representative King's 2011 terrorism hearings even till this day concerned itself with the recent upsurge of radicalization of many Muslim-Americans, while at the same time asking why patriotism amongst American Muslims wasn`t gaining any traction, despite a campaign by the American government dedicated to the contrary. King's inept committee also looked into a growing concern amongst non-Muslim Americans that Muslims are not doing enough to help their country fight the war on terror. Yet it should come as no surprise to Representative King where the Muslim-American community would stand in a national crisis, for the fact is that we Muslims of the West forewarned our respective countries on many occasions that continued support of Muslim-in-name-only despots and imperialistic adventurism will end only in a debacle. Our pleas, however, fell upon the deaf ears of a people who perhaps will only heed a warning once it's too late. Nevertheless, we Muslim believers beg you to understand once again, Mr. King, that peace and reconciliation is useless unless they are preceded by justice! We Muslim Americans demand an end to a foreign policy of doing evil so that good may come. Likewise, the idea that coexistence and tolerance amongst citizens can be a reality, regardless of radical religious or ethnic diversity, lies not in the people's success in rejecting Islam and/ or radical Islam, and embracing secular modernism; for in reality, our diversity here in the secular Western world is our strength, not an obstacle in the development of justice and true prosperity. The right of human dignity cannot be seen as something separate from a just and civil society. Indeed those with an exceptional eye will bear witness that the civilized part of any revolution lies in allowing that divine design of justice to guide our lives, while simultaneously not allowing the fear of each other and the desire for revenge dictate our decisions. The human race did not stumble onto the endangered species list overnight, so why give up this gift of life and it`s vivacity from our lord to end like a passing face?

This obsolete approach to the growing nuclear challenge undertaken by today`s Western leaders presents a formidable challenge; in fact, the mere belief that war can be morally, ethically, and justifiably regulated here on earth is naïve. There is no doubt in my mind that the business of war is hellish, and, as chaos grows, must be won at all costs. Similarly, the business of peace is justice and must be maintained at all costs as wisdom diminishes. These intellectual truths and conventional wisdoms as we know them aren`t an option; they are the key to survival. For I fear that the unlawful enemy combatant coming-of-age has arrived. The odds are that the spooks can't catch every shoe that drops. So it is not beyond the imagination to declare when our interests here in the West conflict with their values; to lower our wing is an act of divine patience. Living in a land that is dominated by the ungodly is a true test of faith for the believing monotheist fundamentalist. To see and not look, to hear and not listen, to know the truth and yet in spite of all that is being said and done all around you is to leave all to Allah`s mercy. Patience!

For many decades now, Muslim-Americans and Muslim Europeans have been forced to pay taxes to support governmental foreign policies of folly that violate our conscience. Our tax money has gone towards efforts that spilled the blood of people of our own faith; likewise, we, the believers, have been asked, shamelessly, to be patriotic for a cause that is morally corrupt and based on lies and imperialism. When a diverse domestic citizenry, such as ours, that includes both secular and religious, share a legitimate national interest, yet differ on how to deal with a particular crisis, namely the current war on terror, the true conflict of interest erupts when a secular majority seeks to go to war over issues that are religious and imperialist in nature, without fully consulting first its minority religious citizens about how best to accomplish peace or war with justice. We fundamentalists condemn the act of pulling the whole nation to war in the first place without a full open public national dialogue of all the basic issues at hand! Consequently, the minority thus destroys the credibility of the majority by declaring both to their compatriots and to the world that the proliferation of injustice is a world full of terrorists. Thus, injustice makes the world full of terrorist! Simply put, hundreds of millions of people here in the secular West denounce so-called acts of terror, yet they themselves both refuse to acknowledge the acts of terror committed by their own governments, and ignore the reasons why their enemies is fighting them! Ignoring the very reasons why Western peoples enemies don't see them as innocent civilians does not help end this war on so-called terror. Such a dilemma is no mystery of grief; however, what will help push back this dark curtain of arrogance and denial, may best be express by that poetic fundamentalist Marianne Moore, who wrote, "The weak overcomes its menace, the strong overcomes itself!"

What is so compelling yet what so many fail to understand, is that a nation of people's well-being is not proof of its virtue. Too often nations are known by what they pretend to stand for instead of what they actually do! So how, then, do we believers "overcome our menace," as Marianne Moore observes? Truth be told, it is time we as a religious people living in the secular West start doing ourselves justice, instead of demanding it from others—to live up to our cherished values regardless of time, place, and the nationalistic idiocy that infects our lands. Time for us to be earnest in our actions and living examples of our own creed come what may!

On the other hand, how will the strong overcome itself? Envision then a day the United States Attorney General Eric Holder enters a federal court in downtown Manhattan with an accused "terrorist," one whom has indeed been tortured and water boarded by U.S. government agents—but a individual, a human being regardless of the charges brought against him—and on that day, Attorney General Holder stands in that courtroom before a federal judge and admits that the accused has been tortured by American officials while awaiting his day in court from prison, as well as evidence introduced against the accused was obtained through torture. Imagine then that federal judge declares contempt of court and a miscarriage of justice despite the political uproar that's bound to follow!

Imagine also, on this day the strong overcomes itself, that neither downtown traffic nor expensive security problems are blamed for the reasons that a trial for the accused cannot be held here in a New York City court room or in any American city court room because of the nefarious government actions done in our name so that we can feel safer here at home! We believe, not bringing an accused to an open public court of law, people who are deemed unlawful enemy combatants who was tortured by their holders brings a certain kind of unnecessary merciless "Karma" our way. America also has a POW in Afghanistan, simply put, would we like it if our POW's are tortured like we do to theirs? The day any Most Wanted faces a fair trial in the courts of our lands without fear of political blowback or public opinion is the day that shameful human practice of victor's justice withers in poverty; unfortunately, the present political climate's weather dictates that the Obama Administration's avenue of justice, much like that of previous administrations, has followed this very same course of fear and revenge, denying fair trials by juries of their peers to men like Mr. Khalid Sheikh Mohammed, Mr. Ali Abdul Azizah, Mr. Ramzi bin Al-Shibh, Mr. Walid Muhammad Sahih Bin Attash, and Mr. Mustafa Ahmed Al-Hawsawi and many others is based solely on ideological grounds and fear. Is the Administration afraid of what these men might say publicly of their treatment of torture in American custody? That, in fact, Osama Bin Laden was killed by information obtained by torture of these and other prisoners in Guantanamo Bay Cuba and elsewhere!

In October 17, 2012 Mr. Khalid Sheikh Mohammed said from the U.S. military court in Cuba, "When the U.S. government feels sad for the death or killings of 3,000 peoples who were killed on 9-11-01 there should also be sorrow that the government has killed thousands of people, millions. Many can kill people under the name of national security and to detain children under the name of national security, underage children."

Oh, humble reader, no one in this country that is accused of a crime should be facing a death sentence at a military tribunal because of the fear of what that person might say of his torture at the hands of his capturers in a civilian public court house of law. The very idea of sentencing a person to death after you have torture him and found him guilty of a crime makes a banana republic a reality here at home.

Never again should a man like Mr. John B. Bellinger III, the legal adviser for the "United States Department of State and the National Security Council" during the George W. Bush presidential administration, be standing in the dock famished of the truth in full world public view before a United Nation Committee against Torture on May 4, 2006. Presumably he was not aware of those torture chambers in Guantanamo Bay, Cuba, and other torture chambers America was shopping out overseas in other countries in its "rendition program" war on terror.

Amazingly, Mr. Jose Rodriguez, the former C.I.A. director of clandestine services, said in justifying the destruction of C.I.A. torture video tapes of prisoners in Guantanamo Bay and other black site locations, "The heat from destroying the torture videos is nothing compared to what it would be if the tapes ever got into the public domain." Sadly, I believe, oh, humble reader, you can never get rid of your shadow. Such ominous episodes only reveals that true divide of our civilian, governmental, and diplomatic frame of mind of contempt upon the very public they suppose to serve.

Rarely do moments in life occur when the accepted way of life by a self-proclaimed civilized society is not tested by a divine tsunami of unforeseen events that has the power to bring to account all those tenets, which the empowered establishments holds dear between citizens and their governments! The fact that prisoners of the West's war on terror can't stand before a civilian court and instead must face military tribunals is due solely to the torture these prisoners endured under the custody of the American government, and to the fear of what they might say to the world in an open court while in enemy's hands. Regardless, as far as the United Nations Committee against Torture is concern, these so-called unlawful enemy combatants have rights regardless of the crimes they are alleged to have committed, solely because in justice lies the foundation of our collective humanity. As such, we as human beings who share this earth with jinn`s (demons) will be unable to solve our disputes and move forward as a species until we realize that justice—true justice—is the means to a peaceful world.

Likewise, we Salafists believe that justice is a means to an end, which heralds a true revolution of humanity.[84] Yet when justice can`t emerge into the light of day because of our governmental policies holding that revenge justifies the means, then we the people must acknowledge the true nature of the society in which we are living in and be willing to suffer the consequences all together, as a people collectively guilty— far from the claims of innocents. For it is impossible to be the civilized nation we claim to be—to be the world's purveyors of truth, justice, and human rights—by permitting torture to justify the capture and death of an enemy. Therefore, Amnesty International starts right here at home until there is a policy change from the grassroots up.

Despite our living in a modern world where ideas are, in fact, more powerful than guns, where the awakening of an independent social media demands for a more equitable redistribution of ideals of justice, our collective humanity is still nowhere near to being utilized to its fullest capacity. Indeed, in justice lies not just the opportunity for human beings to express their freedom of judgment and fear of that

---

[84]   Quran 42:38-43

divine one; the self-evident purpose of justice is to promote greater public welfare. It's that understanding the very idea that "it's not your weapon that matters—it's your aim." For there is no more stunning feat of jihad in motion than literally taking it to the streets and passing that torch of justice hand to hand, Olympic-style, so as to administer the values we hold dear.

If there is any hope for Islam in the secular West, the people here must see justice and truth in us. Likewise, we must remain patient and on guard living here amongst the kufr[85]. "*Strain not thine eyes. Wistfully at what we have bestowed on certain classes of them: but lower thy wing in gentleness to the believers. And say: I am indeed he that warns openly and without ambiguity, Of just such wrath as we sent down on those who divided scripture into arbitrary parts;*" (Quran 15:88-90) otherwise, regardless of how innocent we cry out to each other in despair, we as a nation of peoples must all share in the pain of our nation's crimes.

That classic thirst of justice, which we see dawning in this Islamic revolutionary season (otherwise known as the Arab Spring), is a reflection of a youthful new world order, one that is providing hope while also leading to the great Arab authoritarian meltdown. For those Arab despots who governed by fear, the problem is that their people don't fear them anymore, now that their torture, brutality, and inhumanity is broadcast worldwide by the likes of Facebook, Twitter, YouTube, Al Jazeera, and the Internet. Likewise, the crucial test of our own allegiance to our very own creed lies in our not complying with those carpetbagger politicians of the secular West who govern by duplicity and by hijacking that social currency of trust. Viewing the world with a more rational and sentient mind-set. We fundamentalists, fearing only Jehovah, Allah, simply have to look at ourselves and our lives to see what that guiding intelligent design has in store for us once we want for others what we want for ourselves, and to likewise understand the consequence of not changing our hearts and obeying our Lord.

At present, President Barack H. Obama is trying to come to terms with the true nature of reality after the bombing attack at the Boston Marathon on April 15, 2013. He had addressed the American nation on April 19, 2013, and stated, "Why did young men who grew up and studied here, as part of our communities and our country, resort to such violence?" Why did Mr. Tamerlan Tsarnaev and his younger brother Dzhokhar Tsarnaev, an American citizen attack the citizens

---

[85] Quran 15:88-99

of their own adopted country? Why? Well, this is truly insane the act
of denial. It is an inconvenient truth as with any open heart surgery,
time is unique in a dreadful way not on the side of the imperialist or
colonialist or number one arms merchant of the world. Why they the
national media expect the sacred to be there beneath the patriotic
rhetoric I still just don't know. Those downtown video surveillance
cameras in Boston on April 15, 2013, could not pick out and see the
why, only just mankind's acts of denial and inhumanity in our society,
which is emblematic of how the terrible consequences of these events
on the world stage will play itself out.

At present, the British Prime Minister David Cameron is also
trying to come to terms after the attack and death of Mr. Lee Rigby,
an off-duty soldier, a bandsman, and machine-gunner in the Royal
Fusiliers who had been in combat in Helmand Province, Afghanistan.
This happened in front of his London headquarters of the Royal
Artillery Barracks in Woolwich, London, England. The deed was
committed by Mr. Michael Adebolajo and Mr. Michael Adebowale
both Muslim British citizens on May 22, 2013. Similarly, both Western
leaders stressed in public 'why' did two young men who both lived
and grew up in their Western countries as citizens and part of their
community but resorted to such violence? Yes, it is strange that
imperialist Western leaders talk about in public the 'why' that sheer
brutality. Yet in actuality, in private, they knew why. So the 'why' talk
of sheer brutality is nothing to the actions of plain denial. The fact
that the episode like in Boston was recorded in detail by passerby
witnesses with their cell phone cameras in their goings about town,
thus the nations of the English speaking world heard the reasons
and is aware of the inconvenient truth of 'why.' It was in both cases
acts of consequences for American and British military oppressive
deployments in Muslim countries, the ongoing present stationing
of more than 70,000 American troops and 10,000 British troops in
Afghanistan. And, so they say, because of the oppression, invasion,
murder, torture, rape, kidnapping, and bombing of the Muslim people
in Afghanistan and Iraq. Yes, we believe for a fact that the Western
political powers understand the political and religious dilemma they
are in privately; but publicly they prefer the philosophy of evasion in
asking questions instead of answering them. Acknowledging the reality
of the consequence before them that this war on terror has now come
home to roost in their own communities because of their refusal to end
imperialistic goals without a fight if needs be is indeed a bitter pill. This
idea that they, the leaders of Western nations can buy the silence of
their Muslim citizens by toting nationalistic patriotism is not strange or

unusual, but it is ironic because legend has it, thou I feel at times it is true, when you hear that politics is what men do when metaphysics fall short from reality, the proof is self evident all around the media hype of denial, national patriotism, and arrogance.

Is this now that tipping point, oh, humble reader, who understands that the spooks can't catch every shoe that drops in this war on terror when facing that "stateless government" that has no borders? Are we hearing the sincere concern response to the outcry of the Islamic puritans living among the secular's anxious era of fear here in America? Thus on the first year anniversary on April 15, 2014, of the Boston bombings in Boston, Massachusetts, the newly elected New York mayor Bill de Blasio and police commissioner William Bratton has disbanded the "Demographics Unit" in the New York Police Department. Whose goal was like the goals of many other major and minor police departments nationwide and in Europe—which is to infiltrate, spy, intimidate, and do surveillance on Muslim communities, institutions, and activities here in America. A governmental policy once again, of stifling free speech, undermining freedom of associations, sowing suspicion, and fear. An occasion once more for unconstitutional mass spying on 'people program' solely based on their religion.

This "Demographics Unit" idea is the so called brainchild of a NYPD officer, Lawrence Sanchez who is also an agent of the CIA (Central Intelligence Agency). With the sole purpose of undermining the US First and fourth Amendment, they recruited undercover Pakistani American officers who were sent into Pakistani communities and mosques, Arabic speaking American officers were as well dispatched into Arab speaking communities to infiltrate Mosques and Muslim business. Thereafter employing a tactic dubbed "create and capture," where the informant would try to start a conversation about terrorism or other controversial topics, record the response elicited, and share it with the NYPD who in turn share it with the CIA and Homeland Defense.

So what's really happening here? Is this really a change of heart by the ruling élite, a quid pro quo, away from that domestic—the 'end justify the means' policy tactics in their war on terror? Is this a sincere shift, oh, humble reader, advancing liberty, and civil rights to us that was denied for our trust? Or an unseemly political message to that "stateless government" with no borders, that what happen in Boston, April 15, 2013, they don't want it to happen in New York City, therefore they shall ease their agenda of oppression, knowing the grim consequences for all that may follow.

Remember how the unbelievers plotted against thee, to keep thee in bonds, or slay thee, or get thee out, they plot and plan, and Allah too plans, but the best of planners is Allah (Quran 8:30).

Just how did America made me become a better Muslim? Well, the answer to that is quite simple. It is an accepted fact that America is known worldwide as the land of immigrants; however, only a handful of nations recognize the value in the idea that all nations of peoples are made up of immigrants who come together unto the land for their survival and the hope for a better future. Forthrightly only a small number of nations of peoples understand that we are all foreigners unto these lands no matter how long our ancestors been living there. The Constitution of the United States, says of all its citizens that "we the people are equal with inalienable rights," which are deeds of accomplishments and a reality for some and an unpromising boast unto others. Having been raised in such a land, I have seen more than a glimpse of a life that promises neither the certainty of prosperity nor the fulfillment of aspirations, yet does provide the priceless opportunity to have what you stand for heard freely without the threat of death or imprisonment. I too, cannot ignore a civil war at home that was fought so that no state can withdraw the Constitutional rights of its citizens whomsoever they may be, either slave or non-slave. At the same time I cannot ignore that America as well had a civil war and a million of its citizens died fighting here at home who were family members to each other and neighbors in our own civil war. However, no foreign government invaded America with their armed forces and aided one brother to fight his brother or neighbor for profit or political gain in our civil war in order to scavenge with the greed of buzzards in our domestic disputes of justice, politics and human rights! Yet sadly knowing this my government is still in the business of proliferation of civil wars and subversion in many Muslim and Third world countries!

Still, it is fair to ask in verbatim. Just how did America make me a better Muslim?

In answer to this question, I'd say that it's because of my realization that a secular democracy, with its noble guarantees of "liberty and justice for all," has brought hundreds of millions of people together under one roof, and has guided us to all work together, hopefully, without at times intentionally demonizing one another, or intentionally oppressing one another, because of our religious beliefs or ethnic backgrounds! America has made me a better Muslim because I now understand the sobering consequence of what "do as they say but not as they do" means in regards to justice and oppression! Living in America, I also understand that the miracle is not in our hands in spite of us we the people calling ourselves a superpower. Thus, in the name of personal liberty, I fully comprehend that Islam is superior to any present secular democracy, since its key ingredient—the demand for justice (Quran 4:58, 5:8, 7:181, 10:4, 39:75, 57:25)—is applied directly alongside faith. For Islam's demand for justice—justice for all—is superior, in its creed, in that it is under obligation and indebted to a monotheistic divine being that is aware of all our hearts and actions at all times. Whereas the people of a secular democracy's demand for justice is innately inferior simply because of its reliance on a court of laws defined by the whims, and values of a people's court, of different creeds and faiths, who cannot all see the heart of the accused or aware of the full actions of individuals at all times! The conventional wisdom for all Muslims, then, is that any deviation from Sharia law and justice—even for the sake of security, liberty and peace—is seen, and believed, as an act of treason unto Allah! In contrast, the conventional wisdom in the democratic secular West is that any deviation from its constitution and justice in the rule of law— even for the sake of security, liberty and peace—can be imagined, and seen as a necessary sacrifice. To this, then, I ask, "Who will be punished most severely, the former or the latter, once the hearts of the people therein have been revealed to be in contempt, error, and fault even in the cold night of now in the sight of that divine beholder?" In retrospect, "who will be rewarded and protected most securely, the former or the latter, once the hearts of the people therein have been revealed to be in admiration, truthful, and faithful even in this pragmatic light of now in the sight of that divine beholder?"

America has made me a better Muslim because I have come to understand the difference in the nature of human sovereignty and divine sovereignty, and the seen and unseen consequences racing against the clock that punishment of ignoring these mandates. For believing in "In God we Trust" is not just an ideal for a world of mature people living, praying, and working together with patience and tolerance; it is also a fundamental and continuous purge of the land unto that one and only divine being who demands only generosity to say unto itself, "So you found me." Amen!

I, Muhammad Dawud shall give my government one year after the publication of this book of mine; to end the oppression of my Muslim people otherwise we shall begin in America a Jihad for the mercy of Allah, which only Allah will be able to stop.

Index

CPSIA information can be obtained at www.ICGtesting.com
Printed in the USA
BVOW03s1415210914

367650BV00001B/69/P

9 781499 027266